Lecture Notes in Computer Science

Lecture Notes in Computer Science

Edited by G. Goos and J. Hartmanis

315

K. Furukawa H. Tanaka
T. Fujisaki (Eds.)

Logic Programming '87

Proceedings of the 6th Conference
Tokyo, Japan, June 22–24, 1987

Springer-Verlag

Berlin Heidelberg New York London Paris Tokyo

Editors

Koichi Furukawa
ICOT Research Center
Mita Kokusai Building 21F, 4-28 Mita 1-chome
Minato-ku, Tokyo 108, Japan

Hozumi Tanaka
Department of Computer Science, Faculty of Engineering
Tokyo Institute of Technology, 12-1, Oh-okayama 2-chome
Meguro-ku, Tokyo 152, Japan

Tetsunosuke Fujisaki
IBM, Thomas J. Watson Research Center
P.O. Box 704, Yorktown Heights, New York 10598, USA

CR Subject Classification (1987): B.6, C.1, D.1, D.3, I.2.4–7

ISBN 3-540-19426-6 Springer-Verlag Berlin Heidelberg New York
ISBN 0-387-19426-6 Springer-Verlag New York Berlin Heidelberg

Library of Congress Cataloging-in-Publication Data. Logic programming '87: proceedings of the
6th conference, Tokyo, Japan, June 22–24, 1987 / K. Furukawa, H. Tanaka, T. Fujisaki, eds.
p. cm.–(Lecture notes in computer science; 315) "Papers presented at the Sixth Logic Programming Conference"–Fwd.
ISBN 0-387-19426-6 (U.S.)
1. Logic programming–Congresses. I. Furukawa, Koichi II. Tanaka, H. (Huzumi) III. Fujisaki,
T. (Tetsunosuke) IV. Logic Programming Conference (6th: 1987: Tokyo, Japan) V. Title. VI. Series.
QA76.6.L58762 1988 006.3–dc 19 88-17625

Printing and binding: Druckhaus Beltz, Hemsbach/Bergstr.
2145/3140-543210

Foreword

This volume of the Springer Lecture Notes in Computer Science contains most of the papers presented at the Sixth Logic Programming Conference (June 22-24, 1987 Tokyo). It is the successor of volumes 221 and 264.

The contents cover foundations, programming, architecture and applications. There are 20 papers in all. Topics of particular interest are constraint logic programming and parallelism. In this respect, we are fortunate to be able to include the paper of the invited talk "Constraint Logic Programming" presented by Dr. Jean-Louis Lassez from IBM Watson Research Center. The effort to apply logic programming to large-scale realistic problems is also a significant direction in which this subject is moving.

We thank program committee members, referees and authors for their cooperation and patience. We extend our special thanks to referees from IBM Watson Research Center for their thorough efforts to improve the quality of the English.

Tokyo, Spring 1988   Koichi Furukawa
                                         Hozumi Tanaka
                                         Tetsunosuke Fujisaki

Table of Contents

Invited Paper

Constraint Logic Programming

Program Synthesis

Programming Languages and Implementation

Parallel Architecture and Programming

Foundations

Natural Language Processing

Applications

From Unification to Constraints

Joxan Jaffar and Jean-Louis Lassez
I.B.M. Thomas J. Watson Research Center

Abstract
The constraint paradigm plays a more and more important role in knowledge based systems and declarative programming. This is because because it caters for implicit information and the representation of fundamental domains of computation. In particular constraint solving can advantageously replace unification as it corresponds better to programming practice and existing trends in language design. Furthermore the introduction of constraints in Logic Programming preserves and enhances very naturally the desirable semantic properties of Logic Programs. We give here a brief exposition of the motivations that led to the CLP theory, an overview of the language CLP($\mathcal{R}$), an example of application in Stock Options Trading and finally we mention a number of important activities in the area of Constraints and Logic Programming.

Introduction

The Constraint Logic Programming (CLP) Scheme is a framework for the formal foundations of a class of programming languages. This framework is designed to encapsulate both the paradigms of constraint solving and logic programming, it is presented in Jaffar and Lassez [7, 8]. The constraint solving paradigm allows concise and natural representation of complex problems because of two main reasons:

(a) the constraints state properties directly in the domain of discourse as opposed to having these properties coded into Prolog terms or Lisp lists.
(b) the constraints have the ability of representing properties implicitly as opposed to having bindings to variables. The logic programming paradigm, on the other hand, suggests an overall rule-based framework to reason about constraints.

This article is intended as a brief exposition on three aspects of Constraint Logic Programming: for the theory aspect, we will discuss what it means for CLP to be a Scheme and how, consequently, all the resulting languages have the same essential semantic properties. It is important to note here that these semantic properties are the same as those of conventional Logic Programs. So the introduction of constraints in Logic Programming increases the expressive power without a loss in semantic properties. For the implementation and application aspects, we will choose the particular domain of real arithmetic, and describe CLP($\mathscr{R}$), an instance of the scheme initially defined in Jaffar and Michaylov [9]. A more involved paper by Jaffar, Michaylov, Stuckey and Yap [10] is forthcoming. We highlight the above points that the CLP($\mathscr{R}$) arithmetic constraints are meant to be interpreted exactly in the usual way people understand arithmetic, and also that the ability to state arithmetic properties implicitly is indeed part of a powerful programming methodology.

We illustrate the expressive power of CLP($\mathscr{R}$) with an example in economics, taken from work by C. Lassez, K. McAloon and R. Yap [13]. In a last section, we indicate a number of recent works relating Constraints and Logic Programming and suggest or mention a number of potentially significant directions where substantial work is in progress.

We begin with an informal discussion on constraints in the context of programming.

Implicit and explicit information

Constraint solving is a paradigm that is widely used in graphics, engineering, knowledge representation, etc. as it allows great expressive power from a declarative point of view. Typically, we want to design systems over well understood domains such as sets, graphs, Boolean expressions, integers, rationals, real numbers, etc. These domains have natural algebraic operations associated with them such as set or graph intersection, disjunction, multiplication, etc. They also have associated privileged predicates such as set equality, graph isomorphism and various forms of inequalities such as set inclusion, $<$, $\geq$, $\neq$, etc. These predicates are examples of what we call constraints. Note that the various forms of equality are just a very particular type of constraints.

The key property of constraints is that they allow the user to define objects *implicitly*. Consider the following elementary examples:

(1) A set of names of people is given explicitly as a list
$S = $ *(John Doe, Barbara Smith, ...)*, this same set can also be defined implicitly with the constraints $S = \{x : salary(x) \geq 35000 \ \& \ status(x) \neq manager\}$. The first definition is suitable for some operations like mailing letters to these people, the second definition, however, conveys information that is not apparent in the first one and would be more suitable if one wanted to design an automatic system to help in deciding increases in salaries.

(2) In a different domain, consider the implicit and explicit definitions of a typical conic: $ax^2 + by^2 + cxy + dx + ey + f = 0$ and $x=u(t)/w(t), y=v(t)/w(t)$ where u, v, w are quadratic polynomials. The explicit representation is clearly the one to use to generate a picture of this conic, but to determine whether a given point is above or below the surface or curve the implicit representation is more appropriate.

Implicit and explicit representations play important and complementary role and to be able to pass from one representation to the other is a crucial problem in many fields. In particular, implicit representations are necessary when finite explicit representations are impossible to obtain. For instance, the set of points (x,y) defined by $x \neq y$ or $x \geq y$ cannot be represented explicitly in a finite way and a listing of these points is obviously out of the question, it would not even be countable. Let us mention why this point illustrates a fundamental weakness in conventional Logic Programs. Output from Logic Programs are substitutions, that is strictly of the explicit type, $x = f(u,v)$, $y = g(u)$ for instance. Negation on the other hand allows you to define sets implicitly, for instance $x \neq f(u,u)$. Such a set cannot be finitely represented by substitutions. Implications of this remark on explicit versus implicit representations have been discussed in Lassez and Marriott [14], Lassez, Maher and Marriott [15]. It is shown there that only in very restricted cases is it possible to transform an implicit representation (via terms and complements or system of equations and inequations) into a finite explicit one. It was also mentioned that a major shortcoming of the negation as failure rule comes from the fact that negative information appears implicitly in a program, but bindings are performed only on explicitly defined objects. So the problem arises of transforming implicit information into explicit form. But it is in general impossible to finitely replace the implicit information by an explicit one.

A conflict arises: we are allowed to state implicit information but can compute, input and output only in an explicit manner via unification. So the expressive power of the language we use to write programs allows us to reason about objects that we cannot output. In fact it is clear that in general adding negation to a language strictly adds to its expressive power, a further example is that the complement of a recursively enumerable set cannot be described as a recursively enumerable set. But even in cases where negation could be eliminated in principle it may be more natural or efficient to keep it. Consider the finite set $\{a,b,c,d,e,f,....,z\}$ One could systematically replace expressions such as $x \neq a$ by $x = b \lor x = c \lor .... \lor x = z$. But the implicit definition using $\neq$ is certainly more economical and may convey a more useful type of information.

So the points we made here are that we may need or prefer for many applications to use implicit representations rather than restrict ourselves to explicit ones because it is more natural or because we in fact have no choice.

The CLP Scheme

If we introduce via constraints such implicit representations in Logic Programming, we can expect to derive languages with strictly more expressive power. A clue on how to do it is to replace the Herbrand universe by a user's domain of computation and unification by constraint solving. This is a fairly drastic change and it is not quite clear a priori to see how the formal semantics of logic programs will be affected. In fact the key semantic properties of Logic Programs are preserved in this generalization. We are making here a very strong statement namely that Logic Programming does not depend in any essential way on unification and the Herbrand universe, and that we can as well do Logic Programming on real numbers and arithmetic constraints, or sets or graphs and their associated constraints, to cite a few possibilities. To fully understand this, one of course has to go through all the theorems and proofs to be found in Jaffar and Lassez [8]. Nevertheless a good understanding of the difference between unification and constraint solving can provide an informal and clear clue to why the semantics are indeed preserved, as we show now.

There are two aspects to unification. One is that the unification algorithm is a decision procedure which tells us if the equation t1=t2 has a solution. The other aspect is that it gives us as output a substitution (mgu) which represents the set of all solutions. But one could argue that the equation t1=t2 also represents the set of all solutions. Why is the mgu needed? It is needed only for syntactic convenience, it is simpler to handle x=a rather than f(x,x)=f(a,a). But we could in principle refuse this syntactic simplification without affecting any of the soundness and completeness, fixed points and least model theorems or their proofs. The price to pay would be only that as output we would have a non-simplified system of equations instead of a more concise mgu. But of course they would be equivalent, representing the same solutions. The mgu is a finite explicit representation of the set of solutions, t1=t2 is an implicit representation of the same set. When we deal with a domain where an mgu (or finite collection of mgu's) exists then it is convenient to use, but we know that in many instances such a finite explicit representation does not exist. So what is fundamental here is the decision aspect of unification, not its mgu aspect. Which means the essential aspect of unification is its constraint solvability aspect. The same algorithm which tells us if t1=t2 is solvable also tells us if $t1 \neq t2$ is solvable. So $t1 \neq t2$ is a constraint of the same standing as t1=t2, and both of them can appear in the input, program, goals, and output. Those familiar with the various theorems mentioned will realize that this use of the constraint $\neq$ effectively doe not essentially affect the theorems or their proofs. What essentially matters is that the constraint is solvable, the nature of the constraint and its representation are irrelevant. Similarly one could take other specific domains and constraints and check case by case, theorem by theorem. This remark and example should provide an intuitive justification why unification is just a particular case of constraint solving and that logic programming systems can use in the same way other types of constraints. Nevertheless a fair amount of work was needed to find an appropriate formalism to handle the general case.

The key concept of a scheme, first introduced in Jaffar, Lassez and Maher [6] plays a crucial role here and this is what we discuss now. An analogy with the notion of vector space will be useful to understand the notion of a scheme which provides in an abstract way the same semantics to a class of languages. We first have axioms which define the abstract notion of vector space. Any mathematical object which satisfies these axioms is a vector space. And we have a whole collection of theorems established in the abstract setting, that hold for all these objects. The power of this notion comes from the fact that objects of apparently very different nature such as R^n, sets of matrices, sets of polynomials, etc, are vector spaces and are shown to have substantial structural properties in common. So when we study a new mathematical object if we can verify first that it satisfies the axioms of vector space, we have for free a lot of theorems, which is more satisfactory than the brute force approach of establishing them one by one.

In our context of semantics what plays the role of the vector space axioms, is the abstract notion of *solution compact*. The collection of theorems include soundness and completeness results for success, finite failure and negation as failure, and various least and greatest fixpoint and model theorems. These results are used to formalize the declarative aspects, the operational aspects and establish their relationships. Therefore they provide a high level rigorous definition of a class of languages and their implementation.

Informally we consider a domain whose objects are described by a language of constraints. Essentially this domain will be solution compact if the language of constraints allows us to define limit elements and is precise enough that we can distinguish any object which does not satisfy given constraints from those objects which do. There are a number of interesting aspects to this notion. First it represents a very weak requirement, so that we can claim that if a domain and associated language of constraints was not solution compact, then we would not consider it for computational purposes as the syntax would not allow a precise definition of the objects. All finite or countable domains are solution compact in a trivial manner. Uncountable domains such as reals and infinite trees are also solution compact. So if the notion of solution compact helps us establish the theorems of the scheme, it is important to note that the reverse is true, that is if the theorems of the scheme hold for a particular domain, then it has to be solution compact.

So we have a powerful tool to generate semantics for a variety of languages which cater for different domains but use the rule based paradigm of Logic Programming. We can choose these domains to be user's domains rather than artificial symbolic ones, and therefore enhance the important semantic properties of Logic Programs.

The CLP($\mathcal{R}$) Language and Operational Model

We will now describe a particular instance of the scheme, which caters for real arithmetic constraints. It was chosen as a first illustration of the scheme as the domain of real numbers is of great importance and, as far as we know there is no formally defined or implemented programming language that effectively deals with real numbers. The terms are built using uninterpreted functors and real arithmetic terms in such a way that the functors may have real arithmetic terms as arguments, but not vice versa. Constraints are built from the usual equality and inequality relations between real number terms, and equality between terms which may contain functors.

A CLP($\mathcal{R}$) program consists of a finite number of rules, and these are of the form:

$$A_0 :- c_1 , c_2, ..., c_n, A_1 , A_2, ..., A_m.$$

where c_i, $0 \leq i \leq n$, are primitive constraints and A_i, $0 \leq i \leq m$, are atoms.

Thus rules in CLP($\mathcal{R}$) have much the same format as those in PROLOG except that an un-ordered collection of primitive constraints may appear together with atoms in the body. The same applies to a CLP($\mathcal{R}$) goal; this is of the form

$$?- c_1, c_2, ... , c_n, A_1 , A_2, ... , A_m.$$

where c_i, $0 \leq i \leq n$, are primitive constraints, A_i, $0 \leq i \leq m$, are atoms, and $n + m \geq 1$.

Let P denote a CLP($\mathcal{R}$) program. Let G_1 be a goal containing the collection C_1 of primitive constraints. We say that there is a *derivation step* from G_1 to goal G_2 if G_1 is of the form

$$?- C_1, A_1, A_2, ..., A_m.$$

where $m \geq 1$, C_1 is solvable, and P contains a rule of the form

$$B_0 :- C_2, D_1, D_2, ..., D_k.$$

where $k \geq 0$, and G_2 is of the form

$$?- C_1, C_2, A_i = B_0, A_1, ..., A_{i-1}, D_1, ..., D_k, A_{i+1}, ..., A_m.$$

where $1 \leq i \leq m$, and C_1, C_2, $A_i = B_0$, is solvable. We say that the A_i in G_1 above is the *selected atom*. Equivalently, A_i is the subgoal of G_1 chosen to be *reduced*.

A *derivation sequence* (or simply sequence) is a possibly infinite sequence of goals wherein there is a derivation step to each goal from the preceding goal. A derivation sequence is *successful* if it is finite and its last goal contains only constraints. Such constraints are called *answer constraints*. They constitute the output of CLP($\mathcal{R}$) programs, and facilitate an outstanding feature of the language: *symbolic* output. Finally, a *finitely failed* sequence is a finite sequence where no derivation step, using the selected atom, is possible from the last goal in the sequence.

Thus a CLP($\mathcal{R}$) program and goal are executed by a process of continuously reducing any remaining atoms in the subgoal. There are two nondeterministic aspects in obtaining a derivation sequence as we have defined above. An *atom selection rule* determines in a goal which atom should be reduced next. A *search strategy*, on the other hand, determines which rule is to be used in the reduction of a given atom in the subgoal. In present implementations CLP($\mathcal{R}$) uses the atom selection and search strategies as in PROLOG. Of course, other strategies may be considered without interfering with the theoretical aspects.

Consider an example of a CLP($\mathcal{R}$) program. This program relates some simple parameters in a mortgage. The feature displayed here is that CLP($\mathcal{R}$), via its answer constraints, can produce symbolic answers.

```
mortgage(P, Time, I, MP, B) :-
        0 < Time, Time ≤ 1,
        Int = Time * (P * I/1200),
        B = P + Int - (Time * MP).
mortgage(P, Time, I, MP, B) :-
        Time > 1,
        Int = P * I/1200,
        mortgage(P + Int - MP, Time - 1, I, MP, B).
```

The parameters considered above are the principal, life of mortgage (in months), interest rate (in %), monthly payment, and finally the outstanding balance. The amount of interest to be paid is adjusted monthly.

The following goal represents a typical query for the monthly payment given all the other parameters:

```
?- mortgage(123456, 120, 12, MP, 0).
```

The answer constraint MP = 1771.23 is obtained, as it can be from a straightforward rewrite of the above program in any other imperative language. CLP($\mathcal{R}$) however enjoys the advantage of being a relational language, and so we may ask the reverse question:

```
?- mortgage(P, 120, 12, 1771.23, 0).
```

and obtain P = 123456. These examples, however, fall far short illustrating the expressive power of CLP($\mathcal{R}$). Consider the following goal in which only the time and interest are given:

```
?- mortgage(P, 120, 12, MP, B).
```

The CLP($\mathcal{R}$) system will return the *relationship* between the principal, monthly payment and balance:

```
B = 0.302995*P - 69.700522*MP.
```

This answer may be viewed as another program obtained as a result of partially evaluating the original program with respect to T = 120 and I = 12.

For more examples, see [4].

We conclude this sub-section by emphasizing that constraints in the domain of $\mathscr{R}$ provide a natural implicit representation for real numbers. It is important to distinguish "real" from "rational" here. For example, one could argue that since we finitely represent numbers in computers, we should base our theory on rational numbers. It then would follow that the program and goal below

```
ohmlaw(V, I, R) :- V = I * R.
?-ohmlaw(2, X, X)
```

would lead to failure (because $X^2=2$ has no rational solution) when it clearly should succeed. More generally, with constraints we can represent exactly, and reason about real numbers such as square root of two, defined as $x^2=2, x \geq 0$.

The CLP($\mathscr{R}$) Interpreter

In principle, one can build a CLP system from an easy marriage between a PROLOG-like engine and a constraint solver for the kinds of constraints at hand. In practice, this is not feasible. This is primarily because general purpose solvers are typically aimed at large and static problems. In CLP($\mathscr{R}$), on the other hand, we are dealing with dynamically created and typically smaller and specialized kinds of constraints. The number of such constraints, however, may be very large.

As indicated by the examples above, two central observations dominate the implementation issues in building any CLP system:

- each derivation step requires a solvability test for a collection of constraints, and
- these collections progressively grow larger.

It follows that two properties below are important to have in the handling of constraints:

- *incrementality:*
  This means that whenever a collection of constraints is determined to be solvable, the solvability problem resulting from adding a new constraint does

not necessitate the repetition of all the work already done in determining the solvability of the original collection.

- *canonicality:*
  This is taken to mean that there is standard, simplified representation of the collection which uses a minimal number of constraints. Appropriate canonical representations can have numerous advantages, for example, they can enhance efficiency because all equalities entailed by the collection will in fact appear explicitly in the collection.

It should be pointed out here that one can take for granted that equation solving algorithms are canonical and return a simple and useful canonical form. However for more general constraints the problems of finding incremental algorithms and appropriate canonical forms maybe very complex, this will be discussed in forthcoming publications. The underlying philosophy behind the CLP($\mathscr{R}$) implementation is that a priority is given upon several classes of constraints, and this priority roughly reflects both the computational cost and the expected relative frequency of constraints in a given class. For example, an equation between two variables is of the highest priority whilst a multivariate polynomial equation is of the lowest.

The first four of the five modules below (see figure 1) reflect our four priority classes:

- the *engine*;
  This module is at the center of the entire system and is based upon a standard PROLOG engine. The important feature here concerning constraints is that the engine deals with the highest priority constraints without invoking any other modules.

- the *interface*;
  This module transforms constraints into a standard form. This is done mainly for software engineering reasons, to help make the engine and the constraint solver relatively independent of each other. Like the engine, the interface does some constraint satisfaction on its own, thus lessening the need to use the solvers.

- the *linear equality solver*;
  This module keeps a satisfiable collection of linear equations in parametric solved form, that is, some variables arising from program execution are described in terms of parametric variables. The method of solution used is a variant of Gaussian elimination. This module controls, and contains the only calls to, the linear inequality solver.

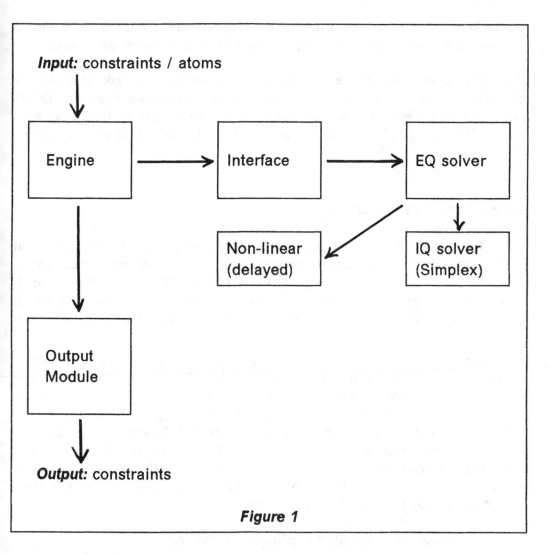

Figure 1

- the *linear inequality solver*;
  This module is implemented using a sparse-matrix representation of a Simplex tableau and a modified form of the Simplex algorithm. It may operate without invoking any other module. However, it can, for efficiency, communicate a certain amount of information back to the equality solver. It does this whenever an equality is inferred from the collection of (non-strict) inequalities.
- the *output* module;
  The purpose of this module is two-fold. Firstly it de-parameterizes the constraints as much as possible so that answer constraints reflect relationships only between the variables in the goal. It then transforms these resulting constraints into a canonical form. This serves both the purpose of standard-

ization, e.g. two sets of constraints defining the same solution space should look alike, and the purpose of having the output as compact as possible.

Non-linear equations, in the present implementations, are not checked for solvability. Instead, they are stored away and inspected only when a sufficient number of variables in a non-linear equation become ground so that it becomes linear. This "delaying" and "waking" activity is controlled by the equality solver.

An example: option pricing

The world of finance is a great user of computer power. As many financial applications contain a mixture of mathematical computation and expert knowledge, they are well suited to a language like CLP($\mathcal{R}$). We present here some elements of a program that determines the price of stock options and which illustrates well the unique nature of the language. The following is derived from [12].

An option gives its owner the right to buy or sell a particular stock at a given price for a limited time. For instance an XYZ July 50 call option is the right to buy 100 shares of XYZ stock at $50 per share until the July expiration date regardless of the market price of the XYZ stock. Similarly an XYZ July 45 put option is the right to sell 100 shares of XYZ stock at $45 per share. The *Black-Scholes* formula (9) given below computes the theoretical price of an option in terms of stock price (p), strike price (the exercise price of the option) (s), time to expiration (t), current risk-free interest rate (r) and volatility (v) of the underlying stock measured by annual standard deviation:

Theoretical option price $= pN(d_1) - se^{-rt}N(d_2)$

$$d_1 = \frac{ln(\frac{p}{s}) + (r + \frac{v^2}{2})t}{v} \sqrt{t} \ , \ d_2 = d_1 - v\sqrt{t}$$

(*ln* is the natural log and *N(x)* the cumulative normal distribution).

The Black-Scholes formula is written as a CLP($\mathcal{R}$) clause

```
black_scholes(Th,P,S,T,R,V) :-
      Th = P * normal(D1) - S * exp(-R*T) * normal(D2),
      D1 = (ln(P/S) + (R + pow(V,2)/2 * T)/(V * sqrt(T)),
      D2 = D1 - V * sqrt(T).
```

where normal, exp, ln, pow and sqrt are system functions. The next two goals return respectively the option price and the stock price for a given option.

```
?-black_scholes(X,40,44,90,0.15,0.60).

--------------------
answer ---> X = 8.129


?-black_scholes(8.129,40,X,90,0.15,0.60).

------------------
answer ---> X = 44
```

This simple program can be incorporated in a larger one implementing for instance a buying strategy that typically requires the computation of the expected returns on all options in a given class. CLP($\mathcal{R}$) inherits from Logic Programming its incrementality which makes the task of expanding an existing program easy. In the Black-Scholes model, one parameter of particular importance is the volatility which is not always known. It can be computed statistically but the necessary data on the underlying stock are not always available and furthermore studies have shown that the statistical model is not always accurate. However, the volatility can also be computed using the Black-Scholes model under what is known as the *fair market assumption* which assumes that the actual option price equals the theoretical price. The Black-Scholes formula can then be used *in reverse* to compute the volatility. This requires solving a non-linear equation, but this is easily programmed in CLP($\mathcal{R}$) using a standard method to find the roots of a non-linear equation. This is illustrated in the next example which uses Steffensen's formula:

$$x_{n+1}=x_n - \frac{f(x_n)}{g(x_n)}, \ g(x_n)= \frac{f(x_n + f(x_n)) - f(x_n)}{f(x_n)}$$

The clause

```
getnext(X, NX) :-
    NX = X - F/G
    eval(X, F),
    eval(X + F, FF),
    G = (FF - F)/F.
```

expresses the formula with $X = x_n$, $NX = x_{n+1}$. The predicate eval is defined by:

```
eval(X, F) :-
    black_scholes(Th,P,S,T,R,X),
    market_price(Ma),
    F = Ma - Th.
```

The Black-Scholes formula is replaced by the equation

$$F = Ma - pN(d_1) - se^{-rt}N(d_2) = 0$$

which is solved for the volatility. This is done by the routine solve which takes an initial value for X and an accuracy factor Epsilon.

```
solve(X, Epsilon) :-
    eval(X, F),
    abs(F) < Epsilon.
solve(X, Epsilon) :-
    getnext(X,NX),
    solve(NX, Epsilon).
```

It terminates successfully when the value of F for the last computed value of X is less than the accuracy factor Epsilon otherwise it calls itself recursively with NX, the next value of X.

Finally, a new clause is added to the previous definition of black_scholes to deal with the case when the volatility is unknown. Provided the market price of the option is given as well as the parameters for solve, the system will compute the volatility as is shown next (unknown succeeds when its parameter is ground -has been given a value- and fails otherwise).

```
black_scholes(Th,P,S,T,R,V) :-
    unknown(V), initial_value(X0),
    accuracy(E), solve(X0,E).


?-black_scholes(_,40,X,90,0.15,V), market_price(8),
    initial_value(0.10), accuracy(0.0005).


----------------------
answer ---> V = 0.598
```

An options buying program must combine expertise to develop strategies with numerical computation to evaluate parameters of those strategies. CLP($\mathscr{R}$) which combines the expressive power of logic programs with the numeric computational capability of a traditional algorithmic language is particularly well suited for this type of applications. A more thorough treatment for this application is to be found in [13].

Other domains of applications have been investigated and interesting applications have been reported in the domain of electrical engineering [3]. These early reports confirm the real usability of CLP($\mathscr{R}$) in domains that were up to now considered to be outside the range of logic programming languages.

Future Directions

Constraint solving is a topic of great importance in Artificial Intelligence, Mathematical Programming and Operations Research. It is clear that progress in these fields will have a deep influence on the CLP theory, on its algorithmic aspects and implementations. Preliminary results will be found in forthcoming papers Lassez and McAloon [16] and Lassez, Maher and Stuckey [17]. At that point in time we do not want to elaborate on these connections as the problem is far too involved, but it opens major new research directions. Our aim here will be more limited and we will suggest or report on recent developments which have a direct connection with CLP.

First as we previously mentioned, many extensions to Prolog can be viewed as instances of the CLP scheme, even though they were not necessarily conceived in that framework. A most notable one is Colmerauer's Prolog-III, which caters for rational arithmetic constraints and boolean constraints [1]. Another language is Mukai's CIL [22]; it is of great interest as is caters for a new and challenging type of constraints of non-numerical nature. Work is in progress to formally establish the connection with the CLP scheme. The work done by Van Hentenryck and Dincbas at ECRC is of particular interest (see e.g. [24]) as they attack successfully real industrial problems, such as cutting stock problems and disjunctive scheduling. Their language caters for finite domains and incorporates general control strategies.

So a first task is to identify languages which are instances of the scheme and inherit its semantic properties. This entails the formalization or axiomatization of domains of computation and languages of constraints. Some recent works along that line are now mentioned. Kunen [11] replaces unifiers by boolean expressions over Herbrand terms which allows the finite representation of negative information. Maher [18] makes a systematic study of this problem extending it to domains of rational and infinite trees. Related work by Mancarella, Martini and Pedreschi [20] is also worth mentioning as well as Wallace's work on negation [25].

We have previously mentioned that we can "lift" Logic Programming by using constraint solving instead of unification. But all the semantics and examples were given related to definite clause programming. This is not what Logic Programming reduces to. Two other main areas are concurrent languages and Data or knowledge bases. Maher has shown in a recent paper [19] that indeed one could also lift aspects of concurrent Logic Programming to handle constraints. Other work in this direction is in progress at Xerox with Saraswat, in Tokyo with Mizoguchi and in New York with McAloon. For data or knowledge bases, it seems clear that the paradigm of constraints in CLP can be pushed further than it has been up to now for languages. Indeed here the full generality of the concept of implicit definitions can be used, in principle a constraint can be "anything" that is a formula as well as a program if one wishes. This is considered by Kannellakis and independently Ramakrishnan who have forthcoming papers that could herald a new and significant area where they analyze and exploit the expressive power of constraints. The work of Imielinski on intelligent queries [5] should also be reexamined in the context of CLP as there are strong conceptual links. If a constraint can be "anything", then it can be a theorem. Indeed Aiba and Sakai [23] in their CAL system which corresponds to an instance of the scheme for non-linear equalities are building a novel form of theorem provers which has great potential. As with all the works previously mentioned the use of constraints raises a number of challenging problems, an important one being the compromise between expressive power and efficiency. There are also aspects of this work which can be relevant to areas outside of Logic Programming. For instance the notion of scheme has been a very powerful tool to analyze semantics properties of languages in our context. But of course this concept can and should be used in other contexts. Constraints are also introduced in rewriting systems. Work by Kapur, in particular jointly with Mohan and Srivas [21] and Comon [2], among others, on systems of equations and inequations and inductive reducibility is clearly relevant and both fields should benefit from a thorough analysis of the connections.

Acknowledgments

We wish to thank C.Lassez and M. Maher for comments on this paper.

Bibliography

1. A. Colmerauer, "Opening the PROLOG-III Universe", Byte Magazine, Special Issue on Logic Programming, August 1987.

2. H. Comon, "Unification et Disunification: Theorie et Applications", PhD Thesis, Grenoble 88.

3. N.C. Heintze, S. Michaylov, P.J. Stuckey, "On the Applications of CLP to Some Problems in Electrical Engineering", Proc. ICLP-4, Melbourne, 1987.

4. N.C. Heintze, J. Jaffar, C.S. Lim, S. Michaylov, P.J. Stuckey, R. Yap, C.N. Yee, "The CLP($\mathcal{R}$) Programmer's manual", Technical Report, Dept. of Computer Science, Monash University, June 1986.

5. T. Imielinski, "Intelligent query answering in rule based systems", Journal of Logic Programming 4(3), Sept 1987.

6. J. Jaffar, J-L. Lassez and M.J. Maher, "A Logic Programming Language Scheme", in Logic Programming: Relations, Functions and Equations", D. DeGroot and G. Lindstrom (Eds), Prentice-Hall, 1985.

7. J. Jaffar and J-L. Lassez, "Constraint Logic Programming", Proc. POPL-87, Munich, 1987.

8. J. Jaffar and J-L. Lassez, "Constraint Logic Programming", Technical report, Department of Computer Science, Monash University, June 1986.

9. J. Jaffar and S. Michaylov, "Methodology and Implementation of a CLP system", Proc. ICLP-4, Melbourne, 1987.

10. J. Jaffar, S. Michaylov, P. Stuckey and R. Yap, "The CLP($\mathcal{R}$) Language and System", To Appear.

11. K. Kunen, "Answer Sets and Negation-as-Failure", Proc. ICLP-4, Melbourne, May 1987.

12. C. Lassez, "Constraint Logic Programming", Byte Magazine, Special Issue on Logic Programming, August 1987.

13. C. Lassez, K. McAloon and R. Yap, "Constraint Logic Programming and Option Trading", IEEE Expert, Special Issue on Financial Software, August 1987.

14. J-L. Lassez and K. Marriott, "Explicit Representation of Terms defined by Counter Examples", Journal of Automated Reasoning, Sept 87 (also IBM Research Report 1986).

15. J-L. Lassez, M. Maher and K. Marriott, "Unification Revisited", to appear in Foundations of Deductive Databases and Logic Programming, J. Minker editor, Morgan Kaufman 1987 (also IBM Research Report 1986).

16. J-L Lassez and K. McAloon, "A Canonical Form for Generalized Linear Arithmetic Constraints", to appear.

17. J-L Lassez, M. Maher and P. Stuckey, In preparation.

18. M. Maher, "Complete axiomatizations of the algebras of finite, rational and infinite trees", Proc. LICS-88, Edinburgh 1988.

19. M. Maher, "Logic Semantics for a Class of Committed-Choice Programs", Proc. ICLP-4, Melbourne, May 1987.

20. P. Mancarella, S. Martini and D. Pedreschi, "Complete Logic Programs with domain closure axioms", To appear in the Journal of Logic Programming.

21. C.K. Mohan, M.K. Srivas and D. Kapur, Forward Reasoning in Systems of Equations and Inequations, to appear, Journal of Logic Programming.

22. K. Mukai and H. Yasukawa, "Complex Indeterminates in PROLOG and its application to discourse models", New Generation Computing 3, 1985.

23. K. Sakai and A. Aiba, "Introduction to CAL", ICOT Memo, 1987

24. P. van Hentenryck and M. Dincbas, "Forward Checking in Logic Programming", Proc. ICLP-4, Melbourne, May 1987.

25. M. Wallace, "Negation by Constraints - a sound and efficient implementation of negation in deductive databases", Proc. SLP-4, San Francisco, 1987.

CS-Prolog:

A Generalized Unification Based Constraint Solver

Toshio KAWAMURA, Hayato OHWADA and Fumio MIZOGUCHI

Dept. of Industrial Administration, Science Univ. of Tokyo

Noda, Chiba 278 , Japan

1. Introduction

Most of recent researches about logic programming present new logic programming language system as extension to PROLOG. Constraint Logic Programming is an attractive new approach. There are several approaches to it. For example, the integration of functional programming and logic programming, and introducing data types etc. However, there are same in the sense of Constraint Logic Programming. Jaffar[Jaffar 86] shows the common framework which he calls "CLP Schema" and gives us formal foundations for these approaches.

Unification can be viewed as equality constraint solver and we can use PROLOG as constraint solver. But it is not sufficient for using the unification of standard PROLOG (DEC10-PROLOG, C-PROLOG etc.) as constraint solver. For example, PROLOG can not handle equality between arithmetic terms (unify $1+2$ with 3, obtain substitution $x= -1$ by unifying $3+x$ with 2). Generalized unification is a basic approach to constraint logic programming. For example PROLOG-II[Colmerauer 84] generalizes the unification to solve equations over the structure of infinite trees and PROLOG-Q[Jaffar 86b] generalizes the unification to solve linear arithmetic equations using Gaussian method.

We aim to develop a powerful constraint solver in logic programming framework. And we have been developing constraint logic programming language. Our design goal is as follows.

(i)   The language must be a natural extension to PROLOG.

(ii) The language is based on the generalized unification.

(iii) The language is small, portable and easy to develop.

(iv) The language is efficient.

To achieve this design goal, we choose PROLOG for the target language for following reasons:

(i)   Meta programming gives easy way to develop a new logic programming language.

(ii) Partial evaluation gives efficient program execution.

(iii) There is no effort to develop a basic logic programming feature such as syntactic equality, inference engine and memory management etc.

(iv) PROLOG (Quintus Prolog on Sun-3) has efficient compiler.

This paper describes a new constraint logic programming language CS-Prolog (Constraint Solver Prolog) and is organized as follows. Chapter 2 discusses the delay mechanism in standard logic programming language. The constraint is regarded as relationships over variables, and delay mechanism manipulate the constraint by its variable instantiation. Chapter 3 shows how to solve linear arithmetic equations. CS-Prolog solves it using 4 rules over PROLOG data structure(i.e. arithmetic terms). Domain concept is presented in [Dincbas 86], chapter 4 firstly gives this and we naturally extends it to real arithmetic. In real arithmetic "Domain Concept" can be viewed as inequation. It is difficult to solve inequations. Thus CS-Prolog has 2 versions. One is an ordering relation between two variables, and another is a general inequation solver using the modified(incremental) SUP-INF Method[Shostak 77].

2. Freeze

PROLOG programmer must care to ordering of literals for efficient execution. Some ordering leads to very fast execution, some ordering leads to very slow execution due to backtracking. We usually write PROLOG programs as generate & test type. But we often interleave the test part into the generate part for efficiency, and there is a transformation technique from the generate & test type to the interleaved version[Seki 86]. The basic approach is reordering literals so as to execute the test part immediately after the test part become evaluable.

The constraint is a test part of the generate & test program. Generally, it is not easy to interleave the test part into the generate part, because the constraint is dynamically created and the constraint predicates have many input-output mode to its arguments. Thus we can not analyze program statically. Data driven mechanism enables to handle this problem. Recent logic programming language supports this as delay mechanism. For example, `freeze(Var,Goal)` in Prolog-II, `Var^Goal` in CIL[Mukai 85] and `bind_hook(Var,Goal)` in ESP(KL0)[Chikayama 84], where `"Goal"` is executed when the variable `"Var"` is instantiated. We get the same effect to write test & generate type. CS-Prolog has the same delay mechanism `freeze(Var,Goal)`, and this is a basic constraint feature of CS-Prolog.

3. Equation Constraint

3.1 Equation Solver

CS-Prolog solves linear arithmetic equations and nonlinear equation is delayed until it becomes linear which is implemented by freeze. This chapter describes how to solve linear equations over PROLOG data structure(i.e. arithmetic term). An example of equation solver in CS-Prolog is shown bellow. The predicate `fact(N,F)` means that F is a factorial of N, which is defined by CS-Prolog program(Figure-2), here, inequality constraint ">" is delayed until it becomes evaluable.

```
| >> 2*X-Y=8,X+3*Y=-3.

SUCCESS (2*3- -2=8,3+3* -2+ -2)

| >> X=X-3.

FAIL

| >> X*X-Y=2,X=2.

SUCCESS (2*2-2=2,2=2)

| >> X*X-Y=2,Y=2.

SUCCESS (X*X-2=2,2=2)

| >> fact(N,6),fact(N,F).

SUCCESS (fact(3,6),fact(3,6))
```

Figure-1: An example of equation solver

```
fact(0,1)
fact(N,N*F)  :- N>0,fact(N-1,F).
```

Figure-2: The program of factorial

3.2 Solving Equations

The arithmetic term as compound term is defined as bellow and represented as tree structure in PROLOG. CS-Prolog uses 4 rules to solve linear equations over arithmetic terms.

The definition of arithmetic term:

i)   Real number and variable are arithmetic terms

ii) if L and R are arithmetic terms, then L+R,L-R,L*R and L/R are also arithmetic terms.

The following 4 rules operate on these tree structures.

(1) variable elimination(VE)

If the equation is of the form X=AT where X is a variable and AT is an arithmetic term, then replace these other occurrences of X by AT'. AT' is a solved form of X which is obtained from solving the equation X=AT. The procedure of this, which we call tree evaluation(TE), is that translating X=AT to equivalent equation T*X=K*X+C in which the function "/" must not occur and the arithmetic term C must not contain the variable X.

When TE has finished, we can determine the original equation X=AT to one of the following 4 conditions.

(i)   If C=0 and (T-K)=0, then X=AT is an equivalent equation.

(ii) If C\==0 and (T-K)=0, then X=AT is a contradictory equation.

(iii) If C/(T-K) is evaluated as real number, then X=AT is a solvable equation.

(iv) Otherwise X=AT is a delayed equation.

AT' can be obtained from T,K and C corresponding to the above conditions.

(i) AT' is X itself.

(ii) AT' can not be obtained.

(iii) AT' is the evaluated real number of C/(T-K).

(iv) AT' is the tree structure C/(T-K) itself.

Figure-3 shows the tree evaluation program. The predicate tree_eval(X,AT,T,K,C,F) means that tree evaluate X=AT and obtain T,K and C. The sixth argument F indicates that the equation has the condition (iv) or not. The predicate bound(AT,V) succeeds when it is able to evaluate arithmetic term AT to real number V. Otherwise it fails. The seventh clause of tree_eval/6 indicates the elimination of function "/". For example, we apply TE to X=2*X/6+4, we get an equivalent equation 6*X=2*X+24. Therefore, AT'=24/(6-2)=6.

(2) tree rewriting(TR)

Rewrite equation to be applicable rule (1) using following rules. These rules have simple estimate function "bound", so as to become left hand side of equation to be variable quickly.

```
(i)    if bound(R) then L+R=AT --> L=AT-R else L+R=AT --> R=AT-L
(ii)   if bound(R) then L*R+AT --> L=AT/R else L*R=AT --> R=AT/L
(iii)  if bound(R) then L-R=AT --> L=AT+R else L-R=AT --> R=L-AT
(iv)   if bound(R) then L/R=AT --> L=AT*R else L/R=AT --> R=L/AT
```

```
tree_eval(X,AT,1,0,1,on)  :- X==AT,!.
tree_eval(X,AT,1,0,V,off)  :- bound(AT,V),!.
tree_eval(X,AT,1,0,AT,ena)  :- var(AT),!.
tree_eval(X,L+R,T,K,C,F)  :-
    tree_eval(X,L,T1,K1,C1,F1),
    tree_eval(X,R,T2,K2,C2,F2),
    T=T1*T2,K=K1*T2+K2*T1,C=C1*T2+C2*T1,
    add_sub_flag(F1,F2,F).
tree_eval(X,L-R,T,K,C,F)  :-
    tree_eval(X,L,T1,K1,C1,F1),
    tree_eval(X,R,T2,K2,C2,F2),
    T=T1*T2,K=K1*T2-K2*T1,C=C1*T2-C2*T1,
    add_sub_flag(F1,F2,F).
tree_eval(X,L*R,T,K,C,F)  :-
    tree_eval(X,L,T1,K1,C1,F1),
    tree_eval(X,R,T2,K2,C2,F2),
    T=T1*T2,K=K1*K2*X+K1*C2+K2*C1,C=C1*C2,
    mult_divi_flag(T,K,C,F1,F2,F).
tree_eval(X,L/R,T,K,C,F)  :-
    tree_eval(X,L,T1,K1,C1,F1),
    tree_eval(X,R,T2,K2,C2,F2),
    T=T1*(K2*X+C2),K=K1*T2,C=C1*T2,
    mult_divi_flag(T,K,C,F1,F2,F).
```

Figure-3: The tree evaluation program

(3) equation anteposition(EA)

If both the rule (1) and (2) are not applicable, then replace the equation L=R by R=L.

(4) back substitution(BS)

If the variable x is replaced by tree structure C/(T-K) in rule (1), then the variable x may be able to evaluate as real number when the variable, which occurs in T, K or C, is instantiated. Thus, we redefine the third clause of tree_eval/6 program as follows using freeze. The predicate `eval/1` evaluates tree structure `C/(T-K)` by using the following `tree_eval/6`:

```
tree_eval(X,AT,1,0,AT,ena) :- var(AT),!,freeze(AT,eval(X)).
```

We show a trace of equation solver in Figure-4, which was demonstrated in Figure-1.

equation sets	applied rule
{2*X-Y=8,X+3*Y= -3}	(TR)
{Y=2*X-8,X+3*Y= -3}	(VE)
{X+3*((2*X-8)/(1-0))= -3}	(TR)
{3*((2*(X-8)/(1-0))=-3-X}	(TR)
{(2*X-8)/(1-0)=(-3-X)/3}	(TR)
{2*X-8=(-3-X)/3}	(TR)
{2*X=(-3-X)/3+8}	(TR)
{X=((-3-X)/3+8)/2}	(VE)
{X=3}	(BS)
{X=3,Y= -2}	

Figure-4: Trace of Equation Solver

4. Domain Concept

4.1 What is the Domain Concept ?

Constraint is solved in a passive manner in chapter 2 and 3, i.e. constraint is evaluated when it becomes evaluable. Contradiction(Failure) caused by constraint leads to backtracking. This backward reasoning is a basic mechanism of PROLOG. However, using constraint in an active manner enable to reduce backtracks and reason forward. Therefore, we get an efficient constraint solver.

Dincbas[Dincbas 86] presents "Domain Concept" that enable us this forward reasoning and active constraint. Generally, in the constraint satisfaction problem the domain of the variable is a finite domain. For example, we know the name of towns in traveling salesman's problem and the candidate of colors in map coloring problem. This finite domain is usually defined implicitly in the generate part of generate & test program. But we use this explicitly, which is basic idea of his, for efficient search.

The domain of the variables of logic program is defined in terms of the Herbrand universe. The domain concept defines the domain of the variables explicitly as a subset of the Herbrand universe. The unification of the domain concept is generalized to obtain the updated domain of the variables instead of obtaining answer substitution in standard logic programming. He introduces a domain variable and defines the unification and some built_in predicates over the variables.

This chapter firstly shows his method with map coloring example, and naturally extends it to the domain of real numbers. In the domain of real numbers the domain concept can be viewed as inequation, and we explain how to solve inequation.

4.2 Unification based on the Domain Concept

This section presents the general unification procedure based on the domain concept. In the following X:D denotes the variable X which has the domain D.

(i) C=X:D where C is a constant
    If C is a member of D then assign C to X, otherwise the unification fails.

(ii) Y=X:D where Y is a variable

Unify X with Y, therefore Y has the same domain of the variable X.

(iii) X:Dx=Y:Dy , let D be the intersection of Dx and Dy

(iii-1) If D is empty then the unification fails.

(iii-2) If D has one element V then unify X with Y and assign V to X.

(iii-3) If D has more than an one element then unify X with Y and assign the new domain D to X.

In this procedure, (iii-2) and (iii-3) indicates the forward reasoning.

4.3 Built_in predicates based on the Domain Concept

Introducing the domain concept causes the redefinition of some built_in predicates. Inequality predicates are most important ones. This section describes the inequality predicate \==(not equal). The other inequality predicates are defined in the same way.

(i) C\==X:D where C is a constant

(i-1) If C is not a member of D then succeeds.

(i-2) If C is a member of D, let R be a domain eliminated C from D .

(i-2-1) If R is empty then succeeds.

(i-2-2) If R has an one element V, then assign V to X else assign new domain R to X.

(ii) Y\==X:D where Y is a variable

Delay this until Y is instantiated.

(iii) X:Dx\==Y:Dy, let D be the intersection of Dx and Dy

If D is empty then succeeds else delays this until X or Y is instantiated.

In this procedure forward reasoning is (i-2-2).

4.4 List Domain

If the domain of the variable is enumerable then we can represent it as a list in PROLOG. This section describes a redefined unification and not-equal procedure written in the PROLOG program. The number of each procedure corresponds to previous sections. In the following program, assign(X,V) assigns the value V to the variable X and domain(X,D) assigns the domain D to the variable X.

```
1) C=X:D :- !,member(X,D),assign(X,C).
2) Y=X:D :- X=Y,!.
3) X:Dx=Y:Dy :-
        intersection(Dx,Dy,D),
        (D==[],!,fail ;
         D=[V],!,X=Y,assign(X,V) ;
         X=Y,domain(X,D)).
```

Figure-5: The unification procedure of list domain

```
1) C\==X:D :- not(member(C,D)),!.
   C\==X:D :-
        delete(C,D,R),
        (R==[],!,fail ; R=[V],!,assign(X,V) ; domain(X,R)).
2) Y\==X:D :- freeze(Y,Y\==X:D).
3) X:Dx\==Y:Dy :- all_different(Dx,Dy),!.
   X:Dx\==Y:Dy :- freeze(X,X:Dx\==Y:Dy),freeze(Y,X:Dx\==Y:Dy).
```

Figure-6: The not-equal procedure of list domain

As an example of list domain, we show map coloring which is coloring each areas in such a way two adjacent area must not have the same color. In this example, we must paint 5 areas using 4 colors(green, yellow, red and blue).

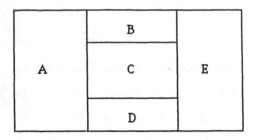

Figure-7: Map Coloring Problem

Figure-8 shows the PROLOG program for solving this and Figure-9 shows the domain concept program. In that program indomain(X) assigns the arbitrary member of the domain of the variable X to the variable X.

```
color([A,B,C,D,E]) :-
    next(A,B),next(A,C),next(A,D),
    next(B,C),next(B,E),
    next(C,D),next(C,E),
    next(D,E).

next(green,yellow).    next(green,red).    next(green,blue).
next(yellow,green).    next(yellow,red).   next(yellow,blue).
next(red,green).       next(red,yellow).   next(red,blue).
next(blue,yellow).     next(blue,green).   next(blue,red).
```

Figure-8: PROLOG program for map coloring

```
color([A,B,C,D,E]) :-
        domain(A,[green,yellow,red,blue]),
        domain(B,[green,yellow,red,blue]),
        domain(C,[green,yellow,red,blue]),
        domain(D,[green,yellow,red,blue]),
        domain(E,[green,yellow,red,blue]),
        next(A,B),next(A,C),next(A,D),
        next(B,C),next(B,E),
        next(C,D),next(C,E),
        next(D,E).


next(X,Y) :- indomain(X),X\==Y.
```

Figure-9: Domain concept program for map coloring

The program in Figure-9 executed as follows. `current_domain(X,Domain)` means that the domain of the variable X is `Domain` at each step.

```
i)   execute each domain predicates
current_domain(A,[green,yellow,red,blue])
current_domain(B,[green,yellow,red,blue])
current_domain(C,[green,yellow,red,blue])
current_domain(D,[green,yellow,red,blue])
current_domain(E,[green,yellow,red,blue])
ii)  execute next(A,B),next(A,C) and next(B,C)
current_domain(A,[green])
current_domain(B,[yellow,red,blue]) *
current_domain(C,[yellow,red,blue]) *
current_domain(D,[yellow,red,blue]) *
current_domain(E,[green,yellow,red,blue])
iii) execute next(B,C) and next(B,E)
current_domain(A,[green])
current_domain(B,[yellow])
current_domain(C,[red,blue]) *
current_domain(D,[yellow,red,blue])
current_domain(E,[green,red,blue]) *
```

```
iv)  execute next(C,D) and next(C,E)
current_domain(A,[green])
current_domain(B,[yellow])
current_domain(C,[red])
current_domain(D,[yellow,blue]) *
current_domain(E,[green,blue]) *
v)   execute next(D,E)
current_domain(A,[green])
current_domain(B,[yellow])
current_domain(C,[red])
current_domain(D,[yellow])
current_domain(E,[green,blue])
```

In the above execution steps, "*" indicates the forward reasoning. For example, when the variable A is assigned to green, the green is eliminated from the domain of the variables B, C and D. Finally we get an answer A=green, B=yellow, C=red, D=yellow and E=green or blue. To the contrary, PROLOG program causes many useless backtracking in the execution of the next predicate. However, backtracking which occur in the domain concept program will be almost shallow backtracking and we gain the efficiency. For example, when we get an answer E=green in the previous example, if we want to get an alternative answer then we can get the answer E=blue quickly.

4.5 Interval domain

In the previous section the domain of the variable is enumerable, therefore we can implement it easily using list manipulation. However, if the domain of the variables is real number then we can not enumerate it, but can define it as interval. The relation between these variables are inequation. Thus we need to solve inequations. It is hard to solve the inequations, therefore CS-Prolog has 2 versions for it. One is a ordering relation between two variables and general inequation between arithmetic terms are not considered. Another is the general inequation solver using modified(incremental) SUP-INF Method[Shostak 77]. We show the example of inequation solver in Figure-10, firstly, and describe 2 versions precisely.

```
| >> X>Y,Y>Z,X>Z.

SUCCESS (X>Y,Y>Z,X>Z)

| >> X>Y,Y>Z,Z>X.

FAIL

| >> P>=Q,P>=R,R>=S,S>=Q.

SUCCESS (P>=Q,Q>=Q,Q>=Q,Q>=Q)

| >> P>=Q,P>=R,R>=3,3>=P.

SUCCESS (3>=Q,3>=3,3>=3,3>=3)
```

Figure-10: An example of inequation solver

4.5.1 A simple inequation solver

CS-Prolog solves inequation using the following axioms.

axiom 1) X=<X (reflexive law)
axiom 2) X=<Y & Y=<X --> X=Y (anti-symmetric law)
axiom 3) X=<Y & Y=<Z --> X=<Z (transitive law)

In addition to these axioms we use the following 3 transitive laws.

axiom 4) X<Y & Y<Z --> X<Z

axiom 5) X=<Y & Y<Z --> X<Z

axiom 6) X<Y & Y=<Z --> X<Z

We assign the types of the variable by its upper bound and lower bound. The upper and lower bounds are also the typed variable, therefore partial order graph is constructed between these variables. The node is a variable and the arc is a relation(<, =<). Generally the variable has more than an upper and a lower bound. It is enough to type the variable its least upper bound(LUB) and greatest lower bound(GLB). For example, the following inequations construct a partial order graph in Figure-11.

X<Z & X=<Y1 & Y1<Z & X<Y2 & Y2=<Z

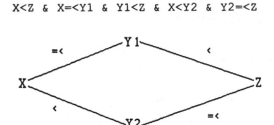

Figure-11: Partial order graph

Inequation solver reasons over this partial order graph. Before we define the inequality predicates "<" and "=<", we prepare the auxiliary predicates is_great/2 and is_greateq/2. These predicates satisfy the following specification and it is easily implemented by graph search technique.

if Y<X & not(Y=<X) then is_great(X,Y)

if Y=<X & not(Y<X) then is_greateq(X,Y)

The predicate "<" is defined in Figure-12. The first clause is in the case of valid, the second and the third is in the case of unsatisfiable and the last needs the refinement of the partial order graph. In the case of partial order graph refinement, it is enough to type the variable with LUB and GLB. If the new upper(lower) bound is less(more) than current LUB(GLB), then updates its LUB(GLB) by its new upper(lower) bound: Otherwise nothing is done. And if there were 2 constraints X=<Y and X<Y we prefer the strict constraint X<Y, thus X=<Y is ignored.

```
X<Y :- is_great(Y,X),!.
X<Y :- is_great(X,Y),!,fail.
X<Y :- is_greateq(X,Y),!,fail.
X<Y :- update_upper_bound(X,Y),update_upper_bound(Y,X).
```

Figure-12: The predicate "<"

If upper or lower bound is a real number, partial order graph is divided that point. We modify is_great/2 and is_greateq/2 to reason such case. Finally we define the "=<" predicate as follows:

```
X=<Y :- is_greateq(Y,X),!.
X=<Y :- is_greateq(X,Y),!,equate_interval(Y,X).
X=<Y :- is_great(Y,X),!.
X=<Y :- is_great(X,Y),!,fail.
X=<Y :-
    update_eq_upper_bound(X,Y),update_eq_lower_bound(Y,X).
```

Figure-13: The predicate "=<"

The first and the third clause are in the case of valid, the fourth clause is in the case of unsatisfiable and the fifth is in the case of refinement of the partial order graph. The second clause indicate the case of anti-symmetric law, in this case CS-Prolog does not only unify X with Y, but also unifies X and Z where Z is the variable which satisfies X=<Z and Z=<Y.

4.5.2 General inequation solver

Here, we need more axioms about inequality to solve the inequations. Figure-14 shows some of them. Using the first axiom we can reason the validity of P<Q --> P+Q<Q+R. However, it is difficult to find the applicable axiom. For example, we must find X=P, Y=R and Z=Q from P+Q=X+Z and Q+R=Z+Y in this case. And it is not enough to reason inequality using the axioms shown in Figure-14.

```
X<Y --> X+Z>Y+Z
X<Y --> X-Z<Y-Z
X<Y --> Z-Y<Z-X
X<Y & 0<Z --> X*Z<Y*Z
X<Y & Z<0 --> Y*Z<X*Z
X<Y & 0<Z --> X/Z<Y/Z
X<Y & Z<0 --> Y/Z<X/Z
```

Figure-14: Axioms for inequation

To overcome this problem CS-Prolog uses modified SUP-INF Method[Shostak 77]. Original his method is the decision procedure for the set of inequations. However, we modified it in an incremental manner.

5. Related work

CS-Prolog is one of the Constraint Logic Programming language based on the generalized unification. This chapter summarizes other logic programming languages similar to ours.

Prolog-II[Colmerauer 84] generalizes the unification to solve equations over the structure of infinite trees. Prolog-II overcomes "occur check" problem, which is omitted in standard PROLOG systems for efficiency, and unification time is proportional to the length of terms.

PROLOG-Q[Jaffar 86b] generalizes the unification to solve linear arithmetic equations using Gaussian method. CLP[Heintze 86] is a real system of this. CS-Prolog will be able to incorporate trigonometric functions which can be written in CLP in the same way, i.e. using delay mechanism.

Term description[Nakashima 85] is a term with constraint on it. `<term:constraint>` denotes the term description and means that "term" must satisfy "constraint". For example `X:member(X,[1,2,3])` means that the variable `X` has the constraint `member(X,[1,2,3])`. A constraint is executed when the term description unified with non-variable term. Therefore, we can delay the predicate using term description. Term description is one of the simplest approach to constraint logic programming.

CIL[Mukai 85] is a logic programming language for natural language understanding based on situation semantics. However, it can be viewed as one of the constraint logic programming language.

6. Conclusion

We have described the constraint logic programming language CS-Prolog. CS-Prolog is written in PROLOG about 1,500 lines. This is a very small as oppose to similar system CLP which is written in C about 12,000 lines, but less efficient than CLP. However, CS-Prolog solves equations and inequations in reasonable time and this paper shows the simple approach to constraint logic programming using PROLOG and this technique is very useful for constraint logic programming language system on top of PROLOG machine.

[REFERENCES]

[Bundy 83] A.Bundy,
The Computer Modelling of Mathematical Reasoning,
Academic Press, 1983.

[Chikayama 84] T.Chikayama,
ESP Reference Manual, ICOT TR-044, 1984.

[Colmerauer 84] A.Colmerauer,
EQUATIONS AND INEQUATIONS ON FINITE AND INFINITE TREES,
Proc. of FGCS '84, 1984.

[Dincbas 86] M.Dincbas,
CONSTRAINTS, LOGIC PROGRAMMING and DEDUCTIVE DATABASE,
France-Japan AI and Computer Science Symposium '86, 1986.

[Heintze 86] N.Heintze et al,
The CLP Programmer's Manual,
Dept. of Computer Science, Monash Univ., 1986.

[Jaffar 86] J.Jaffar and J. Lassez,
A Logic Programming Language Schema,
In D. DeGroot and G.Lindstrom, Eds., LOGIC PROGRAMMING: Functions,
Relations, and Equations, Prentice Hall, 1986.

[Jaffar 86a] J.Jaffar and P.J.Stuckey,
Logic Program Semantics for Programming with Equations,
3rd ICLP, Springer-Verlag, 1986.

[Mukai 85] K.Mukai,
Unification over Complex Indeterminates in Prolog,
Proc. of LPC '85, 1985.

[Nakashima 85] H.Nakashima,
Term Description:A Simple Powerful Extension to Prolog Data Structures, IJCAI '85, 1985.

[Seki 86] H.Seki and K.Furukawa,
Notes on Transformation Technics for Generate and Test Logic Programs, ICOT TM-0240, 1986.

[Shostak 77] Robert E. Shostak,
On the SUP-INF Method for Proving Presburger Formulas,
JACM '77, 1977.

[Simmons 86] R.Simmons
COMMONSENCE ARITHMETIC REASONING, AAAI-86, 1986.

[Steele 80] G.L.Steele Jr.,
The Definition and Implementation of A Computer Programming Language based on CONSTRAINTS, MIT Ph.D Dissertation, 1980.

Update Propagation Network
- A Framework for Constraint Programming

Masayuki Numao

Tokyo Research Laboratory, IBM Japan Ltd.
5-19 Sanbancho, Chiyoda-ku, Tokyo 102, Japan

ABSTRACT

As a framework for constraint programming, a Network model named Cell&Relation Model(CRM) is proposed and an update propagation mechanism is developed on top of the network. The model is used both to describe description of constraint programming and to offer a graphic model for logic programming. An update propagation mechanism, which is useful for on-line interactive systems, is selected as a constraint propagation mechanism. To deal with many-to-many and bidirectional mappings, the mechanism consists of a hypothesis-generating propagator and an evaluator. These components work concurrently; while the former is generating a hypothesis dynamically, the latter evaluates it and controls the propagation. Some heuristics are incorporated to localize the effects of the propagation. An extension to Prolog, named Constraint Prolog, is also included to deal with hypothetical reasoning and lazy evaluation. Constraint Prolog is the interpreter of the update propagation mechanism.

1. INTRODUCTION

Many problems in AI fields are formalized in the framework of constraint programming (Sussman 1980). In scheduling problems, for example, due date requirements, cost requirements, and machine capabilities are all constraints. Consequently, representing such constraints and solving the problems are considered a part of the constraint programming. Intelligent CAD systems are another case. They are required to have a function such that when a user modifies a parameter of a component, the system automatically updates the parameters of other components to satisfy the relations between them. A major research issue in AI, therefore, is to provide a good framework for representing constraints and a good mechanism for solving them.

In this paper, we will propose a Cell & Relation Model(CRM) and explain an update propagation mechanism on top of the model. In the model, variables and relations between them are represented by two kinds of node, Cell and Relation respectively. All the problems are therefore represented in the CRM network. Furthermore, all the relations in the network are always satisfied by the system; this is achieved by a constraint propagation mechanism.

Among many methods for constraint propagation, we focus on the update propagation method. In this method, whenever the user changes the value of any cell, the system updates the values of the other cells so that all the relations are re-satisfied. The advantage of this technique is that the effects of the changes can be localized and minimized. It is therefore suitable for an interactive environment such as an intelligent spreadsheet.

Several update propagation systems were implemented in an object oriented framework. For example, ThingLab (Borning 1981) is written in Smalltalk. However, some difficulty exists in representing a constraint between objects, particularly when the constraint is represented by bidirectional relations. The problem is where to define such relations. If there is a composite object, it is natural for it to have relations with element objects. Otherwise we have two alternatives: one is to invent a special object which plays the role of a composite object, the other is to use a message passing mechanism between objects. In the former case, the special object is used only for managing relations, and does not correspond to anything in the real world. In the latter case, we have to replicate one constraint for many related objects.

We believe that logic programming is appropriate for describing such relational constraints. This is apparent if we consider what languages are suitable for representing bidirectional relations: logic programming language, functional language, and procedural language. CRM can also be considered as a representational model of logic programming language; because a predicate corresponds to a relation and an argument to a cell. The update propagation mechanism also gives a procedural meaning to the model.

This paper is divided into four sections. The first introduces CRM and defines its graphic representations. The difference between the representation of Prolog and of CRM's is also discussed. In the second section we explain the update propagation mechanism, its problems and functions to solve these problems. In the third section we extend a Prolog language to deal with hypothesis and lazy evaluation, which are necessary to describe the update propagation mechanism on Prolog. The fourth section concludes our work.

2. CELL AND RELATION MODEL

The Cell and Relation Model (CRM) is represented by a graph which has two kinds of nodes, Cell and Relation, and a link which connects the cell nodes and the relation nodes. This model is not only suitable for describing constraint problems, but it is also considered as a representational model of logic programming. Furthermore, as a visual language, the model is useful for visualizing a program and its execution process. In this section we show graphic representations of the model, and then compare the model with Prolog.

2.1 Representations

1. Cell

   A cell is represented by a rectangular node which has a cell-id and a cell-value as its elements. There are two kinds of nodes: a free cell node and a fixed cell node with a double bottom line.

2. Relation

   A relation is represented by an ellipse node which has a term with cell-ids as arguments. There are two kinds of nodes: a relation node and a definition node with a double boundary line.

3. Link

   A link is represented by a line connecting a relation and the cell whose cell-id is the same as one of the arguments of the relation.

Each representation is shown in Fig. 1.

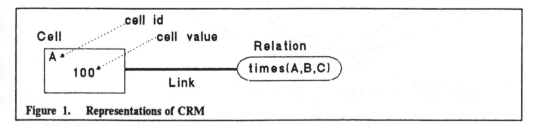

Figure 1. Representations of CRM

The meanings of the cell's elements are as follows:

Cell-id: The cell's name. The relation refers a cell by this id.

Cell-value: The cell's value. The relation evaluates a cell by using this value. The value of the
fixed cell is unchangeable during propagation.

The relation node defines a relation between the values of cells. The definition node forms a new
relation between cells. For example, Figure 2. shows a Celsius-to-Fahrenheit convertor: in this
case the relation is between Celsius and Fahrenheit temperatures. The node *times(A,B,C)* defines the relation among cells *A*, *B*, and *C* such that the product of the values of cells *A* and *B*
is the value of cell *C*. The node *sum(C,D,E)* defines the relation among cells *C*, *D*, and *E* such
that the sum of the values of cells *C* and *D* is the value of cell *E*.

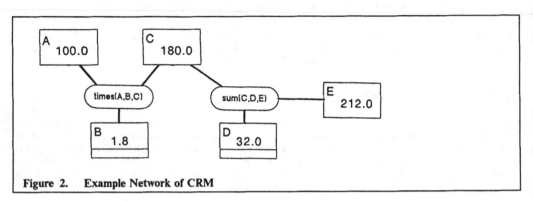

Figure 2.   Example Network of CRM

The value of any cell can be modified by the user, and an update propagation mechanism en-
sures that all the relations are satisfied. This mechanism gives a procedural meaning to the
model, and will be explained in section 3.

2.2 Comparison with Logic Programming Language

CRM can be interpreted in the framework of logic programming language by comparing the
relation to the predicate and the cell to the argument of the predicate. For example, the CRM
representation shown in Fig. 3(a) corresponds to the Prolog program shown in Fig. 3(b).

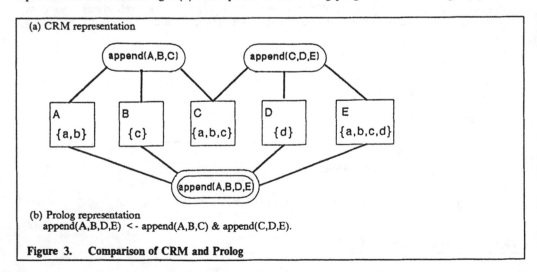

(b) Prolog representation
     append(A,B,D,E) < - append(A,B,C) & append(C,D,E).

Figure 3.   Comparison of CRM and Prolog

However, there are two major differences. One lies in whether the focus is on, data or procedure. The Prolog representation lays emphasis on the procedure: Prolog arguments are subordinate to the predicates, so variables with the same name appear in more than two predicates. The programmer also has to pay attention to which variable is bound in which predicate. On the other hand, the CRM representation lays emphasis on the data: cells in CRM have their own nodes independent of relations. There is no distinction between the roles of cells; any cell can become any input variable or output variable, and thus the user can change the value of any cell. The other difference is in the order of execution; that is, the order in which we should evaluate predicates or relations. In the CRM representation, no order of execution is implied among relations. In Prolog, however, an implicit execution order seems to exist among subgoals, from left to right. These differences are derived from the difference between a 2-dimensional graph representation and a 1-dimensional string representation.

In Prolog, there is a powerful function for matching the patterns of structures, and it is easy to construct a new structure from other structures or to decompose a structure. In CRM, however, it is necessary to use special relations, like cons, car and cdr in Lisp, to construct or decompose a structure.

3. UPDATE PROPAGATION

In the CRM network, all relations should be satisfied, and the constraint propagation mechanism works for that purpose. In this paper we focus on update propagation as a method of constraint propagation. It is formalized as follows: Initially each cell is set a value such that all the relations are satisfied. Whenever the user changes the value of any cell, the system checks whether the relations connected to the cell are satisfied, and updates the value of the cells which are other ends of the relations. The update propagation continues until all the relations are satisfied. This mechanism is adopted as an on-line algorithm, as opposed to off-line algorithms, which compute over the whole network simultaneously. In this mechanism, the smaller the modification, the smaller the computation for the update propagation. Hence it is suitable for an interactive environment, because the user can modify several parameters and see the apparent effect on the whole system interactively, until he finds the best combination of values for the parameters.

In this section, we enumerate the functions necessary for the update propagation mechanism, and explain the algorithm. The algorithm is written in Constraint Prolog which is an extension of Prolog that adds a hypothetical reasoning function and lazy evaluation function. We will explain Constraint Prolog in section 4.

3.1 Functions for Update Propagation Mechanism

When the value of a cell is modified in the network, the relations connected to the cell might cease to be satisfied. If they are not satisfied, the system has to modify other cells connected to the relations so that they will be re-satisfied. This is the one step of update propagation. This modification also influences other relations, causing another step of update propagation, and so on until all the relations are re-satisfied.

There are three major problems in update propagation: (1) which cells to modify, (2) how to modify and (3) in what order to modify. There follows a detailed description of each problem and our system's solution to it.

(1) If a relation has more than two arguments, it means that the relation connects to more than two cells, and that there are several alternative propagation paths. Therefore, the path cannot be uniquely decided. For example, suppose that the value of C in the relation $A + B = C$ is modified. Which cell's value should be modified, $A's$, $B's$, or both $A's$ and $B's$? In our system, we use a search algorithm for the problem. It tries the possible paths one by one until it can find a successful path; i.e. a path along which all relations are satisfied. We call this algorithm the

hypothetical propagation algorithm, because at each step the algorithm makes a hypothesis which consists of the relation and the flag that indicates which cell is modified or fixed.

(2) The second problem is how to decide the value of the modified cell. For example, in the above relation $A + B = C$, suppose that the value of C is modified and the system decides to modify the value of both A and B. How should $C's$ value be divided between $A's$ and $B's$? The value can not be decided uniquely. In our system, we use a lazy evaluation function for the problem. It waits until a relation can be evaluated before attempting to do so. In the above example, the evaluation of the relation is suspended until one of the values of cell A and cell B is determined.

(3) The third problem is the propagation strategy. Since there is much freedom in the selection of propagation paths and values, many solutions exist for one modification. In our system, we use heuristics to localize the effect of the modification, ordering the hypotheses so that the effect of the modification would be minimized.

The update propagation mechanism is divided into two major parts: a hypothesis generator and a hypothesis evaluator. During propagation, the former generates hypotheses and the latter evaluates them and controls the former by a backtracking mechanism. We will explain these parts and the heuristics in the remainder of this section.

3.2 Hypothesis Generator

Figure 4 shows a Prolog program to realize the hypothesis generator. The basic flow of the program is as follows. First, the if-part of the program (lines 2-6) checks whether there is any relation which has not yet been evaluated (line 3) and which connects to the cell which was modified by the user or by the system (lines 4-6). If there is such a relation, then the other cells (*FocusCells*, line 8) connected to the relation are divided into two groups: fixed cells (*NewFixCell*) or modified cells (*NewModCell*, lines 9,10). This classification (flag) and the relation itself become a hypothesis. The hypothesis is then passed to the evaluator (line 11). This is the end of the first step of propagation. In this step, if the evaluator fails and backtracking occurs, then an alternative combination of the fixed cell and the modified cell is selected as another hypothesis, and the evaluator evaluates this in turn. Finally, the program ends by calling the next step; to do this, it adds the newly modified cells to the already modified cells.

```
propagate( ModCellList, UsedRelationList ) < -
  ( relation( Rid, Relation ) &
    ¬member( Rid, UsedRelationList ) &
    Relation  = .. ( Predicate . Arglist ) &
    intersect( ModCellList, ArgList, ModCells ) &
    ModCells  ¬ = {} )
  - >
  ( set_difference( ArgList, ModCells, FocusCells ) &
    subset( NewModCells, FocusCells ) &
    set_difference( FocusCells, NewModCells, NewFixCells ) &
    register_relation( Relation, NewFixCells ) &
    append( ModCellList, NewModCells, ModCellList1 ) &
    propagate( ModCellList1, Rid . UsedRelationList ) ).
```

Figure 4.   Program of Hypothesis Generator

Figure 5 illustrates the propagation process in the case of ternary relations. Here ↓ stands for a modified cell and ⊥ for a fixed cell.

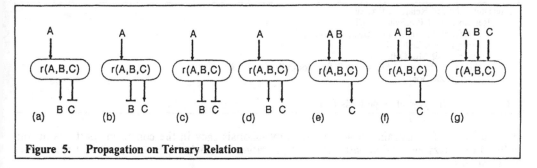

Figure 5. Propagation on Ternary Relation

(1) When one of the three cells (*A*) is already modified, there are four alternatives (Fig. 5-a,b,c,d).

(2) When two of the three cells (*A*,*B*) are already modified, there are two alternatives (Fig. 5-e,f).

(3) When all of the three cells are already modified, there are no alternatives (Fig. 5-g).

3.3 Hypothesis Evaluator

In the propagation cycle, the generator dynamically generates the hypotheses, while the evaluator checks the consistency of hypotheses. If there is any inconsistency, a backtracking mechanism operates in Constraint Prolog, and a new alternative hypothesis is generated by the propagator, making the generator change the direction of propagation. Here we explain how the evaluator checks the hypothesis, which consists of a flag and a relation.

For the flag, the evaluator checks whether any fixed cells are unmodified by the system. This is especially necessary if there is a loop path in the network.

For the relation, the evaluator first replaces its arguments; if the flag is fixed then the cell-id is replaced by the current value of the cell, and if modified then it is replaced by an unbound variable of Prolog.

The evaluator then evaluates the relation as a Prolog goal, using the so-called lazy evaluation mechanism. This is necessary because, if the relation cannot be evaluated immediately, then the evaluation has to be suspended until the necessary bindings of the arguments occur. When it becomes possible, the relation is evaluated to check whether it is satisfied or not, and also to bind the unbound variable.

We will describe the evaluation process with the evaluator program shown in Fig. 6. The evaluation process is separated into two phases: First, a constraint pattern is constructed from a flag, and is registered in Constraint Prolog (lines 4,5). The constructed pattern can be either a fixed pattern «*fix(Id)*» or a modified one «*mod(Id)*». The consistency of the pattern is then checked, to ensure that both the fixed pattern and the modified pattern were not registered for a single cell. Next, a lazy evaluation pattern «*eval(R)*» is constructed from a relation *R* (line 6), and is registered in Constraint Prolog (line 7). When it can be evaluated, The relation is normally evaluated as a Prolog goal.

```
register_relation( Relation, FixCells ) <-
    Relation = .. ( Predicate . Arglist ) &
    set_difference( Arglist, FixCells, ModCells ) &
    register_fix( FixCells ) &
    register_mod( ModCells ) &
    make_goal( Predicate, Arglist, FixCells, ModCells, Goal ) &
    register_goal( Goal ).
```

Figure 6.   Program of Hypothesis Evaluator

In both cases, if Constraint Prolog detects any inconsistency in the constraint patterns or any failure in the lazy evaluation patterns, the registration subgoals (lines 4,5,7) fail and this causes backtracking.

Figure 7 illustrates how update propagation proceeds when the user changes the value of cell *A* from 100 to 50 in the network shown in Fig. 2. It also shows the registered constraint patterns and lazy evaluation patterns.

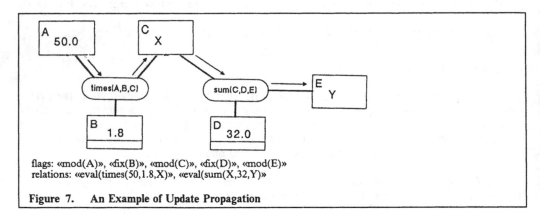

flags: «mod(A)», «fix(B)», «mod(C)», «fix(D)», «mod(E)»
relations: «eval(times(50,1.8,X)», «eval(sum(X,32,Y)»

Figure 7.   An Example of Update Propagation

3.4 Propagation Heuristics

When the values of a few cells in a large network consisting of many cells and relations are modified, it is desirable that the effects of the propagation are minimized. This is necessary to improve the efficiency of the propagation, and also because the user expects little effect from the small changes. To achieve this, some propagation strategies are necessary. In our system, the strategies are realized by two heuristics which set the precedence of the hypotheses:

(1) Fixed cell first
The hypothesis which generates more fixed cells precedes. This is because no more propagations proceed from the fixed cell.

(2) Leaf cell first
The hypothesis which modifies the cell with fewer links precedes. This is because, if a cell is modified, then the relations connected to the cell have to be evaluated during the next propagation, and consequently many links imply a large propagation.

4. CONSTRAINT PROLOG

Constraint Prolog is an extension of Prolog to deal with hypothetical reasoning and lazy evaluation. The constraint pattern and the lazy evaluation pattern discussed in the previous sections are evaluated by Constraint Prolog. The mechanism of Constraint Prolog is based on the language ProBoole (Morishita 1987), which has free Boolean algebra as its truth value domain. In Boolean algebra, symbols can be regarded as truth values. Furthermore, we can define various relationships between symbols. For example, if we define the mutually exclusive relationship between the elements p and q, then the predicates whose values are p and q cannot succeed at the same time. Thus the framework of ProBoole is suitable for representing constraint relationships between Horn-clauses and goals. This characteristic is very useful for constraint programming. Constraint Prolog emphasizes on this practical usefulness rather than theoretical aspects, because ProBoole has many restrictions due to its theoretical background. In Constraint Prolog, multi-valued characteristics vanish and the constraint pattern generated by a special predicate controls the execution.

4.1 System Architecture

The system consists of four parts: a Prolog interpreter, a rule base, a constraint watcher, and a constraint rule base. The former two components are the same as those of Prolog, except that there is a special predicate for constraint pattern generation. The pattern generator predicate has the form «P» and when it is evaluated, the pattern P is registered by the constraint watcher. The major extension of Constraint Prolog is the external execution control mechanism, using the latter two components. During execution, the registered patterns are kept in the pattern list. Each is then compared with the pattern in the constraint rule, and if the matching succeeds, then either the pattern is substituted or external failure occurs.

4.2 Constraint Rules

The constraint rule is defined independently from the Horn-clause. It has the form

rule(SubPattern, Condition, ReplacedPattern).

or

rule(SubPattern, Condition, fail).

This constraint rule checks for the occurrence of the *SubPattern* in the pattern list during the resolution. If it occurs, then the condition part of the rule *Condition* is evaluated. If this succeeds, then the first form of the rule substitutes the sub pattern *SubPattern* in the list with the *ReplacedPattern*, and the second form of the rule causes a backtracking.

For example, If one wants to define that the pattern p implies the pattern q, one should adopt the following rule:

rule({p}, true, {q}).

If one wants to define that the patterns p and q are mutually exclusive, one should adopt the following rule:

rule({q,r}, true, fail).

The rule for the hypothesis flag check is as follows:

rule({fix(Id), mod(Id)}, true, fail).

This means that if the hypotheses that fixed and modified the value of the same cell are both generated, then a backtracking occurs.

4.3 Lazy Evaluation Function

A function which attaches conditions to the variables even they are unbound increases the describability of constraints, since the user does not have to worry about whether the argument variables are bound or unbound when the predicate is called. In Constraint Prolog, we can realize such a function by suspending the predicate until the argument variables are bound. The "freeze" mechanism of Prolog-II (Colmerauer 1982) and the "wait declaration" of MU-Prolog (Naish 1986) also realized the same function.

To represent the lazy evaluation predicate in our system, let us introduce a special pattern named eval. Eval is notated as follows:

$eval(Condition, Predicate)$.

The meaning of this pattern is that the execution of the predicate *Predicate* is suspended until the condition *Condition* is satisfied. For example, the pattern

$eval(\neg var(X) \& \neg var(Y), X < Y)$.

compares the variables X and Y when the two variables are bound.

For the pattern to take effect, the following two rules should be adopted:

$rule(\{eval(Cond, Pred)\}, Cond \& Pred, \{\})$.

$rule(\{eval(Cond, Perd)\}, Cond \& \neg Pred, fail)$.

The meaning of the first rule is that, if the condition succeeds and the predicate also succeeds, then the pattern is removed from the pattern list. The meaning of the second is that, if the condition succeeds but the predicate fails, then it causes a backtracking. In both rules, if the condition fails, the pattern remains in the pattern list, which means that the predicate is suspended.

Figure 8 is an example program using the lazy evaluation pattern. It is a sorting program using the generate-and-test technique. In this case, however, the top-level goal first evaluates the test-part predicate *ordered(R)*, which in turn checks whether the generated list is ordered; it then evaluates the generate-part *perm(L,R)*, which in turn generates permutation lists from the input list. This is the reverse of the generate-and-test order. However, the execution is efficient when compared with the normal order, because the suspended predicate *ordered(R)* checks the sub-list during the intermediate stages of constructing the permutation list, so it is not necessary to generate the whole list if it is not sorted.

Furthermore, the patterns left in the pattern list when the top-level goal succeeds are interpreted as the condition for the goal's success. For example, if you input a variable list $\{A, B\}$ to the above program by

$< - sort(\{A,B\}, R)$,

it returns two answers,

$R = \{A, B\}$, *suspended predicate* $= A < B$

and

$R = \{B, A\}$, *suspended predicate* $= B < A$.

These mean that if $A < B$, then the sorted list becomes $\{A, B\}$, but if $B < A$, then it becomes $\{B, A\}$.

```
sort( L, R ) < - ordered( R ) & perm( L, R ).

perm( {}, {} ).
perm( L, {X|R} ) < - del( L, X, Y ) & perm( Y, R ).

del( {X|Y}, X, Y ).
del( {X|Y}, T, {X|R} ) < - del( Y, T, R ).

ordered( {} ).
ordered( {X} ).
ordered( {X, Y|R} ) < - «eval( ¬ var(X) & ¬ var(Y), X ≤ Y )» & ordered( R ).
```

Figure 8.   A Sort Program using the Lazy Evaluation Function

This mechanism enables the propagation mechanism to be connected to the external constraint solver. It requires many kinds of constraint solvers, according to the problem's domain. For example, the Gaussian elimination method is needed for solving linear equations. CLP(R) (Jaffar 1987) solves constraints of the real domain.

5. CONCLUSION

The Cell and Relation Model gives a common framework for constraint programming and logic programming. The model gives a basic framework to constraint programming from the view point of logic programming. Constraint programming can also be considered as a high-level application of logic programming, because the propagation mechanism requires not only the unification and backtracking mechanism of Prolog, but also lazy evaluation, goal reordering and hypothetical reasoning functions which are expected to be achieved by future logic programming systems.

The model was designed for general constraint problems. However, several extensions are necessary to describe actual problems. For example, currently there are only two kinds of cell: a modified cell and a fixed cell. The user would want to order the modifiability of the cell by some kind of index, e.g. weight for controlling the propagation path. As for the heuristics of propagation, besides the localization heuristics which is adopted by the current system, the user would want to distribute the changes to a certain group of cells, or to propagate the changes so that an evaluation function would be maximized. Therefore, future work should identify the direction of such extensions in order to represent the actual problems and develop a general framework.

References

Borning A.(1981), "The Programming Language Aspect of ThingLab - a Constraint-Oriented Simulation Laboratory", ACM TOPLAS, Vol.3, No.4.
Colmerauer A.(1982), "Prolog-II Manual de Reference et Modele Theoretique", Groupe Intelligence Artificelle, Universite d'Aix-Marsaille.
Jaffar J., Michaylov S.(1987), "Methodology and Implementation of a CLP System", 4th International Logic Programming Conference, MIT Press.
Morishita S. et al.(1987), "Symbolical Construction of Truth Valued Domain for Logic Programs", 4th International Logic Programming Conference, MIT Press.
Naish L.(1986), "Negation and Control in Prolog", Lecture Notes in Computer Science 238, Springer-Verlag.
Sussman G., Steele Jr G.(1980), "Constraints - A Language for Expressing Almost-Hierarchical Descriptions", Artificial Intelligence, Vol.14.

MENDELS: CONCURRENT PROGRAM SYNTHESIS SYSTEM
USING TEMPORAL LOGIC

Naoshi Uchihira, Kazunori Matsumoto, Shinichi Honiden,
and Hideo Nakamura
Systems & Software Engineering Lab.
TOSHIBA Corporation
Yanagicho 70, Saiwai-ku, Kawasaki, Kanagawa 210, JAPAN

ABSTRACT

A concurrent program synthesis system called MENDELS is proposed. A
concurrent programming language MENDEL/87, that is a target language
for program synthesis, is also provided. MENDELS consists of two
parts: (1) retrieving and interconnecting reusable components from I/O
data specifications and (2) synthesizing a synchronization supervisor
from a propositional temporal logic specification. MENDELS has been
implemented in PROLOG on a PROLOG machine. MENDELS is a subsystem of
the intelligent programming environment MENDELS ZONE.

1. INTRODUCTION

The two major purposes of program synthesis and automatic
programming are to generate a program that is assured of being
correct, and to increase software productivity. Our main goal is to
achieve these different purposes while maintaining a good balance,
especially for concurrent programs.

Recently, software reuse is expected to greatly increase software
productivity. In fact, many attempts have been made on research and
practical levels, and in various ways. Because of these many efforts,
sofware reuse is just getting under way. Accordingly, much research on
software components interconnection and software-resuse-based program
synthesis has been presented. However most of them are only for
sequential programs, not for concurrent programs. Also, they are
lacking assurance that the synthesized program is correct.

For concurrent programs, verification has been investigated for a
long time. Some efforts involve verification using a linear time
propositional temporal logic (PTL). In this case, PTL is a

specification language, and a PTL decision procedure is able to verify whether the specification is consistent or not. As PTL is decidable and has various decision procedure algorithms [P186,FT85], verification is accomplished automatically.

Manna and Wolper [MW84,Wo82] use PTL for program synthesis. They show a theorem proving method which can synthesize synchronization parts of a concurrent program using PTL or extended temporal logic (ETL). In this method, a model graph, which is generated in the decision procedure, is considered as a state transition diagram for processes. From this state transition diagram, CSP programs which execute synchronization are generated.

There are other works about synthesis using temporal logic in addition to Manna and Wolper's work. Clarke and Emerson [CE81] propose a synthesis method for the synchronization skeletons of a concurrent program using branching time temporal logic. Fujita, Tanaka, and Moto-oka [FTM84] show a synthesis method of state transition diagrams using PTL for specifying hardware. Katai and Iwai [KI82] propose a method to generate scheduling rules of concurrent system from PTL specification and a Petri net. ENVISAGER system [GU87] is a visual programming environment, similar to MENDELS. This system adopts Interval Temporal Logic as a specification language, and is implemented on the UNIX workstation. But Interval Temporal Logic is used only for simulation, not for program synthesis.

We think the most practical approach to automatic programming in large scale applications is a program synthesis utilizing automated reasoning mechanism with reusable components. Because automated reasoning approach can synthesize only small scale programs and can not support large scale applications. In Manna and Wolper's synthesis method, a synchronization part is generated automatically. However, another part, say a functional part, must be created by the programmer. This paper proposes a new synthesis method which is a combination of software reuse and Manna and Wolper's method. This method consists of two major parts: (1) retrieval and interconnection of reusable components and (2) synthesis of a synchronization supervisor. This method generates a MENDEL/87 program. MENDEL/87 is a Prolog-based concurrent object-oriented language [HUK86]. The program synthesis system based on this method is called MENDELS (MENDEL program Synthesis system). MENDELS has been implemented on a Prolog machine.

2. PROGRAMMING MODEL

This section provides a programming model for a concurrent program, which is more or less restricted but very simple and intuitive. This model is based on the following concepts:

(1) Data stream oriented programming

The program consists of a number of processes which can run concurrently. A process itself is a sequential program. Processes communicate with and synchronize each other only by the data stream through communication pipes; so have no shared variables. Communication pipes are statically defined before execution in the same way as Occam [Oc83].

(2) Software Reuse

Assume that a large enough number of processes have already been created and stored in a library. In principle, a goal program can be synthesized by interconnecting some of the processes in a library. In this case, a process is a reusable component, which cannot be modified when reusing it. Sometimes it is called a "black box" reusable component. Each process looks like an IC. Just as an electronic circuit is composed by connecting a number of LSIs, a program can be synthesized by interconnecting a number of processes.

(3) Synchronization Supervisor

When a programmer prepares reusable processes, he does not know how these processes will be interconnected. A reusable process should be independent from other processes, while synchronization is regarded as interaction between processes. It is difficult and undesirable that the synchronization codes be written in the internal part of each reusable process. The synchronization supervisor should be separated from reusable processes, such as a path expression [Ha76,An79]. Therefore, processes are retrieved and interconnected first, then the synchronization supervisor is provided on these processes (Fig. 1).

3. MENDEL/87

a. Overview

We suggest a concurrent object-oriented programming language with something like Occam + OPS5 + PROLOG; call this language MENDEL/87.

MENDEL/87 program consists of several objects; the object consists of several methods. The object can be regarded as a process. Each object has finite pipe caps and can transmit messages only through the pipe caps. An attribute is assigned to each pipe cap and is used to identify input/output messages. The message is transmitted between objects through the transmission pipe connected with pipe caps, as shown in Fig. 2. The pipe is a one-to-one asynchronous one-way path. Initial messages are sent through the input nodes, and goal messages are extracted from the output nodes. The gate and the signal gate are used for message stream control.

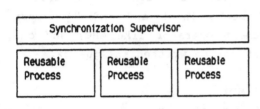

Fig.1 Synchronization supervisor
     separated from reusable
     processes

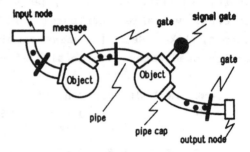

Fig.2 Objects, pipes, and messages
       in MENDEL/87

b. Object

A MENDEL/87 object consists of a declaration part, a method part and a junk part.

```
<object name>
{
     dec : {   <declaration part> }
     meth : {  <method part>      }
     junk : {  <junk part>        }

}
```

The declaration part includes declarations of five items :
1) Input pipe cap attributes
          inpipe(<attribute>, ...).
2) Output pipe cap attributes
          outpipe(<attribute>, ...).
3) Input signal attributes
          insignal(<attribute>, ...).
4) Output signal attributes

        outsignal(<attribute>, ...).
5) Internal state variables
        state(<attribute>!<initial value>,...).

The method part includes several methods. The method is described
as follows :

    method (<attribute> ? <term>, ... , <attribute> ! <term>, ...)
            <- <guard> | <Prolog goals>.

where, <attribute> means pipe cap attribute, signal attribute, or
internal variable attribute; "?" means input and and " ! " means
output, like CSP; "|" means commitment operator like GHC; and only
Prolog predicates with no side effect can be written in <guard>.

    ex. method(hour ? H, minute ! M)
            <- H >= 0 | M is H*60, write(M), nl.

The method is selected when :
(1) Each of the terms after <attribute>? can be unified with a
received message from the pipe, signal, or state variable indicated by
the attribute.
(2) All predicates in <guard> succeed.


```
KeyCheck
{
    dec :(
        inpipe(keyword.word).
        outpipe(ckeck_data).
        state(keywordlist![]).
    )
    meth :(
                % receive a keyword and store it in the keywordlist.
        method(keyword?KW.keywordlist?KWL.keywordlist!(KW:KWL)).
                % receive a word and if it is a keyword. send it to check_data.
        method(word?W.keywordlist?KWL.check_data!W) <-
            menber(W.KWL)! true.
                % receive a word and if it isn't a keyword. do nothing.
        method(word?W).
    )
    junk:(
        member(_.[]) :- !.fail.
        member(X.[X!_]).
        member(X.[_:Y]):- !.member(X.Y).
    )
}
```

Fig.3 MENDEL/87 Object Example (KeyCheck)

When the method is selected, all Prolog predicates in <**Prolog goals**> are evaluated. Each term after <**attribute**>!, which has been unified in <**Prolog goals**>, is sent as a message into the pipe, signal, or state variable indicated by the attribute. If <**Prolog goals**> fails, warn-ing messages are given to the user and the method terminates without sending output messages.

This method selection mechanism is similar to a Dijkstra's guarded command, Occam's alternative construct, and GHC. Moreover, the method can be considered as a production rule in a production system, such as OPS5.

The junk part includes some Prolog clauses, which may be called by methods or other Prolog clauses. One example of MENDEL/87 object is shown in Fig. 3.

c. Gate and Gate controller

In MENDEL/87, a simple synchronization mechanism is given by a method selection mechanism. The object is suspended until it can receive all required messages. However, it is so simple that a complicated synchronization requires complicated pipe interconnection (many of them are only for control stream, not for data stream), so an additional synchroni-zation mechanism using the gate and the gate controller is introduced. Every pipe has only one gate which controls the message stream. The gate opens, lets only one message pass through and then shuts. This is an atomic action of the gate. With no message in the gate, the gate cannot be opened. The gate is similar to the transition of a Petri Net (Fig. 4). The gate controller controls all gates, that is the synchronization supervisor.

d. Signal gate and end_of_gate

The signal gate itself is regarded as a kind of gate. When the input signal gate opens, it generates one signal message which has no value and is sent to an object only for the method selection, like a binary semaphor. When the output signal gate opens, it consumes one signal message which is sent from an object.

The end_of_gate is a system output signal gate. When detecting that there are no more messages passing through the gate g in the future, the system (interpreter) sends one signal message to output signal gate **eog(g)** (end of gate g). The end_of_gate fills the role of a terminal symbol, such as end_of_file and end_of_string in C language. As a terminal symbol itself is not a data, but a control signal, it should not be treated in the same way as other messages. In

MENDEL/87, the signal message and the signal gate are distinguished from the ordinary message and gate.

4. OBJECT RETRIEVAL AND INTERCONNECTION

MENDEL/87 objects can be retrieved and interconnected in two main ways; manually and automatically.

a. Manual

Select an object from an object library and interconnect these objects with pipes manually. These oparations are carried out using a graphic editor in MENDELS.

b. Automatic

Give program specifications as a set of input/output attributes. That is a kind of I/O data type. Objects are then selected from an object library and interconnected automatically, according to the given I/O attributes. Automatic retrieval and interconnection are carried out, according to the following principles:

(1) A pair of pipe caps having the same attributes can be interconnected.

(2) All required output attributes must be reachable from given input attributes through connected objects and pipes.

For example, if the following attributes are given, object B, C, and D are retrieved and interconnected as shown in Fig. 5.

Input attribute a, b ;
Output attribute e ;

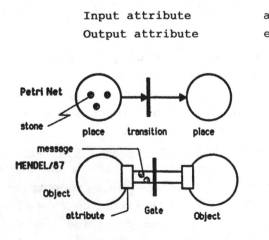

Fig.4 Petri net and MENDEL/87

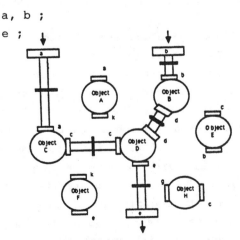

Fig.5 Automatic object retrieval and interconnection

c. More Flexible Automatic Binding

This automatic retrieval and interconnection, which we call "automatic binding", seems to be not enough powerful enough. The binding mechanism depends on the simple pattern matching between output and input attribute names. In some cases, it might find no candidate to fit the given I/O attributes, or a lot of candidates in other cases. More information must be needed to select the most adequate candidate.

To overcome this problem, we adopt a kind of semantic network (called "Attribute Network" [UKMH87]) which represents the attribute structure and define a metric to order the candidates on the semantic network.

By the way, the main topics of this paper are the how to synthsize the synchronization supervisor from PTL specification and how to utilize the supervisor in the concurrent program prototyping system. Therefore we use only simple attributes for clear understanding of main topics.

5. SYNCHRONIZATION SUPERVISOR SYNTHESIS

a. Specification language for synchro-nization

(1) PTL

PTL is a linear time propositional temporal logic which has the following temporal operators in addition to usual logical symbols ('&' -- AND, '#' -- OR, '-' -- NOT, '=>' -- IMPLY) :

[]f (read always f) :
          f is true for all future states
<>f (read eventually f) :
          f is true for some future state
@f   (read next f) :
          f is true for the next state
f1 $ f2 (read f1 until f2) :
          f1 is true until f2 becomes true

(2) Model

An atomic proposition in PTL corresponds to an atomic action of the gate (includes signal gate) in MENDEL/87. That is, "g is true for the state" means "gate g opens, lets only one message pass through, and then shuts at the state". In the same way, "<>g is true" means "gate g will open at some future state", and "[]g is true" means "gate g is always open". Moreover, it is assumed that only one gate can open at the same state (this assumption is called the single-event condition). The single event condition means that only one atomic proposition is true for each state. For example, a specification that "gates g1 and g2 open by turns in Fig.6" is expressed by the following PTL formulas:

$$[](g1 => @g2)$$
$$[](g2 => @g1)$$

b. Scheduling rule synthesis for the gate controller

In MENDEL/87, the synchronization supervisor synthesis means synthesis of scheduling rules, by which the gate controller selects a gate to be opened. While the gate controller selects a gate according to the rules synthesized from a specification, the order of selected gates satisfies the specification. This synthesis method is based on Manna and Wolper's tableau-like PTL decision procedure [MW84]. A brief summary of the synthesis method is as follows:

(Step1) First initial PTL formulas are decomposed into current formulas, which include no temporal operator, and future formulas by the decomposition procedure. Future formulas are also decomposed into current and future formulas from the next state point of view. After every kind (a finite number) of future formulas has been repeatedly decomposed, a graph is derived. Each edge of that graph corresponds to current formulas for each decomposition. This graph is an incomplete model satisfying specifications other than eventuality formulas, such as <>F, -[]F and -(-F1 $ F2).

(Step2) Edges with unsatisfiable eventuality formulas are deleted from the graph by the elimination procedure. The graph remaining after the elimination procedure is a complete model of the initial PTL specification.

(Step3) This model graph can be regarded as a state transition diagram. Scheduling rules are translated from this model graph. Each rule corresponds to a transition on the model graph. These scheduling rules are completed by adding the following fairness strategy:

Fairness Strategy: If there are several possible transitions/rules, one which has never been selected or for which the most time has elapsed from the last selection should be selected.

The state transition diagram and scheduling rules for the previous example are shown in Fig. 7.

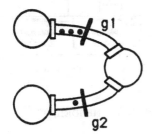

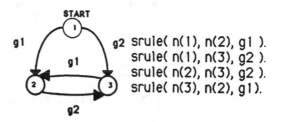

srule(n(1), n(2), g1).
srule(n(1), n(3), g2).
srule(n(2), n(3), g2).
srule(n(3), n(2), g1).

Fig.6 An example of gates

Fig.7 State transition diagram and scheduling rules synthesized from PTL

6. MENDELS

A MENDEL program synthesis system (MENDELS) is based on the method mentioned above, which consists of four steps. (Step1) Make MENDEL/87 objects and store in a library. (Step2) Retrieve and interconnect objects. (Step3) Synthesize scheduling rules for the gate controller. (Step4) Set input data and Execute.

Since MENDELS supports software prototyping, it is possible to go back to an arbitrary previous step (Fig.8). The system provides six windows as the user interface: (1) Command window, (2) Object window which displays MENDEL reusable objects in an object library, (3) I/O window which shows I/O specification of a goal program, (4) PTL window which shows a synchronization specification written by PTL, (5) Diagram window which illustrates objects and interconnections between their attributes, and (6) System message window, as shown in Fig. 9.

For each prototyping step, details will be described below.

(Step1) Make objects and store in a library.

Make MENDEL/87 objects in an integrated editor and store them in an object library. Synchronously, objects are compiled into intermediate codes. Objects in an object library are displayed in the object window.

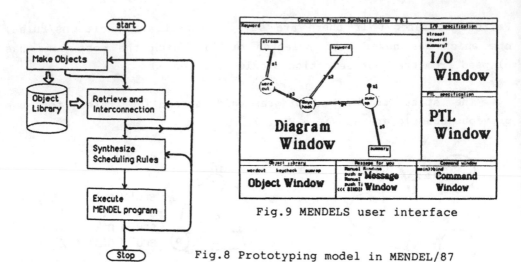

Fig.9 MENDELS user interface

Fig.8 Prototyping model in MENDEL/87

(Step2) Retrieve and interconnect objects.

The system retrieves and interconnects objects manually and automatically as described in section IV. It is also possible to mix these two methods; objects are retrieved and interconnected automatically first and then modified manually. I/O specifications are entered using the I/O window, and the interconnection result is displayed on the diagram window.

(Step3) Synthesize scheduling rules.

While looking at interconnected objects and gates in the diagram window, the user provides a synchronization specification which define the order of gates to be opened, using the PTL window. The system then generates a state transition diagram from the PTL specification, and translates it into scheduling rules.

(Step4) Set data and execute.

From step1 to step3, the system can obtain the following.
* Compiled intermediate codes of objects
* Interconnection information
* Scheduling rules of the gate controller

The system generates executable codes by appending new codes to compiled intermediate codes to perform interconnection. The interpreter executes these codes. Execution is pseudo-concurrent on one CPU. The gate is implemented as a mail box. Therefore, the interpreter selects one of the objects waiting at the mail box and lets it receive a message according to the scheduling rules derived in step 3. This part of the interpreter that schedules a waiting object queue at each mail box is called the gate controller. A process of execution is displayed on the diagram window.

MENDELS has been under construction using the object oriented Prolog (ESP [Ch84]) on a PROLOG machine (PSI [Ta84]).

7. SYNTHESIS EXAMPLE: KEY WORD COUNT Program

We are going to synthesize the Key Word Count Program. This program reads a text (stream of characters) and a key word list, and then checks occurrence of key words in the text and reports its summary.

(STEP1) It is assumed that there are many objects, especially text processing objects, in an object library.

(STEP2) In this example, the user selects the automatic mode and provides I/O attributes for a goal program using the I/O window,

```
      goal program :
      Input attribute          stream, keyword ;
      Output attribute         summary ;
```

and chooses the menu command "automatic". The system then shows several objects in the diagram window, which have been retrieved and interconnected automatically (Fig.10). Here, three objects are selected:

```
        WordCut :
      Input attribute          stream ;
      Output attribute         word ;


        KeyCheck :
      Input attribute          keyword, word ;
      Output attribute         check_data ;


        SumRep :
      Input attribute          check_data ;
      Output attribute         summary ;
```

WordCut reads a character stream and analyzes them to obtain words. KeyCheck reads keywords and sequence of words, checks for words that match one of keywords, and returns the result of checking. (This object was shown in Fig. 3.) SumRep sums up check data and makes a summary report.

(STEP3) While looking at a diagram in the diagram window, the user inputs a PTL specification in the PTL window. The user may require the following :
(1) Both keyword and stream are finite. (Messages going through g1, g3, and g4 are finite.)
(2) WordCut and KeyCheck can be processed concurrently. But KeyCheck must not receive words from WordCut and not start checking until all keywords have been received. (Does not open g2 until there is no more message through g3.)
(3) SumRep analyzes all check data after KeyCheck has finished checking. (Does not open s1 until there are no more messages through g4.)
(4) As an exception, g5 is always open (i.e. out of synchronization).
(5) SumRep must make a summary report at last.

These requests are represented by the following PTL specification:
(1) FINITE(g1), FINITE(g3), FINITE(g4)
(2) - g2 $ eog(g3)
(3) - s1 $ eog(g4)
(4) g5 doesn't appear in PTL.
(5) <> s1, [](s1 => @halt), HALT
where FINITE and HALT are "macros" of this specification language. Each "macro" is expanded into the following PTL:

FINITE(g)   -->
 <>eog(g) & [](eog(g)=>@([](-eog(g)&-g)))
The total number of messages passing through gate g is finite, and after all message have passed through the gate g, the system signal gate eog(g) must be opend only once.

HALT -->   <>halt& [](halt=>@([]halt))
The program eventually terminates.

If an atomic proposition g dosen't appear in PTL, the gate g must be always open.

From these PTL formulas, the system generates a state transition diagram (Fig. 11) and translates it into scheduling rules.

(STEP4) The user inputs two kind of data, a list of keywords and a text stream. The system then executes a synthesized MENDEL/87 program and outputs a summary report (Fig. 12).

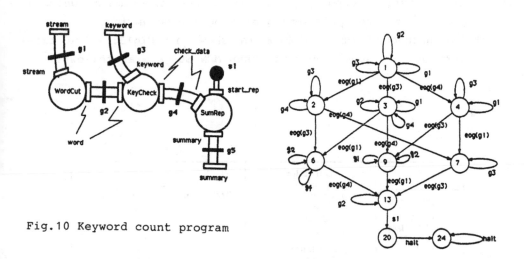

Fig.10 Keyword count program

Fig.11 State transition diagram for the keyword count program

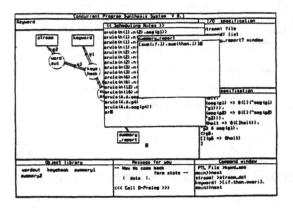

Fig.12   Execution of the keyword count program
in MENDELS

8. MENDELS ZONE

MENDELS is a subsystem of a intelligent programming environment, called MENDELS ZONE, which is based on software reuse assuring the program correctness.

The MENDELS ZONE objectives are to :

(1) Assure the correctness of programs.

(2) Enhance software reuse.

(3) Support the distributed system development using the rapid prototyping methodology.

(4) Assure consistent support for an intelligent programming which is based on object-oriented programming and logic programming.

The structure of MENDELS ZONE is shown in Fig13. The brief explanations of each subsystem other than MENDELS are as follows.

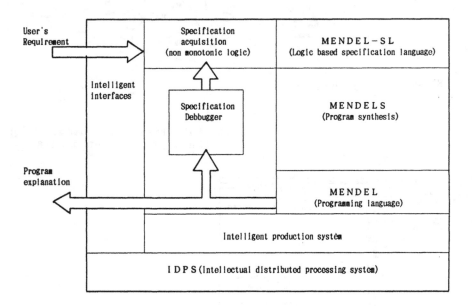

Fig.13 Intelligent programming environment MENDELS ZONE

1. MENDEL

MENDEL is an object-oriented concurrent programming language for prototyping. Each object works concurrently. Inner descriptions of objects are written by guarded Prolog. MENDEL/87 is an instance of MENDEL.

2. MENDEL-SL

A logical specification of each MENDEL object is described by the specification language MENDEL-SL (MENDEL Specification Language). Specifications for object interconnection and synchronization are also described by MENDEL-SL. MENDEL-SL is based on some logics, which includes PTL which specifies the synchronization supervisor as you see in the previous section. Automated reasoning mechanism can verify given specification and transform it to MENDEL program.

3. Specification Acquisition System

User specification may be ambiguous. Based on non-monotonic logic, the specification with ambiguity is transformed to the complete specification of MENDEL-SL.

4. Specification Debugger

User specification may not satisfy user real requirement. While watching the execution of MENDEL program, user can detect a gap between specification and real requirement, and feed it back to the specification aquisition phase. In the specification acquisition phase, specifications can be modified by this feedback.

5. Intellectual Distributed Processing System (IDPS)

IDPS [Ta87] offers a distributed processing environment including Operating System for MENDEL program execution. MENDEL interpreter will be implemented on IDPS.

6. Intelligent Production System

It controls prototype evaluation cycle which evaluates other constraints not appeared in program specifications, and manages software module construction and its history.

7. Intelligent Interfaces

Logical specification may not be user-friendly. It is useful to transforms natural language-like specifications to logical specification. At least, it is possible to define some syntax sugar on PTL.

9. CONCLUSION

We have proposed a concurrent program synthesis method and its system (MENDELS). MENDELS consists of two major parts: (1) Retrieving and interconnecting components from I/O data specifications (2) Synthesizing the gate controller from propositional temporal logic specification. MENDELS is also illustrated with one example. Unique features of MENDELS include: (1) A combination of software reuse and synchronization supervisor synthesis using temporal logic. (2) A new synchronization mechanism using gate, signal gate, and end_of_gate. We believe this approach will become practical enough to help programming on a qualified domain, such as parallel text processing and concurrent business transactions.

At present, much remains to be explored:

(1) More expressive specification language than PTL should be investigated. We are now considering Conditional Proposotional Temporal Logic. On the other hand, it is another practical way to execute temporal logic specification directly as a program [Mo86].

(2) We think that the object interconnection method based on the I/O specification has enough potential. But the current method is not fully satisfactory.

(3) The PTL specification has nothing to do with an internal program of each object. It is desirable to associate PTL specification with internal programs of objects.

(4) A more efficient implementation of the tableau-like PTL decision procedure should be developed.

(5) The degree of concurrency is low because of the limitation wherein the gate controller can only open one gate at a time. It seems possible to relax this limitation for some independent gates.

(6) A transformation technique that distributes synchronization supervisor function into each object is necessary for the Intellectual Distributed Processing System (IDPS) which has no supervisor.

ACKNOWLEDGMENT

This research has been supported by the Japanese Fifth Generation Computer Project and its organizing institute ICOT. We would like to thank Toshio Yokoi, Hidenori Itoh, and Ryuzo Hasegawa of ICOT for their encouragement and support. We are also grateful to Seiichi Nishijima and Takeshi Kohno of Systems & Software Engineering Laboratory, TOSHIBA Corporation, for providing essential support.

REFERENCES

[An79] Andler, S., Predicate Path Expres-sion, Proc. of ACM 6th POPL, 1979.

[Ch84] Chikayama, T., Unique features of ESP, Proc. of the international conference on FGCS1984, 1984.

[GU87] Gonzalez,J.P., Urban,J.E., ENVISAGER: A Visual, Object-Oriented Specification Environment for Real-Time Systems, Proc of 4th International Workshop on Software Specification and Design, 1987.

[FT85] Fusaoka, A. and Takahashi, K., On QFTL and the refutation procedure on w-graphs, ICOT Technical Report TR-132, 1985.

[MW84] Manna, Z. and Wolper, P., Synthesis of communicating processes from temporal logic specification, ACM Trans. on Programming Languages and Systems, Vol.6, No.1, pages 68-93, 1984.

[CE82] Clarke, E. M. and Emerson, E. A., Design and synthesis of synchro-nization skeletons using branching time temporal logic, Logics of programs (Proceedings 1981), Lecture Notes in Computer Science 131, Springer-Verlag, pages 52-71, 1982.

[FTM84] Fujita, M., Tanaka, H.,and Moto-oka, T., Specifying hardware in temporal logic & efficient synthesis of state-diagrams using Prolog, Proc. of FGCS'84, 1984.

[KI82] Katai, O. and Iwai, S., Construction of Scheduling Rules for Asynchronous, Concurrent Systems Based on Tense Logic (in Japanese), Trans. of SICE (Japan) vol.18 no.12, 1982.

[Ha76] Habermann, A. N., Introduction to Operating System Design, SRA, 1976.

[HUK86] Honiden, S., Uchihira, N., and Kasuya, T., MENDEL: PROLOG BASED CONCURRENT OBJECT ORIENTED LANGUAGE, Proc. of COMPCON'86, pages 230-234,1986.

[Oc83] Occam Programming manual,INMOS Ltd., 1983.

[Pl86] Plaisted, D. A., A Decision Procedure for Combinations of Propositional Temporal Logic and Other Specialized Theories, Journal of Automated Reasoning 2, pages171-190, 1986.

[Ta84] Taki, T. et al., Hardware Design and Implementation of the Personal Sequential Inference Machine (PSI), Proc. of the international conference on FGCS1984, 1984.

[Ta87] Tamura,S.,et al., Development of Intellectual Distributed Processing System, Proc. of IFAC 10th World Congress, 1987.

[UKMH87] Uchihira, T., Kasuya, T., Matsumoto,K., and Honiden, S., Concurrent Program Synthesis with Reusable Components Using Temporal Logic, Proc of COMPSAC87, 1987.

[Mo86] Moszkowski, B., Executing temporal logic programs, Cambridge Univ. Press, 1986.

[Wo82] Wolper, P., Synthesis of communicating processes from temporal logic specification, STAN-CS-82-925, Stanford University, 1982.

[Wo86] Wolper, P., Expressing Interesting Properties of Program in Propositional Temporal Logic, Proc of POPL, 1986.

Appendix

Keyword Count Program (WordCut, SumRep)

```
WordCut
(
    dec :(
        inpipe(stream).
        outpipe(word).
        state(inbuf![]).
    )
    meth :(
        method(stream?' '.inbuf?[]).
        method(stream?' '.inbuf?CList.inbuf![].word!Word) <-
            true!rev(CList.RCList2).name(Word.RCList).
        method(stream?C.inbuf?CList.inbuf![C!CList]).
    )
    junk:(
        rev(L1.L2):-revzap(L1.[].L2).
        revzap([X!L].L2.L3):-revzap(L.[X!L2].L3).
        revzap([].L.L).
    )
)


SumRep
(
    dec :(
        inpipe(check_data).
        outpipe(summary).
        insignal(start_rep).
        state(sumlist![]).
    )
    meth :(
        method(check_data?W.sumlist?X.sumlist!Y) <-
            true!countup_sum_list(W.X.Y).
        method(start_rep?_.sumlist?SL.summary!SL).
    )
    junk :(
        countup_sum_list(W.[].[sum(W.1)]).
        countup_sum_list(W.[sum(W.N)!SumList].[sum(W.M)!SumList]) :-
            M is N + 1.
        countup_sum_list(W.[Sum!SumList1].[Sum!SumList2]) :-
            !.countup_sum_list(W.SumList1.SumList2).
    )
)
```

Analogical Program Synthesis from Program Components

Takeshi IMANAKA, Kuniaki UEHARA, and Jun'ichi TOYODA

The Institute of Scientific and Industrial Research
Osaka University, Ibaraki 567, Japan

1 Introduction

In these days, there has been increasing activity in the field of automatic programming. The goal of this effort is to develop a system for deriving programs systematically from given specifications. In automatic programming, the most widely used approach is called progressive refinement. The method of progressive refinement is to start with an abstract specification to be programmed, and to gradually decompose it into specificational components, then to refine and transform them to an appropriate level to obtain an efficient program. This approach requires a large amount of programming knowledge, such as common sense knowledge, domain specific knowledge, the syntax and semantics of a target language, and so on. However, a program synthesis system based on this approach, such as AutoPro(Uehara 1986), has limited capability for synthesizing programs, since generated programs are limited to at most combinations of existing program components.

To overcome this weakness, it is necessary for a system to have the capability of modifying an existing program component to obtain the desired one. For this purpose, we should first define the notion of similarity between two programs and use it as the basis for modifying a given program component to meet a specification. Secondly, we should develop a mechanism for searching for a modifiable program component among many stored components. Thirdly, we should develop a mechanism for modifying a retrieved component to satisfy the required specification.

We are now developing a system called APSS (Analogical Program Synthesis System) whose task domain is manipulation of relational databases. APSS has the ability of retrieving several modifiable programs by using analogical reasoning based on a similarity measure defined by the authors. Analogical reasoning is one tool that automatic programming systems can use to learn from experience, just as programmers do. In this paper, we shall focus our attention on a method of selecting program components based on analogical reasoning.

2 Program component retrieval

2.1 Program specification and planning

APSS accepts a natural language specification, regarding it as the goal, and tries to make a plan to meet the user's requirement (Elliot 1985). The resultant plan is the database manipulation sequence represented in terms of what the author called 'internal requirement specifications'. An internal requirement specification consists of both 'manipulation requirements' and 'data specification terms'. Manipulation requirements and data specification terms are concerned with what kinds of manipulation are performed on data and which data

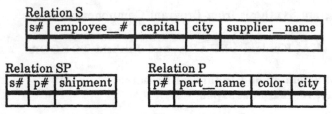

Figure 1: Relational Database 1

are manipulated, respectively. The former comprises three kinds of manipulation: data registration, data retrieval, and data deletion. The latter refers to terms whose functors are either attribute names or procedure names, and whose arguments specify the objects of manipulation. An attribute name is a name of an attribute given to a column of a relational table. A procedure name is a name given to a program of procedural processing. For example, as shown in Figure 1, $s\#$ (which is a supplier number), $employee\_\#$ (which is an employee number), ... are attributes. A program for computing an average has naturally the procedure name $average$. We now define data specification terms, with which we shall henceforth be concerned.

Definition
A data specification term of the form $x(y_1,\ldots,y_n), 1\leq n$, is defined as follows;

1. Assume that x is an attribute name and $y1$ is a numeric constant or a string. Let $x(y_1)$ be the set of tuples the values of whose x attribute is y_1. The example in Figure 2 shows that $A(a)$ is $\{tuple1, tuple3, tuple4\}$

2. Assume that x is an attribute name and y_1 is a data specification term as defined in definition 1. Let $x(y_1)$ be the set of values of the attribute x in the set of tuples y_1. In Figure 2, $B(A(a))$ is a set of values $\{c, e, d\}$; i.e., the set of values of the attribute B in $A(a)$.

3. Suppose that x is an attribute name and y_1 is a data specification term as defined in definition 2. Let $x(y_1)$ be the set of values of the attribute x in the set of tuples each of which has an attribute value in y_1. Thus, in Figure 2, $C(B(A(a)))$ is the set of values $\{f, a\}$ of the attribute C retrieved from $tuple5$ and $tuple7$ which has an attribute value in $\{c, e, d\}$.

4. Let x be a procedure name, and let each y_i $(1\leq i\leq n)$ be assigned to a set of values or a real number. Then, let $x(y_1,\ldots,y_n)$ $(1\leq i\leq n)$ be the output of the procedure x with the input y_i $(1\leq i\leq n)$. Assume that $average$ is a procedure name of program computing an average. In the relational database in Figure 2, $D(A(a))$ denotes $\{80, 300, 220\}$ by definition 2, so that $average(D(A(a))) = 200$. Once the average is computed, we can consider another program, $beyond\_average$, picking up items whose values are larger than the average. Thus, $beyond\_average(D(A(a))) = \{300, 220\}$.

5. Let x be an attribute name and y_i $(1\leq i\leq n)$ be a retrieval condition. Then, $x(y_1,\ldots,y_n)$ is the set of tuples such that the value of attribute x satisfies the retrieval condition y_i

	A	B	D
tuple1	a	c	80
tuple2	b	d	230
tuple3	a	e	300
tuple4	a	d	220

	B	C
tuple5	c	f
tuple6	a	c
tuple7	d	a

Figure 2: Relational Database 2

$(1 \leq i \leq n)$. As retrieval conditions, simple operations such as *larger_than, less_than,...* are used in general. In Figure 2, $D(larger\_than(200)) = \{tuple2, tuple3, tuple4\}$.

To make our idea clear, we now review this definition by using examples given in Figure 1. Definition 1 states that *part_name(p2)* represents the tuple set such that the part name is *p2*. Definition 2 states that *p♯(part_name(p2))* is the part number of a part p2. Definition 3 states that *s♯(p♯(part_name(p2)))* expresses the supplier number who supplies the part *p2*. Definition 4 says that *article_total(C)* and *total(C)* show the number of data belonging to *C* and total number of data belonging to *C*, respectively. The *article_total* and *total* are both procedure names, and the variable *C* represents a value set. And definition 5 states that *employee_♯(larger_than(X))* is the tuple set such that the number of employees is larger than *X*.

Assembling the above defined terms makes it possible to represent any data satisfying complex conditions. For example, the data specification term below means, "obtain the total number of employees belonging to suppliers who ship red-colored parts, and then obtain the total of capitals of suppliers who have larger than one half the number of that total" with procedure name, *total* and *one_half*.

$$total(capital(s♯(\\
\qquad employee\_♯(larger\_than(\\
\qquad\qquad one\_half(\\
\qquad\qquad\qquad total(employee\_♯(\\
\qquad\qquad\qquad\qquad s♯(p♯(color(red)))))))))))).$$

2.2 Program component

Each program component has an input part and an output part, and an output part of each program component can be connected to an input part of another one just like a daisy chain. The resulting connected pair can be used as a new program component. Input and output relations closely correspond to assumption and conclusion in a deduction procedure. Thus, the process of retrieving program components is carried out by deductive inference.

APSS, taking this correspondence into consideration, uses a rule-based representation of program components. Each rule has both a condition part, which specifies the input constraint, and an action part, which specifies a single output. For example, "retrieving the supplier who delivers the part $p2$" and "the total number of employees which is the attribute of the tuple having the attribute value as signed to the cursor variable $Cursor$" (which is a result table to store retrieval answers), are represented by the following rules;

(C1) $dealer\_\sharp(part(part\_name(p2)))\leftarrow.$

(C2) $total(employee\_\sharp(Cursor))\leftarrow cursor(Cursor).$

If the output obtained in a rule's action part satisfies the input constraint in another rule's condition part, then the new action will be derived and two rules can be successfully connected in a cascade. This relation holds in reverse. Let's consider the internal requirement specification as the goal and execute the backward inference from it. If this backward inference succeeds in executing the goal, the inputs and outputs of rules in this inference procedure are well connected with each other. And the reverse-ordered rule chain is the sequence of program components, which satisfies the internal requirement specifications.

For example, if we execute $total(employee\_\sharp(s\sharp(part(part\_name(p2)))))$ as a goal, rules C2 and C1 are activated in that order and the execution of this goal succeeds. This means that the input/output connection of C2 and C1 makes it possible to synthesize the program component "seeking the total of the number of employees who deliver the part $p2$".

2.3 Program component Retrievals

2.3.1 Notation of similarity

APSS uses analogical reasoning to retrieve program components. An analogy is based on a similarity relation defined below. When two terms $t(a, b)$ and $s(b, a)$ are similar, the similarity is written as $t(a, b)\sim s(b, a)$. And when two function names f and g are similar, '$\sim\sim$' is used to express this similarity; e.g., '$g\sim\sim f$'. Using this similarity, extended definitions are given as follows;

1. Let t and s denote terms. If $t = s$, then $t\sim s$.

2. Let f and g denote function names. If $f = g$, then $f\sim\sim g$.

3. If $t_i\sim s_i(1\leq i\leq n)$ and $f\sim\sim g$, then $f(t_1,\ldots,t_n)\sim g(s_1,\ldots,s_n)$.

If $jane\sim mary$ and $girl\sim\sim lady$, hold, for example, then $girl(jane)\sim lady(mary)$ hold.

2.3.2 Analogical reasoning based on the similarity relation

Analogical reasoning is a powerful mechanism for searching past experience in planning and problem solving (Carbonell 1983). In this section, we shall outline a theory of analogical reasoning based on an extension to Winston's analogy-based reasoning (Winston 1983).

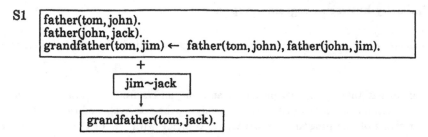

Figure 3: Analogical reasoning

Analogy-based reasoning has been developed to extract knowledge from past experiences that bear a strong similarity to the current situation. Nonetheless, his idea has simply been proposed without suggesting how to implement a mechanism for it.

On the other hand, computational methods for analogical reasoning have been discussed by many researchers. Among them, Haraguchi (Haraguchi 1985) has defined similarity between terms, and formalized analogical reasoning in terms of a logic programming language, i.e., Prolog. He has also shown that Winston's approach can work well in a conventional logical reasoning mechanism. Consider, for instance, the rule expressing the relation of *grandfather* in terms of that of *father* in Figure 3. A condition *father(john, jim)* of the rule, is not directly asserted in the set of clauses $S1$. The similarity of *jim∼jack*, however, holds, so that that of *father(john, jim)* and *father(john, jack)* hold. Thus, *grandfather(tom, jack)* is analogically inferred from the rule.

In addition to the similarity relation '∼' described above, we also have defined similarity between functors of terms using the notation '∼∼'. To introduce this similarity into analogical reasoning, we shall now define the following relation;

$$A{\sim}f(a_1,\ldots,a_n)$$

where the variable A refers to all terms which are similar to $f(a_1,\ldots,a_n)$. Such a variable is a metavariable. Introducing the metavariable and adding some new conditions to the condition part of each rule enables analogical reasoning to be carried out by conventional logical reasoning mechanism. For example, the rule

$$grandfather(tom, jim){\leftarrow}father(tom, john), father(john, jim).$$

is converted as follows;

$$A{\leftarrow}A{\sim}grandfather(tom, jim), father(tom, john){\sim}B, father(john, jim){\sim}C, B, C.$$

This rule specifies the following two assertions. (1) The terms which are similar to *father(tom, john)* and *father(john, jim)*, are expressed by meta-variables B and C, respectively. (2) If B and C hold, then the term A which is similar to *grandfather(tom, jim)* is inferred as a consequence.

2.3.3 Similarity between program components

In APSS, similarity between database manipulation programs is limited to the following three cases;

case1: Assume that there exist two programs and one differs from the other only in the numeric constant or characteristic string specifying the retrieval condition. If the variable or string of one program is rewritten to coincide with one of the other, the two programs will become an equivalent program retrieving the same data. In this case, the two programs are considered to be similar.

case2: Assume that there exist two programs and only specified attribute names are different from each other. If one attribute name in them is rewritten to another one, they will be equivalent to one retrieving the data of the same attribute. Then, two programs are considered to be similar.

case3: Assume that there exist two programs whose attributes and relations are quite different from each other and each program specifies some attributes belonging to only one relation. If all of the attribute names in the retrieval command are rewritten to others, these two programs will coincide and they will retrieve the data of the same relation and attributes. Then, the two programs are said to be similar.

As was described above, since APSS manages program components by the rule representation, then the above similarity should be translated to the similarity between data specification terms expressed in the action part of each rule. The three similarities are paraphrased as follows;

1. Two data specification terms which have different constants or strings used in their retrieval conditions of data specification terms themselves, are considered to be similar.

2. If function names expressing attribute names in data specification terms are different from each other and if all of the attribute names belong to only one relation, then these two data specification terms are considered to be similar.

3. If function names of attribute names in data specification terms are different from each other and their attributes belong to different relations, and if all of the attribute names in data specification terms belong to the same relation, these two data specification terms are considered to be similar.

Figure 4 illustrates these three cases of similarity defined in 1), 2) and 3). These rules show that iff $X{\sim}Y$ is true, then X is similar to Y. In Figure 4, $constant(X)$ is a predicate having the value $true$ if the variable X is substituted for the constant. And the predicate $procedure(X)$ finds out whether the variable X is substituted for the term whose functor corresponds to the procedure name or not.

The predicate $data\_type(X, Y)$ returns $real$ or $cursor$ to Y depending upon the type of X. The predicate $relation\_name(X, Y)$ returns the names of the relation of the attribute X to Y. The predicate $break(X, Y)$ returns the functor and arguments of the term X to Y in list form. And the predicate $all\_in\_one\_relation(X)$ takes the value $true$ iff all attributes in the list X belong to one relation.

(R1)   X~Y   ← constant(X), constant(Y).
(R2)   X~~Y   ← attribute__name(X), attribute__name(Y),
                          relation__name(X, T), relation__name(Y, T).
(R3)   X~Y   ← break(X, Atom__list1), break(Y, Atom__list2),
                          all__in__one__relation(Atom__list1),
                          all__in__one__relation(Atom__list2).

Figure 4: Similarity between data specification terms

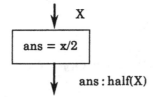

Figure 5: Program component 1

2.4   The algorithm for program component retrieval

As was already described in section 2.2, whether the program which satisfies the internal requirement specification can be synthesized or not is determined through the execution of the data specification term of the internal requirement specification. If the goal (the data specification term) is successfully executed, the set of activated rules corresponds to the necessary program components for the program synthesis.

Now we show an example of retrieving and selecting program components from the internal requirement specification in section 2.1. Assume that there exist program component sets of C1, C2 in section 2.2, and program components 1, 2 of Figure 5 and Figure 6.

The first step is to describe two program components 1, 2 in a rule representation as follows:

(C3) $half(X) \leftarrow real(X)$.

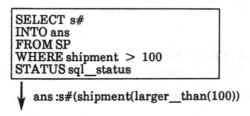

Figure 6: Program component 2

$$X \sim Y \quad \leftarrow X = Y.$$
$$X \sim \sim Y \quad \leftarrow X = Y.$$
$$X \sim Y \quad \leftarrow X = ..[F1|A1], Y = ..[F2|A2], F1 \sim \sim F2, A1 \sim A2.$$

Figure 7: Rule representation of similarity

(C4) $s\sharp(shipment(larger\_than(X))) \leftarrow real(X).$

Then to make a selection of program components in Prolog, by use of analogy, each rule of C1, C2, C3 and C4 is translated into the following:

(C1') $get(Y) \leftarrow Y \sim s\sharp(p\sharp(part\_name(p2))).$

(C2') $get(Y) \leftarrow Y \sim total(employee\_\sharp(X)), cursor(X), get(X).$

(C3') $get(Y) \leftarrow Y \sim half(X), real(X), get(X).$

(C4') $get(Y) \leftarrow Y \sim s\sharp(shipment(larger\_than(X))), real(X), get(X).$

The above translation is based on the algorithm described in section 2.3.2. A predicate $get(X)$, however, corresponds to the metavariable. Since the similarity between limitations for inputs of program component, are not considered, such a predicate as $cursor(C)$ remains untranslated.

With the above preparation and the set of rules in Figure 7, we can proceed to the next step. Given an internal requirement specification such as the one given in section 2.1, we can obtain the following goal, where get is the predicate name for selecting program components.

(G1) $get(total(capital(s\sharp(employee\_\sharp(larger\_than($
$$half(total(employee_\sharp(s\sharp(p\sharp(color(red))))))))))))).$

Then we execute the above goal G1. We immediately find that though the head of C1' is matched with G1, the execution of the body of C1' fails. Now, we execute the body of C2' as a goal, in the following order:

(B1) $total(capital(s\sharp(employee\_\sharp(larger\_than($
$$half(total(employee_\sharp(s\sharp(p\sharp(color(red)))))))))))) \sim total(employee_\sharp(X)).$

(B2) $cursor(s\sharp(employee\_\sharp(larger\_than(half(total(employee\_\sharp(s\sharp(p\sharp(color(red))))))))))).$

(B3) $get(s\sharp(employee\_\sharp(larger\_than(half(total(employee\_\sharp(s\sharp(p\sharp(color(red))))))))))).$

B1 is successfully executed because the similarity rule can be activated. B2 is also successfully executed because the predicate '*cursor*(X)' of APSS for judging if '*X*' is a cursor variable or not, is activated. And when executing B3, just as when executing G1, the execution begins with the body of C1'. Execution of bodies of C1', C2' and C3' totally failed, and the body of C4' is executed as a goal. This execution succeeds because the similarity rule is activated. Rules C3', C2' and C1' are subsequently activated, and finally the goal G1 successfully executed. As a result, the sequence of rules {(C2'), (C4'), (C3'), (C2'), (C1')}, in executing the goal, is selected as the sequence of program components.

2.5 Finding program component vacancy

Suppose the situation in which no appropriate program component can be found among stored components. In this case, the execution of the goal $get(X)$, which searches for a program component, fails. If the execution of the goal fails, APSS, as does a regular Prolog program, backtracks and tries to find another program component combination. If APSS backtracks and again fails, it is said that the appropriate program component is vacant. The following algorithm is applied to find out the vacancy of the program component.

1. Extract the data specification term $p(X)$ which fails.

2. Detach the function name p from $p(X)$ and consider the X as an input. And then, assuming the existence of the component having the output $p(X)$, retry the goal.

3. If the retry of the goal fails, repeat step 2. As a result, the outermost function name is detached and the remaining part is considered as an input, just as in step 2. If the execution of the new goal succeeds, the vacant program component is the one which is assumed to exist in step 2.

To clarify this algorithm, an example is given below;

Consider the example in section 2.4. If the program component shown in Figure 6 does not exist, execution of the following goal fails.

$$get(s\sharp(employee\_\sharp(larger\_than(\\ half(total(employee\_\sharp(s\sharp(\\ p\sharp(color(red))))))))))).$$

Then, $s\sharp$ and $employee\_\sharp$ are detached in that order. But every goal fails. At the point when $larger\_than$ is detached, we assume the existence of the program component which outputs

$$s\sharp(employee\_\sharp(larger\_than(half(total(employee\_\sharp(s\sharp(p\sharp(color(red))))))))).$$

for the input

$$half(total(employee\_\sharp(s\sharp(p\sharp(color(red)))))).$$

Under the assumption above, the re-execution of the goal succeeds. So, we can conclude that the program component expressed by the following rule does not exist.

$$s\sharp(employee\_\sharp(lager\_than(X)))\leftarrow real(X).$$

Once discovering such a vacancy, APSS gives the user a message such as "I can't synthesize the program retrieving the *dealer_number*, the number of whose employees is larger than X".

3   Program synthesis from selected program components

3.1   Program component modification

Program components selected by the algorithm in section 2.4 are modified and reformed as follows;

1. Any program components selected without any consideration of the similarity principle is not reformed at all.

2. For program components selected by the use of rule R1, the retrieval condition in the database retrieval command is rewritten to express the required specification.

3. For program components selected by rule R2, the attribute name in the database retrieval command is rewritten to express the required specification.

4. For program components selected by rule R3, both the attribute name and relation name are rewritten to express the required specification.

To enhance the reader's understanding, the above modification algorithm can be paraphrased as follows; 2 insists that numeric constants and characteristic strings of program components selected by similarity between numeric constants and character strings, must be modified. 3 states that attribute names of program components selected by similarity between attributes are also to be modified. And 4 asserts that all relations and attribute names of program components selected by similarity between relations must be renamed.

For instance, in section 2.4's example, since the program component expressed by the rule (C1') must be modified by 2 and 3. So the attribute name *part_name* and the constant $p2$ in the retrieval condition are replaced by *color* and *red*, respectively.

3.2   Program synthesis by program component combination

After all program components are modified, they are arranged in reverse order of the application of rules, and input and output are connected with each other to make them a complete program. Finally, some processing, such as resolution of variable name conflicts, is done and the stable program in Figure 8 is obtained. Executing this program, the variable *count2* is bound to the value which satisfies the internal requirement specification in section 2.1.

```
SELECT  s#                          SELECT s#
INTO   cursor1                      INTO cursor2
WHERE  P.color = "red"              FROM S
       AND P.p# = SP.p#             WHERE employee__# > half
STATUS  sql_status1                 STATUS sql__status4
label1:                             label3:
    FETCH  FROM  cursor1                FETCH  FROM  cursor2
    SET  get_s1                         SET  get_s3
    STATUS  sql_status2                 STATUS  sql__status5
    if(.not.STATUS__OK(sql_status2))    if(.not.STATUS__OK(sql_status5))
          goto  label2                        goto  label4
    SELECT  employee_#                  SELECT  capital
    INTO  get_s2                        INTO  get_s4
    FROM  S                            FROM  S
    WHERE  s# = get_s1                  WHERE  s# = get_s3
    STATUS  sql_status3                 STATUS  sql_status6
    count = count1 + get_s2            count2 = count2 + get_s4
    goto label1                        goto label3
label2:                             label4:
    half = count1/2                    write(*,*) count2
```

Figure 8: Synthesized program

4 Conclusion

In this paper, we defined the notion of similarity between components, and presented a method for both selecting necessary program components and discovering vacant ones. To verify our concept, the prototype system called 'APSS' was constructed. In this system, we have already included some other similarities not presented in this paper. For example, we consider that a program component for retrieving the largest number from some numerical data set is similar to the one for retrieving the largest three numbers. These two components are similar since they are both containing a process which retrieves an element and compare it with all other elements in the same data set. This type of similarity can be defined using some mathematical definition of numerical elements. We will discuss these similarity relations in the forthcoming paper.

References

Carbonell JG (1983) Learning by analogy : Formulating and generating plans from past experience. In: Ryszard S et al.(eds.), Machine Learning, Morgan Kaufmann, pp.137-161

Elliot S (1985) Learning to Program = Learning to Construct Mechanisms and Explanations. Communications of ACM, 29-9, pp.850-858

Haraguchi M, Arikawa S (1985) Analogical Reasoning using Transforma tions of rules. In: Wada E (ed) Logic Programming '85. Springer, Berlin Heidelberg New York, pp.56-65

Uehara K, Fujii K, Toyoda J (1986) A Technique for Prolog Program Synthesis from Natural Language Specification. Computer software, 3-4, pp.55-64

Winston PH, Binford TO, Katz B, Lowry M (1983) Learning Physical Descriptions from Functional Definitions, Examples, and Precedents. Proc. of AAAI-83, pp.433-439

Deriving a Compilation Method for Parallel Logic Languages

Youji KOHDA

International Institute for Advanced Study
of Social Information Science,
FUJITSU LIMITED
1-17-25, Shinkamata,
Ota-ku, Tokyo 144, JAPAN

Jiro TANAKA

Institute for New Generation
Computer Technology,
21F, Mita Kokusai Building
1-4-28, Mita,
Minato-ku, Tokyo 108, JAPAN

Abstract

It is already known that a Concurrent Prolog program can be compiled into an equivalent Prolog program. Using a Concurrent Prolog interpreter written in Prolog, we converted Concurrent Prolog programs step by step to compiled codes in Prolog. Each conversion step was successfully executed on a Prolog language processor. We examined how each conversion step contributed to performance improvement, using sample Concurrent Prolog programs such as a meta interpreter.

1. Introduction

Concurrent Prolog (CP) is an AND parallel logic language developed by Shapiro [3]. He also developed an interpreter for CP written in Prolog. The interpreter was considered significant as a working specification; however, it suffered from poor execution performance. Ueda and Chikayama have solved this problem by developing a compiling technique from CP to Prolog [4]. Their compilation technique is based on the scheme of Shapiro's CP interpreter. Therefore, it seems feasible to derive their compilation method from the CP interpreter scheme.

The concept of partial evaluation is familiar. It is widely known that the partial evaluation of an interpreter for language *L2* in language *L1* and a program in *L2* results in a compiled code in *L1* for that program. In our case, *L1* and *L2* correspond to Prolog and CP. However, we do not give a precise way to make a partial evaluator in this paper. Instead we will give a method of partial evaluation from CP to Prolog by *derivation*. It should be emphasized that a derivation path from CP to Prolog exists.

In program transformation, only an initial program is given, and it is transformed in small stages. The final program after program transformation will usually be too complicated to understand. This means that the correctness of each conversion step is very important in ensuring the correctness of the total transformation. This paper gives both initial and final programs, our interest lying in how to bridge the gap between them. This is why we use the term *derivation* instead of *transformation*.

We use an append program as a working example throughout this paper. We begin with Shapiro's CP interpreter and an append program in CP, and modify them step by step. Finally, the append is compiled into Prolog. This is identical to what Ueda and Chikayama have developed.

The derivation method is useful both theoretically and practically. It can help us to design a compiled code; each conversion step can be executed directly on a Prolog processor, and by observing the execution speed, the effectiveness of specific conversion methods can be studied. We can experiment with many new compiling techniques before deciding upon the final one. Kursawe gave a full account of this idea in his paper [2]. He showed that successive conversion of an append program in Prolog can finally yield a *Warren-type Abstract Prolog Machine Code*.

2. CP and CP Interpreters

A CP program is a set of *guarded Horn clauses*. A Horn clause has the form: $H:-G|B$. Here, H is a predicate called the *head*, G is a sequence of subgoals called the *guard* part, B is a sequence of subgoals called the *body* part. When G is *true*, the Horn clause is abbreviated as $H:-B$. When B is also *true*, it is simply written out as H. CP is characterized by the *commit* operator, |, introducing nondeterminism, and the *read-only* annotation, ?, introducing data driven control.

Computation in CP is a series of reductions. To reduce a given goal, first, choose a set of clauses each of whose heads is unifiable with the goal, including only the clauses whose guard part is recursively reducible. Second, randomly select one of these clauses. That is, the clause is *guarded* at the | from the rest in the set. Finally, replace the given goal by the body part of the selected clause. Each new goal is subjected to successive reductions. The commit operator, |, achieves coordination among parallel executing goals.

The symbol ? can be attached to any variable to indicate that the variable is used only for a *read-out* operation; a read-only variable cannot be unified with non-variables until some value is assigned to it. This assures a unidirectional flow of information. The read-only annotation, ?, achieves cooperation among parallel executing goals.

(1) CP interpreter in CP

The reduction process of CP can be written in CP as shown below [1]. This is a meta interpreter.

```
(M0)   mcall(true).                                        % halt
       mcall((A,B)) :- mcall(A?), mcall(B?).               % fork
       mcall(G) :- system(G) | G.                          % system
       mcall(G) :- nonsystem(G), G≠true, G≠(A,B) |         % reduce
                   reduce(G?,Body), mcall(Body?).
```

When clause goals conjoined by , are given, *mcall/M0*† reduces each goal recursively. When a single goal is given, it tries to reduce the goal. If the goal is *true*, it simply terminates. If the goal is a system-defined predicate, it executes the predicate directly. Otherwise, the reduction is carried out by *reduce*, and the returned body goals are solved recursively by *mcall/M0*.

(2) CP interpreter in Prolog

Shapiro's CP interpreter written in Prolog is shown below [3]. Notice that the overall program structure is similar to that of *mcall/M0*. The core of the interpreter consists of *solve/S0* and *reduce/R0*.

```
(S0)   solve(['$END'],_,_) :- !.                           % halt
       solve(['$END'|H],[],d) :- !, fail.
       solve(['$END'|H],['$END'|T],nd) :- !,
             solve(H,T,d).
       solve([A|H],T,_) :-                                 % system
             system(A), !, A,
             solve(H,T,nd).
       solve([A|H],T,F) :-                                 % reduce and fork
             reduce(A,B,F,NF),
             schedule(B,H,T,NH,NT), !,
             solve(NH,NT,NF).
(R0)   reduce(A,B,_,nd) :-                                 % reduce
             guarded_clause(A,G,B),
             schedule(G,X,X,H,['$END'|T]),                 % create a new queue
             solve(H,T,d), !.                              % solve guard G in it
       reduce(A,suspended(A),F,F).
(G0)   guarded_clause(A,G,B) :-
```

---

† *The Name/Identifier* format is used to distinguish different versions of clauses.

```
                  guarded_clause(A,B1), find_guard(B1,G,B).
            guarded_clause(A,B) :-
                  functor(A,F,N), functor(A1,F,N),
                  clause(A1,B), unify(A,A1).                       % CP unify
            find_guard((A|B),A,B) :- !.
            find_guard(A,true,A).
(C0)        schedule(true,H,T,H,T) :- !.                          % breadth-first
            schedule(suspended(A),H,[A|T],H,T) :- !.
            schedule((A,B),H,T,H2,T2) :- !,
                  schedule(A,H,T,H1,T1),
                  schedule(B,H1,T1,H2,T2).
            schedule(A,H,[A|T],H,T).
```

Solve(H,T,F) has a goal queue as a difference list, *H* and *T*, and a deadlock detection flag, *F*. The queue has a cycle marker *'$END'* to inform *solve/S0* that every goals in the queue has been tried. *Solve/S0* takes a goal out of the head of the goal queue and attempts to reduce it. *Reduce/R0* tries to reduce the goal. When the reduction succeeds, i.e., when a clause unifiable‡ with the goal is found and its guard is successfully solved, *reduce/R0* returns its body goals to the second argument. When the reduction fails, it returns *suspended(A)*, where *A* is the suspended goal. The third and fourth arguments of *reduce/R0* are the deadlock flags. When the given goal has been reduced, *nd (no deadlock)* is forced to be set to the fourth argument. When it has been suspended, the deadlock flag at the third argument is passed through to the fourth argument. Initially, *d (deadlock)* is set to the deadlock flag. Deadlock can be detected by confirming that the deadlock flag has never fallen to *nd* while the goal queue goes round.

Schedule/C0 schedules the reduction result in the goal queue breadth-first; the goals are appended at the tail of the queue. A depth-first scheduling strategy can also be used; the goals are inserted in front of the head of the queue. In that case, *schedule/C1* shown below is used instead of *schedule/C0*. When the given goal is marked as *suspended*, however, it is a suspended goal, and is always scheduled breadth-first.

```
(C1)        schedule(true,H,T,H,T) :- !.                         % depth-first
            schedule(suspended(A),H,[A|T],H,T) :- !.
            schedule((A,B),H,T,H2,T2) :- !,
                  schedule(B,H,T,H1,T1),
                  schedule(A,H1,T1,H2,T2).
            schedule(A,H,T,[A|H],T).
```

3. Compilation Techniques

As already stated in Section 1, Ueda and Chikayama developed a compiling technique from CP to Prolog. Their method is twofold. The first idea eliminates the overhead of goal invocations. The goal queue and deadlock detection flag in *solve* are included in each goal as extra arguments, thereby eliminating the processing time via *solve*.

The second idea implements depth-first scheduling which can manage the depth of a reduction tree; when depth-first reduction reaches the current depth limit, the search path is suspended and the current depth limit is increased in preparation for the coming deeper search, then another unreached path is tried. To implement this idea, a decrement counter is included in each goal as an extra argument. The counter remembers how many times reductions can take place before reaching the current depth limit. They called

---

‡ *Unify* in *guarded_clause/G0* is a special unification procedure; it has been tailored for CP to handle the read-only annotation, ?.

this scheduling strategy *N-bounded depth-first* scheduling, where N is the step size of the depth limit. The counter is initialized to N every time it reaches zero.

Because these two ideas are independent of each other, we can produce four variations as shown below.

Scheduling strategy	Interpreting	Compilation
Breadth/Depth-first	(i) Shapiro's interpreter	(ii) Breadth/Depth-first compilation
N-bounded depth-first	(iii) Enhanced interpreter	(iv) N-bounded depth-first compilation

Variation (i) is Shapiro's CP interpreter. Variation (ii) adopts the first idea; CP programs are compiled incorporating either breadth-first or depth-first scheduling. Variation (iii) adopts the second idea; it is an enhanced CP interpreter incorporating N-bounded depth-first scheduling. Variation (iv) adopts both ideas; CP programs are compiled incorporating N-bounded depth-first scheduling.

We will derive (ii) from (i) in Section 4, and (iv) from (iii) in Section 5. Enhanced interpreter (iii) incorporating N-bounded depth-first scheduling will be shown in Subsection 5.1. Sample compilations for (ii) and (iv) are shown in Subsections 4.4 and 5.2, respectively.

4. Compilation Incorporating Breadth-first or Depth-first Scheduling

This and the following sections will show that programs in CP can be converted to a Prolog program. The CP interpreter is incorporated into CP programs gradually in this derivation process. The CP interpreter in this section uses a simple scheduling strategy, which is either breadth-first or depth-first. The compiled code derived here is a simplified version of Ueda and Chikayama's compiled code. The following section will show a full derivation using N-bounded depth-first scheduling.

The derivation process consists of four major stages, some of which may consist of several minor steps. The first stage converts a CP program to its Prolog version using the definition of *reduce/R0*. The program is further modified in the second stage using the definition of *solve/S0*. In the third stage, indirect goal invocations are replaced by direct invocations. In the final stage, auxiliary predicates are unfolded to obtain the target code.

As stated before, we use an append program as an example for the derivation. *Append/A0* below is a CP program.

```
(A0)    append([X|Xs],Ys,[X|Zs]) :-          % CP program
                append(Xs?,Ys?,Zs).
        append([],Ys,Ys).
```

4.1 First Stage

In the first stage, *append/A0* in CP is converted to its Prolog version, *append/A1*.

(1) Partial evaluation of reduce/R0

Reduce/R0 is partially evaluated, with respect to *append/A0*. Since *reduce/R0* is written in Prolog, the result is also a Prolog program.

First, consider the second clause of *reduce/R0*, as it is simpler than the first clause. It deals with reduction failure. It reports the failure by returning the suspended goal wrapped by *suspended*, and transmits the deadlock flag. The following clause has the same effect.

```
reduce(append(L,M,N),suspended(append(L,M,N)),F0,F0).
```

Now turn to the first clause of *reduce/R0*. It searches a clause whose head is unifiable with the given goal by *guarded_clause/G0* and tries to solve the clause's guard by *solve/S0*. Because *append/A0* consists of two clauses, both of whose guards are *true*, *guarded_clause/G0* eventually returns the two clauses. The following clauses have the same effect.

```
reduce(append(L,M,N),append(Xs?,Ys?,Zs),F0,nd) :–
        unify(append(L,M,N),append([X|Xs],Ys,[X|Zs])),
        schedule(true,X,X,H,['$END'|T]), solve(H,T,d), !.
reduce(append(L,M,N),true,F0,nd) :–
        unify(append(L,M,N), append([],Ys,Ys)),
        schedule(true,X,X,H,['$END'|T]), solve(H,T,d), !.
```

The evaluation process can go further. First, **schedule(true,X,X,H,['$END'|T]),solve(H,T,d)** always turns out *true*, and can be deleted. Second, *unify* can proceed whenever arguments are given even partially. Two auxiliary predicates, *ulist* and *unil* are introduced to help *unify* proceed. They take charge of the subcomputation of *unify*, and are the same as those used in [4]. *Ulist(A,H,T)* and *unil(L)* have the same meaning as *unify(A,[H|T])* and *unify(L,[ ])*, but they are optimized enough.

Thus, the final result of this stage is *append/A1* below.

```
(A1)    reduce(append(A1,Ys,A3),append(Xs?,Ys?,Zs),_,nd) :–
                ulist(A1,X,Xs), ulist(A3,X,Zs), !.
        reduce(append(A1,A2,A3),true,_,nd) :–
                unil(A1), unify(A2,A3), !.
        reduce(append(X,Y,Z),suspended(append(X,Y,Z)),F,F).
```

4.2 Second Stage

In this stage, *append/A1* and *solve/S0* are converted step by step to *append/A4* and *solve/S4*. It is the key point of this stage that, in *solve/S0*, *schedule* and *solve* are always invoked after *reduce* returns. We will successively move them from *solve/S0* to *append/A1*.

(1) Migration of schedule to append

Solve/S0 includes two successive invocations as follows:

```
        reduce(A,B,F,NF), schedule(B,H,T,NH,NT)
```

They are integrated into the single invocation below by eliminating shared local variable *B*. This results in *solve/s2* and *append/A2*.

```
        reduce_schedule(A,H,T,NH,NT,F,NF)
```

At the same time, *append/A1* is converted to *append/A2*; *schedule* is moved from *solve/S0* to *append/A1*.

```
(A2)    reduce_schedule(append(A1,Ys,A3),H,T,NH,NT,_,nd) :–
                ulist(A1,X,Xs), ulist(A3,X,Zs), !,
                schedule(append(Xs?,Ys?,Zs),H,T,NH,NT).
        reduce_schedule(append(A1,A2,A3),H,T,NH,NT,_,nd) :–
                unil(A1), unify(A2,A3), !,
                schedule(true,H,T,NH,NT).
        reduce_schedule(append(X,Y,Z),H,T,NH,NT,F,F) :–
                schedule(suspended(append(X,Y,Z)),H,T,NH,NT).
(S2)    solve(['$END'],_,_) :– !.
        solve(['$END'|H],[],d) :– !, fail.
        solve(['$END'|H],T,nd) :– !,
                schedule(suspended('$END'),H,T,NH,NT),
                solve(NH,NT,d).
        solve([A|H],T,_) :–
                system(A), !, A,
```

```
                    solve(H,T,nd).
            solve([A|H],T,F) :-
                    reduce_schedule(A,H,T,NH,NT,F,NF),
                    !, solve(NH,NT,NF).
```

(2) Migration of solve to append

Solve/S2 involves two successive invocations as follows:

```
            reduce_schedule(A,H,T,NH,NT,F,NF), !, solve(NH,NT,NF)
```

They are integrated into the following invocation by eliminating shared local variables *NH*, *NT*, and *NF*. This results in *solve/s3* and *append/A3*.

```
            $(A,H,T,F)
```

! above is negligible, because *reduce_schedule* fails immediately when it backtracks and the clause including the ! is the last clause of *solve/S2*. At the same time, *append/A2* is converted to *append/A3*; *solve* is moved from *solve/S2* to *append/A2*.

```
(A3)    $(append(A1,Ys,A3),H,T,_) :-
                ulist(A1,X,Xs), ulist(A3,X,Zs), !,
                schedule(append(Xs?,Ys?,Zs),H,T,NH,NT),
                solve(NH,NT,nd).
        $(append(A1,A2,A3),H,T,_) :-
                unil(A1), unify(A2,A3), !,
                schedule(true,H,T,NH,NT),
                solve(NH,NT,nd).
        $(append(X,Y,Z),H,T,F) :-
                schedule(suspended(append(X,Y,Z)),H,T,NH,NT),
                solve(NH,NT,F).
(S3)    solve(['$END'],_,_) :- !.
        solve(['$END'|H ],[],d) :- !, fail.
        solve(['$END'|H ],T,nd) :- !,
                schedule(suspended('$END'),H,T,NH,NT),
                solve(NH,NT,d).
        solve([A|H],T,_) :-
                system(A), !, A,
                solve(H,T,nd).
        solve([A|H],T,F) :-          % !,
                $(A,H,T,F).
```

(3) Deletion of solve

Next, *solve* is deleted. *Solve/S3* invokes *$*, which, in turn, invokes *solve/S3*. Thus, *solve/S3* is merely used as an intermediary and can be deleted completely. *Solve/S3* really does two things: taking a goal out of the goal queue, and classifying the goal and reducing it according to its type. We will move the first action into *append/A3*. In preparation, *solve/S3* is divided into two.

```
(S3')   solve([A|H],T,F) :-
                    '$2'(A,H,T,F).
        '$2'('$END',[],_,_) :- !.
        '$2'('$END',H,[],d) :- !, fail.
        '$2'('$END',H,T,nd) :- !,
```

```
                    schedule(suspended('$END'),H,T,NH,NT),
                    solve(NH,NT,d).
        '$2'(A,H,T,_) :–
                    system(A), !, A,
                    solve(H,T,nd).
        '$2'(A,H,T,F) :–
                    $(A,H,T,F).
```

All the *solve* invocations are unfolded, consulting *solve/S3'*. For example, solve(NH,NT,d) is unfolded into NH=[G|NH2],'$2'(G,NH2,NT,d). All the '$2' invocations can be also replaced by $ invocations. This replacement is safe on the assumption that no user-defined predicates are the same as either '$END' or system-defined ones. As a side effect, system-defined predicates must be explicitly handled as shown below. Only *unify* is shown as a representative. The other system-predicates must be programmed in the same way.

```
(A4)    $(append(A1,Ys,A3),H,T,_) :–
                    ulist(A1,X,Xs), ulist(A3,X,Zs), !,
                    schedule(append(Xs?,Ys?,Zs),H,T,NH,NT),
                    NH=[G|NH2], $(G,NH2,NT,nd).
        $(append(A1,A2,A3),H,T,_) :–
                    unil(A1), unify(A2,A3), !,
                    schedule(true,H,T,NH,NT),
                    NH=[G|NH2], $(G,NH2,NT,nd).
        $(append(X,Y,Z),H,T,F) :–
                    schedule(suspended(append(X,Y,Z)),H,T,NH,NT),
                    NH=[G|NH2], $(G,NH2,NT,F).
(S4)    $('$END',[],_,_) :– !.
        $('$END',H,[],d) :– !, fail.
        $('$END',H,T,nd) :– !,
                    schedule(suspended('$END'),H,T,NH,NT),
                    NH=[G|NH2], $(G,NH2,NT,d).
        $(unify(X,Y),H,T,_) :– !,
                    unify(X,Y),
                    H=[G|H2], $(G,H2,T,nd).
```

4.3 Third Stage

Now both *append/A4* and *solve/S4* consist solely of $ clauses. The $ clause actually invoked is determined only by its first argument. The symbol $ is, therefore, redundant and can be eliminated by promoting the first argument to a predicate. This is performed in two steps. The first step is transient and deletes $ from the head of a clause. The second step deletes $ from the body.

(1) Deletion of $ from the head

$ is deleted from the head. First, the first argument of each head is promoted to a new predicate; the argument's principal functor becomes a new predicate name. Second, the new predicate is extended and takes the remaining arguments H, T, and F as shown below, where X, Y, and Z are the original arguments of *append*.

> append(X,Y,Z,H,T,F)

The result of this step is shown below. All the $s have been successfully deleted from all the heads. Note how the arguments of *solve/S0* are added to the original arguments of *append/A0*. $ in the body, however, still remains unchanged. To compensate for this discrepancy, $ clause marked as (#) in *solve/S5* below is temporarily reintroduced. This $ will be deleted in the next step.

(A5)   append(A1,Ys,A3,H,T,_) :–
                ulist(A1,X,Xs), ulist(A3,X,Zs), !,
                schedule(append(Xs?,Ys?,Zs,H0,T0,F0),H,T,NH,NT),
                NH=[G|NH2], $(G,NH2,NT,nd).
        append(A1,A2,A3,H,T,_) :–
                unil(A1), unify(A2,A3), !,
                schedule(true,H,T,NH,NT),
                NH=[G|NH2], $(G,NH2,NT,nd).
        append(X,Y,Z,H,T,F) :–
                schedule(suspended(append(X,Y,Z,H0,T0,F0)),H,T,NH,NT),
                NH=[G|NH2], $(G,NH2,NT,F).
(S5)   '$END'([],_,_) :– !.
        '$END'(H,[],d) :– !, fail.
        '$END'(H,T,nd) :– !,
                schedule(suspended('$END'(H0,T0,F0)),H,T,NH,NT),
                NH=[G|NH2], $(G,NH2,NT,d).
        unify(X,Y,H,T,_) :– !,
                unify(X,Y),
                H=[G|H2], $(G,H2,T,nd).
(#) $(G,H,T,F) :–
                functor(G,_,A),
                arg(A,G,F),
                A1 is A−1, arg(A1,G,T),
                A2 is A−2, arg(A2,G,H),
                call(G).

(2) Deletion of $ from the body

The auxiliary $ introduced in the previous step is deleted. When $ is invoked, it gives its extra arguments to a goal which is also given as an argument, and invokes the goal. Fortunately, a $ invocation is always immediately preceded by a *take-out* queue operation. By changing the goal queue structure, taking a goal out of the queue and setting extra arguments in the goal are accomplished by a single operation using the following technique. This technique was originally developed by Ueda and Chikayama.

Let each element in the goal queue have the following form:

$(head($A_1,..,A_m,B_1,..,B_n$),$B_1,..,B_n$)

Head($A_1,..,A_m,B_1,..,B_n$) is an extended goal, where $A_1,..,A_m$ are the original arguments of the goal, and $B_1,..,B_n$ are the extra arguments. This form has a function similar to the λ-expression. $B_1,..,B_n$ serve as formal arguments; each argument B_i in *head* can be initialized by unifying a value and the B_i outside the *head*.

In the case of *append*, this λ-like expression has the form like this:

$(append(X,Y,Z,H0,T0,F0),H0,T0,F0)

where H0,T0, and F0 are the extra arguments coming from *solve/S0*. The following program fragment does two things: taking a goal G from a goal queue H, and setting NT and NF to H0 and T0. At the same time, the rest of the goal queue, H2, is set to H0.

H=[$(G,H2,NT,NF)|H2]

Five unifications occur simultaneously: $G=append(X,Y,Z,H0,T0,F0)$, $H2=H0$, $NT=T0$, $NF=F0$, and $H=[\_|H2]$. These unifications accomplish the intended task as a whole.

The result of this step is shown below. All the $ invocations have been successfully deleted from all the bodies, thereby successfully deleting all the $ invocations from all the clauses. Instead, as can be seen in *append/A6* and *solve/S6*, a substitute for $ appears in the goal queue.

(A6)   append(A1,Ys,A3,H,T,_) :–
        ulist(A1,X,Xs), ulist(A3,X,Zs), !,
        schedule($(append(Xs?,Ys?,Zs,H0,T0,F0),H0,T0,F0),H,T,NH,NT),
        NH=[$(G,NH2,NT,nd)|NH2],
        call(G).
    append(A1,A2,A3,H,T,_) :–
        unil(A1), unify(A2,A3), !,
        schedule(true,H,T,NH,NT),
        NH=[$(G,NH2,NT,nd)|NH2],
        call(G).
    append(X,Y,Z,H,T,F) :–
        schedule(suspended($(append(X,Y,Z,H0,T0,F0),H0,T0,F0)),H,T,NH,NT),
        NH=[$(G,NH2,NT,F)|NH2],
        call(G).

(S6)   '$END'([],_,_) :– !.
    '$END'(H,[],d) :– !, fail.
    '$END'(H,T,nd) :– !,
        schedule(suspended($('$END'(H0,T0,F0),H0,T0,F0)),H,T,NH,NT),
        NH=[$(G,NH2,NT,d)|NH2],
        call(G).
    unify(X,Y,H,T,_) :– !,
        unify(X,Y),
        H=[$(G,H2,T,F)|H2],
        call(G).

4.4 Final Stage

Once the scheduling strategy is fixed, *schedule* can be unfolded. *Append/A7* and *solve/S7* shown below are obtained by unfolding *schedule*, consulting *schedule/C0*. The result is compiled code incorporating breadth-first scheduling, which corresponds to variation (ii) in Section 3.

(A7)   append(A1,Ys,A3,H,T,_) :–
        ulist(A1,X,Xs), ulist(A3,X,Zs), !,
        T=[$(append(Xs?,Ys?,Zs,H0,T0,F0),H0,T0,F0)|NT],
        H=[$(G,H2,NT,nd)|H2],
        call(G).
    append(A1,A2,A3,H,T,_) :–
        unil(A1), unify(A2,A3), !,
        H=[$(G,H2,T,nd) |H2],
        call(G).
    append(X,Y,Z,H,T,F) :–
        T=[$(append(X,Y,Z,H0,T0,F0),H0,T0,F0)|NT],
        H=[$(G,H2,NT,F)|H2],

```
                        call(G).
(S7)    '$END'([],_,_) :- !.
        '$END'(H,[],d) :- !, fail.
        '$END'(H,T,nd) :- !,
                        T=[$('$END'(H0,T0,F0),H0,T0,F0)|NT],
                        H=[$(G,H2,NT,d)|H2],
                        call(G).
        unify(X,Y,H,T,_) :- !,
                        unify(X,Y),
                        H=[$(G,H2,T,F)|H2],
                        call(G).
```

Now let us turn to another scheduling strategy. *Append/A8* is obtained by unfolding *schedule/C1* which performs depth-first scheduling. *Append/A8* equals *append/A7* except for the first clause. Thus, only the first clause of *append/A8* is shown below. *Solve/S8* is the same as *solve/S7*, and it is omitted here. *Append/A8* can be converted further to *append/A8'*, because it is useless to put a goal at the head of the goal queue and immediately take it out. The result is a compiled code incorporating depth-first scheduling, which also corresponds to variation (ii) in Section 3.

```
(A8)    append(A1,Ys,A3,H,T,_) :-
                        ulist(A1,X,Xs), ulist(A3,X,Zs), !,
                        NH=[$(append(Xs?,Ys?,Zs,H0,T0,F0),H0,T0,F0)|H],
                        NH=[$(G,NH2,T,nd)|NH2],
                        call(G).
(A8')   append(A1,Ys,A3,H,T,_) :-
                        ulist(A1,X,Xs), ulist(A3,X,Zs), !,
                        append(Xs?,Ys?,Zs,H,T,nd).
```

5. Compilation Incorporating N-bounded Depth-first Scheduling

This section shows an enhanced CP interpreter incorporating N-bounded depth-first scheduling. To incorporate N-bounded depth-first scheduling into Shapiro's CP interpreter, the execution information of each goal must be explicitly specified, because such an enhanced interpreter must access the information at will to govern the whole reduction process. We will call such an information block a *PCB* (Process Control Block). The interpreter schedules each goal, referring to the information in the PCB attached to the goal.

A PCB and a goal are attached to each other by @ in the following way.

```
        goal@Pcb
```

An enhanced CP interpreter handling the PCB is outlined below.

```
(R1)    reduce(Head@PCB,Body,_,nd) :-
                        firmware(policy,PCB,GuardPCBs,BodyPCBs),
                        guarded_clause(Head,Guard0,Body0),
                        attach(Guard0,GuardPCBs,Guard),
                        schedule(Guard,X,X,H,['$END'|T]),
                        solve(H,T,d), !,
                        attach(Body0,BodyPCBs,Body).
        reduce(Goal@PCB,suspended(Goal@SuspendedPCB),F,F) :-
                        firmware(policy,PCB,SuspendedPCB).
```

Reduce/R1 handles the form *goal@Pcb*. *Solve* in *reduce/R1* is the same as *solve/S0* in the original CP interpreter. *Firmware* calculates two PCB lists of child goals from the PCB of the parent goal, referring to the specified *policy*; *policy* decides how to calculate the PCB lists. *Attach* is an auxiliary predicate only for matching; it combines a goal list with a PCB list sequentially, and produces a *goal@Pcb* list.

5.1 Interpreter Incorporating N-bounded Depth-first Scheduling

Here, PCB is the form *(B,BC)*, where *B* is a decrement counter which limits the depth of a reduction tree and *BC* is the initial value for the counter. *Reduce/R2* incorporating N-bounded depth-first scheduling is shown below. *Reduce/R2* combined with *solve/S0* corresponds to variation (iii) in Section 3.

Here, the *policy* is defined as "If *B* has not yet reached 0, reduction can continue and *B* is decremented by 1. If not, reduction is suspended, and *BC* is set to *B*."

(R2) reduce(Head@(B,BC),Body,_,nd) :-
$\qquad$ B>0, NB is B−1,
$\qquad$ guarded_clause(Head,Guard0,Body0),
$\qquad$ attach(Guard0,(BC,BC),Guard),
$\qquad$ schedule(Guard,X,X,H,['$END'|T]),
$\qquad$ solve(H,T,d), !,
$\qquad$ attach(Body0,(NB,BC),Body).
$\quad$ reduce(Goal@(_,BC),suspended(Goal@(BC,BC)),F,F).

Since all the child goals that generated from a parent goal have the same PCB, *attach* here is simpler than *attach* in *reduce/R1*.

N.B.: *Schedule* in *solve* is *schedule/C1*, because breadth-first scheduling is meaningless here.

5.2 Compilation Incorporating N-bounded Depth-first Scheduling

A compiled code incorporating N-bounded depth-first scheduling is obtained by performing the program conversion described in Section 4, using *reduce/R2* instead of *reduce/R0*. The first stage is the only exception; it needs special consideration. *Reduce/R2* is partially evaluated, with respect to *append/A0*. This results in *append/A9* below.

(A9) reduce(append(A1,Ys,A3)@(B,BC),append(Xs?,Ys?,Zs)@(NB,BC),_,nd) :−
$\qquad$ B>0, ulist(A1,X,Xs), ulist(A3,X,Zs), !, NB is B−1.
$\quad$ reduce(append(A1,A2,A3)@(B,BC),true,_,nd) :−
$\qquad$ B>0, unil(A1), unify(A2,A3), !.
$\quad$ reduce(append(X,Y,Z)@(_,BC),suspended(append(X,Y,Z)@(BC,BC)),F,F).

Here, the PCB can be included as extra arguments of each goal without any trouble, because it always goes with the goal. This results in *append/A9'* below.

(A9') reduce(append(A1,Ys,A3,B,BC),append(Xs?,Ys?,Zs,NB,BC),_,nd) :−
$\qquad$ B>0, ulist(A1,X,Xs), ulist(A3,X,Zs), !, NB is B−1.
$\quad$ reduce(append(A1,A2,A3,B,BC),true,_,nd) :−
$\qquad$ B>0, unil(A1), unify(A2,A3), !.
$\quad$ reduce(append(X,Y,Z,_,BC),suspended(append(X,Y,Z,BC,BC)),F,F).

In the remaining stages, the clauses are converted to *append/A10* in the procedure described in Section 4. *Append/A10* corresponds to variation (iv) in Section 3.

(A10) append(A1,Ys,A3,B,BC,H,T,_) :−
$\qquad$ B>0, ulist(A1,X,Xs), ulist(A3,X,Zs), !, NB is B−1,
$\qquad$ append(Xs?,Ys?,Zs,NB,BC,H,T,nd).
$\quad$ append(A1,A2,A3,B,BC,H,T,_) :−
$\qquad$ B>0, unil(A1), unify(A2,A3), !,

```
                H=[$(G,H2,T,nd)|H2],
                call(G).
        append(X,Y,Z,_,BC,H,T,F) :-
                T=[$(append(X,Y,Z,BC,BC,H0,T0,F0),H0,T0,F0)|NT],
                H=[$(G,H2,NT,F)|H2],
                call(G).
```

6. Compiling a CP Meta Interpreter

The *append* we have used as an example so far is really a simple program. All the guards that appeared in *append* are *true*, i.e., *append* is merely a FCP program. FCP is a subset of CP where all guards are either *true* or system-defined predicates. The CP programs used in [4] are really FCP programs. Now we will develop a compilation technique for full CP. We use *mcall/M0* as the next example.

Mcall/M1 is a working version of *mcall/M0* in Section 2. *Mcall/M1* invokes several auxiliary predicates, system-defined *system*, *exec*, *clauses* and user-defined *resolve*. *System* detects a system-defined goal and *exec* executes it. *Clauses* collects candidate clauses that are unifiable with the given goal. *Resolve* selects one reducible clause from the candidate clauses.

```
(M1)    mcall(true).
        mcall((A,B)) :- mcall(A?), mcall(B?).
        mcall(A) :- system(A) | exec(A).
        mcall(A) :- clauses(A,Clauses) |
                    resolve(A,Clauses,Body), mcall(Body?).
(#)     resolve(A,[(Head:-Guard|Body)|Cs],Body) :-
                    unify(A,Head), mcall(Guard) | true.
        resolve(A,[(Head:- Body)|Cs],Body) :-
                    unify(A,Head), Body≠(_|_) | true.
        resolve(A,[C|Clauses],Body) :-
                    resolve(A,Clauses,Body) | true.
```

Mcall/M1 is really a full CP program, because the first clause includes **mcall(Guard)** and the third clause includes **resolve(A,Clauses,Body)** as a guard, and both are user-defined.

Compilation proceeds as before. We need no more tricks. In the first stage, *reduce/R0* is partially evaluated, with respect to *mcall/M1*. To make the following explanation brief, we will concentrate on the (#) clause in *mcall/M1*. The following clause is the intermediate result of unfolding *reduce(resolve(L,M,N),B,F0,F1)*, consulting the (#) clause above.

```
(#1)    reduce(resolve(L,M,N),true,F0,nd) :-
                unify(resolve(L,M,N),resolve(A,[(Head:-Guard|Body)|Cs],Body)),
                schedule((unify(A,Head),mcall(Guard)),X,X,H,['$END'|T]),
                solve(H,T,d), !.
```

The first *unify* can proceed to a further computation. The second *unify* can be moved out of *schedule*, because *unify* is system-defined and is executed immediately by *solve*. The (#2) clause below is the second intermediate result.

```
(#2)    reduce(resolve(A,Arg2,Body),true,_,nd) :-
                ulist(Arg2,(Head:-Guard|Body),Cs),
                unify(A,Head),
                schedule(mcall(Guard),X,X,H,['$END'|T]),
                solve(H,T,d), !.
```

The rest of the task proceeds in the same way as *append*. The (#3) clause below is the final code after the derivation, incorporating depth-first scheduling. This result corresponds to variation (ii) in Section 3.

```
(#3)    resolve(A,Arg2,Body,H,T,_) :-
            ulist(Arg2,(Head:-Guard|Body),Cs),
            unify(A,Head),
            NH=[$('$END'(H0,T0,F0),H0,T0,F0)|NT],
            mcall(Guard,NH,NT,d), !,
            H=[$(G,H2,T,nd)|H2],
            call(G).
```

7. Performance Improvement in Practice

Sections 4 and 5 showed how to compile a CP program in Prolog. Since each program obtained this way is a complete Prolog program, it can be executed on any Prolog processor. The effect of each step on performance can be measured by checking the execution speed. Performance was measured by the total execution time of three sample problems.

The sample problems used in the measurement are as follows:

(a) *Reverse* a list three times through a pipe

nreverse(3,[1,2,3,4,5,6,7,8,9,10,11,12,13,14,15,16],S).

i.e.,   reverse([1,2,3,4,5,6,7,8,9,10,11,12,13,14,15,16],X), reverse(X?,Y), reverse(Y?,S).

(b) Sort a random list using the *quick sort* algorithm

qsort([17,26,13,21,5,1,20,9,3,27,15,25,11,30,24,8,2,
            28,29,4,23,19,16,22,31,6,10,14,32,12,7,18],S).

(c) *Quick-sort* a short random list on *meta interpreter*

mcall(qsort([4,2,3,5,1],S)).

We used **Quintus Prolog**™ Release 1.5 that has a Prolog compiler. The experimental results are summarized in Table 1 on the next page.

The table organizes the results along two axes:

- Eight derivation steps among four stages

  Three problems in every step:

  nreverse, *qsort*, and *mcall*

- Two selections either using or not using the Quintus Compiler

  Three scheduling strategies in each selection:

  depth-first, breadth-first, and 10-bounded depth-first scheduling¶

The rows at the *first stage* contain real processing time in seconds. The other rows contain the ratio of the processing time in the stage to the corresponding time in the *first stage*. For example, when using the Quintus Prolog Interpreter and depth-first scheduling, *nreverse* took 14.83 sec in the *first stage*. *Nreverse* at the *initial stage* took 7.15 times as many seconds as in the *first stage*; it took 106.0 sec = 14.83 sec × 7.15.

Compiling considerably affected the performance improvement in the derivation process. The improvement in the Prolog interpreter is apparent from Table 1. In the case of Prolog compiler, on the other hand, the improvement is dependent upon the selections of the problems and the scheduling strategies.

In both cases, the performance improved considerably in the first stage of the derivation, because the execution cost of *reduce/R0* or *reduce/R2* was substantially decreased. No improvement was found in the second stage, because some goal invocations in *solve* were simply moved to each *append*. The performance improved somewhat more in the third stage than in the second stage, because indirect invocations to the

---

¶ *N* is 10; the step size of depth limit is 10.

Table 1   Performance Improvement in the Derivation Process

Derivation	Problem	Quintus Prolog Interpreter			Quintus Prolog Compiler		
		Depth	Breadth	10-Depth	Depth	Breadth	10-Depth
Initial Stage	*nreverse*	7.15	5.01	6.05	20.4	14.4	8.89
original CP	*qsort*	7.67	4.59	5.44	22.2	15.3	8.74
program	*mcall*	5.32	5.38	5.05	4.79	4.84	4.35
First Stage	*nreverse*	14.83 sec	25.97 sec	18.10 sec	0.77 sec	1.35 sec	1.70 sec
partial evaluation	*qsort*	10.42 sec	41.67 sec	16.22 sec	0.50 sec	1.78 sec	1.52 sec
of reduce	*mcall*	3.90 sec	14.05 sec	15.12 sec	2.82 sec	2.83 sec	3.20 sec
Second Stage	*nreverse*	1.03	1.04	1.02	1.00	0.98	0.99
migration	*qsort*	1.01	1.01	1.04	1.03	0.87	0.99
of schedule	*mcall*	1.01	1.01	1.02	0.99	0.99	1.02
Second Stage	*nreverse*	0.84	0.84	1.06	0.89	0.93	0.86
migration	*qsort*	0.91	0.87	1.08	0.93	0.76	0.87
of solve	*mcall*	0.96	0.97	1.04	0.98	0.99	0.99
Second Stage	*nreverse*	0.88	0.88	1.09	0.78	0.77	0.80
deletion	*qsort*	0.96	0.94	1.12	0.80	0.68	0.83
of solve	*mcall*	0.99	1.00	1.06	0.98	0.99	0.99
Third Stage	*nreverse*	0.94	1.00	1.07	2.37	2.64	1.24
deletion	*qsort*	0.83	0.81	0.87	1.97	2.13	0.98
of $ from head	*mcall*	0.94	0.97	0.95	1.11	1.12	1.01
Third Stage	*nreverse*	0.60	0.61	0.78	2.24	2.43	1.12
deletion	*qsort*	0.63	0.52	0.69	1.87	1.95	0.91
of $ from body	*mcall*	0.83	0.84	0.85	1.08	1.10	0.99
Final Stage	*nreverse*	0.36	0.53	0.56	0.74	2.23	0.45
unfolding	*qsort*	0.46	0.48	0.56	0.93	1.78	0.60
of schedule	*mcall*	0.77	0.80	0.80	0.99	1.06	0.91

next goal were replaced by direct invocations, but this is only true in the case of the Prolog interpreter. In the case of the Prolog compiler the performance became worse. The performance improved further in the final stage, where the time-consuming scheduling calculation was eliminated.

8. Future Research

Each derivation stage is characterized as follows. The first stage utilizes partial evaluation. The second stage moves common goal invocations into each clause. The third stage promotes the first argument of each clause to a predicate. The fourth and final stage unfolds auxiliary goals, consulting their definitions. Of these four stages, the third stage is somewhat magical; an argument is promoted to a predicate and the goal queue structure is changed. We believe that such magical techniques are necessary to enrich the world of program transformation. Further investigation is necessary.

Section 7 showed that the meta interpreter can be compiled in Prolog. An interesting subject is the automation of a process in which a compiled code is generated from a given meta interpreter and a program, in other words, developing a specialized partial evaluator which can be used as a compiler. All we have to do is to make a meta interpreter which realizes the desired functionality. The specialized partial evaluator will do the rest of the work. It can compile programs written in the new functional style, consulting the meta interpreter. Hirsch has moved closer to this goal in the domain of CP.

9. Conclusion

Ueda and Chikayama developed a compiling technique from CP to Prolog. The technique might look complicated at a first glance. In this paper, we successfully separated several ideas; we derived their compiled code from the CP interpreter and a CP program. Specifically, we used an append program and a meta interpreter in CP as our examples, transforming them step by step and incorporating the CP interpreter gradually.

Acknowledgements

This research was conducted as part of the Fifth Generation Computer Project. We wish to thank the members of the First Research Laboratory at ICOT and Dr. Kitagawa and Dr. Enomoto at IIAS-SIS, FUJITSU LIMITED for giving us the opportunity to complete this study.

References

[1]   Hirsch, M., Silverman, W. and Shapiro, E., Layers of Protection and Control in the Logix System, *CS86-19*, Weizmann Instit., 1986

[2]   Kursawe, P., How to Invent a Prolog Machine, in *Proc. of 3rd Inter. Conf. on Logic Prog.*, 1986, pp. 134-148

[3]   Shapiro, E., A Subset of Concurrent Prolog and Its Interpreter, *Tech. rep. TR-003*, ICOT, 1983

[4]   Ueda, K., and Chikayama, T., Concurrent Prolog Compiler on Top of Prolog, in *Proc. of Symp. on Logic Prog.*, 1985, pp. 119-126

The Art of Building
a Parallel Logic Programming System
or
From Zero to Full GHC in Ten Pages

Martin Nilsson   Hidehiko Tanaka
The Tanaka Lab., Dept. of Electrical Engineering,
The University of Tokyo, Hongo 7-3-1, Bunkyo-ku, Tokyo 113

Abstract: We show how a parallel logic programming system is produced as the result of stepwise improvements of a series of minimal interpreters. This paper exposes typical problems and solutions in a clear way. One result is a full implementation of the language Fleng, including built-in functions, suspension mechanism, and one-way unification. We also give a version of the same interpreter using a freeze primitive. The Fleng interpreter is further developed into a Flat GHC interpreter, and then into a Full GHC interpreter.

Key words: Parallel, Logic Programming, Prolog, Committed choice, Interpreter, Fleng, GHC.

1   Introduction

We will gradually, through a series of interpreters, build up a complete implementation of a parallel logic programming language. We start with a minimal interpreter, and improve it successively. Although small in size (about a page), we reach a full implementation of the language Fleng [7], including built-in functions, idle detection, and suspension mechanism. Other results of the process are Flat and Full GHC [12], [4] interpreters.

This paper has two main points: One is demonstrating a way in which parallel logic programming languages such as Fleng and GHC can be implemented. The other is the educational value in the stepwise development of a parallel logic programming implementation: The steps are small and easy to understand. All steps are clearly motivated from general considerations about parallelism, and are applicable to general parallel implementations, not only Fleng and GHC. We will assume that the reader is familiar with some common Prolog implementation such as C-Prolog [9]. We will use standard Prolog features, so the reader should have no problem to port the interpreters to other Prolog systems.

It may be argued that the real problem in implementing a language like this is implementing not the parallelism, but garbage collection and logical variables. This is, however, a common problem of all logic programming languages. In this paper we assume the level of Prolog, and concentrate on the problem of implementing *parallelism*. We have observed that the implementation of parallel logic programming languages is not obvious even for skillful Prolog programmers.

We would like to point out that we do not discuss meta-interpreters here, i.e. interpreters for a language written in the language itself. All our interpreters are executable Prolog programs. A reader of an earlier version of this paper asked: "But where is the parallelism?" This paper describes how to *simulate* parallelism. The interpreters are sequential Prolog programs, of course, but the Fleng programs they interpret will behave as if they were run on a parallel computer. In fact, the structure of the interpreters can be likened to that of a parallel system.

First of all, we suggest a basic interpretation cycle for the language. We will then modify this interpreter to detect idling, handle built-in functions, and optimize the suspension mechanism. In the three final sections we give interpreters for the languages Fleng, Flat GHC, and Full GHC.

2   Related work

The first paper which deals with small interpreters for parallel logic programming languages as a major point is probably the original paper on Concurrent Prolog by Shapiro [10]. Starting with this paper, Shapiro has written a large number of meta-interpreters for different versions of Concurrent Prolog. A recent article [1] also contains a nice small interpreter of (Flat) Concurrent Prolog.

Our paper has grown out of the experience of Ueda [12]. Ueda's approach is a compiler from Flat GHC into Prolog, and he gets quite a fast implementation as a result. Ueda's thesis builds upon the results of [11], which describes implementations of a compiler from Concurrent Prolog to Prolog.

One aspect in which our approach is different from the mentioned is that we consider a simpler language than Concurrent Prolog or GHC. This makes it possible to implement the entire language. We believe this helps in seeing the consequences of an implementation. Still, the language is general enough to encompass the same power as Flat GHC [6].

As for the basic approach to parallel logic programming languages we have learnt very much from, and agree very much with [12], but have designed these interpreters as maybe a somewhat easier way to understand the basic mechanisms of Fleng and GHC than Ueda's compiled approach.

3 Basic Interpretation Cycle

Let a program consist of a set of clauses, looking like Prolog clauses, each clause with a head part and a body of goals:

```
H :- G1,G2,...,Gn.
```

One can imagine several reasonable Prolog-like interpretation cycles for such programs. We choose the following cycle, which is one of the simplest, and which also follows the "committed-choice" philosophy of execution:

- A program is executed by giving it a set Q of goals. All goals are executed independently, in some arbitrary order. A goal G is executed by removing it from Q, and matching it with the head of all clauses in the program. For the first clause with matching head, that clause is selected, and the body goals of that clause are added to Q.

- Matching is like unification, but variable bindings may not be made in G (exported) during the matching. This kind of unification is also called "one-way unification." If a match of a variable in G with a non-variable (or some other variable from G) is attempted, this matching is suspended, and resumes when the variable becomes bound somewhere else.

An interpreter for this basic cycle is given in figure 1.

```
cycle([(G1,G2)|Goals]) :- cycle([G1,G2|Goals]).
cycle([Goal|Goals]) :-
  functor(Goal,F,Arity), functor(Head,F,Arity), clause(Head,Body),
  oneway_unify(Goal,Head), enqueue(Body,Goals),
  cycle(Goals).
cycle([Goal|Goals]) :- enqueue(Goal,Goals),  cycle(Goals).
```

enqueue and oneway_unify are defined in figure 2.

Figure 1: Basic interpreter cycle.

A note on the policy of cut ('!'): The only predicate in this paper which generates more than one result by backtracking, is the system predicate clause. Thus, one can improve the efficiency of the interpreters by adding cut to the end of every clause. However, we have not done this since it is unnecessary and just clutters the look of the program. (Of course, if we ask for several solutions from the top level call to cycle, several answers may be generated, but only the first one makes sense.)

The set Q is treated as a queue and represented in the program as a list whose tail is an unbound variable. Goals to execute are taken from the front of the list, which is the first argument of the procedure cycle, and a new goal is added to the end of the list by attaching it to the tail variable. The predicate enqueue goes down a list (its second argument) until it finds the tail variable, and binds it to a cell containing the element to be inserted, and a new tail variable. For instance, if X=[a,b,c|_] and we call enqueue(d,X), X becomes [a,b,c,d|_].

The procedure oneway_unify may already be built into a well-equipped Prolog system, but we show one way of defining it in figure 2. The strategy is to first test if one-way unification *can* be done, and if so, perform the unification. The predicate **protect** protects variables in the calling goal from being bound, by temporarily binding them to the symbol **$protected**.

```
enqueue(X,L) :- var(L), L=[X|_].
enqueue(X,[_|L]) :- enqueue(X,L).

oneway_unify(X,Y) :- without_binding((protect(X),match(X,Y))), X=Y.

without_binding(X) :- \+ (\+ call(X)).

match(X,Y) :- (var(X); var(Y)), !, X=Y.
match(X,Y) :- (X='$protected'; Y='$protected'), !, fail.
match(X,Y) :- (atomic(X); atomic(Y)), !, X=Y.
match([X|Y],[U|V]) :- !, match(X,U), match(Y,V).
match(X,Y) :- (X=[_|_]; Y=[_|_]), !, fail.
match(X,Y) :- X=..U, Y=..V, match(U,V).

protect(X) :- atomic(X), !.
protect('$protected') :- !.
protect([X|Y]) :- protect(X), protect(Y), !.
protect(X) :- X=..Y, protect(Y), !.
```

Figure 2: Subroutines: Enqueueing and One-way unification.

The test **match** is almost identical to traditional unification. Only the second clause is different: It makes sure that attempts to bind protected variables will fail. After this testing, we have to undo all temporary bindings. This is accomplished by encapsulating the call to **match** in a double negation by failure, expressed by the operator **\+**. The call to the procedure **without_binding** will succeed if and only if its argument succeeds, but without binding any variables in the argument. Finally, if the test was successful, we perform a unification.

Consider the following example:

```
a(X) :- b(X), c(17).
b(17) :- true.
c(X)  :- true.
```

This program can be called by:

```
?- cycle([a(X)|_]).
```

The reader is encouraged to type in this program, and trace through its execution.

Let us see what happens when this call is executed: The call matches the second clause of the interpreter. The two calls to **functor** causes Head to be bound to a copy of Goal, but with fresh variables in all argument positions. The call to **clause** through backtracking then generates all clauses which could match Goal. In this case, the call to **clause** binds Body to (b(X),c(17)). These parentheses pop up because a definition

```
a(X) :- b(X), c(17).
```

is actually stored as

```
a(X) :- (b(X), c(17)).
```

The call to **oneway_unify** is successful, and **cycle** is called recursively. Note that _ (the anonymous variable) in our original query has now become bound to [(b(X), c(17)) | _], with the result that the new call becomes:

```
cycle([(b(X), c(17)) | _ ])
```

The new call matches the first clause. The purpose of this clause is just to flatten the compound goals into a list, so the next call to **cycle** becomes:

```
cycle([b(X), c(17) | _ ])
```

This time the second clause matches the call. However, oneway_unify(b(X),b(17)) fails since we try to bind X to 17. The goal suspended, and so we put it back at the end of the queue. This is taken care of by the second clause, which calls cycle recursively by

```
cycle([c(17), b(X) | _ ])
```

For c(17), the call oneway_unify(c(17),c(X)) is successful.

After running the interpreter for some time, we discover that it falls into an infinite loop, where the queue contains the goals b(X) and true. Whenever they are tried, matching fails, and they are put back into the queue again. We would like to stop execution if this kind of idling happens.

```
cycle([chkpoint|Goals],idle).
cycle([chkpoint|Goals],busy) :-
  enqueue(chkpoint,Goals), cycle(Goals,idle).

cycle([(G1,G2)|Goals],Busy) :- cycle([G1,G2|Goals],Busy).
cycle([Goal|Goals],_) :-
  functor(Goal,F,Arity), functor(Head,F,Arity), clause(Head,Body),
  oneway_unify(Goal,Head), enqueue(Body,Goals),
  cycle(Goals,busy).
cycle([Goal|Goals],Busy) :- enqueue(Goal,Goals), cycle(Goals,Busy).
```

enqueue and oneway_unify are defined in figure 2.

Figure 3: Interpreter with Idle Detection.

We can detect whether the interpreter is idle by putting *checkpoints* in the queue. Whenever a checkpoint is encountered, we check a *busy-flag* if anything "interesting" has happened since last time we saw the checkpoint. If nothing has happened, i.e. the interpreter is idle, we stop execution. If something *has* happened, we put the checkpoint back at the end of the queue, reset the busy-flag, and continue execution. We implement the busy-flag as a second argument of cycle. The flag is idle until some operation sets it to busy. The resulting interpreter now looks as in figure 3. The interpreter is called by

```
?- cycle([a(X),chkpoint|_],idle).
```

The interpreter is still a bit boring, because subgoals may not export any bindings, so they can never return any results. Also, we lack the ability to do simple arithmetic operations, comparisons, etc. For this reason, we add some *built-in functions* to the interpreter.

4 Built-in functions

We add three built-in functions to the interpreter: unify, compute, and call:

- unify(R,X,Y)
  This procedure may bind any variables, and export bindings. It is similar to Prolog unification, but has an extra argument R. R will be bound to true if X unifies with Y. R will be bound to false if X doesn't unify with Y. Otherwise R will remain unbound. This extra argument allows us to detect when unify completes execution, and allows synchronization with other procedures which depend on the unification.

- compute(Op,X,Y,R)
  This procedure performs various binary operations on primitive data structures, e.g. arithmetic. The argument Op represents a binary operation and may be bound to one of the following: +, -, *, /, (arithmetic), and, or, xor, (bitwise), =, <, sametype (comparison). = and sametype allow unbound variables as arguments. Completion of this built-in function can be detected since R then becomes instantiated to a non-variable (true or false).

- call(X)
  This is a metacall primitive. It adds the term X to the queue as a goal, and allows us to call a data structure as a program. It does not need a result parameter, since the result is supposed to be reported by a subterm of X.

These three built-in functions can be implemented as five `cycle` clauses and added to the beginning of the interpreter. The resulting interpreter is shown in figure 4.

```
cycle([call(X)|Goals],_) :- cycle([X|Goals],busy).
cycle([unify(true,X,X)|Goals],_) :- cycle(Goals,busy).
cycle([unify(false,X,Y)|Goals],_) :- cycle(Goals,busy).
cycle([compute(Op,X,Y,R)|Goals],_) :-
    member([Op,Expr],[['+',X+Y],['-',X-Y],['*',X*Y],
      ['/',X//Y],[and,X/\Y],[or,X\/Y],[xor,X^Y]]),
    R is Expr, cycle(Goals,busy).
cycle([compute(Op,X,Y,R)|Goals],_) :-
    member([Op,Pred],[['=',X==Y],['<',X<Y],
      [sametype,(type(X,T),type(Y,T))]]),
    (call(Pred), R=true; R=false), cycle(Goals,busy).
```

The rest of `cycle` is defined in figure 3.
`member` and `type` are defined in figure 5.

Figure 4: Built-in functions.

Here, we have used a Prolog bitwise exclusive-or operator ^. Some Prolog systems does not have this, so instead one has to write X^Y as a combination of the Prolog operators for bitwise and, or, and not. The **sametype** operation of **compute** uses a procedure **type**, which we have defined in figure 5. We have also defined the procedure **member**.

```
member(X,[Y|Z]) :- X=Y; member(X,Z).

type(X,var) :- var(X).
type(X,number) :- integer(X).
type(X,symbol) :- atomic(X), \+ integer(X).
type(X,compound) :- nonvar(X), \+ atomic(X).
```

Figure 5: Subroutines: **member** and **type**.

The careful reader may wonder what happens if an arithmetic operation is applied to operands which are not yet instantiated to numbers. Our interpreter does not wait, but directly applies the operation, with an error as the result. Avoiding this kind of problem is discussed in detail in the next section.

5   Waiting for Constant Terms

Suppose that we have a Fleng definition

```
a(X,X) :-...
```

If we execute a call a(Y,Y), the call will suspend, according to our interpreter. This is because the **match** procedure does not allow binding a variable in the caller, even if the variable becomes bound to itself. This may at first seem to be an unnecessary restriction, but there are some less than obvious important reasons for suspending the call: First, suppose that the call is a(Y,Z). Clearly, it must be suspended. But if we later unify Y and Z, should the goal be activated? It is desirable that the suspension of a query Y=Z, a(Y,Z) does not depend on the order of execution of the goals. Activation trigged by unification of Y and Z is quite hard on the implementor.

Second, suspension of calls such as a(X,X) provides us with a very powerful mechanism for waiting until an argument becomes ground, i.e. does not contain any variables. Consider the following example: We would like to define a predicate wcompute, which is like compute, but which waits until the operation and the operands are instantiated to non-variables. One way to do this in Fleng is

```
wcompute(Op,X,Y,R) :-
```

```
        compute(sametype,Op,_,R1),
        compute(sametype,X,_,R2),
        compute(sametype,Y,_,R3),
        wcomp(R1,R2,R3,Op,X,Y,R).
    wcomp(false,false,false,Op,X,Y,R) :- compute(Op,X,Y,R).
    wcomp(true,_,_,Op,X,Y,R) :- wcompute(Op,X,Y,R).
    wcomp(_,true,_,Op,X,Y,R) :- wcompute(Op,X,Y,R).
    wcomp(_,_,true,Op,X,Y,R) :- wcompute(Op,X,Y,R).
```

Although this is a possible way, it is quite inefficient, because of the busy waiting scheme.

Using the suspension method we can instead write:

```
    wcompute(Op,X,Y,R) :- wcomp(Op,Op,X,X,Y,Y,R).
    wcomp(Op,Op,X,X,Y,Y,R) :- compute(Op,X,Y,R).
```

So far, we have not made any difference between *failed* matchings and *suspended* matchings, since this is important only for efficiency. In the next section, we will improve the interpreter in this respect.

6 Suspended vs. Failed Matchings

Until now, we have put all unsuccessful goals back into the queue. This is quite a waste if we *know* that matching can never succeed. How can we know? If the goal will not match any clause head even for a "normal" unification, we know that it is just wasted effort to put it back into the queue. We implement this by splitting the last clause in figure 3 into two, one for suspension, and one for failure. In figure 6 we have collected all cycle clauses together.

```
    cycle([call(X)|Goals],_) :- cycle([X|Goals],busy).
    cycle([unify(true,X,X)|Goals],_) :- cycle(Goals,busy).
    cycle([unify(false,X,Y)|Goals],_) :- cycle(Goals,busy).
    cycle([compute(Op,X,Y,R)|Goals],_) :-
      member([Op,Expr],[['+',X+Y],['-',X-Y],['*',X*Y],
        ['/',X//Y],[and,X/\Y],[or,X\/Y],[xor,X^Y]]),
      R is Expr, cycle(Goals,busy).
    cycle([compute(Op,X,Y,R)|Goals],_) :-
      member([Op,Pred],[['=',X==Y],['<',X<Y],
        [sametype,(type(X,T),type(Y,T))]]),
      (call(Pred), R=true; R=false), cycle(Goals,busy).

    cycle([chkpoint|Goals],idle).
    cycle([chkpoint|Goals],busy) :-
      enqueue(chkpoint,Goals), cycle(Goals,idle).

    cycle([(G1,G2)|Goals],Busy) :- cycle([G1,G2|Goals],Busy).
    cycle([Goal|Goals],_) :-
      functor(Goal,F,Arity), functor(Head,F,Arity), clause(Head,Body),
      oneway_unify(Goal,Head), enqueue(Body,Goals),
      cycle(Goals,busy).
    cycle([Goal|Goals],Busy) :-
      functor(Goal,F,Arity), functor(Head,F,Arity), clause(Head,Body),
      without_binding(Goal=Head), enqueue(Goal,Goals),
      cycle(Goals,Busy).
    cycle([Goal|Goals],Busy) :- cycle(Goals,Busy).
```

without_binding, enqueue and oneway_unify are defined in figure 2.
member and type are defined in figure 5.

Figure 6: Complete Interpreter.

7 "Freeze" instead of busy waiting

Until now, all interpreters have employed busy waiting for suspension: Suspended goals have been put back in the queue. If there are many suspensions, this is clearly an inefficient method, as the queue becomes full of suspended goals.

Some Prolog implementations have a built-in primitive called **freeze**, or, in French, **geler** [3]. Although **freeze** is not available in all common Prolog systems, it is a very useful feature and not very hard to implement, so it can be expected to be included as a standard feature in production-quality Prolog systems in the future.

```
cycle(Goals) :- var(Goals).

cycle([call(X)|Goals]) :- cycle([X|Goals]).
cycle([unify(true,X,X)|Goals]) :- cycle(Goals).
cycle([unify(false,X,Y)|Goals]) :- cycle(Goals).
cycle([compute(Op,X,Y,R)|Goals]) :-
    member([Op,Expr],[['+',X+Y],['-',X-Y],['*',X*Y],
        ['/',X//Y],[and,X/\Y],[or,X\/Y],[xor,X^Y]]),
    R is Expr, cycle(Goals).
cycle([compute(Op,X,Y,R)|Goals]) :-
    member([Op,Pred],[['=',X==Y],['<',X<Y],
        [sametype,(type(X,T),type(Y,T))]]),
    (call(Pred), R=true; R=false), cycle(Goals).

cycle([(G1,G2)|Goals]) :- cycle([G1,G2|Goals]).
cycle([Goal|Goals]) :-
    functor(Goal,F,Arity), functor(Head,F,Arity), clause(Head,Body),
    oneway_unify(Goal,Head), enqueue(Body,Goals),
    cycle(Goals).
cycle([Goal|Goals]) :-
    functor(Goal,F,Arity), functor(Head,F,Arity), clause(Head,Body),
    without_binding(Goal=Head),
    collectvars(Goal,Vars), freezelist(Vars,enqueue(Goal,Goals)),
    cycle(Goals).
cycle([Goal|Goals]) :- cycle(Goals).
```

without_binding, enqueue and oneway_unify are defined in figure 2.
member and type are defined in figure 5.
collectvars and freezelist are defined in figure 8.

Figure 7: Complete Interpreter using **freeze**.

freeze(X,Goal) delays execution of Goal until the variable X becomes instantiated. We can use this to implement suspension in a simple and efficient way. Figure 7 shows such an interpreter. In this new interpreter, suspended goals are not put back in the queue, so the termination test becomes simpler: Instead of using a busy-flag, it suffices to check if the queue is empty, i.e. if it is an unbound variable. Thus we can remove the second argument of **cycle**, and the idle checking clauses. The only other difference is the expression **enqueue(Goal,Goals)** which is changed into the equivalent:

```
collectvars(Goal,Vars), freezelist(Vars,enqueue(Goal,Goals))
```

collectvars and **freezelist** are defined in figure 8. As the name indicates, **collectvars(Goal,Vars)** collects all variables occurring in Goal into a list Vars. **freezelist(Vars,Goal)** is defined in terms of **freeze**, and sees to that Goal is activated, when any of the variables in the list Vars becomes bound. **freezelist** must ensure that Goal is only activated once, even if more than one variable from Vars is bound. The shared variable **Alternative** in the definition of **freezelist** is used for this purpose.

```
collectvars(X,L) :- collectvars1(X,[],L).
collectvars1(X,L,[X|L]) :- var(X).
```

```
collectvars1(X,L,L) :- atomic(X).
collectvars1([X|Y],L1,L2) :-
  collectvars1(X,L1,L3), collectvars1(Y,L3,L2).
collectvars1(X,L1,L2) :- X=..Y, collectvars1(Y,L1,L2).

freezelist(L,Goal) :- freezelist1(L,Goal,0,Alternative).
freezelist1([X|L],Goal,N,Alternative) :-
  freeze(X,(Alternative=N,call(Goal);true)),
  N is N+1, freezelist1(L,Goal,N,Alternative).
freezelist1([],_,_,_).
```

Figure 8: Freezing subroutines.

8   A Flat GHC interpreter

Starting from the interpreter in figure 3, we can define a Flat GHC interpreter, as we have done in figure 9. We have defined the complete set of built-in predicates as defined in [4], except for I/O primitives.

```
:- op(1070,xfx,'|').
:- op(700,xfx,[':=','\=']).

cycle([true|Goals],_) :- cycle(Goals,busy).
cycle([X=X|Goals],_) :- cycle(Goals,busy).
cycle([X:=Y|Goals],_) :- ground(Y), X is Y, cycle(Goals,busy).

cycle([chkpoint|Goals],idle).
cycle([chkpoint|Goals],busy) :-
  enqueue(chkpoint,Goals), cycle(Goals,idle).

cycle([(G1,G2)|Goals],Busy) :- cycle([G1,G2|Goals],Busy).
cycle([Goal|Goals],_) :-
  functor(Goal,F,Arity), functor(Head,F,Arity),
  clause(Head,(Guard|Body)), oneway_unify(Goal,Head),
  without_binding((protect(Goal),guard(Guard))),
  guard(Guard), enqueue(Body,Goals), !, cycle(Goals,busy).
cycle([Goal|Goals],Busy) :- enqueue(Goal,Goals), cycle(Goals,Busy).

guard(true).
guard((Goal1,Goal2)) :- guard(Goal1), guard(Goal2).
guard(wait(X)) :- \+ (X='$protected').
guard(X=Y) :- match(X,Y).
guard(X:=Y) :- ground(Y), X is Y.
guard(X\=Y) :- ground(X), ground(Y), X \== Y.
guard(Goal) :- ground(Goal), functor(Goal,Pred,_)
  member(Pred,['>','<','=<','>=','=\=','=:=']), call(Goal).

ground(X) :- without_binding((protect(X),match(X,X))).
```

enqueue, protect, match, oneway_unify, and without_binding are defined in figure 2.
member is defined in figure 5.

Figure 9: Flat GHC interpreter.

Flat GHC programs have a structure different from that of Fleng. Clauses have a *guard* part, a test which consists of built-in predicates and is evaluated in essentially a Prolog fashion. If this additional test fails, matching also fails. In addition to head matching, we need to evaluate the guard goals. This is done just after oneway_unify in the code. The guard is first tested once without binding variables. If successful, it is reexecuted to properly bind variables occurring in the guard. The guard primitives are quite similar to their Prolog counterparts, and are executed by the predicate guard. Notice that guard primitives and body primitives have different definitions.

The first two clauses declare the GHC operators for commitment, assignment, and "not-equal" as infix operators. The definition of ground uses the ideas from section 5, to make the implementation particularly simple. However, ground can be defined in a much more efficient way, similar to the definition of protect in figure 2. We leave this as an exercise to the efficient-minded reader.

9 Full GHC Interpreter

The final interpreter we will show is a Full GHC interpreter. The difference between Flat GHC and Full GHC is that guard goals in Full GHC may be user defined goals, and are executed in parallel, just like the body goals of a clause.

The difference in the code is that a recursive call to cycle has replaced the Prolog-type execution for guard tests. Since it has become meaningful for calls to cycle to fail (this means that a guard either suspended or failed), it is necessary to insert cuts before the calls to cycle. If the queue is empty on termination, the call to cycle succeeds, and if there are still goals in it, the call fails. All primitives are now treated uniformly in the beginning of cycle.

```
cycle([true|Goals],_) :- !, cycle(Goals,busy).
cycle([X=Y|Goals],_) :- match(X,Y), !, cycle(Goals,busy).
cycle([X:=Y|Goals],_) :- ground(Y), X is Y, !, cycle(Goals,busy).
cycle([wait(X)|Goals],_) :- \+ (X='$protected'), !, cycle(Goals,busy).
cycle([X\=Y|Goals],_) :-
  ground(X), ground(Y), X \== Y, !, cycle(Goals,busy).
cycle([Goal|Goals],_) :-
  functor(Goal,Pred,_), member(Pred,['>','<','=<','>=','=\=','=:=']),
  ground(Goal), call(Goal), !, cycle(Goals,busy).

cycle([chkpoint|Goals],idle) :- !, Goals = [].
cycle([chkpoint|Goals],busy) :-
  enqueue(chkpoint,Goals), !, cycle(Goals,idle).

cycle([(G1,G2)|Goals],Busy) :- !, cycle([G1,G2|Goals],Busy).
cycle([Goal|Goals],_) :-
  functor(Goal,F,Arity), functor(Head,F,Arity),
  clause(Head,(Guard|Body)), oneway_unify(Goal,Head),
  Guardtest = cycle([Guard,chkpoint|_],idle),
  without_binding((protect(Goal),call(Guardtest))),
  call(Guardtest), enqueue(Body,Goals), !, cycle(Goals,busy).
cycle([Goal|Goals],Busy) :- enqueue(Goal,Goals), !, cycle(Goals,Busy).
```

enqueue, protect, match, oneway_unify, and without_binding are defined in figure 2.
member is defined in figure 5.
Infix operators and ground are defined in figure 9.

Figure 10: Full GHC interpreter.

A simple and illustrative test program for this interpreter can be run by first defining

```
a(0,Y) :- true | Y = zero.
```

and then executing a query like ?- cycle([a(X,Y),X=0,chkpoint|_],idle).

Prolog is deceiving as an implementation language: It may seem that this final interpreter is the most simple and efficient of all the interpreters in this paper. Actually, just the opposite is true. It is very hard to implement this interpreter efficiently. The problems are causes by the guard tests, which require the full overhead of a recursive call to the interpreter. On the other hand, Flat GHC, for which guard evaluation is much simpler, is sufficient for all practical purposes. These are the reasons why implementations of GHC usually are restricted to Flat GHC. The complications which appear when implementing Flat and Full GHC become more clear if one tries to implement suspension by **freeze**, and differ between failure and suspension, as we did for Fleng in section 6 and 7.

An alternative approach to implementing Flat GHC is by compilation to Fleng [6]. Since Fleng is very easy to implement compactly and efficiently, this gives us a practical way of implementing GHC. Using this method, the authors have implemented a Flat GHC interpreter as a small number of vectorizable loops, and been able to execute programs on a supercomputer, at more than 0.5 million process reductions per second [8].

10 Discussion and Conclusions

We have developed pseudo-parallel interpreters for the parallel logic programming languages Fleng, Flat GHC, and Full GHC, by stepwise improvement of very simple interpreters. The development has shown in a clear way how mechanisms are implemented for handling parallel execution. The interpreters have been easy to express in Prolog, with reasonable efficiency, although we have traded off efficiency for clarity. The particular merit of the interpreters in this paper is that they, despite their simplicity, implement the full semantics of a committed-choice language, including suspension, activation, stream communication, and one-way unification.

The ideas presented here should also be directly applicable to such languages as Oc [5] and Parlog [2], which use the same suspension mechanism as Fleng and GHC, and have many other similarities.

11 Acknowledgements

This work was supported by the Japanese Ministry of Education, and the Swedish National Board for Technical Development. We are very grateful to the University of Tokyo for giving us the opportunity to visit. We have benefited very much from discussions with members of the Special Interest Group of the Inference Engine at the university, and with members of the Parallel Programming Systems Working Group at ICOT, especially Ueda-san and Miyazaki-san. Also special thanks to Seif Haridi for giving us manna in the wilderness, in the form of Sicstus Prolog, a very nice Prolog system with freeze.

References

[1] Anzai, Y.: *Parallel Processing.* bit, Vol 19, No 4, April 1987. p 84-88. (In Japanese)

[2] Clark, K.L. and Gregory, S.: *Parlog: Parallel Programming in Logic.* ACM Trans. on Programming Languages,Vol. 8, No. 1, 1986.

[3] Colmerauer, A.: *Prolog-II - Manuel de reference et modele theorique.* Groupe d'Intelligence Artificielle, Universite d'Aix-Marseille II, 1982.

[4] Furukawa,K. and Mizoguchi,F. (Eds.): *The Parallel Programming Language GHC and its Applications.* Kyoritsu Publishing Co. Tokyo, 1987. (In Japanese).

[5] Hirata, M.: *Self-description of Oc and its Applications.* In Proc. Second National Conf. of Japan Society of Software Science and Technology, 1985. p 153-156. (In Japanese)

[6] Nilsson, M. and Tanaka, H.: *Implementing Safe GHC the Easy Way - by Compilation into Guard-free Form.* In Proc. Information Processing Soc. of Japan, March 1987. p 773-774.

[7] Nilsson, M. and Tanaka, H.: *Fleng Prolog - The Language which turns Supercomputers into Prolog Machines.* In Wada,E. (Ed.): Proc. Japanese Logic Programming Conference. ICOT, Tokyo, 1986. p 209-216. Also in Wada,E.(ed.): Logic Programming '86, Springer Lecture Notes in Computer Science 264. p 170-179.

[8] Nilsson, M. and Tanaka, H.: *Submitted for publication.*

[9] Pereira,F.: *C-Prolog User's Manual version 1.5.* EdCAAD, Univ. of Edinburgh, February 1984.

[10] Shapiro, E.: *A Subset of Concurrent Prolog and its Interpreter.* ICOT Technical Report TR-003, February 1983.

[11] Ueda, K. and Chikayama, T.: *Concurrent Prolog Compiler on Top of Prolog.* ICOT Technical Report TR-092, 1984.

[12] Ueda, K.: *Guarded Horn Clauses.* D.Eng. Thesis, Information Engineering course, University of Tokyo, Japan. March 1986.

Introduction of a package system into Prolog

Hiroaki Etoh,Naoyuki Tamura,Yasuo Asakawa,Toshiyuki Hama and Hideaki Komatsu

IBM Research, Tokyo Research Laboratory, IBM Japan, Ltd.
5-19 Sanban-cho, Chiyoda-ku, Tokyo 102, JAPAN

Abstract

In this paper we introduce a package system enabling Prolog to support modularity and separate compilation. A package system is for the development of large systems and is an important feature when coding is done by a number of programmers.

1. Introduction

Nowadays Prolog is sometimes used to develop large systems, such as expert systems, natural language processing systems, etc. There have been an increasing numbers of studies on Prolog compilers following D.Warren (1983), (Kurokawa 1986), (Turk 1986). Furthermore, the number of Prolog applications are increasing and its programs are getting longer. Therefore, the expectations of Prolog are growing, and in particular for a Prolog compiler system to develop large systems.

However, most current Prolog systems are not designed to support large program development. For example, in the current Prolog language specification, there is no module function to divide a large program into several subprograms or to support large program development. Therefore, we need to extend Prolog for this purpose.

This paper introduces a package system for Prolog and also introduces Prolog language extensions. The package system is to support modularity and separate compilation. We also describe some problems that occur when the package system is introduced into Prolog, and show some built-in predicates to solve these problems.

Please note that this paper uses notations in the mixed syntax of VM/Prolog (IBM 1985). The implication operator is < -. instead of :- as in DEC-10 Prolog (Bowen 1981). The conjunctive operator is & instead of ,. The void variable symbol is * instead of _. The cut operator symbol is / instead of !. Also we use the addax/delax/ax predicates instead of the assert/retract/clause predicates.

2. The package system

In the development of a large system, the effectiveness of dividing the whole program into small parts is well known. By defining the interface to modules, this method allows coding to be done by a number of programmers, and modules to be compiled or debugged separately. Moreover, separate compilation enables a library of frequently used predicates to be created.

However, in the current Prolog language specification, there is no way to avoid conflicts between predicate names among modules. This is because Prolog has only one name space for predicates.

Our Prolog supports the separation of programs by the separation of the predicate name space. That is, programmers can independently define the mapping between predicates and predicate names in each part.

Each predicate name space is called a *package*. Therefore, the pair package name, predicate name (including arity) identifies the predicate. The notation, *Package_name : Predicate_name* (a term whose infix operator is a colon) will be used to represent the pair.

As for ordinal symbols (that is, atoms and functors), a single name space is used, because conflicts between symbols is not a serious problem. In Prolog, a mapping between names and meanings (or values) exists only for predicates, not for symbols.

3. Open/closed packages

A package is a compilation unit. Therefore, the information that the package will not be modified at the time of execution is of use to the compiler. It is possible for a compiler to optimize the object code for unmodifiable packages (such as program transformation, in-line expansion, etc.).

In this Prolog system, packages are categorized into two types :

(1) **Open packages,**
    which can be modified at execution time (by addax/delax)

and

(2) **Closed packages,**
    which cannot be modified at execution time

Packages are written as follows :

Package ≡
        package(*Package_name* [, *Package_type*]).
           Statement ...
        endpackage(*Package_name***).**

Package_name ≡ *Symbol*

Package_type ≡ **open** | **closed**

Statement ≡ *Declaration* | *Clause*

Package_type will be considered as *closed* if it is omitted. The execution of addax/delax in (or for) closed packages will cause an error.

4. Import/export

An interface among packages is specified by import/export declarations. Predicates from other packages are invisible until they are imported, and only exported predicates are visible from other packages. Built-in predicates are automatically imported from the *built-in* package. Import/export declarations are described as follows :

Import_declaration ≡ **import(** [Package_name **:**] Predicate**)**.

Export_declaration ≡ **export(**Predicate**)**.

Predicate ≡ Predicate_name(Variable [, Variable] ...) | Predicate_name

The following program is an example of import/export.

```
package(a).
    export(p(*)).
    import(b:q(*)).
    import(b:r(*)).
    import(c:r(*)).
    p(X) <- q(X).
    p(X) <- b:r(X) & c:r(X).          package(c).
endpackage(a).                            export(r(*)).
                                          r(c).
package(b).                            endpackage(c).
    export(q(*)).
    export(r(*)).
    q(a).
    r(b).
endpackage(b).
```

The important point is that non-imported predicates are invisible. The interface among packages is well defined by import/export declarations. Therefore, it is possible to detect undefined predicates increasing reliability, even though packages are separately compiled.

5. Comparison with other systems

In Ada and Modula-2, packages and modules are introduced to support separate compilation (Ada allows separate compilation of subprograms and subunits). Though they were designed as compiler systems, they established guidelines for supporting large program development.

The packages of Common Lisp (Steele 1984) were also designed as name spaces; however not only function names, but other ordinal symbols are also separate for each package. As mentioned before, Prolog symbols need not be localized as long as they do not have values.

MProlog (Dömölki 1983)(SzKI 1985) supports modules where the predicates are either local (not visible from other modules) or visible from other packages (by exporting). As the source module name cannot be specified at import time, the conflict of visible predicate names is still a problem. MProlog provides the predicate set_module_state to control visibility, but the program is complicated compared with the use of multiple name spaces.

Prefixes in VM/Prolog are comparable with the packages in our Prolog system; that is, predicates are represented by a pair "*Prefix : Predicate_name .*" Prefixes can be omitted except when the predicate name is passed as a parameter to a meta-predicate (but it is possible to write a pre-processor to add prefixes to parameters of meta-predicates). Import/export declarations are not provided.

6. Interpretation in a package.

If there is only one name space, there is no ambiguity in the interpretation of goal terms in the "call" predicate (there exists only one mapping from names to predicates). However, with multiple name spaces, goal terms can be interpreted in several ways depending on which name space is selected to interpret the goal:

1.   In the package where the call is invoked

2.   In the name space consisting of all exported predicates from all packages

3.   In the name space consisting of all predicates of all packages

We take the first interpretation, because this facilitates understanding, by identifying a called term with a defined clause in a package. Moreover, it is important for meta-predicates to preserve the package properties with explicit interfaces between packages.

Another requirement for the "call" predicate is that it should be usable by dynamically created predicate, which can not be specified in import/export declarations. When so-called libraries of pre-defined predicates are being made, it sometimes appears that a predicate is called which cannot be specified by import/export declarations. To meet this requirement, we introduce a new predicate call and lexical closure.

7. Treatment of call

Our approach is to interpret goal terms in the package where the call is invoked. Therefore, call(p) and p execute the same predicate in any package; that is, goal X is equivalent to call(X).

```
/* The string 'a:q is called' will be printed out by */
/* executing the goal p.                              */

package(a).
    export(p).

    p <- my_not(q).
    q <- write('a:q is called') & fail.

    my_not(X) <- call(X) & / & fail.
    my_not(X).
endpackage(a).
```

This is easy to understand by regarding every package as a different predicate call, because every name space has a different interpretation of goals. In other words, the predicate call is defined in each package.

The predicate call is treated as an ordinal user-defined predicate. Therefore, when a user wants to interpret a goal as if it were in another package, he or she can import the call from that package.

```
package(a).
    export(p).
    import(b:call(*)).

    p <- call(q) &          /* a:q is called */
         b:call(q).          /* b:q is called */

    q <- write('a:q is called').
endpackage(a).

package(b).
    export(call(*)).

    q <- write('b:q is called').
endpackage(b).
```

8. Closure

Import/export declarations in this Prolog system specify the interface among packages. It provides a framework for good programming style. However, it will restrict programmers by requiring them to pre-define a predicate which takes another predicate as an argument; for example, a bagof predicate in DEC-10 Prolog which takes a predicate as an argument.

```
package(a).                          package(b).
    export(q(*)).                        export(bagof(*,*,*)).
    import(b:bagof(*,*,*)).           import(a:q(*)).

    p <- bagof(X,q(X),L).                bagof(X,Goal,L) <-
    q(a).                                    .....
    q(b).                                    call(Goal) &
endpackage(a).                               .....
                                     endpackage(b).
```

The built-in predicate "call" interprets its argument as a goal in the name space where "call" is invoked. Therefore, if you want to execute a predicate "q" of package "a", An import declaration for the argument predicate should be included in the bagof package. To pre-define such predicates, we need a way to pass predicates as arguments without import/export declarations.

Lexical closure is introduced for this purpose. Like Common Lisp, a lexical closure is the interpretation of the given term representation; a lexical closure will be executed as if it were at the location where the closure was created.

The built-in predicate "goals" is used to create a closure and call is extended to accept the closure. The built-in predicate "call" will execute the closure in such a way as to observe the rules of lexical scoping properly.

Built-in predicate

goals(*Goal, Closure*)

    Goal   (input) Logical formula to be called.
    Closure (output) a *Closure* of *Goal*

Closure of *Goal* is created and unified with *Closure*.

Built-in predicate

     call(*G*)

     G   (input) a *Goal* or a *Closure*

     When *G* is a *Goal*, it is interpreted as a term representing a goal.

A lexical closure consists of an input goal and the environment in which it was created. When the closure is called by the predicate "call", it is executed as if it were at the place where the closure was created. Therefore it is possible to execute a particular predicate in a particular package without import/export declarations. For example:

```
package(a).
    import(b:bagof(*,*,*)).

    p <- goals(q(X),G) & bagof(X,G,L).
    q(a).
    q(b).
endpackage(a).

package(b).
    export(bagof(*,*,*)).

    bagof(X,Goal,L) <-
        .....
        call(Goal) &
        .....
endpackage(b).
```

The predicate "call" in package "b" can execute the Goal in the name space of the package "a". Therefore, it is no need to declare an import/export for the argument predicate. Lambda abstraction can be implemented by using these predicates "goals" and "call". For this purpose, we prepared two built-in predicates, "closure" and "apply" (see appendix). When a closure created by the built-in predicate "goals" is interpreted applying the value to the variable in the closure, the closure can execute only one time in a deterministic execution. Because, the variable in the closure is a logical variable. But you may execute the closure several times in a deterministic execution after assigning the value to the variable in the copied closure. Lambda abstraction take advantage of usage in the case which the closure is evaluated several times in a deterministic execution, because the predicate "apply" abstracts its input list after duplicating it. The following is an example of a sort program that sorts elements of its input list by using its own predicate gt(*,*).

```
package(general_sort).
    export(sort(*, *, *)).

    sort(Input_list, Output_list, Function) <-
        .......
        apply(Function, [Element1, Element2]) &
        .......
endpackage(general_sort).

package(foo).
    import(sort(*,*,*)).

    p <- closure([X, Y], gt(X, Y), CLS) &
        sort([1, 3, 2], L, CLS).
    gt(X, Y) <- X > Y.
endpackage(foo).
```

9. Conclusion

This paper introduced a package system enabling Prolog to perform separate compilations. We showed the problems of dividing name spaces in Prolog, and explained our approach which involves new control primitives, such as goals, call etc.

This proposed Prolog package system was successfully designed in terms of handling multiple name spaces, and will facilitate the development of large systems. We are now constructing a compiler system of almost 13000 lines, using these language specifications.

References

Warren, D. H. D., An Abstract Prolog Instruction Set, Technical Note 309, Artificial Intelligence Center, Computer Science and Technology Division, SRI Internatinal, 1983.

Kurokawa (1986),T.,Tamura,N.,Asakawa,Y.,and Komatsu,H., A Very Fast Prolog Compiler on Multiple Architecture, Proc. of the 1986 ACM/IEEE Computer Science Fall Joint Computer Conference, pp.963-968,Dallas, 1986.

Turk,A.K. (1986), Compiler Optimizations for the WAM, the Lecture Notes in Computer Science 225, pp.656-662, Springer-Verlag, Berlin, 1986.

Bowen,D.L. (1981), DECsystem-10 PROLOG USER'S MANUAL, Department of Artificial Intelligence, Univ. of Edinburgh,1981.

Steele Jr.,G.L. (1984), Common Lisp : the Language, Digital Press, 1984.

Dömölki (1983),B.,Szeredi,P. Prolog in Practice, Proc. Information Processing 83, pp.627-636, Elsevier Science Publishers B.V., 1983.

SzKI, MPROLOG LANGUAGE REFERENCE (1985), Release 2.1, Logicware Inc., 1985.

International Business Machines Co. (1985), VM/Programming in Logic 5785-ABH Program Description/Operations Manual, SH20-6541-0, 1985.

Wirth,N., Programming in modula-2 (1985), Springer-Verlag, Berlin, 1985.

Appendix

Built-in predicate

```
closure(Vars, F, Closure)

    Vars      ( input)  a Input pattern
    F         ( input)  a Logical Formula
    Closure  (output)  a Closure.
```

Closure of *F* is created. *Closure* is made from *Vars* and Closure.

Built-in predicate

```
apply(Closure, Args)

    Closure  ( input)  a Closure.
    Args     ( input)  a Argument list
```

The closure unified with *Args* is executed as if it is at where the closure is created.

Implementation of closure and apply using goals and call.

```
closure(Vars,F,closure(Vars1,G)) <-
        new_var_copy(Vars,F,Vars1,F1) &
        goals(F1,G).

apply(closure(Vars,G),Args) <-
        new_var_copy(Vars,G,Args,G1) &
        call(G1).

new_var_copy(Vars,X,Vars1,X1) <-
        listvar(X,VL) &
        copy({Vars,VL,X},{Vars1,VL1,X1}) &      /* This is no shared copy. */
        unify_free_vars(VL,VL1,Vars,X,X1).

unify_free_vars({},*,Vars,X,X1) <-
        /.
unify_free_vars({V|VL},{V1|VL1},Vars,X,X1) <-
        memq(V,Vars) &
        / &
        unify_free_vars(VL,VL1,Vars,X,X1).
unify_free_vars({V|VL},{V1|VL1},Vars,X,X1) <-
        V = V1 &
        unify_free_vars(VL,VL1,Vars,X,X1).

memq(V,{V1|Vars}) <-
        V == V1 &
        /.
memq(V,{V1|Vars}) <-
        memq(V,Vars).
```

KPR: A Logic Programming Language-Oriented Parallel Machine

Kiyoshi SHIBAYAMA, Masaaki YAMAMOTO, Hiroaki HIRATA,

Yasushi KANOH, Takanori SANETOH and Hiroshi HAGIWARA

Department of Information Science, Faculty of Engineering,
Kyoto University, Kyoto 606, JAPAN

ABSTRACT

In this paper, we describe the architecture of a multiprocessor system oriented to the logic programming language, called KPR, which can execute a program written in some parallel logic programming languages. The KPR system is controlled on the basis of a new computation model named "Parallel Reduction (PR-) model", which regards execution of a logic program as a combined process of searching assertions and traversing the corresponding AND/OR inference tree. On this PR-model, a logical process is allocated to a node of a process graph that is dynamically produced at execution time. And, the resultant reduction (folding / unfolding) of this AND/OR process graph is executed in parallel. This execution model is implemented by three kinds of processes as follows: (i) 'Or-process' for implementing OR-parallelism of a logic program; (ii) 'Stream-process' for realizing the AND-parallelism by a stream-pipeline processing method; (iii) 'Database-process' for managing an assertion database.

KPR is a heterogeneous-function distributed-processing system, where each process is executed on the specialized processor. The inter-processor network of KPR is realized by a tree-structured topology, each leaf node of which represents a processor element. The processor element is a tightly-coupled processor pair, called ORP (Or Reduction Processor) and ARP (And Reduction Processor). An intermediate network node is called NNU (Network Node Unit) and is provided with a bus-switching mechanism, status flag registers and a shared memory for storing global environment data. Some DBP's (DataBase Processors) will be attached to some of NNU's and the SVP (SuperVisory Processor) will be attached to the root NNU.

An ARP is composed of a PCU-A (Process Control Unit for ARP) which controls process executions and inter-process (processor) communications, and an ARU (And Reduction Unit) which implements a Stream-parallel processing strategy. An ORP is composed of a PCU-O (PCU for ORP) and ORU (Or Reduction Unit) where four sets of unification operations can be executed in parallel by means of four UU's (Unification Units).

[Keywords] Parallel Inference Machine; High-Level Language Machine; Logic Programming Language; Parallel Processing.

1. INTRODUCTION

Inherent parallelism residing in logic programs can be processed effectively by a parallel machine. A wide variety of parallel inference machine architectures each of which can process and execute a logic program at a high-speed are being developed at several research organization.[Shi87]

We have been also developing a parallel machine, called KPR[Shi86] since 1985, designed to execute some of the parallel logic programming languages. We have adopted pure-Prolog as a target language of KPR at the first stage. Since pure-Prolog has no sequential specification in its semantics, the inherent parallelism of a logic program is implicitly represented and easily extracted. Pure-Prolog is a basic language for a parallel-inference machine, and so KPR has much adaptability for nondeterministic AI application problems.

KPR is intended to be a practical multiprocessor system for large-scale applications. A maximum instance of KPR system organization will be composed of 512 processor elements.

2.   OUTLINE OF **KPR** ARCHITECTURE

2.1 Parallel Processing Technique on KPR (The Parallel Reduction Model)

On KPR, the execution of a parallel logic language program is based on the "Parallel Reduction model" (PR-model)[Shi86], where the execution process corresponds to transforming a logical AND/OR inference tree. On the PR-model, an inference can be performed on this process graph where each node represents a processing unit. On each processor node, a logical process may be produced or consumed. These operations correspond to folding or unfolding a process graph respectively, called "graph reduction". Based on the PR-model, KPR implements pure OR-parallelism and pseudo AND-parallelism as follows.

(1) Or-process (O-Process) manages a procedure represented by a clause head. An O-process may produce concurrent child processes all of which have a logical OR-relation with each other, and these child processes can be executed in parallel. The logical Or-parallelism of a logic program is realized by the pure Or-parallel processing strategy.

(2) Stream-process (S-process) evaluates AND goals in a clause body by a stream-pipeline method[Shi87], and then the logical AND-parallelism is realized by a pseudo AND-parallel (Stream-parallel) processing strategy.

(3) Database-process (D-process) evaluates a 'database clause' which belongs to a set of clauses composed of assertions only, as an ad-hoc Or-node in the process graph. A D-process does not produce any child process, and so it is a trigger process of a reduction (unfolding) sequence.

The parallel processing technique of KPR consists of intra-process operations and inter-process communications as follows:

1) In principle, an S-process and an O/D-process are alternately invoked.

2) Inter-process communication is performed between a parent and its child in principle. There are three kinds of communication messages as follows:

a) 'Demand' is a request message from parent to child, and may produce a new process on a process graph.

a1)   'invoke' message requests the invocation of a child process.

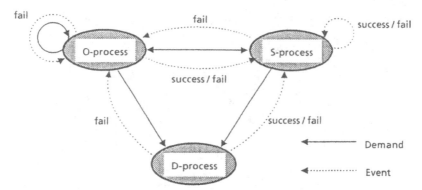

Fig. 1: Logical Processes and Inter-Process Communication Messages on the PR-Model.

b) 'Event' is an acknowledge message from child to parent, and may consume the process.

    b1)   *'success'* message gives a solution of the inference to the parent.

    b2)   *'fail'* message notifies the parent that there are no more solutions from the process.

And, in order to lessen redundant process invocations or overheads in inter-process communications, we have extended the process allocation strategy as follows.

(i) The compiler may eliminate some redundant processes. It analyzes syntactically a process that has a unique child and is on an intermediate node of a demand without any complicated process control. If the rightmost literal is a user-defined predicate in the body goals, the parent O-process does not produce any child S-process and invokes directly a grandchild (O/D-)process. All information about this optimization will be created in advance of the execution (i.e., in the compile time).

(ii) An event may jump over some intermediate process in the inter-process communication. This is named "Event Bypass Optimization (EBO)". The following are the cases where an event message can be directly sent to the grandparent process in order to eliminate redundant processings on an intermediate process: (a) a *success* message that is a solution from the child that corresponds to the rightmost goal in an S-process; (b) a *success* message that is also a solution from a child of an O-process; (c) a *fail* message that is a solution from the unique child invoked by an O-process.

Fig.1 shows all inter-process communication messages in the case of performing the above-mentioned process allocation strategy with two (static and dynamic) optimization techniques.

2.2 System Organization of KPR

KPR is a heterogeneous multiprocessor system, as shown in Fig.2, where each of the function processors specializes in executing the respective one out of a variety of logical processes (O/S/D-processes) based on the PR-model. On KPR, heterogeneous processor modules are connected by a tree-structured interconnection network, each leaf node of which is implemented by a PE (Processor Element). The network is composed of two

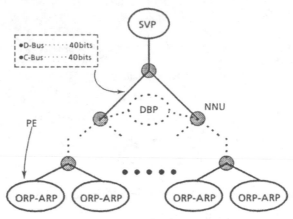

Fig. 2: System Organization of KPR.

parallel buses, called Command-Bus and Data-Bus (40 bits wide respectively). As shown Fig.3, a PE consists of a tightly-coupled processor pair (ARP-ORP). These paired processsors share a register file and a local memory, and cooperate under the control of the PCU.

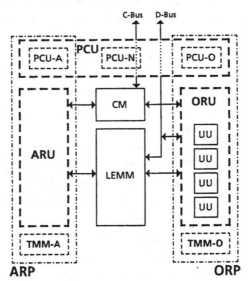

Fig. 3: Hardware Organization of a PE.

ARP (And Reduction Processor): ARP is composed of PCU-A, ARU and TMM-A, and specializes in S-processes.

ORP (Or Reduction Processor): ORP is composed of PCU-O, ORU and TMM-O, and specializes in O-processes.

PCU (Process Control Unit): PCU performs process management in the PE, and consists of three sub-units called PCU-A, PCU-O and PCU-N. PCU-A/O are process managers for ARP/ORP respectively, and PCU-N is a network manager which acts as an interface between a PE and the inter-processor network.

ARU (And Reduction Unit) and ORU (Or Reduction Unit): These are the respective main units in an ARP/ORP, where parallel reductions based on the PR-model will be operated. Especially, ORU is constructed from four UU's (Unification Units) and can simultaneously operate upon up to four unifications.

TMM (Template Memory Module): TMM-A/O contains the instructions of ARP/ORP which down-loaded from the SVP in advance of the execution.

CM (Communication Memory): CM is a large-capacity and high-speed register file where goal arguments or predicate solutions which are to be transferred between PE's through a bus are stored. The capacity of a CM is 4K words (40 bits/word). A CM is divided into pages (32 words/page) under the time-slice arbitration control of the PCU, and may be accessed from the ARU, the PCU (or the network) or each of the UU's.

LEMM (Local Environment Memory Module): LEMM is a shared local memory between an ARP-ORP pair in which environment data which is to be transferred between PE's through a bus is stored. The capacity of an LEMM is 256K words. An LEMM is also divided into pages (but 512 words/page) under the time-slice arbitration control by the PCU, and may be accessed from the ARU/ORU. An LEMM has four independent access ports in order that the ARU/ORU can read data at two different memory locations respectively.

NNU (Network Node Unit): NNU is an intermediate node on the tree-structured network, which is equipped with a bus-switching mechanism, a global memory module called GEMM, its controller and status (of PE's and buses) flag registers called "Flag Board (FB)".

GEMM (Global Environment Memory Module): GEMM is a shared global memory among all the PE's. The root node of these PE's is the NNU including the GEMM. A GEMM is provided with two access ports and double memory banks, each capacity of which is 128K words. A GEMM has the same logical function as an LEMM has. Consequently, the environment memory space of one PE is organized from the LEMM and all GEMM's of intermediate nodes (NNU's) located on the unique bus route from the PE through the root NNU.

SVP (SuperVisory Processor): SVP is attached to the root NNU, and supervises the total operation of the KPR system as follows: (i) it compiles a logic program into such object programs composed of instructions of ARP/ORP, and then broadcasts them to each TMM-A/O; (ii) it invokes the initial process for a question written in a logic programming language; (iii) it executes some built-in predicates such as I/O operations. Since these operations can be executed independent of an inherent operation such as a pure inference and it is very difficult to realize them in hardware, we intend to use a conventional workstation as the SVP.

DBP (DataBase Processor): DBP takes D-processes by means of a high-speed database search mechanism, and so a DBP is provided with a database memory (called DBM) and a hashing mechanism in hardware. DBM has multiple access ports as a shared memory among some NNU's and is divided into memory banks for a parallel search. DBP's will be tightly connected to some NNU near the root.

We are now developing a prototype of KPR, which is composed of a couple of PE's (ARP-ORP pairs), one NNU and one SVP (using the SVP as a DBP also).

KPR has a tag-architecture where each word (40 bits) is composed of a data word (32 bits) and a tag word (8 bits) respectively.

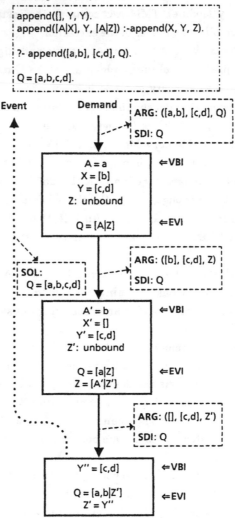

Fig. 4: An Example Data Flow of Environment Data.

2.3 Inter-Processor (Inter-Process) Communication Scheme

The following three kinds of informations are transferred between processors as messages: (1) 'Process Control Data' (PCD); (2) 'goal ARGuments (ARG)'; (3) 'ENVironment data (ENV)'. Command-Bus (C-Bus) is used for transferring PCD and ARG, but Data-Bus (D-Bus) is used for ENV.

Environment data (ENV) consists of some independent sub data structure as follows. (See also Fig.4.)

(a) 'Variable Binding Information (VBI)' shows for each variable in a clause whether it is bound to a value or not, and if it is, its value.

(b) 'External Variable Information (EVI)' is the data about each of characteristic variables called "external variables", unbound and imported from the external of the clause. Each execution of processes on KPR presents an independent environment so that the child process need to send the VBI as solutions to the parent.

(c) 'Solution Designation Information (SDI)' designates which external variable should be returned to the parent process as an answer of evaluating a goal. This information is necessary because adopting the EBO technique may cause that an EVI necessitated by the destination process of the solution does not correspond with the information transferred from the parent.

(d) 'SOLution data (SOL)' represents an EVI identified by an SDI, and it is a part of a *success* message to the (grand)parent.

(e) 'Sub-Process Information (SPI)' represents status of the goal stream just before the evaluation of each AND-goal. An internal process in an S-process of an ARP is called "sub-process". Especially, the lifetime of a sub-process will begin by receiving an *invoke* message from the parent or a *success* message from the child, and will end by invoking a child (O-)process. The Stream-parallel processing can concurrently execute multiple inference streams which are caused to branch away according to (multiple) solutions from one goal stream.

(f) 'ARG' gives a process the parameters on a predicate call, and passes a part of an *invoke* message to an O/D-process.

The inter-processor communications on KPR are implemented by the following two ways:

(A) PCD or ARG transferred through the C-Bus should be immediately received by the receiver (processor). First of all, the sender (processor) locks a physical pass and the data transfer is executed directly between processors.

(B) ENV transferred through the D-Bus is necessary only when the processor executes a process under the environment. First, the sender transmits the data to the global memory GEMM in the root NNU of the processor cluster. The receiver can obtain access to this GEMM when necessary. A PCU will transmit the address data necessary for the access to the GEMM manager in the NNU through the C-Bus in advance.

Since the identifier of an event receiver is fixed beforehand, the NNU can switch the bus by reading the routing information transferred from the sender PCU through a C-Bus.

The process allocation scheme employed can be summarized as follows. A demand causes the receiver kind itself fixed. First, the NNU will mark each load factor of the cluster processor by the flag board (FB). Next, it will take a bus-route to the receiver which can be allocated a new process and which is the nearest one to the sender. By means of such dynamic load balancing strategy, KPR will overcome the following drawbacks with tree-structured networks: (i) its average pass length may be longer than multi-stage network; (ii) the loads of some nodes near the root may become heavy.

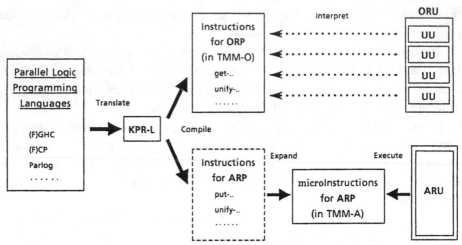

Fig. 5: Flowchart of Processing a Logic Program on KPR.

2.4 Logic Programming Language Processor on KPR

On KPR a logic program will be executed by the following compiler-interpreter method as also shown in Fig.5. (1) First of all, the SVP translates a logic program written in any parallel logic programming language to the object program in the target language of KPR, called "KPR-L", which has the semantics of pure-Prolog and primitive functions for controlling parallelism. (2) Next, the SVP compiles the KPR-L program which mainly consists of rules or facts into the object instruction sequence called "templates". The templates are loaded into each TMM of PE's in advance of the execution. (3) Whenever a question is input through the SVP, the corresponding processor interprets these templates for the inference. (4) If necessary, a solution of the question can be obtained from the SVP.

The functional level of the template representation corresponds to an instruction-set architecture of each processor (ARP or ORP). On KPR, each functional level of three kinds of processors differs with one another as follows:

(1) The instructions for an ORP are stored in the TMM-O. On the ORP, each of four UU's independently fetches and interprets them by microprograms. This technique can be called "two-level instruction control method".

(2) The instructions for an ARP, which are regarded as temporary intermediate codes only in the compile time are expanded into microinstructions and stored in the TMM-A. These microinstructions directly control executions on the ARP.

(3) The instructions for a DBP are stored in the DBM.

The reasons why the instruction-set architecture level of TMM-A differs from the one of TMM-O are as follows:

a) ORP takes a two-level instruction control method. And, ORP does not need any branch instruction inherently. The overhead time in fetching instructions is negligible, because our simulation shows that one instruction of ORP is dynamically interpreted by 4 to 5 microinstructions on an average. Such an instruction control method can lessen the occupied TMM-O capacity and the hardware organization size of UU.

b) However, adopting this control method on ARP may yield overhead time in fetching instructions, because processing an event needs a short instruction sequence. And, microprograms in TMM-A are directly executable on ARU. We can say that TMM-A is a control storage of ARP.

If the target source language of KPR may be changed into another logic programming language, for example such as an AND-parallel type one as GHC, or if the execution model may be modified, or if the processing scheme and the load balancing strategy on a processor may be optimized, KPR can cope by rewriting the firmware (microprograms).

The fundamental instruction-set of ARP/ORP is classified as follows: (i) sequential instructions like these of WAM[War83] (for example put/get/unify operations or built-in predicate ones); (ii) the instruction-set controlling parallelism (for example demand/event operations).

2.5 Architectural Comparison with Other Parallel Inference Machines

KPR is supervised by an 'event-driven method' where a logic program or the intermediate language instruction sequence translated from a logic program will be executed on a reduction machine. We can say that KPR is one of the high-level language machines where semantics of logic programs are executed as the syntax according to goal-rewritings.[Shi87] Consequently, the computation model of KPR architecture is different from the PIM-D of ICOT et al. or other dataflow machines that use data-driven control.

In general we can say in the world of 'symbolic manipulation machines' that such logic programming language-oriented machines as Prolog machines have higher abstraction for architectural function level than such functional programming language-oriented machines as Lisp machines.[Shi87] For example, the ALICE computer of London Univ. is a multi-purpose reduction machine directed to both logic and functional programming languages. On the other hand, KPR is more oriented to logic-programming machine architecture than the ALICE.

We can call the functional degree of a processing unit on a parallel machine "granularity". The design of KPR is pursuing the definite policy that the physical granularity of the machine architecture is adapted to the logical one of the computation strategy as the PR-model. To give another example, each granularity of the KABU-WAKE of Fujitsu and ICOT or the intermediate-stage PIM of ICOT is more coarse, and the granularity of the PIE of Univ. of Tokyo is more fine, as compared with the KPR. We can regard the PIM-R of ICOT et al. as a reduction machine with equal granularity to KPR. However, the PIM-R is a homogeneous multiprocessor system, and KPR is a heterogeneous one as a function-distributed system.

3. HARDWARE ORGANIZATION OF KPR

3.1 Process Control Unit (PCU)

As shown in Fig.6, a PCU consists of three sub-units, called PCU-A, PCU-O and PCU-N. These are tightly coupled with one another. PCU-A shares a Process Description

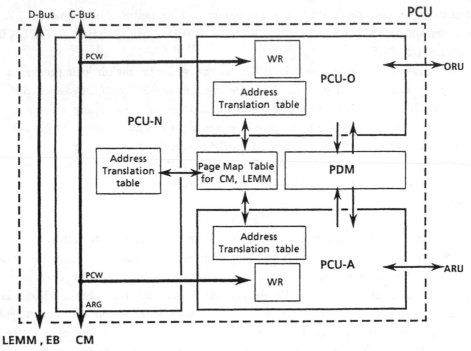

Fig. 6: Hardware Organization of PCU.

Memory (PDM) with PCU-O, and PCU-N shares Working Registers (WR) with PCU-A and PCU-O. The hardware organization of PCU-A is as same as the one of PCU-O. Each of PCU-A, PCU-O and PCU-N is controlled by horizontal-type microinstructions.

PCU-N is an interface unit between a PE and the inter-processor network. In PCU-N a message received through the C-Bus is separated into the Process Control Words (PCW) and the ARG. PCU-A and PCU-O request the coupled PCU-N to send a message to another PE or to obtain access to a GEMM. The network (another PE) requests the PCU-N to receive a message. PCU-N controls inter-processor communications according to these requests.

In the execution of logic programs on the basis of the PR-model, an ARP and an ORP communicate frequently with each other. The communication traffic between paired processors may become heavy especially by adopting a dynamic load balancing strategy where the locality of message communications is very important. On KPR, therefore, we aim at lessening the overhead in the inter-processor communication as much as possible by means of organizing an ARP and an ORP tightly coupled together. As a result, ARU and ORU share a CM and an LEMM, and PCU-A and PCU-O share a PDM. For example, when a PCU-A sends a demand message to the paired PCU-O, the PCU-A will create a new process descriptor and interrupt the PCU-O having its entry point to the PDM.

A process in KPR can be divided logically into the following two tasks; (i) a reduction operation in an ARU/ORU; (ii) management of sub-processes in a PCU itself. KPR is controlled by a function-distributed system under the cooperative control of PCU's. The invocation of a new process in KPR means that a PCU creates a new process descriptor into the PDM.

If the logical granularity of a task executed in the PCU is too fine, overhead such as task switchings will arise. On the contrary, if the granularity is too coarse, the following heavy loads will be overcome the functional degree of a PCU:

(i) PCU has to be able to receive messages (for example, *success* / *fail* events), even if they come continuously to a process;

(ii) When an ARU or an ORU is executing a process, the coupled PCU must not only manage the process but also prepare the execution of the next process at the same time;

(iii) More than one solution may be received as the result of the execution in the ARU / ORU. The PCU has to be able to cope efficiently with such an intricate situation.

In order to solve the above-mentioned problems, on KPR, a PCU creates an environment for controlling S/O-processes on an interrupt from its external. And, a PCU can execute many tasks concurrently by a multi-tasking mechanism, where a task created in the PCU plays the following roles: (1) to reallocate a new page of the CM to the ARU / ORU at the occurrence of a page fault; (2) to dispatch the ARU / ORU to work; (3) to register the result of executions in the ARU / ORU; (4) to transfer a message; (5) to create a new message; (6) to modify the process descriptors.

Consequently, the main objectives of PCU are as follows: (i) to schedule processes so as to achieve efficiency in space and time; (ii) to perform high-speed process switchings in the PE; (iii) to carry out a dynamic load balancing optimization. And so, PCU is provided with various hardware to efficiently realize the following functions: (1) scheduling processes according to priority; (2) operating task queues at a high-speed; (3) handling a wide spectrum of interrupts efficiently.

In the case of developing a special purpose machine, the hardware designer usually chooses conventional microprocessor or sequencer chip as the process control unit of the machine. A PE of KPR, however, consists of a tightly-coupled processor pair, and they have heterogeneous functions with each other. So, we finally chose to have a PCU composed of some distributed-function units, that is PCU-A/O/N and the function of each unit is enhanced by some hardware mechanisms directed to process controls, for example a paged register file, a queue mechanism and so on.

3.2 AND Reduction Processor (ARP)

ARP implements the pseudo AND-parallelism by Stream-parallel processing strategy. There are two main works executed in ARP as follows:

(1) To manage processes executed concurrently on the processor. For example, creating processes according to demands and managing inter-process(processor) communications are executed in the PCU-A of an ARP.

(2) To implement S-process itself. Namely, multiple streams through a body goal sequence are created and updated by the Stream-parallel processing strategy of the ARU.

A PCU-A and an ARU are asynchronous components of an ARP, and cooperate with each other by requests, for example an *invoke* message to the network.

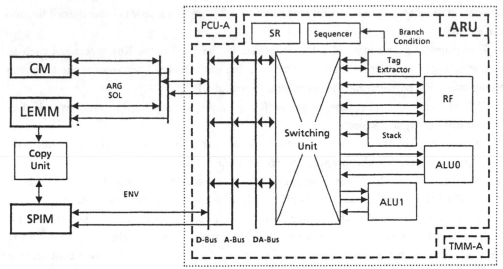

Fig. 7: Hardware Organization of ARU.

ARP manipulates Sub-Process Information (SPI), which represents ENV of sub-process in an S-process and is made of three parts: VBI, EVI and SDI (see an example also in Fig.4). The SPI is stored in SPIM (Sub-Process Information Memory). SPIM is a local memory of ARP, and is used to represent temporary status (SPI) about branches in an inference stream. An environment necessary on invocation of an S-process is transferred from the LEMM to the SPIM under the control of the ARP. This operation is overlapped with the execution of another S-process in the ARU. In case the environment is stored in the GEMM, it is transferred from the GEMM to the SPIM through the LEMM. The capacity of an SPIM is 1M words and is also devided into pages managed by PCU-A. The size of each page is 512 words as the one of LEMM.

In ARP, the processing of one clause body is initiated by a demand message from the parent process, and there are the following two kinds of works.

(a) <u>Demand processing</u>: First, ARP will receive from the parent process (processor) an *invoke* demand including ENV. This data is used in order that ARU may build the ARG of the first (leftmost) goal of the clause body in CM and LEMM. And then, the ARU requests PCU-A to issue another *invoke* demand. ENV is stored into SPIM as the initial SPI about the stream.

Hereafter, sub-processes are successively driven by the *success / fail* event (solution) from the child processes. A *fail* event does not update ENV, so that only PCU-A needs to detect it. Namely, a *fail* event will lead PCU-A to perform management of information about the child processes and memory allocation or deallocation for the LEMM and SPIM. ARU is only concerned about *success* events.

(b) <u>Event processing</u>: ARU updates SPI by using a *success* event from a child process, which contains a solution (SOL). In ARU, built-in predicates which the current goal precedes to are also executed so that SPI is updated. If an event is thrown from the child which corresponds to the last (rightmost) goal, the ARU will build an SOL from the updated SPI and will request the PCU-A to issue a *success* event including this SOL. In other cases, the updated SPI is saved into SPIM, and a child process for evaluating a next goal is invoked like in demand processing.

The work of ARU consists of the following data processings: (a) Creating ARG (for child processes) using ENV; (b) Updating ENV using SOL from child processes; (c) Updating ENV as a result of executing built-in predicates; (d) Making SOL of ENV (and SDI from the parent).

In cases of (a) and (c), their processing flows are fixed by a static analysis of a program at compile time and the processings will be done by executing the microinstructions stored in TMM-A. But, in cases of (b) and (d), the processings depend on the dynamic transformation of the data structure.

The abstract instruction-set of ARP can be classified as follows. These instructions are actually expanded into microinstructions before execution.

(1) Put / unify instructions make ARG of ENV on CM.

(2) Unify-back instructions update ENV by an SOL. These instructions unify an SOL with an entry of the corresponding SDI in SPI.

(3) Built-in predicate instructions update ENV as a result of evaluating built-in predicates, for example arithmetic or logical operations.

(4) Demand or Event instructions build up the message to be transferred and the request interrupt of its invocation to PCU-A.

As shown in Fig.7, in order to realize these operations, ARU is provided with the following facilities and mechanisms in hardware.

a) Copy unit for fast copying of ENV.

b) Multiple buses and a bus switching unit for making fast dereference of pointers and for accessing multiple data simultaneously.

c) Tag extractor for multi-way branching using data tags.

d) Hardware stacks for accessing data with recursive structure efficiently.

e) ALU's for implementing built-in predicates.

f) SR (Special Registers) for communicating with PCU-A.

ARU operations are divided into some primitive functions. In order to achieve efficiency in these primitive functions, hardware facilities of an ARU are connected by multiple buses via a bus switching unit and are executable in parallel under the control of a horizontal-type microinstruction. That is, a kind of low-level (primitive function level) parallelism in this processing unit brings about both efficiency and flexibility.

In addition, providing an ARP with a double communication port between the ARU and the PCU-A will contribute to a decrease of overhead in the data transfer.

3.3 OR Reduction Processor (ORP)

An ORP realizes O-processes on the basis of the PR-model. Each O-process has the following three kinds of works:

(1) Unification: An O-process will try unification between a goal literal and multiple head literals of candidate clauses in parallel.

(2) Execution of built-in predicates: If a unification succeeds, the O-process will evaluate

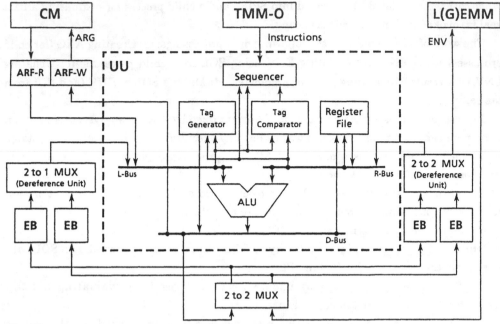

Fig. 8: Hardware Organization of UU.

all of built-in predicates which precede the leftmost user-defined predicates in the candidate clause body.

If both (1) and (2) succeed, the O-process will send an *invoke* demand to a child process and evaluate the rest of the candidate clause body. If all candidate clauses fail in either (1) or (2), the O-process sends a *fail* event to its parent process and aborts itself.

(3) Processing of *fail* events from child processes. Whenever an O-process receives such an interrupt as a *fail* event, it decreases by one the number of the alive child processes in the process management table. And also, when the number goes down to zero, the O-process sends a *fail* event to its parent process and aborts itself.

Thus, ORP implements pure OR-parallelism by the way that one O-process can invoke child processes running in parallel.

An ORP can receive ARG and ENV as an *invoke* demand message from itself or another ARP/ORP. An ORP does not receive any *success* event as the effect of the event bypass optimization (EBO), so that the ORP need not save the ENV into its local memory as against an SPIM of an ARP.

An ORP consists of two sub-processing units: a PCU-O and an ORU. Further, an ORU has four UU's which execute the above-mentioned works: (1) and (2) for four candidate clauses in parallel. And in ORU, there are two memory modules, called Argument Register File (ARF) and Environment Buffer (EB), which interface with CM and (L/G)EMM respectively.

ORU executes mainly the following operations:

i) It assigns individual clause to each of four UU's dynamically and controls the independent unifications.

ii) It broadcasts a request from the PCU-O to each of the four UU's and merges requests from the UU's to PCU-O.

iii) It supplies all of the UU's with ARG and ENV through ARF and EB respectively, in advance of the unifications. Namely, before four UU's begin the executions simultaneously, the ORU requests that the PCU-O should transfer the ARG from the CM to the ARF and load the ENV from the (L/G)EMM into each of four EB's.

Each UU can execute unifications by means of the ARG in the common ARF, the ENV in the EB and a part of instructions (information about a clause head) in the TMM-O.

We adopt the method that each UU renews ENV according to information of each clause head. Each UU must save the ENV in the unification into itself, and each of four UU's needs to be able to access asynchronously and independently the memory for the ENV. Therefore, each UU is provided with a local memory, called EB, which has a double memory bank and stores the ENV of only one O-process. Since data transfers between an (L/G)EMM and an EB can be done simultaneously during unifications, we can make overheads in environment copying time as little as possible.

Moreover each UU is provided with two read ports for an EB so that it can concurrently access two different operands of the EB in one unify operation. Hence one EB for a UU consists of four memory banks, where each of the UU's and the PCU-O can access either of two banks in parallel. The two banks of the EB are exchanged by the ORU. The ENV transferred from GEMM through the network will be directly stored into EB, not through LEMM, in order to lessen the number of accessings to LEMM. And also, a UU is provided with a special hardware mechanism, called "dereferencing unit" as shown in Fig.8, where traversing an intricate binding list can be automatically repeated until detecting a not-reference tag.

A UU does not have a fixed cycle time for dereferencing unit, and so it cannot use the same clock signal as an ARU and an PCU. Each UU of an ORU runs asynchronously of one another and independently of the paired ARU. In addition to a time-slice arbitration technique, an ARF enables four UU's to have asynchronous accesses to the shared CM. An ARF also consists of two register banks, called an ARF-R/W. ARF-R stores ARG transferred from CM and sent to UU's. ARF-W stores ARG and also SOL produced by UU and written into CM.

The compiler on the SVP translates arguments of a clause head into the corresponding instructions in advance of the interpretation. Each of four UU's independently interprets instructions in the TMM-O by the respective microprograms. A combination of two argument tags may decide dynamically the unification sequence in the execution.

The instruction-set of ORU is classified as follows:

(1) Get instructions are executed in unifying the arguments of a clause head with the arguments of a goal literal in an ARF-R;

(2) Built-in predicate instructions are used for executions of built-in predicates, which may modify ENV in EB;

(3) Put instructions load ARG's in CM for producing an *invoke* message to ORP;

(4) Unify instructions correspond to each argument in a structured data and are executed

in unifying with existing structures in EB or in constructing new structures.

(5) <u>Demand instructions</u> put into communication registers of PCU-O the name of a predicate processed by the child process and the identifier of a processor (ARP or ORP) on executing them, and then interrupt PCU-O in order to send an *invoke* demand.

(6) <u>Event instructions</u> correspond to the request that the ORU should send a *success* message to the parent process. There are no event instructions for any *fail* messages, because if the evaluation of a predicate fails, the event is directly reported to the ORU by microinstructions.

These instructions translated by the SVP are stored in all TMM-O's, and then they are expanded to the corresponding microinstructions of UU's. There is no branch operation in the instruction-set so that TMM-O is provided with only one serial access port. In result, one ORP has only two (not four) TMM-O's each of which stores the same contents, and two UU's can commonly read one of TMM-O's.

In the unification, a UU creates new data structure, heaps it on the old ENV and writes directly a value into unbound variables in the old ENV. If on a UU an unbound variable is bound to a data structure in the old ENV, the UU need not copy all data structure into the heap, and has only to write a pointer to the data structure into the unbound variable. But this method has a deficiency that it is necessary to copy as many times as the number of candidate clauses. We cope with this deficiency by the following manners. (1) Before an execution, PCU-O broadcasts ENV into all of four EB's. (2) By a double EB organization, data transfers between EB and EMM and operations of UU's can be performed simultaneously.

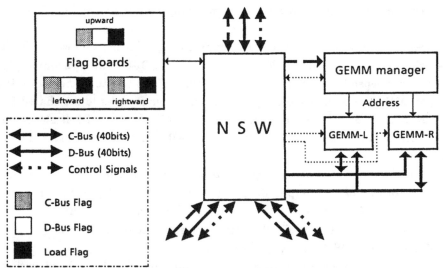

Fig. 9: Hardware Organization of NNU.

3.4 Network Node Unit (NNU)

NNU's are allocated to intermediate nodes of the tree-structured network, and dynamically control inter-processor communications. On executing a program, logical processes communicate with each other, so that communication messages such as events or demands are transferred between physical PE's through more than one NNU. When a communication message is sent from another NNU or a PE, NNU decides which direction it should be transmitted to.

(A) Communicating an event message: The process generating the message can specify a destination processor to which this message should be transferred. When a demand invokes a process which may return an event message, the processor having generated the event can be informed of the identifier of the processor which invoked the demand message. Consequently, when a processor transfers an event message through C-Bus, PCU-N makes up the "routing information" which designates a destination processor. Each NNU can know by a routing information how to transmit a message.

(2) Communicating a demand message: A demand message may invoke a new process on any destination processor. And, any NNU should consider the load balancing of the KPR system whenever it has to decide a destination processor of a demand message.

NNU should grasp the status (factor of loads) of every PE for the load balancing, so that the status information indicates whether a processor can afford to execute a new process (whether it is free or busy). Any PE should know the status of other PE's in real-time. But, judging from the large scale of KPR, it is very difficult to realize the practical mechanism. Therefore, each NNU is provided with status flags, each of which indicates the load factor of each PE connected in a cluster (i.e., a sub-tree where the NNU is the root node). NNU can judge the direction to transmit a demand message by these status flags.

Each NNU can know three kinds of status flags by the flag board (FB) as shown in Fig.9. The rightward (or leftward) FB of them indicates the load factor of the right (or left) cluster. The upward FB indicates the load factor of other PE's except the cluster PE's. Each PE propagates its own status to the upward NNU. And also, each NNU informs the neighboring NNU or PE of the contents of the FB. In transmitting a demand message, NNU can judge the direction of sending the message by the FB.

When a PE sends a message to another PE, an NNU issues a 'REQuest (REQ)' signal to the upward NNU so that the NNU can allocate a transfer path of the message. And, as soon as an NNU is invoked by an REQ signal, the NNU switches the bus to the destination and transmits an REQ signal to the neighboring NNU's or PE's.

As shown in Fig.9, NNU consists of four sub-units as follows: a FB, a Network SWitch (NSW), a Global Environment Memory Module (GEMM) and a GEMM manager.

Each FB consists of three kinds of flags as follows: 'Load Flag', 'C-Bus Flag' and 'D-bus Flag'. A C/D-Bus Flag respectively shows whether the C/D-Bus in the three directions of the NNU is free or busy. A Load Flag shows whether in the direction there are any PE's which can afford to execute a new process or not.

When an NSW is invoked by an REQ signal, it decides the direction to transmit a message and switches the network bus.

A GEMM is a global memory storing ENV. A GEMM has a double port by the respective D-Bus connected to the PE's side. A GEMM is shared by the PE's belonging to the cluster under the NNU. Namely, the GEMM must not be accessed by the upward

GEMM. The ENV stored into a GEMM from the rightward (or leftward) cluster may be read from any PE of the leftward (or rightward) cluster respectively. As a result, a NNU is provided with a double bank organization of a GEMM, called GEMM-R/L, as also shown in Fig.9.

In the case of implementing an AND-parallel type language on KPR, a logical 'channel' for a shared value among processes is allocated on a GEMM. The content of a channel can be read out from PE's of both the rightward and leftward cluster. Therefore, in order to implement a channel, a PE writes the same value to both GEMM-R and GEMM-L, and the value may be read out from either of the GEMM-R/L.

A GEMM manager is a memory processor composed of three sub-units as follows: a control unit, a processing unit, and an address table. A GEMM manager is controlled by microprograms, and it manages a GEMM by a paging strategy where it allocates or deallocates a page in a GEMM whenever a request is transferred to a GEMM.

Since the information which is necessary to make load balancing among PE's is dynamically propagated to all NNU's in real-time, any NNU can know the status of all PE's immediately. This dynamic load balancing mechanism has been made possible based on the binary tree-structured network of KPR.

4. CONCLUSION

We have still some unsolved problems about KPR architecture as follows: (1) We have to evaluate tradeoffs between a PE architecture and the network architecture in practice. Especially, the structure copying strategy may yield overheads in space and time for the copying; (2) We also have to evaluate tradeoffs between an ARP-ORP pair in a PE; (3) For another target language such as an AND-parallel type one, it may be necessary to improve the hardware organization of KPR. Most of our current works shall be devoted to solving these problems by experimenting on a prototype and also simulating it by software.

A prototype hardware organization of KPR, which is composed of two PE's, an NNU and the SVP used also as a DBP, has already become large-scale. What is more, we would like to build KPR with up to 512 PE's prospectively. We have to take possibility of customarizing a KPR's processor element a VLSI chip into current consideration.

We are now implementing a prototype hardware organization with 200 ns as a processor cycle and programming an AND-parallel language processor for KPR. And, we are beginning to refine the design of a DBP architecture.

ACKNOWLEDGEMENT

The KPR project is supported in part by Grant-in-Aid for Scientific Research from the Ministry of Education, Science and Culture, and in part by the Information and Communication Systems Laboratory and the Research and Development Center of

Toshiba Corporation, and in part by the Main Frame Division of Fujitsu Limited. We would like to extend our special thanks to them for their supports.

Last but at least, we would like to express our sincere appreciation to the members of the PIM working group of the ICOT and the members of the Information Systems Research Center of Sony Corporation for their stimulating discussions and valuable advices.

References

[Shi86] Shibayama, K. et al.: The Architecture of a Logic Programming-Oriented Parallel Reduction Machine KPR, *IEICE Technical Report*, EC85-70, pp.43-54 (Mar. 1986). (in Japanese)

[Shi87] Shibayama, K.: Symbolic Manipulation Machine, *Journal of IPS Japan*, 28, 1, pp.27-46 (Jan. 1987). (in Japanese)

[War83] Warren, D.H.D.: An Abstract Prolog Instruction Set, *Report of Stanford University Computer Science Department*, SRI-309, pp.1-30 (Oct. 1983).

A Preliminary Evaluation of a Parallel Inference Machine
for Stream Parallel Languages

Toshiaki Tarui (1), Tsutomu Maruyama (2) and Hidehiko Tanaka
Department of Electrical Engineering, The University of Tokyo
Hongo 7-3-1, Bunkyou-ku, Tokyo 113, Japan
(1) Currently with: Central Research Laboratory, HITACHI, Ltd.
(2) Currently with: C&C Systems Laboratories, NEC Corporation

Abstract

A new architecture is proposed for a parallel inference machine for stream parallel languages. Its performance is evaluated using software simulation. In the architecture, a unit consists of a processor and a logically shared memory, and several units are connected through a network. Based on simulation results, it is confirmed that the main problem is the existence of frequent access to remote memories through the network. It is also determined that it is necessary to introduce a cluster configuration if the system is to consist of more than 64 processors.

1.   Introduction

A new parallel inference engine, PIE [1], is under development. A PIE executes logic programs in parallel and is based on a goal rewriting model. The previously developed PIE can efficiently extract OR-parallelism from logic programs. However, it is difficult to efficiently execute stream parallel languages such as GHC [2] with this PIE's architecture.

To design a parallel inference machine for stream parallel languages and introduce an efficient system for it, the following aspects must be evaluated before an appropriate parallel execution environment can be attained:
(1) the load distribution between processors
(2) the status of processes, i.e. goals, in each processor
(3) the network traffic required to access the shared variables
This paper presents result of the software simulation of parallel inference machine for stream parallel languages and a discussion of the above aspects.

For simulation, a stream parallel logic programming language, FLENG [3], was used as the target language of the system instead of GHC. This is because FLENG has shared variables and suspension/activation of goals, which are the essence of stream parallel processing, and has no complex controls such as guards. Thus, FLENG makes it possible to easily evaluate the basic performance of a system for a stream parallel language.

2. FLENG

FLENG is a logic programming language like GHC, and its execution mechanism is similar. In FLENG, like in GHC, the binding of variables in parent goals is not allowed in head unification. If binding is attempted, the unification is suspended.

The following are the features that are different from those of GHC:
(1) Guards do not exist, so goal execution committing starts immediately after head literal unification is successful.
(2) The literals in the body of a clause have no logical relationship, so each literal in the committed clause is executed regardless of whether the execution of another goal literal was successful. If a logical AND relationship is needed, it can be written explicitly in the program.

As mentioned above, FLENG is very similar to GHC concerning access to the shared variables, but the execution control mechanism is much simpler than GHC's. In addition, FLENG's language level is lower than GHC's, and almost all GHC programs can be compiled into FLENG very easily.

3. Architecture for a Stream Parallel Language

In designing a parallel inference machine for a stream parallel language, the major consideration is where to store the shared variables. Shared variables may be stored in the central shared memory, such as the structure memory of the previously developed PIE [4]. However, access conflicts would be a problem in such a case. Thus, a distributed shared memory (SM) has been introduced for shared variable storage in the new architecture.

One processing unit is composed of a shared memory and a unify processor (UP). To suppress the access to the SM in other units, the UP is allowed to access the SM in the same unit quickly, i.e. without network overhead.

The inference unit(IU), the execution element of the machine system, consists of a UP, which executes unification, and an SM. This system consists of many IUs, which are connected through two networks. The networks are as follows:

(1) a distribution network(DN).

It is used for goal distribution.

(2) a shared memory network(SMN).

It is used when the values of the shared variables and the structure data are fetched. It is also used for the activation of suspended goals.

The structure of the system model is shown in Fig. 1.

The DN is an omega type network, which was used in the previous PIE [5]. It distributes goals according to the current load of each IU so that the load of each is balanced. The structure of the SMN has not been decided yet. Since the purpose of the system simulation is to measure the exact frequency required to gain access to the network, it is assumed an ideal network, i.e. constant connection time and no blocking, is essential for this model.

The UP and SM are closely connected inside an IU. Therefore, the UP can gain access to the SM without using the SMN. Thus, if the load distribution is optimized, the frequency required for gaining access to the SMN can be decreased.

The structure of an IU is presented in Fig. 2. The function of each element is described below.

- Cache

The cache contains the address and the value of the external SM. It is an associative memory with which the UP can search the contents of the SMs in other IUs using the address of the other SMs, i.e. the IU number and internal address. The value of the shared variables in the other SMs, the value of the structure data in the other SMs, and the addresses of undefined variable cells in the other SMs are contained in the caches.

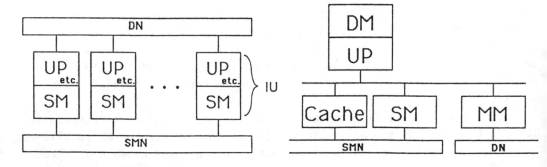

Fig. 1 structure of system model   Fig. 2 structure of inference unit

- SM (shared memory)

   The SM contains the value of the shared variables and structure data.
- MM (memory module)

   The MM contains and maintains the goals.
- DM (definition memory)

   The DM contains the FLENG program. All DMs have the same definition clauses.
- UP (unify processor)

   The UP executes the unification and makes new goals. It can directly access the DM, MM, cache, and SM in the same IU. It accesses the SM of the other IUs through the SMN.

4. FLENG Program Execution Methods

4.1 Goal Representation

   Each goal, which is the basic unit of program execution, consists of one literal. When several literals are generated as the result of head unification, each literal becomes a different goal and is distributed into different MMs. At that time, the pointers to the local SMs (the local SM and the UP that generate the new goal are in the same IU) are dereferenced. The results of the dereferencing are copied in the new goal. This is done to decrease the access to the SMN.

   The pointers to the structure data in the local SMs are handled based on the following two methods. In one method, the structure data are copied in the goal as the structure area of the goal. In the other method, the structure data are not copied, and only the pointers to the structure data are copied in the new goal. Both methods were used in this simulation.

4.2 Allocation of Shared Variables

   When a UP executes a new goal, the cells of all the variables in the definition are placed in the local SM and initialized as an UNDEF (undefined variable). All bindings that occur during head unification are written into the variable cells. When a variable cell is bound to the structure data of the definition, the structure data are copied in the SM, and its pointer is written in the variable cell. When a UP generates new goals, the variables are treated in two ways. For a variable to which the new value is bound, its new values are copied in the new goal. For a variable that is still undefined, the pointer to the variable cell is copied in the new goal.

4.3 Suspension and Activation of Unification

In FLENG, the following two cases cause unification suspension:
(1) the binding of an undefined variable in the parent goal during head unification.
(2) the unification of an undefined variable and a head variable that have a bind-to-non-variable annotation.
Suspended goals can be executed again when some value is bound to the undefined variable cell that causes the suspension.

The suspension and activation of goals are executed in the following way:
(1) The goal address in the MM, i.e. the IU number and internal address, is stored in the undefined variable cell, which causes suspension, when suspension-causing binding occurs during the unification of a head literal (actually, when access to the undefined variable cell occurs to fetch and then bind some value to the cell).
(2) If no alternative succeeds and one or more alternatives are suspended during the head unification of the goal, the goal is removed from the MM's active queue and the state of the goal changes to a suspended one.
(3) After that, the SM will send an activate command to the suspended goal in the MM through the SMN when some value is bound to the undefined variable cell. Then, the goal can be executed again. At the same time, the new value of the variable cell is written in the cache.
If an activate command is sent to a goal that is being executed in the UP, the UP aborts the execution of the goal and restarts the unification with the new value of the variable in the cache.

4.4 Operation in the Cache.

Each IU has a cache buffer with the same contents as that of the SMs in the other IUs. Before the access to the external SM, the UP searches the contents of the cache. If the value of the address that the UP is going to access exists in the cache, i.e. if the cache hits, the UP will continue the execution with the value in the cache, and no access will be made through the SMN. If the cache does not hit, the value of the address will be read through the SMN, and the value read will be stored in the cache. The addresses of undefined variable cells in the external SMs are also stored in the caches, until the execution of one goal ends.

4.5 System Predicate UNIFY

In FLENG, binding to the variables of parent goals is executed only in system predicate UNIFY. If a variable cell to which UNIFY is going to bind a value is already bound by another UP, i.e. if the variable cell is a defined variable, the UP fetches the value that has been written and tries to unify the new value of the variable and the value that the UP is going to write in the cell.

4.6 Load Distribution

The distribution of the load between the IUs is executed by the DN, which distributes goals according to each IU load, i.e. the number of goals in each IU. When a goal is generated by a UP, it is sent to an IU to which the UP can be connected and that has the least number of active goals. (If several IUs have the same number of active goals, the new goal is sent to the IU with the least number of suspended goals). However, when no active goal exists in the local MM, the new goal is returned to the local MM and no access through the DN is made.

5. Simulation Assumption

The following points were assumed regarding the simulation:
(1) Each UP should have the same performance as the UP hardware of the previous PIE [6]. Additionally, it should be possible to simulate it on the micro instruction level. The simulation time (simulation clock) must be the same as that of a real processor.
(2) The network should be an ideal circuit switch network that can always be connected in the same amount of time.
(3) By varying the time for connecting the SMN from 0 to 20 clocks, the effects of network connecting time on machine performance can be examined. In the case of ordinary simulations, the time for connecting the SMN is 5 clocks.
(4) The cache is an associative memory. It must be possible to quickly find necessary data in the cache.
(5) The caches are big enough.
(6) The SM and MM are multi-bank memories that have two ports so fetch access from the external network and from the UP can be executed at the same time. However, when write access is performed from one port, the SM has to be locked and no access can be made from the other port.
The simulation was conducted using the C language and a UNIX operating system. The simulation had about 10,000 steps.

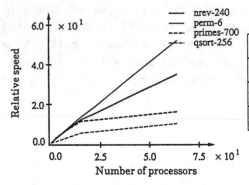

Fig. 3 Relative execution speed

Table 1 Number of suspensions
and activations

	nrev	qsort	primes	perm
number of suspended goals	7351	4935	26226	0
number of hooks	32120	15518	52497	4990
number of activate commands	32075	13176	44070	4990

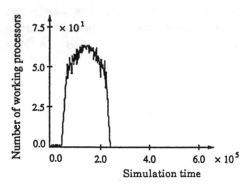

Fig. 4 Number of working
processors (NREV)

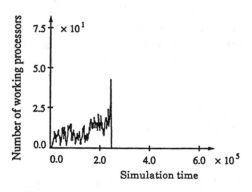

Fig. 6 Number of working
processors (QSORT)

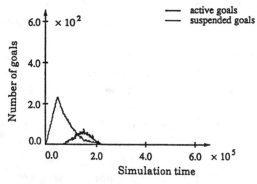

Fig. 5 Number of goals
in MM (NREV)

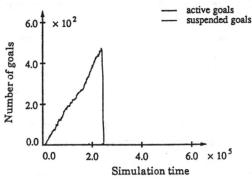

Fig. 7 Number of goals
in MM (QSORT)

6. Simulation Results

The following programs were used as benchmarks:
(1) nreverse240 (NREV) -- naive-reverse of list with length 240.
(2) qsort256 (QSORT) -- quick-sort of list with length 256.
(3) primes700 (PRIMES) -- generation of prime numbers below 700.
(4) perm6 (PERM) -- the making of all permutations of a list with length
     6.

6. 1 Parallelism

The relationship between the number of IUs, which varied from 1 to 64,
and system performance is shown in Fig. 3.   The number of working IUs and
the number of goals in the MMs of each benchmark program are presented in
Figs.   4 to 11 in the case of 64 IUs.   The number of suspensions and
activations are given in Table 1.

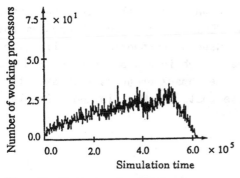

Fig. 8   Number of working
             processors (PRIMES)

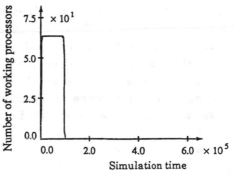

Fig. 10 Number of working
             processors (PERM)

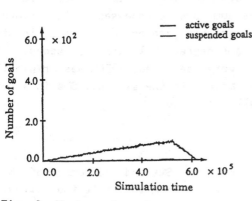

Fig. 9   Number of goals
             in MM (PRIMES)

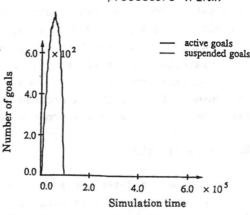

Fig. 11 Number of goals
             in MM (PERM)

No parallelism appears in the first part of NREV because the list is divided sequentially (Fig. 4). Many "append" goals are created as the result of list division, and the goals are suspended in MM (Fig. 5). When the list is completely divided, the "append" goals that are suspended in the MMs are gradually activated and executed in the stream parallel method. Thus, the system shows very high parallelism.

In QSORT (Figs. 6 and 7), many of the UPs work in parallel because stream parallel operation is performed between the "partition" goal, which divides the list, and the two "qsort" goals, which are called recursively. When the division of the list ends, concatenation of the list is performed, like in NREV, and the number of IUs that work in parallel increases. However, unlike in NREV, concatenation of the list is first because differential lists are used.

In PRIMES (Figs. 8 and 9), many of the UPs work in parallel. In addition, the number of suspensions and activations is large. This is because many prime number filters work in a stream parallel way and these filter processes are suspended and activated one after another. The average suspending time of a goal is not as large as for such programs as NREV.

PERM (Figs. 10 and 11) displays much higher parallelism than the other benchmark programs. This is because PERM is a full-search program that executes no stream operations and that causes no suspension or activation.

As mentioned above, parallelism is very high in a program like PERM that collects all answers. However, in other benchmark programs that execute in stream parallel, the number of executable goals in MMs is not so large because many goals are suspended in the MMs.

6.2 Locality of SM Access

The number of accesses to SMs is presented in Table 2. In the programs that execute stream parallel operations, i.e. NREV, PRIMES and PERM, accesses to the local SMs, except access to the variable cell in the definition clause, are 2 or 3 times as numerous as accesses to the external SMs. Although accesses to the shared variables are not considered in the goal distribution, there seems to be some degree of locality of access. In PERM, accesses to the external SMs are very few because PERM was originally an OR-parallel benchmark program and access to the external SMs is seldom performed, except when the program collects answers.

6.3 Cache Effects

The number of fetch accesses to the external SMs and the number of hits in the caches are presented in Table 3. From the table the following things can be determined:

(1) The hit ratio of the caches is at most 20 or 30 percent.
(2) The number of hits of undefined variable addresses is about half of the all cache hits, even though the addresses of the undefined variable cells are cleared from the cache at the end of the unification of a goal.
(3) Almost all the other cache hit data , except the hits of the addresses of undefined variable cells, are entered in the cache when the goal is activated.
(4) Cache data previously entered by other goals rarely hit.

The contents of most of the pointers to the SMs are read only once. This is because, when the contents of the pointers are read, they are copied in the new goal during the goal creating process. Thus, most cache hits, except the hits of data entered in activation, occur during the unification of alternatives clause for one input goal.

Accesses to the shared variables do not decrease very much when the addresses of the undefined variable cells in the caches are cleared at the end of the unification of a goal. Thus, the addresses of the undefined variables should be registered in the caches in the same manner as the addresses of constant cells, to decrease access to the SM by the caches. When some value is bound to a variable cell, the value must be written in all the caches that have this variable cell entered.

Table 2   Number of accesses to SMs

	nrev	qsort	primes	perm
total accesses to SMs	453875 (100%)	123589 (100%)	435259 (100%)	307370 (100%)
accesses to externnal SMs	129089 (28%)	22525 (18%)	110164 (25%)	4196 (1%)
accesses to local SMs	324786 (72%)	101064 (82%)	325095 (75%)	303714 (99%)
accesses to def's variables	115921 (26%)	36553 (30%)	130755 (30%)	85017 (28%)

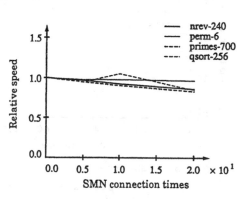

Fig. 12   Effect of SMN connection times

Table 3   Cache Effects

	nrev	qsort	primes	perm
externnal SMs read	100529	16948	82162	2109
total caches hit	15273	5807	26166	22
undef	7560	2612	8658	0
except undef	7713	3195	17508	22
┌ entered by other goals	277	34	46	22
└ entered in activation	7436	3131	17347	0

6.4 Effect of SMN Connection Times

The relationship between the SMN connection times, which vary from 0 to 20 clocks, and the relative speed of the system are shown in Fig. 12. The damage to the system performance caused by an increase in the connection time of the network is about 20 percent. If there is no heavy access traffic in the SMN, an increase to about 10 or 20 clocks in the connecting time of the network does not have an extremely bad effect on system performance.

6.5 Operation with Structure Data

The execution time of each benchmark program is presented in Table 4 for two methods. One is when the structure data in the local SMs is copied with the goal literals. The other is when the structure data is not copied (instead of copying, pointers to the structure data are written in the goals). In NREV and PRIMES, the execution times for both methods are nearly the same. However, in PERM and QSORT, the non-copying method is 25 percent quicker.

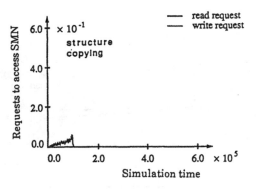

Fig. 13   Requests to
              access SMN (PERM)

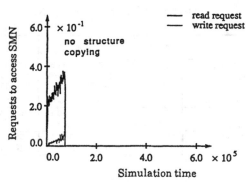

Fig. 14   Requests to
              access SMN (PERM)

Table 4   Copying of structure data and execution time

	nrev	qsort	primes	perm
structure copying	241008	249645	620840	100812
no structure copying	239069	189769	619062	75515

In programs with very large structure data such as PERM, the time for generating new goals increases when all structure data in local SMs are copied with the goals. This is because structure data that need not be copied is copied with the goals and the goals become unnecessarily large. In fact, in PERM, the average generation time of a goal increases from 88 clocks (without copying) to 140 clocks (with copying).

However, requests for access to the SMN become very large in PERM when the structure data are not copied with the goals, as shown in Figs. 13 and 14. This is because fetch access to the structure data through the SMN increases. In the other benchmark programs, requests for access to the SMN are nearly the same for both methods.

Thus, for the present, it is better not to copy structure data with goals. However, some structure data have to be copied with the goals, if there are many requests for access to the SMN and heavy network traffic has a bad effect on system performance. In such a case, however, some optimization has to be carried out, for example, by only copying structure data that is bound to some particular arguments of goals.

6.6 Frequency of Access to the SMN

The maximum and average number of accesses to an SMN with 16 processors using NREV with a length list of 60 is shown in Fig. 15. Note that, for the following simulations, the number of accesses was measured for every 1000 system clocks. Frequency of access to an SMN with 64 processors using NREV and PRIMES is shown in Figs. 16 and 17. Figures 18 to 21 show the write requests and read requests for the 64-processor SMN. The peak number of requests for access to shared variables for each benchmark program is shown in Table 5.

Table 5   Peak access frequency
                   to shared variables

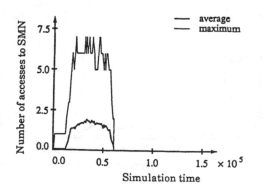

Fig. 15 Number of accesses to SMN
(NREV, 16 IUs)

		IU=16	IU=64
nreverse	read	0.13	0.57
	write	0.05	0.20
quicksort	read	0.06	0.20
	write	0.04	0.17
primes	read	0.05	0.16
	write	0.025	0.07
permutation	read	0.08	0.38
	write	0.014	0.07

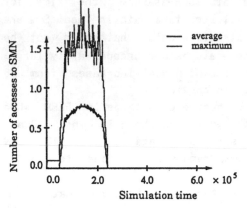

Fig. 16 Number of accesses
         to SMN (NREV)

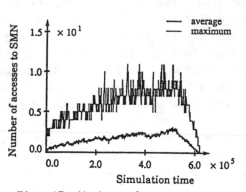

Fig. 17 Number of accesses
         to SMN (PRIMES)

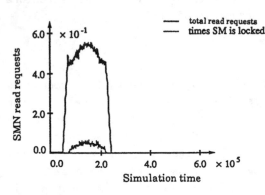

Fig. 18 SMN read requests
         (NREV)

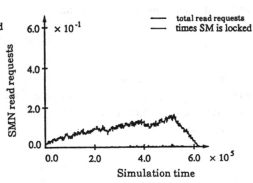

Fig. 19 SMN read requests
         (PRIMES)

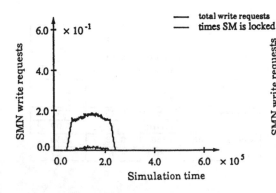

Fig. 20 SMN write requests
         (NREV)

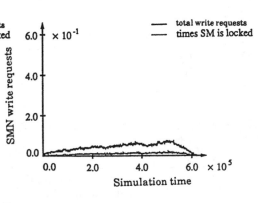

Fig. 21 SMN write requests
         (PRIMES)

Access requests are so frequent that, even with 16 processors, more than two processors are accessing the network at the same time during the access peak of the program (Fig. 15). Thus, the executing method must be improved to construct the SMN by using a bus. Table 5 shows that, at the peak, write access occurs every 20 clocks. The SMN can be made by using a bus if the SMN only has this amount of traffic.

Thus, if the SMN is made using a bus, the following method is required: Each IU must have an adequately large cache and, when read access or write access to a variable cell is performed through the network, the value of the variable must be sent to all the caches in the system.

When the system has 64 processors and when almost all the processors in the system are executing unification (for example, the last part of the NREV program), read access frequency to external SMs through the SMN is once every two clocks (Fig. 18). The write access frequency is once every six clocks (Fig. 20). At such a time, a maximum of 12 (an average of 6) processors is accessing the SMN at the same time (Fig. 16). The average accessing time to the SMN is 10 clocks when it is assumed the SMN connection time is 5 clocks. Thus, networks like an omega network are needed when 64 processors are connected to the same network.

The number of times the SMs are locked when processors access the SMs through the network is very small (Figs. 18 to 21). The main consideration is heavy network traffic when access to the SMs is discussed.

7. Discussion

With the simulations, many characteristics of the modeled machine with distributed shared memories were confirmed. With the model, a stream parallel language program can be executed in parallel for many processors, if the program has parallelism in itself. However, in stream parallel programs, there are many suspensions and activations during execution. Thus, the number of executable goals is not as large as in OR-parallel Prolog.

The load distribution method of the previous PIE described in Section 3, i.e. load minimization with the DN, is applicable to a system with a stream parallel language. However, if decreasing network traffic is desired, it is necessary to develop a load distribution method that also considers access to shared variables.

The main problem in developing the titled system is how to make the network between the shared memories (SMN). From the simulation results, the following two SMN structures are possible.

(1) a network (such as an omega network) with 64 processors.
(2) a bus with 16 processors. (In this case, broadcasting the values of the SMs is needed to decrease the access frequency through the network.)

In the case that an SMN is made using an omega network, the following problems must be investigated:
(1) Access to the SMs may even conflict with the 64 processors.
(2) It is difficult to connect many (256 or more) processors with a single omega network. Consequently, cluster architecture must be made that includes an omega network as the inside network of the cluster. Unfortunately, an omega network is too complex to be the inside network of a cluster.

In the case that an SMN is made using a bus, the following is a problem:
(1) The cluster system must be introduced because of bus throughput in the case that more than 64 processors are connected. However, the number of clusters becomes larger. This problem is not serious because the number of connections between clusters is not so large. However, a goal distribution method that enables goals to be efficiently distributed between numerous clusters must be developed.

In consideration of the complexity of system hardware, the SMN should be made by using the bus mentioned in (2) above and the system should have cluster architecture. Thus, future work must focus on an evaluation of a system with cluster architecture.

8. Conclusion

In this paper, execution of stream parallel language programs on a parallel inference machine was presented. Machine performance and operation were evaluated using software simulation. In the simulation model, units consisting of a processor and a logically shared memory were connected through a network.

The execution method and network configuration of the system were examined and discussed using the simulation results. It was confirmed that the main problem in developing the system is the existence of frequent access to the external shared memories through the network. It was also determined that it is necessary to introduce a cluster configuration if the system is to consist of more than 64 processors.

In future work, the following points will be included.
(1) the detailed architecture of a cluster system.
(2) the evaluation of a cluster system.
(3) a load distribution that considers access to shared variables.

Acknowledgements

The authors would like to thank the people in the 8th department of the Hitachi Central Research Laboratory, especially Dr. Mamoru Sugie, for their advice in writing this paper. The authors would also like to thank the individuals in the Tanaka Laboratory, especially Mr. Martin Nilsson, for their discussions and advice.

References

[1] Moto-oka, T., Tanaka, H. et al, The Architecture of a Parallel Inference Engine - PIE -, FGCS '84, ICOT, 1984.

[2] Ueda, K., Guarded Horn Clauses, PhD thesis, Information Engineering Course, The University of Tokyo, 1986.

[3] Nilsson, M. and Tanaka, H., - FLENG Prolog - the language which turns supercomputers into parallel prolog machines, Proc. of the Logic Programming Conference '86, ICOT, 1986.

[4] Hirata, K., Tanaka, H. and Moto-oka, T., A model of structure memory for PIE, Architecture Workshop In Japan '84, IPSJ, 1984 (in Japanese).

[5] Sakai, S., Interconnection Networks In A Highly Parallel MIMD Computer, PhD thesis, Information Engineering Course, The University of Tokyo, 1986.

[6] Yuhara, M., Koike, H., Tanaka, H. and Moto-oka, T., A Unify Processor Pilot Machine for PIE, Proc. of the Logic Programming Conference '84, ICOT, 1984.

[7] Tarui, T., Maruyama, T. and Tanaka, H., Execution Method of FLENG Prolog in PIE, Proc. of 32nd Annual Convention, 5B-4, IPSJ, 1986 (in Japanese).

[8] Tarui, T., Maruyama, T. and Tanaka, H., A Preliminary Evaluation of Execution Method of FLENG Prolog in PIE, Proc. of 33nd Annual Convention, 4P-11, IPSJ, 1987 (in Japanese).

Managing Search in Parallel Logic Programming

Hayato Ohwada and Fumio Mizoguchi

Dept. of Industrial Administration,
Science Univ. of Tokyo
Noda, Chiba(278), Japan

Abstract

This paper explores a new parallel logic programming technique for managing state-space search in problem solving. The technique can be characterized as a parallel search strategy to obtain reasonable solutions efficiently in contrast with any sequential search strategy. Using the strategy, it is possible to search a solution space in a parallel exhaustive manner, focus on possible alternatives simultaneously and control all search processes for efficient search. These capabilities are due to expressive power of parallel logic programming; particularly parallelism and communication via shared variables. To demonstrate its expressive power, we show several simple programs written in Flat GHC on top of DEC-10 Prolog. These programs illustrate that the parallel search strategy allows to implement search programs efficiently within Horn-clause logic differently from other programming techniques.

1. Introduction

Most problem solving systems are built by state-space search to obtain desired solutions. They are often confronted with problems to select possible alternatives in searching through a solution space. In a naive problem solver such as (sequential) Prolog [Bowen *et al.*, 1983], this task may be performed by selecting one alternative in a non-deterministic way and by resuming the previous point through backtracking after the selected one is incorrect. The search strategy could focus on only one point in a search tree at a time inherently. Therefore it will be a difficult and complex task for sequential search programs to compare several alternatives for efficient search.

One straightforward approach to the above problem is to provide a parallel search strategy based on parallel logic programming. In parallel logic programming languages such as Concurrent Prolog, Parlog, GHC etc., a goal clause can be regarded as a process and a conjunctive goal as parallel processes with communication channels [van Emden and de Lucena, 1982] [Takeuchi and Furukawa, 1986]. If the process represents a state at each stage on state-space search, the parallel search strategy lies on parallel logic programming inherently.

In this paper, we will explore a new parallel logic programming technique for managing state-space search in problem solving. The technique is motivated by a requirement to obtain reasonable solutions from possible alternatives. To satisfy the requirement, we provide a parallel search strategy underlying the computation mechanism of parallel logic programming. This strategy consists of the following properties:

(1) State-space search is achieved by parallel search which traverses all

possible alternatives in a parallel exhaustive manner.

(2) Each search process can be monitored by a control process through communication channels.

(3) To obtain reasonable solutions in the solution space, the control process focuses on all search processes simultaneously.

These properties are due to expressive power of parallel logic programming; particularly parallelism and communication via shared variables.

In addition to managing state-space search, two attractive features are provided in parallel search. One is the ability to naturally implement deterministic exhaustive search programs as a special case of the state-space search formalism. In this framework, each search process representing one of possible alternatives will independently proceed with keeping its partial solution, so that it is possible for the search program to obtain all solutions in a parallel exhaustive manner. The resulting programs are interesting because they are quite similar to those of Ueda's method presented in   [Ueda, 1986a].

The other is to improve efficiency of generate-and-test programs by pruning a search tree at intermediate search stage. The 'test process' monitors the 'generate process' state through shared variables in the same way as state-space search management. Unlike efficient implementation techniques such as meta-level programming and program transformation, this method can be achieved without much effort.

The next section describes parallel search formalism so as to implement on existing parallel logic programming languages. In Section 3, several programming techniques for managing parallel search process are presented. Section 4 presents two attractive features that   exhaustive search and efficient generate-and-test programs can be naturally implemented in parallel search.   Section 5 presents a performance result on experiments on sequential computer. Section 6 describes related works. Lastly, we describe a summary and a realistic application to state-space search management as concluding remarks. All programs shown throughout the paper are written in Flat GHC [Ueda, 1985] on top of DEC-10 Prolog.

2. Parallel Search

Deduction processes of parallel logic programming are executed in parallel. Viewing parallel logic programming as problem solving, it may be possible to directly apply parallel search to state-space search. To realize it in the existing parallel languages, we impose the following restrictions on the search program:

(1) State-space search is done by invoking all search processes that express the possible alternatives.

(2) Each search process proceeds independently by means of AND-parallelism.

(3) Each search process must keep the history of its process states leading from the initial one to previous one for checking whether the state is cyclic or not.

The first two restrictions are trivial in writing parallel search programs. (1) can be achieved by calling the predicate which represents a search process. In (2), we suppose that target languages exploit AND-parallelism at least in a computational model. Fortunately, even Flat GHC which is the simplest parallel logic programming language satisfies this restriction. To the contrary, (3) requires a data structure for keeping the history.

We consider the following simplest form for representing a search process: `search_process(State)`. The variable `State` should express both the current process state and the history at least, so that it is represented by the term `'S'(CurrentState,History)` where `History` takes the nesting form: `'S'(S1,'S'(S2,...,'ROOT'))`. The term `'S'(State,'ROOT')` indicates the initial state.

Specified a data structure representing a process state, the simplest parallel state-space search program may be as follows:

```
search_process(State,Operator,Goal) :- State=Goal | true.
search_process(State,Operator,Goal) :- otherwise |
     operate(State,Operator,NewStates),
     fork_search_process(NewStates,Operator,Goal).


fork_search_process([],_,_) :- true | true.
fork_search_process([State|Rest],Operator,Goal) :- true |
     search_process(State,Operator,Goal),
     fork_search_process(Rest,Operator,Goal).
```

The predicate `search_process(State,Operator,Goal)` expresses a search process where `State` is a data structure representing an intermediate search state, `Operator` is a generator of possible new states, and `Goal` represents a desired solution. The first clause examines the terminate condition that the process state is equal to the goal state. The second clause generates possible new states by the predicate `operate/3`, then forks search processes as possible new processes by the predicate `fork_search_process/3`. In forking the process, current process state must be saved as part of the history.

As a typical example of the state-space search, an eight-puzzle program is shown in Figure 1 (The entire program is shown in Appendix A). In the eight-puzzle program, a state of the search process is represented by the term `'S'(State,History,D)`, where `State` is a data structure representing board configuration, History is a set of states leading from the initial state to previous state, and D is the depth of node in the search tree. The predicate operate(State,N) produces new possible states from the current state and the check_cycle(N,NewStates,[],History) predicate eliminates a cycle state from them and returns remaining new states to the variable NewStates. Then the new states will be forked as the process eight_puzzle('S'(X,S,D),Depth,Goal) by the predicate fork_eight_puzzle/5. In the program, the variable Depth indicates the depth bound for making search-space finite. The search program never proceeds beyond the depth bound.

```
eight_puzzle('S'(Goal,_,_),_,Goal) :- true | true.
eight_puzzle('S'(State,History,D),Depth,Goal) :- State\=Goal |
     operate(State,N),
     check_cycle(N,N0,[],History),
     D1:=D+1,
     fork_eight_puzzle(N0,'S'(State,History,D),Depth,D1,Goal).


fork_eight_puzzle([],_,_,_,_) :- true | true.
fork_eight_puzzle(_,_,Depth,D,_) :- Depth<D | true.
fork_eight_puzzle([X|Y],S,Depth,D,Goal) :- Depth>=D |
     eight_puzzle('S'(X,S,D),Depth,Goal),
     fork_eight_puzzle(Y,S,Depth,D,Goal).
```

Figure 1: An Eight-puzzle Program

Given the following goal statement for example,
```
:- eight_puzzle('S'([2,8,3,1,6,4,7,space,5],'ROOT',0),5,
                [1,2,3,8,space,4,7,6,5]).
```

the program will search through the space of all possible solutions in a parallel exhaustive manner. The search strategy is parallel using the default control structure of parallel logic programming. There is no control information except for the depth bound.

3. Managing Parallel Search Processes

To determine which process should fork, suspend or terminate for managing parallel search processes, we will start out to distinguish two processes, *ie*. search process and control process within a program. The search process is a normal search process (or inference process) through the solution space, while the control process controls search processes by message passing through communication channels. This section describes several types of search programs managing parallel search processes effectively.

3.1 Communication between a search process and a control process

One search program is a program which controls one search process. A stream communication channel works as a medium between a search process and a control process. A general search program controlling a search process is shown in Figure 2. The goal statement `manager(Msg)` is added as a controller of the search process `search_process(State,Operator,Goal,Msg,[])` through the stream communication channel `Msg`. In this case, the search process does not proceed eagerly. Before forking, it sends the message to the control process, waits until the response from the search process is sent, and then determines whether it should fork or terminate. Thus each search process proceeds dependently to the response sent from the control process.

```
:- search_process(State,Operator,Goal,Msg,[]),manager(Msg).

search_process(State,Operator,Goal,Msg,M1) :- true |
     Msg=[(State,Control)|M0],
     search_process(Control,State,Operator,Goal,M0,M1).


search_process(terminate,_,_,_,M,M0) :- true | M=M0.
search_process(fork,State,_,Goal,M,M0) :- State=Goal | M=M0.
search_process(fork,State,Operator,Goal,M,M0) :- State\=Goal |
     operate(State,Operator,NewStates),
     fork_search_process(NewStates,Operator,Goal,M,M0).


fork_search_process([],_,_,M,M0) :- true | M=M0.
fork_search_process([State|Rest],Operator,Goal,M,M1) :- true |
     search_process(State,Operator,Goal,M,M0),
     fork_search_process(Rest,Operator,Goal,M0,M1).

manager([(State,Control)|M]) :- true |
     control_process(State,Control),manager(M).
manager([]) :- true | true.

control_process(State,Control) :- terminate_condition(State) |
     Control=terminate.
control_process(State,Control) :- otherwise | Control=fork.
```

Figure 2: A General Search Program Controlling a Search Process

Here, the message is of the form Msg=[(State,Control)|M0] where the variable State expresses the search process state, Control is an uninstantiated variable for receiving a message from the control process and MO is a new pointer of the communication channel. The variable Control will be instantiated within the control process and used for communication once. In the program, there are three types of messages: *terminate*, *suspend* and *fork*, where *suspend* is implicit for a GHC suspension rule (This rule corresponds to *read-only annotation* in Concurrent Prolog and *mode declaration* in Parlog).

```
:- eight_puzzle(State,Goal,Msg,[]),manager(Msg,Depth).

eight_puzzle(State,Goal,M,M1) :- true |
     M=[(State,Control)|M0],
     eight_puzzle(Control,State,Goal,M0,M1).

eight_puzzle(terminate,_,_,M,M0) :- true | M=M0.
eight_puzzle(fork,'S'(G,_,_),G,M,M0) :- true | M=M0.
eight_puzzle(fork,'S'(State,History,D),G,M,M0) :- State\=G |
     operate(State,N0),
     check_cycle(N0,N1,[],History),
     D1:=D+1,
     fork_eight_puzzle(N1,'S'(State,History,D),D1,G,M,M0).

fork_eight_puzzle([],_,_,Goal,M,M0) :- true | M=M0.
fork_eight_puzzle([NewState|Rest],State,D,Goal,M,M1) :- true |
     eight_puzzle('S'(NewState,State,D),Goal,M,M0),
     fork_eight_puzzle(Rest,State,D,Goal,M0,M1).

manager([],_) :- true | true.
manager([('S'(_,_,D),Control)|M],Depth) :- D>Depth |
     Control=terminate, manager(M,Depth).
manager([(_,Control)|M],Depth) :- otherwise |
     Control=fork, manager(M,Depth).
```

Figure 3: An Eight-puzzle Program Using Incomplete Messages

The program behaves as follows: The search process plays a role of sender to the control process at first. It sends the term (State, Control), then suspends until the variable Control is instantiated to either terminate or fork. The instantiation is achieved by the predicate control_process(State, Control) in the control process. In this case on the other hand, the control process sends to the search process. On instantiating the variable Control, the search process proceeds in the same way as described in Section 2.

The technique presented here is to send a message contained uninstantiated variables to the receiver. This form of the message is called incomplete messages and gives a powerful programming technique to parallel logic programming [Shapiro and Takeuchi, 1983].

An eight-puzzle program using incomplete messages is shown in Figure 3. The variable Depth expressing the depth bound as control information is transferred from the search process to the control process. When the predicate manager(Msg, D) receives a message ('S'(State, History, D), Control) sent from the search process, it could send the message terminate to the search process if the variable D is greater than the depth bound. Otherwise it sends fork.

Although the search process forks new search processes in parallel, the predicate manager(Msg, D) controls the new search processes in depth-first left-to-right precedence. This is due to the fact that the search process does not release the communication channel Msg to other forking processes until it terminates or reaches the goal. Let's consider the definition of the predicate eight_puzzle(State, Goal, M, M1). The variable M means the stream communication channel, so that it will be instantiated from the head to the tail in turn. Therefore the control process will receive messages sequentially. The variable M1 expressing a communication channel for other search processes will be never used for message passing until the new process `eight_puzzle(Control,State,Goal,M0,M1)` terminates. Indeed, the state-space search is carried out by only one search process and other forking processes suspend. This control mechanism is a kind of depth-first search in parallel logic programming.

3.2 A general method for controlling search processes

The control strategy mentioned above has a serious defect which the allocation of messages to the communication channel could be done sequentially. This defect is due to the computation mechanism in which the search process never releases the communication channel to the other forking processes until the search process terminates or reaches the goal. Hence, we will rewrite the search program as follows:

```
search_process(State,Operator,Goal,M,M0) :- true |
    M=[(State,Control)|M0],
    search_process(Control,State,Operator,Goal).
```

The variable `M0` expressing next pointer of the stream communication channel `M` is not transferred to the predicate `search_process(Control,State,Operator,Goal)`. Thus messages to the control process can be fairly allocated among the search processes. Instead, the predicate `search_process(Control,State,Operator,Goal)` must be rewritten as follows:

```
search_process(fork(M,M0),State,Operator,G) :- State\=G |
    operate(State,Operator,NewStates),
    fork_search_process(NewStates,Operator,G,M,M0).
```

As shown in the above program, two new communication channels are added in the first argument. These are used for resuming the communication with the control process and for distributing the communication channel to forking search processes.

On the other hand, the control process must send `fork(M,M0)` with new communication channel if the search process forks. In the previous method mentioned in Section 2.2 the search process takes the initiative in comminicating with the control process, while in this method the control process itself can communicate with all search processes in an active way. A general program controlling the search processes is shown in Figure 4.

```
manager(M) :- true | terminate_process(M,PS),fork_process(PS).

terminate_process([],PS) :- true | PS=[].
terminate_process([(State,C)|M],PS) :- terminate_cond(State) |
      C=terminate, terminate_process(M,PS).
terminate_process([(State,C)|M],PS) :- otherwise |
      PS=[(State,C)|PS0], terminate_process(M,PS0).

fork_process([]) :- true | true.
fork_process(PS) :- otherwise |
      choose_process(PS,P,Others), send_msg(P,Others).

send_msg((State,Control),Others) :- true |
      Control=fork(M,Others), manager(M).
```

Figure 4: A General Program for Controlling All Search Processes

The control process is divided into two processes, *ie.* 'terminate process' and 'fork process'. The predicate `terminate_process(M,PS)` accepts all messages sent from search processes, sends the message `terminate` if the process should terminate, and then returns the other processes to the variable `PS`. The predicate `fork_process(PS)` chooses one process among `PS` and forks the predicate `send_msg(P,Others)` where the variables `P` and

`Others` indicate the message sent from the chosen process and the messages from the other processes respectively.

The predicate `send_msg((State,Control),Others)` plays a role of the sender to the chosen search process. It sends the message `fork(M,Others)` where the variable `M` expresses a new communication channel for receiving messages from the search processes and the variable `Others` indicates the tail part of `M`. Since `Others` contains a set of communication channels to the suspended processes, `M` becomes to express a set of messages sent from all search processes. Thus it is possible for the predicate `manager(M)` to control all of the search processes simultaneously.

Specified control information for the control process, the following types of search strategies are useful.

Depth-first search:

The depth-first search can be done by responding to a message the control process accepts firstly. The process `manager/1` defined by the below schedules search processes in a depth-first left-to-right manner.

```
manager([(State,Control)|Rest]) :- otherwise |
      Control=fork(New,Rest), manager(New,Rest).
```

Distributed search:

The distribued search allows the control process to distribute `manager/1` for efficient search. When the process `manager/1` accepts a message sent from a search process, it distributes and governs the search process only by sending a new channel expressed as `fork(New,[])`.

```
manager([(State,Control)|Rest]) :- otherwise |
      Control=fork(New,[]), manager(New), manager(Rest).
```

Best-first search:

Since `manager/1` controls all of the search processes simultaneously, the best-first search can be naturally implemented within the framework. The programs are as follows:

```
manager(M) :- true |
        choose_best_process(M,Best,Others),
        send_mesg(Best,Others).

send_msg((State,Control),Others) :- true |
        Control=fork(New,Others), manager(New).
```

It is a difficult and complex task for sequential search programs to collect all possible solutions, compare them and select the best one among them, because their search strategy could focus on only one point at a time inherently. If you enforce this task, you should represent a set of search process to be considered as all possible alternatives by a queue and prepare a specific interpreter for the program. In parallel search, each search process is expressed by a first-order predicate and is connected to a control process through communication channels. Thus, there is no interpreter for the program. It allows a programmer to specify a control process for obtaining desired solutions.

An eight-puzzle program based on best-first search is shown in Appendix B. In this case, the sum of the depth of node in the search tree and the number of misplaced tiles is used as a heuristic function.

4. Two Advantages of Parallel Search

4.1 Exhaustive Search

Exhaustive search is equivalent to obtain all answer substitutions for the variables in logic programming. To collect the process obtaining solutions, the extralogical predicates beyond Horn-clause logic are provided in the languages; for example 'setof' and 'bagof' in DEC-10 Prolog. However, it is also important to implement exhaustive search programs within Horn-clause logic. Recent work achieved in [Ueda, 1986a] is intended to generate deterministic exhaustive search programs by transforming a program finding only one solution into one finding all solutions.

It is possible for our parallel search technique to implement exhaustive search programs naturally. This task can be formulated as a special case of state-space search. Let's consider the following list decomposition program for explanatory purpose:

```
decompose(List,Result) :- true |
        decompose('S'(List,'ROOT'),Result,[]).

decompose('S'([],S),R,R0) :- true |
        get_stack(S,L,[]),R=[p(L,[])|R0].
decompose('S'([X|Y],S),R,R1) :- true |
        get_stack(S,L,[]),
        R=[p(L,[X|Y])|R0],
        decompose('S'(Y,'S'(X,S)),R0,R1).

get_stack('ROOT',L,L0) :- true | L=L0.
get_stack('S'(X,S),L,L0) :- true |
        L1=[X|L0],get_stack(S,L,L1).
```

The predicate decompose(List,Result) means the relation that Result is a list whose element is a decomposed pair of List. It invokes the search process decompose('S'(List,'ROOT'),Result,[]) involving a special form of state-space search. The search process state is represented by the term 'S'(List,Stack) where the variable List is a list to be decomposed and the variable Stack is a stack stocking the search process states from initial one to previous one. Unlike the state-space search, each search process state does not require the whole state history but only its head part of the list representing the state.

The first clause of decompose('S'(List,Stack),R,R0) indicates a terminate condition that List is equal to the goal, *ie*. empty list. If the condition is satisfied, all elements pushed into the stack are retrieved as a list L in a reversal form by the predicate get_stack(S,L,[]), and then the term p(L,[]) is recorded as a solution. The second clause decomposes the list into [X|Y], records as a solution p(L,[X|Y]) where L is obtained by the get_stack(S,L,[]) predicate, and then forks a new search process which is of the form decompose('S'(Y,'S'(X,S)),R0,R1).

Here, the predicate get_stack(State,L,L0) plays an important role in obtaining all answer substitutions. It returns the list L whose element is stocked in the variable Stack during search process. Since each search process keeps a part of solution on the stack, the solution can be found in a bottom-up manner. That is all answer substitutions of the variable Result can be obtained by collecting a solution of each search process. This computation process is quite different from the append(X,Y,Z) predicate solving the goal in a top-down manner. In this case, a part of solution is shared among search processes and therefore we must make variants of the partial solution beyond Horn-clause logic.

This framework is quite similar to the Ueda's method. His method pushes a partial solution into stack and gets its solution through continuation processing in sum. To obtain the answers in a bottom-up manner, he introduces the continuation processing, while we implement it by the predicate get_stack(Stack,L,L0).

As an example of a more complex exhaustive search program, permutation program is shown in Figure 5.

```
perm(List,Result) :- true | perm('S'(List,'ROOT'),Result,[]).

perm('S'([],S),R,R0) :- true | get_stack(S,L,[]),R=[L|R0].
perm('S'([X|Y],S),R,R0) :- true |
     del('S'([X|Y],'ROOT'),S,R,R0).

del('S'([],_),_,R,R0) :- true | R=R0.
del('S'([X|Y],S),SS,R,R1) :- true |
     get_stack(S,L,Y),
     perm('S'(L,'S'(X,SS)),R,R0),
     del('S'(Y,'S'(X,S)),SS,R0,R1).
```

Figure 5: An Exhaustive Search Program of Permutation

There exist two processes of perm(State,R,R0) and their subprocess del(State1,State2,R,R1), in the program. The first definition of the predicate perm(State,R,R0) checks whether State is equal to an empty list. If it is satisfied, the list obtained by get_stack(S,L,[]) is recorded as a solution. The second definition invokes its subprocess only. On the other hand, the predicate del(State1,State2,R,R1) distributes the perm(State,R,R0) processes to the number equal to the length of the list L in the term 'S'(L,S) representing the process state. The get_stack(S,L,Y) predicate is used for constructing the list deleted one element from the original list passed by the perm(S,R,R0) predicate.

Viewing the program as the state-space search, the process perm(State,R,R0) can be seen as a 'search_process', while the process del(State1,State2,R,R1) corresponds to 'fork_search_process'. In fact, perm(State,R,R0) specifies its terminate condition only and del(State1,State2,R,R1) distributes the process perm(State,R,R0) keeping the history.

```
n_queens(X,L) :- true |
     perm('S'(X,'ROOT'),L,[],M,[]),manager(M).


perm(S,R,R0,M,M1) :- true |
     S='S'(_,S0),M=[(S0,C)|M0],
     perm(C,S,R,R0,M0,M1).


perm(terminate,_,R,R0,M,M0) :- true | R=R0,M=M0.
perm(fork,'S'([],S),R,R0,M,M0) :- true |
     get_stack(S,L,[]),R=[L|R0],M=M0.
perm(fork,'S'([X|Y],S),R,R0,M,M0) :- true |
     del('S'([X|Y],'ROOT'),S,R,R0,M,M0).


del('S'([],_),_,R,R0,M,M0) :- true | R=R0,M=M0.
del('S'([X|Y],S),SS,R,R1,M,M1) :- true |
     get_stack(S,L,Y),
     perm('S'(L,'S'(X,SS)),R,R0,M,M0),
     del('S'(Y,'S'(X,S)),SS,R0,R1,M0,M1).


manager([('ROOT',C)|M]) :- true | C=fork,manager(M).
manager([('S'(X,S),C)|M]) :- true | qsafe(X,S,1,C),manager(M).
manager([]) :- true | true.


qsafe(_,'ROOT',_,C) :- true | C=fork.
qsafe(X,'S'(Y,S),N,C) :- Y+N=\=X,Y-N=\=X |
     M:=N+1,qsafe(X,S,M,C).
qsafe(_,_,_,C) :- otherwise | C=terminate.
```

Figure 6: An N-queens Program in Parallel Search

4.2 Efficient Improvement of Generate-and-test Programs

The parallel search strategy of state-space search allows the control process to determine which process should fork, suspend or terminate at the intermediate search stage. The technique gives us an improvement of generate-and-test programs. There are a number of techniques for improving search programs efficiently. Metalevel control and program transformation are such techniques, but our method is simpler than these.

We will present an N-queens program in parallel search in Figure 6. The process `n_queens(X,L)` is divided into two processes, `perm('S'(X,'ROOT'),L,[],M,[])` and `manager(M)`. The `perm(S,R,R0,M,M1)` process is the same as that shown in Figure 4 except for adding two variables `M` and `M1` in order to communicate the control process `manager(M)`. Similarly, two variables `M` and `M0` are added to the `del(S1,S1,R,R0,M,M0)` process. The `manager(M)` does not only control the search process `perm(S,R,R0,M,M1)` to prevent the extra processes from forking but also obtain desired solutions for the `n_queens(X,L)` process.

As the same case of state-space search using incomplete messages, the process `perm(S,R,R0,M,M1)` sends the message `(S0,C)` to the `manager(M)` through the stream communication channel `M` before forking. Here, the variables `S0` and `C` indicate the stack of the process and 'uninstantiated variable' respectively. Then the `perm(S,R,R0,M,M1)` process invokes the subprocess `perm(C,S,R,R0,M0,M1)` which will suspend until `C` is instantiated to either `terminate` or `fork`. The `qsafe(State,Stack,N,C)` predicate is a part of the control process to determine whether the process `perm(S,R,R0,M,M1)` should fork or terminate. It can check eagerly whether two queens lie on the same diagonal or not, because `S0` expresses a partial solution represented by stack in `perm(S,R,R0,M,M1)`.

The generate-and-test program in parallel search has an attractive feature for program development. The feature is to separate the control process from the search process clearly without the loss of efficiency. The program shown in Figure 6 illustrates that the process `perm(S,R,R0,M,M1)` is a subprocess of the `n_queens(X,L)` process because of the separation of the process `manager(M)`. Only two variables `M` and `M1` are added as a stream communication channel to the `perm(S,R,R0,M,M1)` process. In naive generate-and-test programs, the 'test routine' is invoked after all solutions are generated by the 'generate routine'. Although these programs are readable for programmers, they are inefficient. In our case, the 'generate process' is monitored by the 'test process' at any time a new process forks. The parallel search contributes to develop generate-and-test programs in a readable and efficient manner.

5. Performance

Table 1 shows the performance result of 8-puzzle programs on the experiment on a sequential machine. All programs are measured using Flat GHC on top of DEC-10 Prolog on DEC2040. The 8-puzzle program interleaved with control information was shown in Figure 1. The method for constructing the programs scheduled in a depth-first, distributed and best-first manner were shown in Section 3.2. Here, we measured two types of best-first search programs: all solutions program and one solution program.

As shown in Table 1, the program interleaved with control information is slightly faster than programs in a depth-first and a distributed manner. This is due to the fact that process switching takes place very often in communicating between a search process and a control process. It is similar to the result of the bounded-buffer communication program in Concurrent Prolog Compiler [Ueda and Chikayama, 1985]. However, this shortcoming seems to be solved on a highly parallel machine if communication overhead is relatively small.

Table 1: Performance of 8-puzzle Programs (Depth bound is 5)

Program	CPU time (in sec)
8-puzzle interleaved with control information	18.4
8-puzzle in a depth-first manner	19.3
8-puzzle in a distributed manner	19.3
8-puzzle in a best-first manner (all solutions)	83.4
8-puzzle in a best-first manner (one solution)	4.1

Compared between programs in a depth-first and a distributed manner, the two programs have the same execution speed. In 8-puzzle programs shown throughout the paper, there is no control information except for depth bound preventing search processes from oversearching. Checking depth for each search process requires computation cost little. Therefore the search program in this case does not improve the efficiency even if control processes are distributed.

The best-first search programs require an additional computation cost in order to compare all search processes and choose the best one among them. In 8-puzzle programs, such computation cost is indicated as the difference of speeds between the best-first search program obtaining all solutions and other exhaustive search programs. As table 1 shows, the best-first search programs executed 4 times as slow as the other programs. On the contrary, the best-first search program obtaining only one solution improved efficiency for the sake of heuristic function if we want to get one solution.

Another performance result is shown in Table 2. The permutation and

N-queens programs shown in Section 4 are included. Also Ueda's permutation and N-queens programs are presented for comparison. His permutation program is in [Ueda, 1986a], and N-queens program in [Ueda, 1986b].

Table 2: Performance of Exhaustive Search and Generate-test Programs

Program	CPU time (in sec)		
	5	6	7 (elements)
Permutation	1.9	15.8	-
Ueda's permutation	2.0	16.5	-
N-queens in a depth-first manner	1.9	7.6	38.0
N-queens in a distributed manner	1.7	6.3	34.1
Ueda's N-queens	1.4	5.8	30.6

For permutation programs, our program is slightly faster than Ueda's. This difference may not be considerable on a sequential machine, but on a parallel machince. In his exhaustive search programs, searching and collecting all solutions are sequentially done through continuation processing because AND goals of source programs are solved being poped from the continuation stack. In our programs, this defect are avoided.

The N-queens program in a distributed manner improves efficiency in comparison with the program in a depth-first manner. For 8-puzzle programs, the distributed search strategy does not contribute to efficient search because there are few control information. On the other hand, the

N-queens program exploites AND-parallelism for the sake of distributing control processes that check whether two queens lie on the same diagonal. This property becomes more useful on a parallel machice.

However, our programs based on parallel search strategy cannot make the original program so speed up as the program transformation technique. Recently Ueda proposes an effective transformation technique which makes exhaustive generate-and-test programs deterministic [Ueda, 1986b]. Using his method, the transformed programs are ten times faster than the orginal programs and are about equal to the optimized programs by hand. Our eight-queens program is slower down than his program as shown in Table 2. Nevertheless, it is evident that parallel search programs can be implemented efficiently without changing the original source programs in a highly parallel machine. This feature allows a programmer to debug his program in source level.

6. Related Work

The technique for managing state-space search in a logic programming framework is concerned with how to control logic programs. Several approaches to the control problem are summarized as follows:

(1) Non-sequential coroutine computation
(2) Metalevel control of deductions
(3) Unfold/fold based program transformation

The first approach is found in the computation mechanism of IC-PROLOG

[Clark *et al.*, 1982]. In IC-PROLOG, there are several non-sequential evaluation mechanisms for implementing coroutine programs. Annotations which specify control allow a programmer to initiate the pseudo parallel computation mechanism. It can specify whether data is transferred from a producer process into a consumer process eagerly or lazily. The two processes can be communicated through annotated logical variables on the sequential execution. In our case, the coroutine computation is supported in the parallel language.

The (2) approach views control information as meta-level knowledge expressing how to use object-level knowledge. In this framework, a number of metalevel expressions are provided in the language. These expressions specify an interpreter demonstrating object-level clauses and hence they allow a programmer to define his own interpreter. This approach is found in [Gallaire and Lasserre, 1982] [Dincbas and Pape, 1984] for example. Our approach is quite different because a control process is solved as a object-level clause in the same way as a search process is done.

The (3) approach takes an advantage of making a naive program efficient in mathematically founded program transformation techniques. In the technique, inefficient search programs can be transformed into efficient ones by using transformation rule [Burstall and Darlington, 1977] [Tamaki and Sato, 1984]. It is interesting that a given program is automatically transformed into equivalent one, but its applicable range is not so wide. Further study with respect to the technique is required for solving practical problems.

Concerned with the third approach, Ueda presents an effective transformation technique for making exhaustive generate-and-test programs deterministic [Ueda, 1986b]. His technique transforms a given program by the three steps, *ie*. mode analysis, precompile and main compile to obtain efficient one. It compiles one solution generate-and-test programs into exhaustive one directly. However, a class of transformable programs is so restricted. The restriction that 'test process' checks data in a top-down manner gives a difficulty in implementing efficient state-space search programs. Indeed, it is impossible for the method to obtain the best solution among possible alternatives.

These approaches mentioned above share a common purpose for controlling logic programs. The purpose is to separate control information from search processs as possible. Although the transformation approach does not require control information in a given program, it requires some conditions with respect to the computation process of the program.

Another approach is found in [Dincbas, 1986]. Its feature is to incorporate the existing logic programming languages into the declarative expression, namely constraints. In the approach, generate-and-test paradigm can be seen as an analogy of constraint satisfaction problem. He proposes a data-driven computation and domain concept for overcoming the problem in an efficient way. His eight-queens program based on constraint programming illustrates the expressive power of the technique. It is quite different from the above approaches in the point that it never introduces control information.

7. Concluding Remarks

We have described the parallel search strategy as a parallel logic programming technique for managing state-space search. The eight-puzzle programs have shown its expressive power to obtain reasonable solutions. Moreover, this technique provides two attractive features for implementing general search programs, namely exhaustive search program and generate-and-test program. The simplest decomposition program illustrates the method of writing an exhaustive search program. The n-queens program is executed efficiently for the sake of 'test process' which monitors 'generate process'. These programs can be implemented without much effort unlike other programming techniques. To illustrate these techniques, we have chosen the simplest parallel logic programming language, Flat GHC as a target language. Therefore, all programs shown throughout the paper seem to be applicable to other languages.

For sequential search, efficient implementation of search programs is laborious work. This is due to poor control facility in sequential logic programming languages. An example is a depth-first strategy in Prolog. Metalevel control and program transformation have been applied in order to provide some rich control facilities. However, these approaches seem to require complex mechanisms since they are concerned with metalevel strategy dealing with logic programs. In parallel logic programming incorporating communication via shared variables and data flow synchronization, efficient implementation can be achieved within the first-order logic.

Acknowledgements

The authors would like to thank Kazuhiro Fuchi, Director of ICOT Research Center for giving us the opportunity to use Flat GHC. We also thank Koich Furukawa and members of ICOT working group for valuable discussions.

References

Bowen, D. L. (ed.), Byrd, L., Pereira, L. M. and Warren, D. H. D. [1983] *DECsystem-10 Prolog User's Manual*, Dept. of Artificial Intelligence, Univ. of Edinburgh.

Burstall, R. M. and Darlington, J. [1977] A Transformation System for Developing Recursive Programs, *J. ACM*, Vol. 24, No. 1, (1977),pp. 44-67.

Clark, K. L., McCabe, F., Gregory, S. [1982] IC-Prolog Language features, In *Logic Programming*, Clark, K. L. and Tarnlund, S. A. (ed.), Academic Press, pp. 253-266.

Dincbas, M. [1986] Constraints, Logic Programming and Deductive Databases, In *Proc. Frans-Japan Arti. Intell. and Computer Science Symp. 86*, pp. 1-27.

Dincbas, M. and Pape, J. L. [1984] Metacontrol of Logic Programs in Metalog, In *Proc. Int. Conf. of Fifth Generation Computer Systems 1984*, ICOT, pp. 361-370.

Gallaire, H. and Lasserre, C. [1982] Metalevel control for logic programs, In *Logic Programming*, Clark, K. L. and Tarnlund, S. A. (ed.), Academic Press, pp. 173-185.

Shapiro, E. Y. and Takeuchi, A. [1983] Object Oriented Programming in Concurrent Prolog, *New Generation Computing*, Vol. 1, No. 1 (1983), pp. 25-48.

Tamaki, H. and Sato, T. [1984] Unfold/Fold Transformation of Logic Programs, In *Proc. Second Int. Logic Programming Conf.*, Uppsala Univ., Sweden, pp. 127-138.

Takeuchi, A. and Furukawa, K. [1986] Parallel Logic Programming Languages, In *Proc. Third Int. Logic Programming Conf*, Imperial College of Science and Technology, London, pp. 242-254.

Ueda, K. [1985] *Guarded Horn Clauses*, ICOT Tech. Report TR-103, Institute for New Generation Computer Technology. Also in *Lecture Notes in Computer Science*, Springer-Verlag, Berlin Heidelberg (1986).

Ueda, K. [1986a] Making Exhaustive Search Programs Deterministic, In *Proc. Third Int. Logic Programming Conf.*, Imperial College of Science and Technology, London, pp. 270-282.

Ueda, K. [1986b] Making Exhaustive Search Programs Deterministic (II), In *Proc. Third National Conf. of Japan Society of Software Science and Technology* (in Japanese), Tokyo, pp (1)-(8).

Ueda, K. and Chikayama, T. [1985] Concurrent Prolog Compiler on Top of Prolog, In *Proc. 1985 Symp. on Logic Programming*, IEEE Computer Society, pp. 119-126.

van Emden, M. H. and de Lucena Filho, G. J. [1982] Predicate logic as a programming language for parallel programming, In *Logic Programming*, Clark, K. L. and Tarnlund, S. A. (ed.), Academic Press, pp. 189-198.

Appendix A: A Parallel Eight-Puzzle Program

```
:- eight_puzzle('S'([2,8,3,1,6,4,7,space,5],'ROOT',0),5,
                [1,2,3,8,space,4,7,6,5],Result,[]).

eight_puzzle(S,_,G,R,R0) :- S='S'(G,_,_) | R=[S|R0].
eight_puzzle('S'(State,H,D),Depth,G,R,R0) :- true |
        operate(State,N),
        check_cycle(N,New,[],H),
        D1:=D+1,
        fork_eight_puzzle(New,'S'(State,H,D),Depth,D1,G,R,R0).

fork_eight_puzzle([],_,_,_,_,R,R0) :- true | R=R0.
fork_eight_puzzle(_,_,_,Depth,D,_,R,R0) :- Depth<D | R=R0.
fork_eight_puzzle([X|Y],S,Depth,D,G,R,R1) :- Depth>=D |
        eight_puzzle('S'(X,S,D),Depth,G,R,R0),
        fork_eight_puzzle(Y,S,Depth,D,G,R0,R1).

operate(S,S1) :- true |
        current_pos(X,S),
        next_state([left,right,up,down],X,S,S1,[]).

current_pos(X,[space|_]) :- true | X=1.
current_pos(X,[H|T]) :- H\=space | current_pos(X1,T),X:=X1+1.

next_state([],_,_,_,R,R0) :- true | R=R0.
next_state([Op|Rest],X,S,R,R1) :- true |
        move(Op,X,S,R,R0),next_state(Rest,X,S,R0,R1).

move(left,X,S,R,R0)  :- X=\=1,X=\=4,X=\=7 |
        X1:=X+1,find(X1,S,Tile),swap(space,Tile,S,S1),R=[S1|R0].
move(right,X,S,R,R0)  :- X=\=3,X=\=6,X=\=9 |
        X1:=X+1,find(X1,S,Tile),swap(space,Tile,S,S1),R=[S1|R0].
move(up,X,S,R,R0)  :- X=\=1,X=\=2,X=\=3 |
        X1:=X+1,find(X1,S,Tile),swap(space,Tile,S,S1),R=[S1|R0].
move(down,X,S,R,R0)  :- X=\=7,X=\=8,X=\=9 |
        X1:=X+1,find(X1,S,Tile),swap(space,Tile,S,S1),R=[S1|R0].
move(_,_,_,R,R0) :- otherwise | R=R0.

find(1,[X|_],Y) :- true | X=Y.
find(X,[_|L],Y) :- X=\=1 | X1:=X+1,find(X1,L,Y).
```

```
swap(_,_,[],L) :- true | L=[].
swap(X,Y,[X|Z],L) :- true | L=[Y|W],swap(X,Y,Z,W).
swap(X,Y,[Y|Z],L) :- true | L=[X|W],swap(X,Y,Z,W).
swap(X,Y,[A|Z],L) :- X\=A,Y\=A | L=[A|W],swap(X,Y,Z,W).

check_cycle([],S,S0,_) :- true | S=S0.
check_cycle([X|Y],S,S1,H) :- true |
        check_cycle0(X,H,S,S0),check_cycle(Y,S0,S1,H).

check_cycle0(X,'ROOT',S,S0) :- true | S=[X|S0].
check_cycle0(X,'S'(X,_,_),S,S0) :- true | S=S0.
check_cycle0(X,'S'(Y,H,_),S,S0) :- X\=Y |
        check_cycle0(X,H,S,S0).
```

Appendix B: An Eight-Puzzle Program Using Heuristic Search

```
:- eight_puzzle('S'([2,8,3,1,6,4,7,space,5],'ROOT',0),
                G,Msg,[],Result,[]),
   manager(Msg,5,G),G=[1,2,3,8,space,4,7,6,5].

eight_puzzle(S,G,M,M0,R,R0) :- true |
     M=[(S,C)|M0],eight_puzzle(C,S,G,R,R0).

eight_puzzle(terminate,_,_,R,R0) :- true | R=R0.
eight_puzzle(fork(M,M0),S,G,R,R0) :- S='S'(G,_,_) | R=[S|R0].
eight_puzzle(fork(M,M0),S,G,R,R0) :- otherwise |
     S='S'(State,History,D),
     operate(State,N),
     check_cycle(N,NewStates,[],History),
     D1:=D+1,
     fork_eight_puzzle(NewStates,S,D1,G,M,M0,R,R0).

fork_eight_puzzle([],_,_,_,_,M,M0,R,R0) :- true | M=M0,R=R0.
fork_eight_puzzle([X|Y],S,D,G,M,M1,R,R1) :- true |
        eight_puzzle('S'(X,S,D),G,M,M0,R,R0),
        fork_eight_puzzle(Y,S,D,G,M0,M1,R0,R1).

manager(M,D,G) :- true |
        terminate_process(M,PS,D,G),
        fork_process(PS,D,G).

terminate_process([],PS,_,_) :- true | PS=[].
terminate_process([(S,C)|M],PS,Depth,G) :-
        S='S'(_,_,D),D>Depth |
        C=terminate,
        terminate_process(M,PS,Depth,G).
terminate_process([(S,C)|M],PS,Depth,G) :- otherwise |
        PS=[(S,C)|PS0],
        terminate_process(M,PS0,Depth,G).

fork_process([],_,_) :- true | true.
fork_process([P|Ps],D,G) :- true |
        choose_process(Ps,P,Best,Others,G),
        seng_msg(Best,Others,D,G).
```

```
choose_process([],P,B,O,_) :- true | P=B,O=[].
choose_process([(S1,C1)|Rest],(S2,C2),B,O,G) :- true |
        cost(S1,X1,G),cost(S2,X2,G),
        choose_process0((S1,C1,X1),(S2,C2,X2),B1,O1),
        O=[O1|O2],
        choose_process(Rest,B1,B,O2,G).

choose_process0((S1,C1,X1),(S2,C2,X2),B,O) :- X1=<X2 |
        B=(S1,C1),O=(S2,C2).
choose_process0((S1,C1,X1),(S2,C2,X2),B,O) :- X1>X2 |
        B=(S2,C2),O=(S1,C1).

send_msg((S,C),O,D,G) :- true |
        C=fork(M,O),manager(M,D,G).

cost('S'(S,_,D),C,G) :- true | wrong(S,G,X),C:=X+D.

wrong([],[],C) :- true | C=0.
wrong([X|Y],[X|Z],C) :- true | wrong(Y,Z,C).
wrong([X|Y],[X1|Z],C) :- X\=X1 | wrong(Y,Z,C1),C:=C1+1.
```

Inductive Inference of Regular Languages based on Model Inference

Hiroki ISHIZAKA

IIAS-SIS, FUJITSU LIMITED

140, Miyamoto, Numazu,

Shizuoka 410-03, Japan

ABSTRACT

This paper is concerned with an algorithm for identifying an unknown regular language from examples of its members and non-members. The algorithm is based on the model inference algorithm given by Shapiro. In our setting, however, a given first order language for describing a target logic program has countably many unary predicate symbols: $q_0, q_1, q_2, \cdots$. On the other hand, the oracle which gives information about the unknown regular language to the inference algorithm has no interpretation for predicates other than the predicate q_0. In such a setting, we cannot directly take advantage of the contradiction backtracing algorithm which is one of the most important part for the efficiency of the model inference algorithm. In order to overcome this disadvantage, we develop a method for giving an interpretation for predicates other than the predicate q_0 indirectly, which is based on the idea of using the oracle and a one to one mapping from a set of predicates to a set of strings. Furthermore, we propose a model inference algorithm for regular languages using the method, then argue the correctness and the time complexity of the algorithm.

1. Introduction

The theory of model inference given by shapiro [5] is in principle applicable to automated program synthesis for logic programs [6]. However, there is a serious problem as follows. In the framework of the theory, a first order language L with finitely many predicate symbols is previously given over which a target theory is described. Furthermore, the oracle which gives information about a target model to an inference machine is assumed to be able to answer the truth of all predicates in L. In automated program synthesis, it seems difficult to assume such a power on the oracle. Because, the assumptions require that a user of a synthesis system should have too much knowledge about the target program.

Now, we shall consider, via a simple example, what will happen when the assumptions are removed.

Suppose that an inexperienced programmer is going to make a program for the predicate *sort(Input_List, Output_List)*, where *Output_List* is a sorted version of *Input_List*, using a system which is an implementation of the model inference algorithm, e.g. Model Inference System. Since he is inexperienced, he has not enough understanding of an algorithm for sorting or he understands an algorithm but he doesn't see what kind of auxiliary predicates (e.g. *insert*(_, _, _) or *partition*(_, _, _, _) etc.) are necessary for the algorithm. So, he gives the first order language with only one predicate symbol *sort*(_, _) to the system, then he starts the task. He patiently continues to input facts about *sort*(_, _). However, if there is no program for sorting which consists of only the predicate symbol, then his efforts will result in failure. On the other hand, suppose that the system discovers the difficulty of the programming with only one predicate *sort*(_, _) then it introduces a new predicate as an auxiliary one. Since the programmer has no interpretation for such a new predicate, he cannot answer the questions from the contradiction backtracing algorithm which plays a central role in the model inference algorithm. Hence he cannot continue the inference process.

Eventually, it seems that the purpose of the inexperienced programmer is not accomplished. However, from the above example, the following two questions arise.

1) Is there no sorting program with only one predicate *sort*(_, _).
2) Is there no method for giving an interpretation, which depends on the user's intended model, to the new predicates introduced by the system.

For applying the theory of model inference to automated program synthesis, it seems very important to answer the above two questions.

In this paper, from the point of view of the second questions, we consider a problem of inferring a class of restricted logic programs that are acceptors of regular languages. In our setting, a target logic program is over a first order language L with countably many predicate symbols: $q_0, q_1, q_2, \cdots$. A given oracle is that for a model M_0 over L_0, the restricted language of L in which only one predicate symbol q_0 is allowed. As mentioned in the above example, in such a setting, the oracle has no interpretation for predicates other than the predicate q_0. This implies that we cannot take advantage of the contradiction backtracing algorithm which is one of the most important part for the efficiency of the model inference algorithm.

In order to overcome this disadvantage, we develop a method for giving an interpretation for predicates other than the predicate q_0, which is based on the idea of using the oracle for M_0 and a one to one mapping from a set of predicates to a set of strings. Furthermore, we propose a model inference algorithm for regular languages using the method, then argue the correctness and the time complexity of the algorithm. We shall also discuss an approach based on the first question in the last section.

2. Regular Model Inference Problem

We introduce a class of Herbrand models called *regular models* and show that the class is equivalent to that of regular languages. Then a model inference problem for regular languages is defined. In what follows, the reader is assumed to be familiar with rudiments of the theory of logic programs [4] and regular languages [3].

Let L be a first order language with countably many unary predicate symbols q_0, q_1, $q_2, \ldots$, a binary function symbol $.$ and finitely many constant symbols $[]$, a_1, $a_2, \ldots, a_m$. L_0 denotes the restricted language of L in which only one predicate symbol q_0 is allowed. Let P be a logic program over L. L_P denotes the language with only predicate, function and constant symbols occurring in P. For simplicity, we shall use the following notations.

$$\Sigma = \{a_1, a_2, \ldots, a_m\}.$$
$$[X \mid Y] = .(X, Y).$$
$$[a_{i_1} a_{i_2} \cdots a_{i_n}] = [a_{i_1} \mid [a_{i_2} \mid [\ldots [a_{i_n} \mid []] \ldots]]].$$
$$\text{Pred}(P) = \text{A set of all predicate symbols occurring in a program } P.$$
$$B_L = \text{The Herbrand base for } L.$$
$$M(P) = \text{The least Herbrand model for } P.$$
$$M(P)_{q_0} = \{q_0([x]) \in M(P) \mid x \in \Sigma^*\}.$$

Definition 1: A *deterministic regular logic program* (DRLP) P is the logic program over L which satisfies the following two conditions.

1) Each clause in P is of one of the following two types:

$$q_i([a_k \mid X]) \leftarrow q_j(X),$$
$$q_i([]).$$

2) For any $q_i \in \text{Pred}(P)$ and $a_k \in \Sigma$, there exists at most one clause in P whose head is $q_i([a_k \mid X])$.

Definition 2: Let $M_0 \subseteq B_{L_0}$. We say M_0 is a *(deterministic) regular model* iff there exists a DRLP P such that $M_0 = M(P)_{q_0}$.

Now, let $L(M_0) = \{x \in \Sigma^* \mid q_0([x]) \in M_0\}$. Then, we have the following theorem. The theorem shows that the class of regular models is equivalent to that of regular languages.

Theorem 1: *For any $M_0 \subseteq B_{L_0}$, M_0 is a regular model iff $L(M_0)$ is a regular language.*

Proof: Let P be a DRLP such that $M(P)_{q_0} = M_0$. Then, construct a (nondeterministic) finite-state automaton $A = (Q, \Sigma, \delta, q_0, F)$, where

$$Q = \text{Pred}(P),$$
$$\delta(q_i, a_k) = q_j \text{ iff } q_i([a_k \mid X]) \leftarrow q_j(X) \in P,$$
$$q_i \in F \text{ iff } q_i([]) \in P.$$

Clearly, for any $q_i \in \text{Pred}(P)$ and $x \in \Sigma^*$, it follows that

$$\delta(q_i, x) \in F \text{ iff } q_i([x]) \in M(P).$$

Hence we have that

$$\delta(q_0, x) \in F \text{ iff } q_0([x]) \in M(P)_{q_0} \text{ iff } q_0([x]) \in M_0.$$

Thus $L(M_0)$ is a regular language.

Conversely, from a (deterministic) finite-state automaton accepting $L(M_0)$, we can construct a DRLP and show the other direction. ☐

Let M_0 ($\subseteq B_{L_0}$) be a regular model. An *oracle* for M_0 is the device which, for any input $a \in B_{L_0}$, returns *'true'* if $a \in M_0$, *'false'* otherwise. *Facts* about M_0 are pairs of the form $<a, V>$, where $a \in B_{L_0}$ and $V \in \{true, false\}$ is the output value of an oracle for M_0 on the input a. Ground atoms in M_0 are called positive facts, while others negative facts. An *enumeration of M_0* is an infinite sequence $F_1, F_2, F_3, \ldots$ where each F_i is a fact about M_0 and every $a \in B_{L_0}$ occurs in a fact $F_i = <a, V>$ for some $i > 0$. We assume that the oracle for M_0 can give any enumeration of M_0 to an inference algorithm.

The main problem considered in this paper is as follows.

Suppose an oracle for some unknown regular model M_0 is given. Find a DRLP P such that $M(P)_{q_0} = M_0$.

According to the definitions of Shapiro [5], we define the notion of a regular model inference algorithm for solving the above problem, illustrated in Figure 1. At each time,

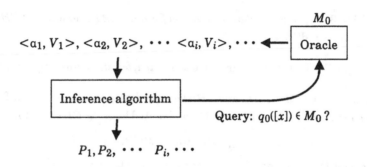

Figure 1.

the algorithm reads one fact $<a_i, V_i>$ from a given enumeration of the target model M_0. Then it makes finitely many membership queries about M_0 to the given oracle. According to answers from the oracle, the algorithm produces a DRLP P_i as its output, called the *conjecture* of the algorithm. While computing a conjecture, such an algorithm usually produces some DRLPs as candidates for the conjecture. We call such DRLPs *hypotheses*.

We say that a regular model inference algorithm *converges in the limit* given an enumeration of a regular model if eventually the algorithm produces some conjecture and never produces a different conjecture. We say that a model inference algorithm *identifies a regular model M_0 in the limit* if it converges on every enumeration of M_0 to a conjecture P such that $M(P)_{q_0} = M_0$.

In the framework of Shapiro's model inference [5, 6], a first order language L with finitely many predicate symbols is given in advance. The Model Inference System (MIS, for short) based on the model inference algorithm requires an oracle for a model M over L. Then MIS efficiently synthesizes a logic program P over L such that $M(P) = M$. The model inference algorithm is equipped with the contradiction backtracing algorithm as a sub-algorithm. The sub-algorithm plays the most important part for the efficiency of the model inference algorithm. With the help of the given oracle, the contradiction backtracing algorithm finds out a wrong clause in a hypothesis unsuitable for a conjecture by checking falsity of clauses in the hypothesis. Note that, in the setting, hypotheses are logic programs over L and a target model M is a Herbrand model over the same language L.

In our setting, however, a given oracle cannot be used directly to check falsity of clauses in a hypothesis P. Because the clauses are over L, while the oracle is for a model over L_0 ($\subseteq L_P$). In order to construct an efficient regular model inference algorithm equipped with the contradiction backtracing algorithm, we should develop some method for checking falsity of clauses over L_P for any hypotheses P. In the next section, we shall argue such a method.

3. An Extended Model of a Regular Model

We introduce a mapping called a *predicate characterization*. With the mapping, we can appropriately extend a regular model over L_0 to a model over L_P for any DRLP P.

Definition 3: A *predicate characterization for a DRLP P*, denoted by CH_P, is a one to one mapping from $\mathrm{Pred}(P)$ to Σ^*.

For any $q_i \in \mathrm{Pred}(P)$, $CH_P(q_i)$ is called the *characteristic string of q_i with CH_P*.

Definition 4: Let $M_0 \subseteq B_{L_0}$ and CH_P be a predicate characterization for a DRLP P. We define an *extended model of M_0 with CH_P*, denoted by $I(M_0, CH_P)$, as follows:

$$I(M_0, CH_P) = \{q_i([x]) \in B_{L_P} \mid q_0([CH_P(q_i) \cdot x]) \in M_0\},$$

where $x \cdot y$ denotes the concatenation of a string x and a string y.

With the above extension of a model over L_0, for the present, we can get a model over L_P. However, it is nonsense that a model over L_0 is arbitrarily extended with a haphazard predicate characterization. The extension should satisfy the following condition:

$$M(P)_{q_0} = M_0 \quad \text{iff} \quad M(P) = I(M_0, CH_P).$$

We show that some restrictions on CH_P lead to such an extension.

Definition 5: Let CH_P be a predicate characterization for a DRLP P. We say that CH_P is *consistent* iff, for any $q_i \in \mathrm{Pred}(P)$, there exists a derivation of $q_0([CH_P(q_i)])$ on P in which $q_i([])$ appears.

The above definition is translated in terms of the theory of finite-state automata as follows. Let P be a deterministic finite-state automaton with a transition function δ, CH_P is consistent iff $\delta(q_0, CH_P(q_i)) = q_i$ for any state q_i in P. From the definition of DRLPs, it is clear that such a derivation is unique if it exists.

Lemma 2: *For any DRLP P, if a predicate characterization CH_P for P is consistent, then $M(P) = I(M(P)_{q_0}, CH_P)$.*

Proof: From the definition of DRLPs and the consistency of CH_P, for any $q_i \in \text{Pred}(P)$ and $x \in \Sigma^*$, it follows that

$$P \vdash q_i([x]) \text{ iff } P \vdash q_0([CH_P(q_i) \cdot x]).$$

Hence we have that

$$
\begin{aligned}
q_i([x]) \in M(P) \quad &\text{iff} \quad q_0([CH_P(q_i) \cdot x]) \in M(P) \\
&\text{iff} \quad q_0([CH_P(q_i) \cdot x]) \in M(P)_{q_0} \\
&\text{iff} \quad q_i([x]) \in I(M(P)_{q_0}, CH_P). \qquad \square
\end{aligned}
$$

Theorem 3: *Suppose CH_P for a DRLP P is consistent and $CH_P(q_0) = \varepsilon$ (an empty word). Then, for any $M_0 \subseteq B_{L_0}$, $M(P)_{q_0} = M_0$ iff $M(P) = I(M_0, CH_P)$.*

Proof: Since the *only if* direction immediately follows from lemma 2, it is sufficient to prove the *if* direction. For any $x \in \Sigma^*$, it follows that

$$
\begin{aligned}
q_0([x]) \in M_0 \quad &\text{iff} \quad q_0([CH_P(q_0) \cdot x]) \in M_0 & \text{(from } CH_P(q_0) = \varepsilon) \\
&\text{iff} \quad q_0([x]) \in I(M_0, CH_P) & \\
&\text{iff} \quad q_0([x]) \in M(P) & \text{(from the assumption)} \\
&\text{iff} \quad q_0([x]) \in M(P)_{q_0}. & \square
\end{aligned}
$$

By the above theorem, the regular model inference problem can be restated as follows.

> *Suppose an oracle for some unknown regular model M_0 is given. Find a DRLP P such that $M(P) = I(M_0, CH_P)$, where CH_P is consistent and $CH_P(q_0) = \varepsilon$.*

With such a predicate characterization, it is possible to take advantage of the contradiction backtracing algorithm. Whenever the algorithm needs information about the truth of some ground atom $q_i([x]) \in B_{L_P}$ in an extended model $I(M_0, CH_P)$, it can get the information by making a query "$q_0([CH_P(q_i) \cdot x]) \in M_0$?" to a given oracle.

4. A Regular Model Inference Algorithm

In this section, we propose a regular model inference algorithm in which an extended model of a target regular model is used for checking falsity of clauses in an unsuitable hypothesis.

First, we present a property of DRLPs which is useful for not only a proof of the correctness of the algorithm but also provides much understanding about an outline of the algorithm.

Definition 6: We say that a clause $A \leftarrow B$ *covers* an atom a in a model M ($\subseteq B_L$) iff there exists a substitution θ such that $A\theta = a$ and $B\theta \in M$. $C(M)$ denotes a set of all ground atoms covered by a clause C in M.

Definition 7: Let $M \subseteq B_L$ and C be a clause. C is *true in* M iff $C(M) \subseteq M$.

Definition 8: Let $M \subseteq B_L$ and C be a clause. C is *sufficient in* M iff $a \in C(M)$ for every $a \in M$ which is unifiable with the head of C.

Definition 9: C is *complete* in M iff C is both true and sufficient in M.

From the above definitions, it is clear that the following two propositions are equivalent.

i) A clause $q_i([a \mid X]) \leftarrow q_j(X)$ is complete in a model M.
ii) For any $x \in \Sigma^*$, $q_i([a \cdot x]) \in M$ iff $q_j([x]) \in M$.

Hence, we have the following proposition.

Proposition 4: *For any DRLP P, every clause in P is complete in $M(P)$.*

With Lemma 2, the following proposition holds.

Proposition 5: *Let CH_P be a consistent predicate characterization for a DRLP P. If $M(P)_{q_0} = M_0$ then every clause in P is complete in $I(M_0, CH_P)$.*

By the above proposition, if there is a clause in P which is not complete in $I(M_0, CH_P)$ for some CH_P, then $M(P)_{q_0} \neq M_0$. Hence, whenever a clause which is not complete in $I(M_0, CH_P)$ exists in a hypothesis P, then the clause must be eliminated from P. Thus in our setting, the clauses that are not sufficient in an extended model are removed from an unsuitable hypothesis, while, in Shapiro's model inference algorithm, only the clauses that are not true in a target model are removed.

Now we state an outline of the algorithm mainly concentrating on the following three:

(a) the way for modifying hypotheses,
(b) a device for generating clauses,
(c) the way for constructing a predicate characterization.

For the present, we assume that, at any time, the predicate characterization CH_P constructed by the algorithm is consistent and $CH_P(q_0) = \varepsilon$.

There are the following two cases in which a hypothesis P must be modified.

(1) The hypothesis is too strong, that is, P succeeds on some negative fact (the first while loop in Algorithm 1).
(2) The hypothesis is too weak, that is, P finitely fails on some positive fact (the second while loop in Algorithm 1).

Input: An oracle for a regular model M_0.
Output: A sequence of DRLPs.
Procedure:
 $P := \varnothing$; $CH_P := \{(q_0, \varepsilon)\}$; $S_{\text{true}} := \varnothing$; $S_{\text{false}} := \varnothing$;
 $State := 0$;
 repeat
  read the next fact $<a, V>$;
  $S_V := S_V \cup \{a\}$;
  repeat
   while $\exists A \in S_{\text{false}}$ s.t. $P \vdash A$ *do*
    $C :=$ **contradiction_backtracing**(A);
    $P := P \setminus \{C\}$;
    $C' :=$ **next_clause**(C);
    $P := P \cup \{C'\}$
   while $\exists A \in S_{\text{true}}$ s.t. $P \nvdash A$ *do*
    $A' :=$ **uncovered_atom**(A);
    $C :=$ **search_for_a_clause**(A');
    $P := P \cup \{C\}$
  until neither of the *while* loop is entered;
  output P
 forever.

Algorithm 1: A regular model inference algorithm.

In the first case, there exists at least one clause in P which is not true in $I(M_0, CH_P)$ (this is shown by the same argument as in the proof of Theorem 3.2 in [6]). Hence the algorithm finds such a clause using the contradiction backtracing algorithm (procedure **contradiction_backtracing**). The clause is removed from the hypothesis. Then an alternate clause constructed by a clause generator (procedure **next_clause**) is added to the hypothesis.

In the procedures **contradiction_backtracing** and **uncovered_atom**, the test of *if* statement "$q_j([x]) \in I(M_0, CH_P)$" is done by asking the oracle and checking whether $q_0([CH_P(q_j) \cdot x]) \in M_0$ or not. The procedure **resolvent** computes and returns a resolvent of its argument on the current hypothesis P. The procedure **character**, on an input q_i, retrieves the pair (q_i, x) in CH_P and returns x. We don't consider the atom in the form of $q_i([])$ as an input for **contradiction_backtracing**. The reason will be described after Proposition 6.

In the second case, there exists a ground atom $q_i([x]) \in I(M_0, CH_P)$ which is not covered in $I(M_0, CH_P)$ by any clause in P (this is shown by the same argument as in the

contradiction_backtracing:
Input:　An atom $q_i([a \cdot x])$ which is in $M(P)$ but not in $I(M_0, CH_P)$.
Output:　A clause in P which is false in $I(M_0, CH_P)$.
Procedure:

$\quad q_j([x]) := \text{resolvent}(q_i([a \cdot x]))$;
$\quad if\ q_j([x]) \in I(M_0, CH_P)\ then$
$\quad\quad\quad \text{return } q_i([a \mid X]) \leftarrow q_j([X])$
$\quad else\ \text{return } \textbf{contradiction\_backtracing}(q_j([x]))$.

next_clause:
Input:　A clause $q_i([a \mid X]) \leftarrow q_j(X)$.
Output:　A clause $q_i([a \mid X]) \leftarrow q_{j+1}(X)$.
Procedure:

$\quad if\ j = State\ then$
$\quad\quad State := State + 1$;
$\quad\quad x := \text{character}(q_i)$;
$\quad\quad CH_P := CH_P \cup \{(q_{j+1}, x \cdot a)\}$
$\quad \text{return } q_i([a \mid X]) \leftarrow q_{j+1}(X)$.

Algorithm 2

proof of Theorem 3.7 in [6]). The procedure **uncovered_atom** finds out such an atom. Then the following two cases are considered.

(i) There is no clause in P whose head is unifiable with $q_i([x])$.

(ii) Although there is a clause C whose head is unifiable with $q_i([x])$, C does not cover $q_i([x])$ in $I(M_0, CH_P)$.

In the case (i), if $x = \varepsilon$, then $q_i([])$ is added to the hypothesis, and if $x = a \cdot w$ ($a \in \Sigma$, $w \in \Sigma^*$), then $q_j([a \mid X]) \leftarrow q_0(X)$ is added to the hypothesis. In the case (ii), according to Proposition 5, C is removed from the hypothesis, then an alternate clause is added to the hypothesis similarly in the case (1). The procedure **search_for_a_clause** works according to each case.

Figure 2 illustrates the outline of modifying hypotheses mentioned above. The dotted line denotes the operation which is made in the case (2)-(i). The two solid lines denote the operations that are made simultaneously in the case (1) and (2)-(ii).

In the model inference algorithm, candidate clauses for constructing hypotheses are generated by a refinement operator [5]. In our setting, clauses to be generated are so restricted that the refinement operator is rather simple. Figure 3 illustrates an example of a refinement graph [5] for clauses in DRLPs. Thus we can exhaustively generate the candidate clauses by increasing the index of the predicate symbol in the body of clauses.

uncovered_atom :

Input :   An atom a which is in $I(M_0, CH_P)$ but not in $M(P)$.

Output :   An atom in $I(M_0, CH_P)$ which is not covered in
                $I(M_0, CH_P)$ by any clause in P.

Procedure :

   if $\exists(A := \text{resolvent}(a))$ *then*

      if $A \in I(M_0, CH_P)$ *then*

         return **uncovered_atom**(A)

      else return a

   else return a.

search_for_a_clause :

Input :   An uncovered atom $q_i([x])$.

Output :   A new clause whose head is unifiable with $q_i([x])$.

Procedure :

   if $x = \varepsilon$ *then*

      return $q_i([])$

   else if $\exists C \in P$ s.t. head(C) is unifiable with $q_i([x])$ *then*

      $P := P \setminus \{C\}$;

      return **next_clause**(C)

   else return $q_i([\text{car}(x) \mid X]) \leftarrow q_0(X)$.

Algorithm 3

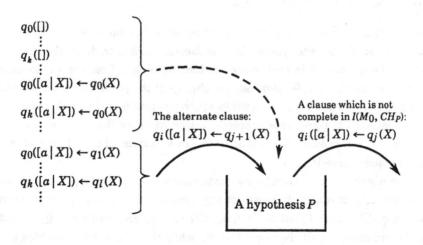

Figure 2: A modification of hypotheses.

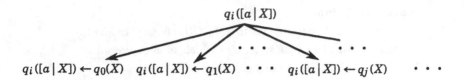

Figure 3: An example of a refinement graph for clauses in DRLPs.

In the algorithm, the predicate characterization is represented as a set of pairs of a predicate symbol and a string. The set is constructed as follows. Let P be the current hypothesis and $CH_P = \{(q_0, \varepsilon), (q_1, x_1), (q_2, x_2), \ldots, (q_k, x_k)\}$ be the current predicate characterization. Now we assume that the algorithm finds out a clause $C = q_i([a \mid X]) \leftarrow q_k(X)$ in P which is not complete in $I(M_0, CH_P)$. Then P is modified in the way mentioned above. Hence C is removed from P and an alternation constructed by the clause generator is added to P. Since the clause generator increases the index of q_k, the alternation has a new predicate symbol q_{k+1} which has never appeared in P before. When such a new predicate symbol is introduced, the algorithm adds a pair $(q_{k+1}, x_i \cdot a)$ to CH_P, that is, a characteristic string of the new predicate symbol is determined by the head of the clause which caused the introduction of the new predicate symbol.

In the following, we shall show the justification of the way for constructing a predicate characterization.

From the definition of an extended model, the following proposition holds.

Proposition 6: *Let P_1 and P_2 be DRLPs such that $Pred(P_1) \subseteq Pred(P_2)$. Suppose that $CH_{P_1}(q) = CH_{P_2}(q)$ for any $q \in Pred(P_1)$. Then, for any $M_0 \subseteq B_{L_0}$ and $q([x]) \in B_{L_{P_1}}$, $q([x]) \in I(M_0, CH_{P_1})$ iff $q([x]) \in I(M_0, CH_{P_2})$.*

The predicate characterization constructed by the algorithm changes with increase of its domain: the set of predicate symbols in hypotheses. This introduces the change of the extended model with the predicate characterization. However, from the way to construct a predicate characterization, it is clear that the change of the predicate characterization by modifying hypotheses satisfies the condition of Proposition 6. Hence the change of the extended model with the predicate characterization satisfies the conclusion of Proposition 6. Thus, once a ground atom is true (false) in an extended model, the atom is true (false) in subsequent models.

Now, in Algorithm 2, we don't consider the atom in the form of $q_i([])$ as an input for **contradiction_backtracing**. Because, at any time on the inference process, there is no case in which $q_i([])$ is in $M(P)$ but not in $I(M_0, CH_P)$. The ground atom $q_i([])$ is in $M(P)$ if and only if there exists a unit clause $q_i([])$ in P, while the clause $q_i([])$ is added to P after the procedure **search_for_a_clause** is called on the input $q_i([])$. Let P' be the current hypothesis, then $q_i([])$ is in $I(M_0, CH_{P'})$. By Proposition 6, we take that $q_i([])$ is in

$I(M_0, CH_P)$ for any subsequent hypothesis P.   Hence, there is no case in which q_i ([]) is in $M(P)$ but not in $I(M_0, CH_P)$.

We can restate Proposition 6 as follows.

Proposition 7: *Let P_1 and P_2 be DRLPs such that $Pred(P_1) \subseteq Pred(P_2)$.   Suppose that $CH_{P_1}(q) = CH_{P_2}(q)$ for any $q \in Pred(P_1)$.   Then, for any $M_0 \subseteq B_{L_0}$ and $C \in P_1$, C is complete in $I(M_0, CH_{P_1})$ iff C is complete in $I(M_0, CH_{P_2})$.*

Lemma 8: *Let P be a DRLP.   Suppose $CH_P(q_j) = CH_P(q_i) \cdot a$, where $a \in \Sigma$ and q_i, $q_j \in Pred(P)$.   Then, for any $M_0 \subseteq B_{L_0}$, the clause $q_i([a \,|\, X]) \leftarrow q_j(X)$ is complete in $I(M_0, CH_P)$.*

Proof: By the definition of an extended model, for any $x \in \Sigma^*$, it follows that

$$q_i([a \cdot x]) \in I(M_0, CH_P)$$
$$\text{iff} \quad q_0([CH_P(q_i) \cdot a \cdot x]) \in M_0$$
$$\text{iff} \quad q_0([CH_P(q_j) \cdot x]) \in M_0$$
$$\text{iff} \quad q_j([x]) \in I(M_0, CH_P).$$

Hence $q_i([a \,|\, X]) \leftarrow q_j(X)$ is complete in $I(M_0, CH_P)$. $\qquad\square$

Theorem 9: *The predicate characterization CH_P constructed by the algorithm is, at any time, consistent and $CH_P(q_0) = \varepsilon$.*

Proof: It is clear that $CH_P(q_0) = \varepsilon$ holds .

Let P be a hypothesis constructed by the algorithm.   From the way for constructing the predicate characterization, for any $q_j \in Pred(P)$ $(j > 0)$, there exists a predicate symbol $q_i \in Pred(P)$ such that $CH_P(q_j) = CH_P(q_i) \cdot a$ for some $a \in \Sigma$.   On the other hand, in defining the characteristic string $CH_P(q_j) = CH_P(q_i) \cdot a$, the clause $q_i([a \,|\, X]) \leftarrow q_j(X)$ is added to the hypothesis at the moment.   Since Lemma 8 ensures the clause being complete in $I(M_0, CH_P)$, it is never removed from the hypothesis.   Hence, for any $q_j \in Pred(P)$ $(j > 0)$, there exist clauses in P that are necessary for such a derivation in Definition 5.

For the predicate symbol q_0, there exists such a derivation at all time, even if P is empty, because $CH_P(q_0) = \varepsilon$. $\qquad\square$

Now we show the correctness of the algorithm, that is, for any regular model M_0, the algorithm identifies M_0 in the limit.   Since the conjectures of Algorithm 1 are consistent with known facts, it is sufficient to show the following:

1. The algorithm produces an infinite sequence of conjectures.
2. The infinite sequence of the conjectures converges a DRLP.

For the former, we must show that the inner *repeat* loop of Algorithm 1 terminates finitely. For the latter, we must show that there are at most finitely many times in which hypotheses are modified.   Finally, it is sufficient to show that the bodies of the two *while* loops are executed at most finitely many times in total.

When the target model is empty, the bodies of the *while* loops are never entered, because the initial hypothesis is empty. Thus, in the following, we assume that the target regular model M_0 is not empty.

Lemma 10: *Let P be an arbitrary hypothesis constructed by the algorithm and let CH_P be the predicate characterization for P. For any $q_i \in Pred(P)$, there exists a string $x \in \Sigma^*$ such that $q_0([CH_P(q_i) \cdot x]) \in M_0$.*

Proof: First, we show that, for any non-unit clause $q_k([a \mid X]) \leftarrow q_j(X) \in P$, there exists a string $x \in \Sigma^*$ such that $q_k([a \cdot x]) \in I(M_0, CH_P)$.

The clause whose head is $q_k([a \mid X])$ occurs for the first time in a hypothesis after executing the last *else* statement in the procedure call of **search_for_a_clause** on an input $q_k([a \cdot x])$. Suppose that P' is the hypothesis at the time of the procedure call. Then $q_k([a \cdot x]) \in I(M_0, CH_{P'})$ and $q_k([a \cdot x]) \notin M(P')$. By Proposition 6, for any subsequent CH_P, it holds that $q_k([a \cdot x]) \in I(M_0, CH_P)$. Thus, for any non-unit clause $q_k([a \mid X]) \leftarrow q_j(X) \in P$, there exists a string $x \in \Sigma^*$ such that $q_k([a \cdot x]) \in I(M_0, CH_P)$.

On the other hand, for any $q_i \in Pred(P)$ ($i > 0$), there exists a predicate symbol $q_k \in Pred(P)$ such that $CH_P(q_i) = CH_P(q_k) \cdot a$ for some $a \in \Sigma$. By the argument in the proof of Theorem 9, there exists a clause $q_k([a \mid X]) \leftarrow q_i(X) \in P$. By the previous discussion, there exists a string $x \in \Sigma^*$ such that $q_k([a \cdot x]) \in I(M_0, CH_P)$ that is $q_0([CH_P(q_k) \cdot a \cdot x]) \in M_0$. Hence, for any $q_i \in Pred(P)$ ($i > 0$), there exists a string $x \in \Sigma^*$ such that $q_0([CH_P(q_i) \cdot x]) \in M_0$.

For the predicate q_0, since M_0 is not empty, there exists a string $x \in \Sigma^*$ such that $q_0([CH_P(q_0) \cdot x]) = q_0([x]) \in M_0$. □

In the following lemma, we consider the DRLP P with the minimum number of predicate symbols satisfying $M_0 = M(P)_{q_0}$. Such a DRLP can be constructed, by a similar method in the proof of Theorem 1, from the minimum deterministic finite-state automaton which accepts $L(M_0)$.

Lemma 11: *Let P' be a DRLP with a minimum number of predicate symbols such that $M_0 = M(P')_{q_0}$. Let P be an arbitrary hypothesis constructed by the algorithm. Then it follows that $|Pred(P)| \leq |Pred(P')|$, where $|S|$ denotes the cardinality of the set S.*

Proof: Let CH_P be the predicate characterization for P constructed by the algorithm. By Lemma 10, for any $q_i \in Pred(P)$, there exists a string $x \in \Sigma^*$ such that $q_0([CH_P(q_i) \cdot x]) \in M_0$. Since $M_0 = M(P')_{q_0}$, there uniquely exists a refutation of $q_0([CH_P(q_i) \cdot x])$ on P'. Hence, for any $q_i \in Pred(P)$, there uniquely exists a predicate symbol $q_i' \in Pred(P')$ such that $q_i'([])$ appears in the derivation of $q_0([CH_P(q_i)])$ on P'. For such q_i', it holds that, for any string $x \in \Sigma^*$,

$$q_i'([x]) \in M(P') \text{ iff } q_0([CH_P(q_i) \cdot x]) \in M(P'). \tag{$*$}$$

Now we consider the mapping τ from Pred(P) to Pred(P') such that $\tau(q_i)=q_i'$. For the proof of the lemma, it is sufficient to show that τ is injective.

Suppose that $\tau(q_i)=\tau(q_j)$ for some $i<j$. Then, for any string $x \in \Sigma^*$, it holds that

$$q_0([CH_P(q_i)\cdot x]) \in M(P')$$
$$\text{iff} \quad q_i'([x]) \in M(P') \qquad \text{(from the property (*))}$$
$$\text{iff} \quad q_j'([x]) \in M(P') \qquad \text{(from the assumption)}$$
$$\text{iff} \quad q_0([CH_P(q_j)\cdot x]) \in M(P'). \qquad \text{(from the property (*))}$$

Hence, we take that

$$q_0([CH_P(q_i)\cdot x]) \in M_0 \quad \text{iff} \quad q_0([CH_P(q_j)\cdot x]) \in M_0.$$

Since $0 \leq i<j$, there exists a predicate symbol $q_k \in$ Pred(P) ($k<j$) such that $CH_P(q_j)=CH_P(q_k)\cdot a$ for some $a \in \Sigma$. Hence, for any $x \in \Sigma^*$, it follows that

$$q_0([CH_P(q_i)\cdot x]) \in M_0 \quad \text{iff} \quad q_0([CH_P(q_k)\cdot a\cdot x]) \in M_0,$$

that is,

$$q_i([x]) \in I(M_0, CH_P) \quad \text{iff} \quad q_k([a\cdot x]) \in I(M_0, CH_P).$$

Thus the clause $C=q_k([a \mid X]) \leftarrow q_i(X)$ is complete in $I(M_0, CH_P)$. Since $i<j$, C is generated by the procedure **next_clause** and added to the hypothesis before the clause $q_k([a \mid X]) \leftarrow q_j(X)$. From Proposition 7, C is complete in any extended model subsequently. Thus C is never removed from subsequent hypotheses. This contradicts that $CH_P(q_j)= CH_P(q_k)\cdot a$. □

Theorem 12: *For any regular model M_0, Algorithm 1 identifies M_0 in the limit.*

Proof: It is clear that the procedure **next_clause** and **search_for_a_ clause** terminate finitely and return the desired output. We can show the correctness of the procedure **contradiction_backtracing** and **uncovered_atom** along to the same line of arguments about the correctness of Algorithm 1 and Algorithm 2 in [6]. Hence the computation in the bodies of the two *while* loops terminates finitely and a operation corresponding to either the two solid lines or the dotted line in Figure 2 is executed. The operation is executed at most once for each clause enumerated in the left hand of Figure 2. Hence, if only finitely many clauses are generated, then the bodies of the two *while* loops are executed at most finitely many times.

On the other hand, by Proposition 7 and Proposition 8, once a predicate symbol is introduced into a hypothesis, the symbol never disappears from the subsequent hypotheses. Hence, by Lemma 11, only finitely many predicate symbols are introduced into the hypotheses. Thus the number of clauses generated is at most finite. □

5. The Time Complexity of the Algorithm

In this section, we argue the time complexity of Algorithm 1. Since the algorithm is based on the notion of *"identification in the limit"* by Gold [2], we don't discuss the whole time spent until the algorithm converges. Because, by an intentional oracle, the time could be increased arbitrary. Therefore, we consider the time between an input of a fact and that of the next fact, that is, the time required in each iteration of the outer *repeat* loop.

In the following, we assume that testing *if* statements and sub-procedures except for the four procedures defined in Algorithm 2 and Algorithm 3 are all executed in one step. Therefore, we shall evaluate the number of steps in computing a resolvent of a ground atom on a hypothesis or in testing of "$q_i([x]) \in I(M_0, CH_P)$" as one step.

Let M_0 be a target regular model and P be a DRLP with a minimum number of predicate symbols satisfying $M_0 = M(P)_{q_0}$. From the arguments in the previous section, the number of predicate symbols introduced into hypotheses is at most $n = |\text{Pred}(P)|$. Hence, for $k = |\Sigma|$, the number of clauses that may be appear in hypotheses is at most $kn^2 + n$. Thus the bodies of the two *while* loops are executed at most $kn^2 + n$ times in total.

For any ground atom $q_i([x]) \in B_L$, define $\text{size}(q_i([x]))$ to be the length of the word x. Let P be an arbitrary hypothesis and β be the resolvent of a ground atom a on P, then it is holds that $\text{size}(\beta) = \text{size}(a) - 1$. Hence $O(\text{size}(a))$ steps are required in checking whether $P \vdash a$ or not and also in computing the procedure **contradiction_backtracing** and **uncovered_atom** on an input a. The procedures **next_clause** and **search_for_a_clause** terminate, for any input, in c steps for some constant c. Thus the time required in an execution of the body of each *while* loop is $O(\text{size}(a))$, for a ground atom $a \in B_{L_0}$ which is found in the test of the *while* loop. The test is executed on every known facts in the worst case. Thus, for $m = \max\{\text{size}(a) \mid a \in S_{true} \cup S_{false}\}$ and $l = |S_{true} \cup S_{false}|$, the time required in each iteration of the *while* loops is at most $O(lm + m)$.

Eventually, the amount of the time required in each iteration of the outer *repeat* loop is at most $O((kn^2 + n)(lm + m)) = O(klmn^2)$.

Angluin [1] gives an algorithm for synthesizing a deterministic finite-state automaton (dfa) in an polynomial time in m and n. In her setting, a given oracle (called a *minimally adequate Teacher*) is assumed to have the following ability. First, the oracle can answer membership queries from the algorithm about the target regular language L. Furthermore, whenever the algorithm produces a conjecture A', the oracle performs a test of whether $L(A')$, the language accepted by A', is equal to L. If they are equivalent, then the oracle terminates the inference process, otherwise, it gives a counter-example and continues the inference process. (A counter-example is an element of the symmetric difference of $L(A')$ and L.) Because of the difference in the power of the oracles, it seems difficult to compare straightforwardly the efficiency of the two algorithms. It would be, however, interesting to study about an influence of the power of the oracle on the efficiency of the inference algorithm.

6. Concluding Remarks

We have discussed the inductive inference of regular languages from the point of view of applying the theory of model inference to automated logic program synthesis. We believe that the presented algorithm is an adequate one for the efficiency. Finally, we conclude this paper by presenting some problems which should be solved in the future.

The idea of extending a model with a predicate characterization is applicable to the class of models other than that of regular models by changing the range of the predicate characterization. In the application, it is important to clarify conditions for the predicate characterization on which a model is appropriately extended and to give an efficient procedure for constructing such a predicate characterization. For a regular model, a predicate characterization has only to satisfy the conditions in Theorem 3 and such a predicate characterization can be constructed by such a simple method in **next_clause**. However, if the condition becomes more complex, then the time required in constructing the predicate characterization will increase. We would like to investigate an application of the idea to other classes of models.

We would like to consider the first question mentioned in the section 1. Shapiro [5] treats the problem of model inference for regular languages by using the following type of program as a finite representation of a regular language.

$$in([\,]).$$
$$in([0, 0 \mid X]) \leftarrow in(X).$$
$$in([1, 1 \mid X]) \leftarrow in(X).$$
$$in([0, 1, 0 \mid X]) \leftarrow in([1 \mid X]).$$
$$in([0, 1, 1 \mid X]) \leftarrow in([0 \mid X]).$$
$$in([1, 0, 0 \mid X]) \leftarrow in([1 \mid X]).$$
$$in([1, 0, 1 \mid X]) \leftarrow in([0 \mid X]).$$

The program corresponds to the acceptor of strings over $\{0, 1\}$ with an even number of 0's and an even number of 1's. If the target program synthesized is such a program with only one predicate symbol, then it is sufficient that the given oracle can answer the truth about only the predicate symbol. Therefore, for an application of the theory of model inference to automated program synthesis, it is important to investigate the power of logic programs with only one predicate symbol or with fully restricted number of predicate symbols. Shapiro [7] shows that an arbitrary alternating Turing machine can be simulated by a logic program with only one 3-ary predicate symbol. In such a logic program, however, the information of each state of the alternating Turing machine is preserved in one of the arguments of the predicate. Therefore, the problem of inferring such a program results in that of inferring a program over the language with countably many predicate symbols. Here we don't mean this kind of reduction on the number of predicate symbols, but are interested in the essential relation between the power of logic programs and the number of predicate symbols allowed.

ACKNOWLEDGMENTS

The author wishes to acknowledge Dr. T. Kitagawa, the president of IIAS-SIS, and Dr. H. Enomoto, the director of IIAS-SIS, for their ceaseless support and advice. He is deeply grateful to Dr. T. Yokomori for reading the draft and giving him many valuable comments. Discussions with his colleagues Y. Takada and Y. Sakakibara were also very fruitful.

REFERENCES

[1] Angluin, D. : Learning regular sets from queries and counter-examples, Technical Report 464, Yale University, Department of Computer Science, March, 1986.

[2] Gold, E. M. : Language Identification in the Limit, Information and Control 10, 447-474, 1967.

[3] Hopcroft, J. E., Ullman, J. D. : Formal Languages and Their Relation to Automata, Addison-Wesley, 1969.

[4] Lloyd, J. W. : Foundations of Logic Programming, Springer-Verlag, 1984.

[5] Shapiro, E. Y. : Inductive Inference of Theories From Facts, Technical Report 192, Yale University, Department of Computer Science, February, 1981.

[6] Shapiro, E. Y. : Algorithmic Program Debugging, MIT Press, 1983.

[7] Shapiro, E. Y. : Alternation and the Computational Complexity of Logic Programs, The Journal of Logic Programming 1, 19-33, 1984.

Polymorphic Type Inference in Prolog by Abstract Interpretation

Kenji HORIUCHI   Tadashi KANAMORI

Central Research Laboratory
Mitsubishi Electric Corporation
8-1-1, Tsukaguchi-Honmachi
Amagasaki, Hyogo, 661 JAPAN

Abstract

We present an abstract interpretation method for polymorphic type inference for Prolog programs. The method is an extension of our monomorphic type inference method, which is one of the examples of analyzing patterns of Prolog goals at calling time and exiting time by *abstract interpretation*. The framework is based on OLDT resolution by Tamaki and Sato, a hybrid of the top-down and bottom-up interpretations of Prolog programs. By abstracting the hybrid interpretation directly, we can compute approximately not only the type information at calling time and exiting time without infinite looping but also just the necessary and relevant information without waste. The monomorphic type inference method is extended to polymorphic types by introducing parameterized type definitions and generalizing operations for manipulating type information accordingly.

1. Introduction

Most programming languages for symbolic processing, like Lisp or Prolog, can work on a variety of objects without type checking. Though such flexibility is useful for programmers to construct programs with less burden, lack of type checking makes it more difficult to find program bugs. Inferring data types of arguments from program texts provides useful information not only to programmers on debugging but also to meta-processing systems, like a compiler.

In Prolog, types can be introduced by defining type predicates, e.g.,

    list([ ]).
    list([$A|L$]) :- list(L).

In general, when the set of all terms satisfying the definition of a type can be uniquely determined from its definition, the type is called a *monomorphic type*. For example, list is a monomorphic type, since the set of all terms satisfying the definition above, denoted by *list*, is uniquely determined. Similarly, the following is the definition of a monomorphic type *num*.

    num(0).
    num(suc(X)) :- num(X).

The expressive power of a monomorphic type system, however, is neither flexible nor sufficient. Suppose that we would like to express a set of terms not only by *list* and *num* but also by lists of *num*, lists of *list* or lists of lists of *num* etc. If we would like to introduce a list of numbers as a type, we can define it as a new monomorphic type *numlist* by

    numlist([ ]).
    numlist([A|L]) :- num(A), numlist(L).

But such an overloading of type constructors [ ] and [|] causes the following problems.

- The sets *list* and *numlist* are not disjoint though they are two distinct types.
- The intersection of *list* and *numlist* is not clear from the syntax.
- Type definitions like this have less syntactical regularity.

The approach to extend monomorphic types to parametric ones, called *polymorphic types*, is investigated in [8],[10],[13]. As for the above example, since the head A of the list $[A|L]$ isn't mentioned at all in the definition of *list*, we can express the type *numlist* by parameterizing the type of the head part in *list* and instantiating it to *num*.

In this paper, a polymorphic type inference method for Prolog programs by abstract interpretation is presented. The method is an extension of our monomorphic type inference method [3], which is one of the examples of analyzing patterns of Prolog goals at calling time and exiting time by *abstract interpretation* [2],[7]. The framework is based on an OLDT resolution by Tamaki and Sato [12], a hybrid of the top-down and bottom-up interpretations of Prolog programs. By abstracting the hybrid interpretation directly, we can compute approximately not only the type information at calling time and exiting time without infinite looping but also just the necessary and relevant information without waste. The monomorphic type inference method is extended to polymorphic types by introducing parameterized type definitions and generalizing operations for manipulating type information accordingly.

After presenting the hybrid interpretation of Prolog programs in Section 2, we will introduce a monomorphic type into Prolog and extend it to a polymorphic type in Section 3. Then we will show a polymorphic type inference method.

In the following, we assume familiarity with the basic terminology of first order logic such as term, atom (atomic formula), formula, substitution and most general unifier (m.g.u.) We follow the syntax of DEC-10 Prolog [11]. As syntactical variables, we use X, Y, Z for variables, s, t for terms and A, B for atoms, possibly with primes and subscripts. In addition we use σ, τ, μ, ν for substitutions.

2. Standard Hybrid Interpretation of Logic Programs

In this section, we will first present a basic hybrid interpretation method of Prolog programs [12], then a modified hybrid interpretation method suitable for the basis of the abstract interpretation presented later.

2.1 Basic Hybrid Interpretation of Logic Programs

(1) Search Tree

A *search tree* is a tree with its nodes labeled with negative or null clauses, and with its edges labeled with substitutions. A *search tree of* negative clause G is a search tree whose root node is labeled with G. The relation between a node and its child nodes in a search tree is specified in various ways depending on various strategies of "resolution". In this paper, the class of "ordered linear" strategies is assumed. (See the explanations of OLDT resolution in the following subsection (4), and of OLD resolution in Section 3.)

A *refutation* of negative clause G is a path in a search tree of G from the root to a node labeled with the null clause $\square$. Let $\theta_1, \theta_2, \ldots, \theta_k$ be the labels of the edges on the path. Then, the *answer substitution of the refutation* is the composed substitution $\tau = \theta_1 \theta_2 \cdots \theta_k$, and the *solution of the refutation* is $G\tau$.

Consider a path in a search tree from one node to another node. Intuitively, when the leftmost atom of the starting node's label is refuted just at the ending node, the path is called a unit subrefutation of the atom. More formally, let $G_0, G_1, \ldots, G_k$ be a sequence of labels of the nodes and $\theta_1, \theta_2, \ldots, \theta_k$ be the labels of the edges on the path. The path is called a *unit subrefutation* of atom A when $G_0, G_1, G_2, \ldots, G_{k-1}, G_k$ are of the form

$$\text{``}A, G\text{''},$$
$$\text{``}H_1, G\theta_1\text{''},$$
$$\text{``}H_2, G\theta_1\theta_2\text{''},$$
$$\vdots$$
$$\text{``}H_{k-1}, G\theta_1\theta_2 \cdots \theta_{k-1}\text{''}$$
$$\text{``}G\theta_1\theta_2 \ldots \theta_k\text{''},$$

respectively, where G, H_1, H_2, ..., H_{k-1} are sequences of atoms. Then, the *answer substitution of the unit subrefutation* is the composed substitution $\tau = \theta_1\theta_2 \cdots \theta_k$, and the *solution of the unit subrefutation* is $A\tau$.

(2) Solution Table

A *solution table* is a set of entries. Each entry is a pair of the *key* and the *solution list*. The key is an atom such that there is no other identical key (modulo renaming of variables) in the solution table. The solution list is a list of atoms, called *solutions*, such that each solution in it is an instance of the corresponding key.

(3) Association

Let Tr be a search tree whose nodes labeled with non-null clauses are classified into either *solution nodes* or *lookup nodes*, and let Tb be a solution table. (The solution nodes and lookup nodes are explained later.) An *association* of Tr and Tb is a set of pointers pointing from each lookup node in Tr into some solution list in Tb such that the leftmost atom of the lookup node's label and the key of the solution list are variants of each other.

(4) OLDT Structure

The hybrid Prolog interpreter is modeled by the OLDT resolution. An *OLDT structure* of the negative clause G is a triple (Tr, Tb, As) satisfying the following conditions:

   (a) Tr is a search tree of G. The relation between a node and its child nodes in a search tree is specified by the following *OLDT resolution*. Each node of the search tree labeled with a non-null clause is classified into either a *solution node* or a *lookup node*.

   (b) Tb is a solution table.

   (c) As is an association of Tr and Tb. The tail of the solution list pointed from a lookup node is called the *associated solution list* of the lookup node.

Example *2.1.1* An OLDT structure of "$reach(a, Y_0)$" is depicted in Figure 2.1.1. The underline denotes the lookup node, and the dotted line denotes the association from the lookup node.

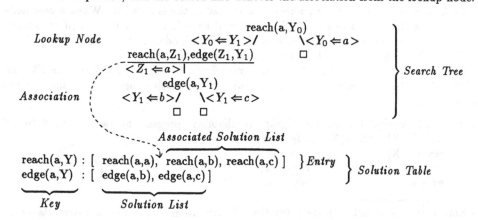

Figure 2.1.1 OLDT Structure

Let G be a negative clause of the form "$A_1, A_2, \ldots, A_n$" ($n \geq 1$). A node of OLDT structure (Tr, Tb, As) labeled with G is said to be *OLDT resolvable* when it satisfies either of the following conditions:

(a) The node is a terminal solution node of Tr, and there is some definite clause "$B_0 :- B_1, B_2, \ldots, B_m$" ($m \geq 0$) in program P such that A_1 and B_0 are unifiable, say by an m.g.u. θ. (Without loss of generality, we assume that the m.g.u. θ substitutes a term consisting of fresh variables for every variable in A_1 and the definite clause.) The negative clause (or possibly null clause) "$B_1\theta, B_2\theta, \ldots, B_m\theta, A_2\theta, \ldots, A_n\theta$" is called the *OLDT resolvent*.

(b) The node is a lookup node of Tr, and there is some solution $B\tau$ in the associated solution list of the lookup node such that A_1 and $B\tau$ are unifiable, say by an m.g.u. θ. (Again, we assume that the m.g.u. θ substitutes a term consisting of fresh variables for every variable in A_1 and the definite clause.) The negative clause (or possibly null clause) "$A_2\theta, \ldots, A_n\theta$" is called the *OLDT resolvent*.

The restriction of the substitution θ to the variables of A_1 is called the *substitution of the OLDT resolution*.

The *initial OLDT structure* of the negative clause G is the triple (Tr_0, Tb_0, As_0), where Tr_0 is a search tree consisting of just the root solution node labeled with G, Tb_0 is the solution table consisting of just one entry whose key is the leftmost atom of G and solution list is the empty list, and As_0 is the empty set of pointers.

An *immediate extension* of the OLDT structure (Tr, Tb, As) in program P is the result of the following operations, when a node v of the OLDT structure (Tr, Tb, As) is OLDT resolvable.

(a) When v is a terminal solution node, let $C_1, C_2, \ldots, C_k$ ($k \geq 0$) be all the clauses with which the node v is OLDT resolvable, and $G_1, G_2, \ldots, G_k$ be the respective OLDT resolvents. Then add k child nodes of v labeled with $G_1, G_2, \ldots, G_k$, to v. The edge from v to the node labeled with G_i is labeled with θ_i, where θ_i is the substitution of the OLDT resolution with C_i. When v is a lookup node, let $B_1\tau_1, B_2\tau_2, \ldots, B_k\tau_k$ ($k \geq 0$) be all the solutions with which the node v is OLDT resolvable, and $G_1, G_2, \ldots, G_k$ be the respective OLDT resolvents. Then add k child nodes of v labeled with $G_1, G_2, \ldots, G_k$, to v. The edge from v to the node labeled with G_i is labeled with θ_i, where θ_i is the substitution of the OLDT resolution with $B_i\tau_i$. A new node labeled with a non-null clause is a lookup node when the leftmost atom of the new negative clause is an instance of some key in Tb, and is a solution node otherwise [†].

(b) Replace the pointer from the OLDT resolved lookup node with the one pointing to the last of the associated solution list. Add a pointer from the new lookup node to the head of the solution list of the corresponding key.

(c) When a new node is a solution node, add a new entry whose key is the leftmost atom of the label of the new node and whose solution list is the empty list. When a new node is a lookup node, add no new entry. For each unit subrefutation of atom A (if any) starting from a solution node and ending with some of the new nodes, add its solution $A\tau$ to the last of the solution list of A in Tb, if $A\tau$ is not in the solution list.

The OLDT structure (Tr', Tb', As') is an extension of OLDT structure (Tr, Tb, As) if (Tr', Tb', As') is obtained from (Tr, Tb, As) through the successive application of immediate extensions.

Example 2.1.2 Consider the following "graph reachability" program by Tamaki and Sato [12].

```
reach(X,Y) :- reach(X,Z), edge(Z,Y).
reach(X,X).
edge(a,b).        edge(b,a).
edge(a,c).        edge(b,d).
```

[†] Note that it is a lookup node when the leftmost atom of the new negative clause is an *instance*, not a *variant*, of some key in Tb. (cf. the definition in our previous papers [3],[4].)

Then, the hybrid interpretation generates the following OLDT structures of "$reach(a, Y_0)$".

First, the initial OLDT structure is generated. The root node of the search tree is a solution node labeled with $reach(a, Y_0)$. The solution table contains only one entry with its key $reach(a, Y)$ and its solution list [ ].

Secondly, the root node "$reach(a, Y_0)$" is OLDT resolved using the program to generate two child nodes. The generated left child node is a lookup node, because its leftmost atom is an instance (a variant) of the key in the solution table. The association associates the lookup node to the head of the solution list of $reach(a, Y)$. The generated right child node is the end of a unit subrefutation of $reach(a, Y_0)$. Its solution $reach(a, a)$ is added to the solution list of $reach(a, Y)$.

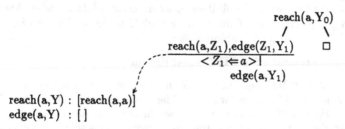

$$reach(a, Y_0)$$
$$<Y_0 \Leftarrow Y_1>/ \qquad \backslash <Y_0 \Leftarrow a>$$
$$reach(a, Z_1), edge(Z_1, Y_1) \qquad \square$$

$reach(a, Y) : [reach(a, a)]$

Figure 2.1.2 Basic Hybrid Interpretation at Step 2

Thirdly, the lookup node is OLDT resolved using the solution table to generate one child solution node. The association associates the lookup node to the last of the solution list.

$$reach(a, Y_0)$$
$$/ \qquad \backslash$$
$$reach(a, Z_1), edge(Z_1, Y_1) \qquad \square$$
$$<Z_1 \Leftarrow a>|$$
$$edge(a, Y_1)$$

$reach(a, Y) : [reach(a, a)]$
$edge(a, Y) \ : [\ ]$

Figure 2.1.3 Basic Hybrid Interpretation at Step 3

Fourthly, the generated solution node is OLDT resolved further using the program to generate two new nodes labeled with the null clauses. These two nodes add two solutions $reach(a, b)$ and $reach(a, c)$ to the last of the solution list of $reach(a, Y)$, and two solutions $edge(a, b)$ and $edge(a, c)$ to the last of the solution list of $edge(a, Y)$.(See Fig. 2.1.1.)

Fifthly, the lookup node is OLDT resolved using the solution table, since new solutions were added to the solution list of $reach(a, Y)$.

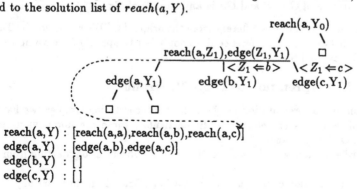

$$reach(a, Y_0)$$
$$/ \qquad \backslash$$
$$reach(a, Z_1), edge(Z_1, Y_1) \qquad \square$$
$$/ \qquad |<Z_1 \Leftarrow b> \quad \backslash <Z_1 \Leftarrow c>$$
$$edge(a, Y_1) \qquad edge(b, Y_1) \qquad edge(c, Y_1)$$
$$/ \quad \backslash$$
$$\square \qquad \square$$

$reach(a, Y) : [reach(a, a), reach(a, b), reach(a, c)]$
$edge(a, Y) \ : [edge(a, b), edge(a, c)]$
$edge(b, Y) \ : [\ ]$
$edge(c, Y) \ : [\ ]$

Figure 2.1.4 Basic Hybrid Interpretation at Step 5

Sixthly, the left new solution node "$edge(b, Y_1)$" is OLDT resolved, and one new solution $reach(a, d)$ is added to the solution list of $reach(a, Y)$.

Lastly, the lookup node is OLDT resolved once more using the solution table, and the extension process stops, because the solution nodes labeled with $edge(c, Y_1)$ and $edge(d, Y_1)$ are not OLDT resolvable.

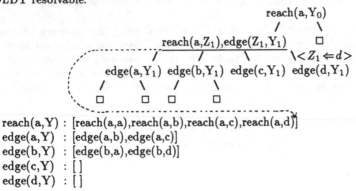

$reach(a, Y)$: $[reach(a,a), reach(a,b), reach(a,c), reach(a,d)]$
$edge(a, Y)$: $[edge(a,b), edge(a,c)]$
$edge(b, Y)$: $[edge(b,a), edge(b,d)]$
$edge(c, Y)$: $[\,]$
$edge(d, Y)$: $[\,]$

Figure 2.1.5 Basic Hybrid Interpretation at Step 7

Though all solutions were found under the depth-first from-left-to-right extension strategy in this example, the strategy is not complete in general. The reasons of the incompleteness are two-fold. One is that there might be generated infinitely many different solution nodes. Another is that some lookup node might generate an infinite number of child nodes so that extensions at other nodes right to the lookup node might be inhibited forever.

(5) Soundness and Completeness of OLDT Resolution

Let G be a negative clause. An *OLDT refutation* of G in program P is a refutation in the search tree of some extension of the OLDT structure of G. The *answer substitution of the OLDT refutation* and the *solution of the OLDT refutation* are defined in the same way as before. It is a basis of the abstract interpretation in this paper that the OLDT resolution is sound and complete. (Do not confuse the completeness of the general OLDT resolution with the incompleteness of the one under a specific extension strategy, e.g., the depth-first from-left-to-right strategy.)

Theorem 2.1 (Soundness and Completeness of the OLDT Resolution)
If $G\tau$ is a solution of an OLDT refutation of G in P, its universal closure $\forall X_1 X_2 \cdots X_n \; G\tau$ is a logical consequence of P.
If a universal closure $\forall Y_1 Y_2 \cdots Y_m \; G\sigma$ is a logical consequence of P, there is $G\tau$ which is a solution of an OLDT refutation of G in P and $G\sigma$ is an instance of $G\tau$.

Proof. Though our hybrid interpretation is different from the original OLDT resolution by Tamaki and Sato [12] in one respect (see [3]), the difference does not affect the proof of the soundness and the completeness. See Tamaki and Sato [12] pp.93–94.

2.2 Modified Hybrid Interpretation of Logic Programs

In order to make the conceptual presentation of the hybrid interpretation simpler, we have not considered the details of how it is implemented. In particular, these are not obvious in the "immediate extension of OLDT structure"
  (a) how we can know whether a new node is the end of a unit subrefutation starting from some solution node, and
  (b) how we can obtain the solution of the unit subrefutation efficiently if there are any.
It is an easy solution to insert a special call-exit marker $[A_1, \theta]$ between $B_1\theta, B_2\theta, \ldots, B_m\theta$ and $A_2\theta, \ldots, A_n\theta$ when a solution node is OLDT resolved using an m.g.u. θ, and obtain the unit subrefutation of A_1 and its solution $A_1\tau$ when the leftmost of a new OLDT resolvent is the special call-exit marker $[A_1, \tau]$. But, we will use the following modified framework. (Though such

redefinition might be confusing, it is a little difficult to grasp the intuitive meaning of the modified framework without the explanation in Section 2.1.)

A *search tree* of the OLDT structure in the modified framework is a tree with its nodes labeled with a pair consisting of a (generalized) negative clause and a substitution. (We have said "generalized", because it might contain non-atoms, i.e., call-exit markers. The edges are not labeled with substitutions any more.) A *search tree of* (G, σ) is a search tree whose root node is labeled with (G, σ). The clause part of each label is a sequence "$\alpha_1, \alpha_2, \ldots, \alpha_n$" consisting of either atoms in the body of the clauses in $P \cup \{G\}$ or *call-exit markers* of the form $[A, \sigma']$. A *refutation of* (G, σ) is a path in a search tree of (G, σ) from the root to a node labeled with $(\Box, \tau)$. The *answer substitution of the refutation* is the substitution τ, and the *solution of the refutation* is $G\tau$. A *solution table* and an *association* are defined in the same way as before.

An *OLDT structure* is a three-part structure of a search tree, a solution table and an association. The relation between a node and its child nodes in search trees of OLDT structures is specified by the following modified OLDT resolution.

A node of the OLDT structure (Tr, Tb, As) labeled with $(\text{"}\alpha_1, \alpha_2, \ldots, \alpha_n\text{"}, \sigma)$ is said to be *OLDT resolvable* when it satisfies either of the following conditions:

(a) The node is a terminal solution node of Tr, and there is some definite clause "B_0 :- $B_1, B_2, \ldots, B_m$" $(m \geq 0)$ in program P such that $\alpha_1\sigma$ and B_0 are unifiable, say by an m.g.u. θ.

(b) The node is a lookup node of Tr, and there is some solution $B\tau$ in the associated solution list of the lookup node such that $\alpha_1\sigma$ and $B\tau$ are unifiable, say by an m.g.u. θ.

The OLDT resolvent is obtained through the following two phases, called *calling phase* and *exiting phase* since they correspond to a "Call" (or "Redo") line and an "Exit" line in the messages of the conventional DEC10 Prolog tracer. A call-exit marker is inserted in the calling phase when a node is OLDT resolved using the program, while no call-exit marker is generated when a node is OLDT resolved using the solution table. When there is a call-exit marker at the leftmost of the clause part in the exiting phase, it means that some unit subrefutation is obtained.

(a) (Calling Phase) When a node labeled with $(\text{"}\alpha_1, \alpha_2, \ldots, \alpha_n\text{"}, \sigma)$ is OLDT resolved, the intermediate label is generated as follows:

  a-1. When the node is OLDT resolved using a definite clause "B_0 :- $B_1, B_2, \ldots, B_m$" in program P and an m.g.u. θ, the intermediate clause part is "$B_1, B_2, \ldots, B_m, [\alpha_1, \sigma], \alpha_2, \ldots, \alpha_n$", and the intermediate substitution part τ_0 is θ.

  a-2. When the node is OLDT resolved using a solution $B\tau$ in the solution table and an instantiation θ, the intermediate clause part is "$\alpha_2, \ldots, \alpha_n$", and the intermediate substitution part τ_0 is $\sigma\theta$.

(b) (Exiting Phase) When there are k call-exit markers $[A_1, \sigma_1], [A_2, \sigma_2], \ldots, [A_k, \sigma_k]$ at the leftmost of the intermediate clause part, the label of the new node is generated as follows:

  b-1. The clause part is obtained by eliminating all these call-exit markers. The substitution part is $\sigma_k \cdots \sigma_2 \sigma_1 \tau_0$.

  b-2. Add $A_1\sigma_1\tau_0, A_2\sigma_2\sigma_1\tau_0, \ldots, A_k\sigma_k \cdots \sigma_1\tau_0$ to the last of the solution lists of $A_1\sigma_1$, $A_2\sigma_2, \ldots, A_k\sigma_k$, respectively, if they are not in the solution lists.

The precise algorithm is shown in Figure 2.2.1. The processing at the calling phase is performed in the former **case** statement, while that of the exiting phase is performed in the latter **while** statement successively.

OLDT-resolve$(("\alpha_1, \alpha_2, \ldots, \alpha_n", \sigma)$: label) : label ;
    $i := 0$;
    case
        when a solution node is OLDT resolved with "$B_0 :\text{-} B_1, B_2, \ldots, B_m$" in P
            let θ be the m.g.u. of $\alpha_1\sigma$ and B_0 ;
            let G_0 be a negative clause "$B_1, B_2, \ldots, B_m, [\![\alpha_1, \sigma]\!], \alpha_2, \ldots, \alpha_n$" ;
            let τ_0 be the substitution θ ;   — (A)
        when a lookup node is OLDT resolved with "$B\tau$" in Tb
            let θ be the m.g.u. of $\alpha_1\sigma$ and $B\tau$;
            let G_0 be a negative clause "$\alpha_2, \ldots, \alpha_n$" ;
            let τ_0 be the composed substitution $\sigma\theta$;   — (B)
    endcase
    while the leftmost of G_i is a call-exit marker $[\![A_{i+1}, \sigma_{i+1}]\!]$ **do**
        let G_{i+1} be G_i other than the leftmost call-exit marker ;
        let τ_{i+1} be $\sigma_{i+1}\tau_i$;   — (C)
        add $A_{i+1}\tau_{i+1}$ to the last of $A_{i+1}\sigma_{i+1}$'s solution list if it is not in it ;
        $i := i + 1$;
    endwhile
    $(G_{new}, \sigma_{new}) := (G_i, \tau_i)$;
    return (G_{new}, σ_{new}).

Figure 2.2.1 Modified Hybrid Interpretation

Note that when a node is labeled with (G, σ), the substitution part σ always shows the instantiation of atoms to the left of the leftmost call-exit marker in G. When there is a call-exit marker $[\![A_j, \sigma_j]\!]$ at the leftmost of the clause part in the exiting phase, we need to update the substitution part by composing σ_j in order that the property above still holds after eliminating the call-exit marker. The sequence $\tau_1, \tau_2, \ldots, \tau_i$ denotes the sequence of updated substitutions. In addition, when we pass a call-exit marker $[\![A_j, \sigma_j]\!]$ in the **while** loop above with substitution τ_j, the atom $A_j\tau_j$ denotes the solution of the unit subrefutation of $A_j\sigma_j$. The solution $A_j\tau_j$ is added to the solution list of $A_j\sigma_j$.

A node labeled with $("\alpha_1, \alpha_2, \ldots, \alpha_n", \sigma)$ is a lookup node when the leftmost atom $\alpha_1\sigma$ is an instance of an already existing key in the solution table, and is a solution node otherwise $(n \geq 1)$.

The *initial OLDT structure* of (G, σ) is a triple (Tr_0, Tb_0, As_0), where Tr_0 is a search tree of G consisting of just the root solution node labeled with (G, σ), Tb_0 is a solution table consisting of just one entry whose key is the leftmost atom of G and the solution list is [ ], and As_0 is the empty set of pointers. The *immediate extension of OLDT structure*, *extension of OLDT structure*, *answer substitution of OLDT refutation* and *solution of OLDT refutation* are defined in the same way as before.

Example 2.2 Consider the example in Section 2.1 again. The modified hybrid interpretation generates the following OLDT structures of $reach(a, Y_0)$.

First, the initial OLDT structure below is generated. Now, the root node is labeled with $("reach(a, Y_0)", <>)$.

Secondly, the root node $("reach(a, Y_0)", <>)$ is OLDT resolved using the program to generate two child nodes. The intermediate label of the left child node is
    $("reach(X_1, Z_1), edge(Z_1, Y_1), [\![reach(a, Y_0), <>]\!]", <Y_0 \Leftarrow Y_1, X_1 \Leftarrow a>)$.
It is the new label immediately, since its leftmost is not a call-exit marker. The intermediate label of the right child node is
    $("[\![reach(a, Y_0), <>]\!]", <Y_0 \Leftarrow a, X_1 \Leftarrow a>)$.

By eliminating the leftmost call-exit marker and composing the substitution, the new label is $(\square, <Y_0 \Leftarrow a, X_1 \Leftarrow a>)$. (When the clause part of the label is $\square$, we will omit the assignments irrelevant to the top-level goal in the following figures, e.g., $<X_1 \Leftarrow a>$.) During the elimination of the call-exit marker, $reach(a, a)$ is added to the solution table.

$$reach(a, Y_0)$$
$$<>$$

$$\text{reach}(X_1, Z_1), \text{edge}(Z_1, Y_1), [\![\, reach(a, Y_0), <> \,]\!] \qquad \square$$
$$<Y_0 \Leftarrow Y_1, X_1 \Leftarrow a> \qquad\qquad <Y_0 \Leftarrow a>$$

$$reach(a, Y) : [reach(a, a)]$$

Figure 2.2.2 Modified Hybrid Interpretation at Step 2

Thirdly, the left lookup node is OLDT resolved using the solution table to generate one child solution node.

Fourthly, the generated solution node is OLDT resolved using a unit clause "$edge(a, b)$" in program P to generate the intermediate label

$$(\text{"}[\![edge(Z_1, Y_1), <Y_0 \Leftarrow Y_1, X_1 \Leftarrow a, Z_1 \Leftarrow a>\,]\!], [\![reach(a, Y_0), <>\,]\!]\text{"}, <Y_1 \Leftarrow b>).$$

By eliminating the leftmost call-exit markers and composing substitutions, the new label is $(\square, <Y_0 \Leftarrow b, X_1 \Leftarrow a, Z_1 \Leftarrow a, Y_1 \Leftarrow b>)$. During the elimination of the call-exit markers, $edge(a, b)$ and $reach(a, b)$ are added to the solution table.

Similarly, the node is OLDT resolved using a unit clause "$edge(a, c)$" in program P to generate the intermediate label

$$(\text{"}[\![edge(Z_1, Y_1), <Y_0 \Leftarrow Y_1, X_1 \Leftarrow a, Z_1 \Leftarrow a>\,]\!], [\![reach(a, Y_0), <>\,]\!]\text{"}, <Y_1 \Leftarrow c>)$$

By eliminating the leftmost call-exit markers and composing substitutions similarly, the new label is $(\square, <Y_0 \Leftarrow c, X_1 \Leftarrow a, Z_1 \Leftarrow a, Y_1 \Leftarrow c>)$. This time, $edge(a, b)$ and $reach(a, b)$ are added to the solution table during the elimination of the call-exit markers. The process of extension proceeds similarly to obtain all the solutions as in Example 2.1.2.

$$reach(a, Y_0)$$
$$<>$$

$$\text{reach}(X_1, Z_1), \text{edge}(Z_1, Y_1), [\![\, reach(a, Y_0), <> \,]\!] \qquad \square$$
$$<Y_0 \Leftarrow Y_1, X_1 \Leftarrow a> \qquad\qquad <Y_0 \Leftarrow a>$$

$$edge(Z_1, Y_1) [\![\, reach(a, Y_0), <> \,]\!]$$
$$<Y_0 \Leftarrow Y_1, X_1 \Leftarrow a, Z_1 \Leftarrow a>$$

$$\square \qquad\qquad \square$$
$$<Y_0 \Leftarrow b> \qquad\qquad <Y_0 \Leftarrow c>$$

$$reach(a, Y) : [reach(a, a), reach(a, b), reach(a, c)]$$
$$edge(a, Y) : [edge(a, b), edge(a, c)]$$

Figure 2.2.3 Modified Hybrid Interpretation at Step 4

Remark. Note that we no longer need to keep the edges and the non-terminal solution nodes of search trees. In addition, we can throw away assignments in θ for the variables in $B\tau$ at step (B), and those in τ_i for variables not in $A_{i+1}\sigma_{i+1}$ at step (C) in Figure 2.2.1.

3. Polymorphic Type Inference by Abstract Interpretation

Suppose that a goal "$map\text{-}plus(X,Y,Z)$" is executed with the second argument instantiated to a number and the others to any term, where $map\text{-}plus$ and $plus$ are defined by

> map-plus([ ],M,[ ]).
> map-plus([A|L],M,[C|N]) :- plus(A,M,C), map-plus(L,M,N).
> plus(0,Y,Y).
> plus(suc(X),Y,suc(Z)) :- plus(X,Y,Z).

Then, the first and third arguments of $map\text{-}plus$ are always instantiated to a list when the execution succeeds. But we would like to know more detailed type information if possible. In fact, these arguments are always instantiated to lists of numbers. How can we show it mechanically ?

In this section, we introduce a monomorphic type into Prolog and extend it to a polymorphic type, and show how a polymorphic type is inferred in the framework based on the OLDT resolution in Section 2.

3.1 Polymorphic Type Inference

(1) Monomorphic Types

We introduce "**type**" construct into Prolog to separate definite clauses defining data structures from others defining procedures, e.g.,

> **type**.
> list([ ]).
> list([X|L]) :- list(L).
> **end**.

type defines a unary relation by definite clauses. The head of definite clause takes a term defining a data structure as its argument, either a constant b called a *bottom element* or a term of the form $c(t_1, t_2, \ldots, t_n)$ where c is called a *constructor*. The body shows type conditions on proper subterms of the argument.

Note here that the set of terms is prescribed by type predicates. The set of all terms t such that the execution of $p(t)$ succeeds is called the *type* of p, and denoted by $\underline{p}$.

Example 3.1.1 Let the definition of a type num be

> **type**.
> num(0).
> num(suc(X)) :- num(X).
> **end**.

Then $\underline{num}$ is a set $\{0, suc(0), suc(suc(0)), \ldots\}$. Note that terms in each type are not necessarily ground, since the execution of $p(t)$ sometimes succeeds without instantiation of variables in t. For example, we include $[X]$ in $\underline{list}$, since the execution of $list([X])$ succeeds without instantiation of the variable X.

Suppose there are k type predicates $p_1, p_2, \ldots, p_k$ defined using the **type** constructs such that $\underline{p_1}, \underline{p_2}, \ldots, \underline{p_k}$ are disjoint modulo renaming variables. A *type* is one of the following $k + 2$ sets of terms.

$\underline{any}$: the set of all terms,
$\underline{p_1}$: the set of all terms satisfying the type definition of p_1,
$\underline{p_2}$: the set of all terms satisfying the type definition of p_2,

$\quad \vdots$

$\underline{p_k}$: the set of all terms satisfying the type definition of p_k,
$\emptyset$: the empty set.

(2) Polymorphic Types

We extend the "**type**" construct in the above to a polymorphic one, e.g.,

    type.
      list$\langle\alpha\rangle$([ ]).
      list$\langle\alpha\rangle$([A|L]) :- α(A), list$\langle\alpha\rangle$(L).
    end.

In the definition of *numlist* in Section 1, its body, i.e., num(A) and numlist(L), is its type condition. In the definition above, the *num* is parameterized to α and *numlist* is to *list*$\langle\alpha\rangle$.

In general, we introduce polymorphic types by parameterizing the predicates of their type conditions (directly or indirectly) as follows:

$$p\langle\alpha_1,\alpha_2,\ldots,\alpha_k\rangle(b_1).$$
$$\vdots$$
$$p\langle\alpha_1,\alpha_2,\ldots,\alpha_k\rangle(b_m).$$
$$p\langle\alpha_1,\alpha_2,\ldots,\alpha_k\rangle(c_1(X_{11},X_{12},\ldots,X_{1n_1})) :- p_{11}(X_{11}),p_{12}(X_{12}),\ldots,p_{1n_1}(X_{1n_1}).$$
$$\vdots$$
$$p\langle\alpha_1,\alpha_2,\ldots,\alpha_k\rangle(c_h(X_{h1},X_{h2},\ldots,X_{hn_h})) :- p_{h1}(X_{h1}),p_{h2}(X_{h2}),\ldots,p_{hn_h}(X_{hn_h}).$$

where p is a new polymorphic type predicate, b_i is a new constant called *bottom element*, c_i is a new function symbol called *constructors*, p_{ij} is either a type predicate of an arbitrary polymorphic (or monomorphic) type (including <u>any</u>) or type parameter α_l.

A type definition obtained from $p\langle\alpha_1,\ldots,\alpha_k\rangle$ by substituting type predicates $u_1,\ldots,u_k$ for parameters $\alpha_1,\ldots,\alpha_k$ is called an *instance of* $p\langle\alpha_1,\ldots,\alpha_k\rangle$, and denoted by $p\langle u_1,\ldots,u_k\rangle$. The corresponding set of terms is called a *type instance of* $p\langle\alpha_1,\ldots,\alpha_k\rangle$, and denoted by $\underline{p}\langle u_1,u_2,\ldots,u_k\rangle$. The set of terms $\underline{p}\langle any,\ldots,any\rangle$ is denoted simply by $\underline{p}$. The parameter α_i is called a *type parameter*, and the part enclosed with '$\langle$' and '$\rangle$' is called the *parameter part*.

Example 3.1.2 Let <u>num</u> be defined as before. Then, we can express a list of numbers, *numlist* in Section 1, as a type instance of *list*$\langle\alpha\rangle$, i.e., the set of all lists of <u>num</u> is denoted by <u>list</u>$\langle\underline{num}\rangle$, where a polymorphic type definition of *list*$\langle\alpha\rangle$ is

      list$\langle\alpha\rangle$([ ]).
      list$\langle\alpha\rangle$([A|L]) :- α(A), list$\langle\alpha\rangle$(L).

<u>list</u>$\langle any\rangle$ means <u>list</u> of a monomorphic definition, and <u>num</u> can't be denoted by any other expressions. A list of lists of <u>num</u> is denoted by <u>list</u>$\langle\underline{list}\langle\underline{num}\rangle\rangle$.

Example 3.1.3 Suppose that <u>list</u> is defined in the same way as Example 3.1.2. A binary tree whose node is labeled with some term in <u>list</u> is defined as follows.

      ltree$\langle\alpha\rangle$(ϕ).
      ltree$\langle\alpha\rangle$(ltr(L,N,R)) :- ltree$\langle\alpha\rangle$(L), list$\langle\alpha\rangle$(N), ltree$\langle\alpha\rangle$(R).

Then, a term in the type <u>ltree</u>$\langle\underline{num}\rangle$ is a binary tree with its node labeled with a term in <u>list</u>$\langle\underline{num}\rangle$.

In general, polymorphic types $\underline{p}\langle\ldots\rangle$ and $\underline{p}\langle\ldots\rangle$ are not necessarily disjoint, while $\underline{p_i}\langle\ldots\rangle$ and $\underline{p_i}\langle\ldots\rangle$ are disjoint whenever p_i and p_j are different type predicates. For example, <u>list</u>$\langle\underline{num}\rangle$ and <u>list</u>$\langle any\rangle$ are not disjoint, and <u>list</u>$\langle\underline{num}\rangle$ and <u>list</u>$\langle\underline{list}\rangle$ are disjoint.

(3) Orderings of Polymorphic Types

Suppose that there are k type predicates $p_1,p_2,\ldots,p_k$ such that $\underline{p_1},\underline{p_2},\ldots,\underline{p_k}$ are disjoint. Then, a type is either <u>any</u>, some type instance of $p_1\langle\mathcal{A}_1\rangle,p_2\langle\mathcal{A}_2\rangle,\ldots,p_k\langle\mathcal{A}_k\rangle$ or $\emptyset$, where <u>any</u> is the set of all terms, $\mathcal{A}_i$ is a sequence of type parameters, and $\emptyset$ is the empty set.

Polymorphic types are ordered in two different ways. One is the instantiation ordering. A type instance $\underline{p}\langle u_1,\ldots,u_m\rangle$ is said to be *smaller than* a type instance $\underline{q}\langle v_1,\ldots,v_n\rangle$ w.r.t. *the instantiation ordering* iff any terms in $\underline{q}\langle v_1,\ldots,v_n\rangle$ are instances of terms in $\underline{p}\langle u_1,\ldots,u_m\rangle$, and denoted by $\underline{p\langle u_1,\ldots,u_m\rangle} \preceq \underline{q\langle v_1,\ldots,v_n\rangle}$. The instantiation ordering between polymorphic types is defined as follows:

(a) $\underline{any} \preceq \underline{p\langle u_1,u_2,\ldots,u_m\rangle}$

(b) $\underline{p\langle u_1,u_2,\ldots,u_m\rangle} \preceq \underline{\emptyset}$

(c) $\underline{p\langle u_1,u_2,\ldots,u_m\rangle}$ and $\underline{q\langle v_1,v_2,\ldots,v_n\rangle}$ are incomparable when p and q are different type predicates,

(d) when p and q are the same type predicate,

   (i) $\underline{p\langle u_1,u_2,\ldots,u_m\rangle} \preceq \underline{q\langle v_1,v_2,\ldots,v_n\rangle}$, when $\underline{u_j}$ and $\underline{v_j}$ are the same type or $\underline{u_j} \preceq \underline{v_j}$ for any $\underline{u_j}$ and $\underline{v_j}$,

   (ii) $\underline{q\langle v_1,v_2,\ldots,v_n\rangle} \preceq \underline{p\langle u_1,u_2,\ldots,u_m\rangle}$ when $\underline{u_j}$ and $\underline{v_j}$ are the same type or $\underline{v_j} \preceq \underline{u_j}$ for any $\underline{u_j}$ and $\underline{v_j}$,

   (iii) otherwise, $\underline{p\langle u_1,u_2,\ldots,u_m\rangle}$ and $\underline{q\langle v_1,v_2,\ldots,v_n\rangle}$ are incomparable.

Example 3.1.4 Let *num* and *list* be defined as before. Then,

$\underline{list} \preceq \underline{list\langle num\rangle}$,

$\underline{list\langle list\rangle} \preceq \underline{list\langle list\langle num\rangle\rangle}$.

$\underline{list\langle list\rangle}$ and $\underline{list\langle num\rangle}$ are incomparable.

Example 3.1.5 Suppose that the type definition of *dtree* is

dtree$\langle\alpha_1,\alpha_2\rangle$(dlf(A,B)) :- α_1(A), α_2(B).

dtree$\langle\alpha_1,\alpha_2\rangle$(dtr(L,A,B,R)) :- dtree$\langle\alpha_1,\alpha_2\rangle$(L), α_1(A), α_2(B), dtree$\langle\alpha_1,\alpha_2\rangle$(R).

Then, $\underline{dtree\langle list,num\rangle}$ and $\underline{dtree\langle num,list\rangle}$ are incomparable.

The other ordering is the set inclusion ordering. A type instance $\underline{p\langle u_1,\ldots,u_m\rangle}$ is said to be *smaller than* a type instance $\underline{q\langle v_1,\ldots,v_n\rangle}$ w.r.t. *the set inclusion ordering* iff $\underline{p\langle u_1,\ldots,u_m\rangle}$ is included in $\underline{q\langle v_1,\ldots,v_n\rangle}$, and denoted by $\underline{p\langle u_1,\ldots,u_m\rangle} \subseteq \underline{q\langle v_1,\ldots,v_n\rangle}$.

Example 3.1.6 Let *num* and *list* be defined as before. Then,

$\underline{list\langle num\rangle} \subseteq \underline{list}$,

$\underline{list\langle list\langle num\rangle\rangle} \subseteq \underline{list\langle list\rangle}$.

$\underline{list\langle list\rangle}$ and $\underline{list\langle num\rangle}$ are disjoint.

(4) Join and Union of Polymorphic Types

We define the join and union operations of polymorphic types reformulating the monomorphic one. The join operation w.r.t. the instantiation ordering, denoted by $\vee$, is defined as follows:

$$\underline{p\langle u_1,\ldots,u_m\rangle} \vee \underline{q\langle v_1,\ldots,v_n\rangle} = \begin{cases} \underline{p\langle u_1,\ldots,u_m\rangle}, & \text{when } \underline{q\langle v_1,\ldots,v_n\rangle} \text{ is } \underline{any}; \\ \underline{q\langle v_1,\ldots,v_n\rangle}, & \text{when } \underline{p\langle u_1,\ldots,u_m\rangle} \text{ is } \underline{any}; \\ \underline{\emptyset}, & \text{when } p \text{ and } q \text{ are different, or} \\ & \text{either } \underline{p\langle u_1,\ldots,u_m\rangle} \text{ or} \\ & \underline{q\langle v_1,\ldots,v_n\rangle} \text{ is } \underline{\emptyset}; \\ \underline{p\langle\ldots,u_i \vee v_i,\ldots\rangle}, & \text{when } p \text{ and } q \text{ are identical.} \end{cases}$$

Similarly, the union operation w.r.t. the set inclusion ordering, denoted by $\cup$, is defined as follows:

$$\underline{p\langle u_1,\ldots,u_m\rangle} \cup \underline{q\langle v_1,\ldots,v_n\rangle} = \begin{cases} \underline{p\langle u_1,\ldots,u_m\rangle}, & \text{when } \underline{q\langle v_1,\ldots,v_n\rangle} \text{ is } \underline{\emptyset}; \\ \underline{q\langle v_1,\ldots,v_n\rangle}, & \text{when } \underline{p\langle u_1,\ldots,u_m\rangle} \text{ is } \underline{\emptyset}; \\ \underline{any}, & \text{when } p \text{ and } q \text{ are different, or} \\ & \text{either } \underline{p\langle u_1,\ldots,u_m\rangle} \text{ or} \\ & \underline{q\langle v_1,\ldots,v_n\rangle} \text{ is } \underline{any}; \\ \underline{p\langle\ldots,u_i \cup v_i,\ldots\rangle}, & \text{when } p \text{ and } q \text{ are identical.} \end{cases}$$

Example 3.1.7 Let *num* and *list* be defined as before. Then,

$$\underline{list\langle num\rangle} \vee \underline{list\langle any\rangle} = \underline{list\langle num\rangle}$$
$$\underline{list\langle list\rangle} \vee \underline{list\langle num\rangle} = \emptyset$$
$$\underline{list\langle list\rangle} \cup \underline{list\langle num\rangle} = \underline{list\langle any\rangle}$$

Example 3.1.8 Let $\underline{dtree}\langle\alpha_1, \alpha_2\rangle$ be defined as before.

$$\underline{dtree\langle any, num\rangle} \vee \underline{dtree\langle num, any\rangle} = \underline{dtree\langle num, num\rangle},$$
$$\underline{dtree\langle any, num\rangle} \cup \underline{dtree\langle num, any\rangle} = \underline{dtree\langle any, any\rangle}.$$

(5) Polymorphic Type Inference

A *type substitution* μ is an expression of the form

$$<X_1 \Leftarrow \underline{p_1}, X_2 \Leftarrow \underline{p_2}, \ldots, X_l \Leftarrow \underline{p_l}>,$$

where $\underline{p_1}, \underline{p_2}, \ldots, \underline{p_l}$ are types. The type assigned to variable X by type substitution μ is denoted by $\mu(X)$. We stipulate that a type substitution assigns $\underline{any}$, the minimum element w.r.t. the instantiation ordering, to variable X when X is not in the domain of the type substitution explicitly. Hence the empty type substitution $<>$ assigns $\underline{any}$ to every variable.

Let A be an atom in the body of some clause in $P \cup \{G\}$ and μ be a type substitution of the form

$$<X_1 \Leftarrow \underline{p_1}, X_2 \Leftarrow \underline{p_2}, \ldots, X_l \Leftarrow \underline{p_l}>.$$

Then $A\mu$ is called a *type-abstracted atom*, and denotes the set of all atoms obtained by replacing each variable X_i in A with a term in $\underline{p_i}$. Two type-abstracted atoms $A\mu$ and $B\nu$ are said to be unifiable when $A\mu \cap B\nu \neq \emptyset$. A list of type-abstracted atoms $[A_1\mu_1, A_2\mu_2, \ldots, A_n\mu_n]$ denotes the set union $\cup_{i=1}^n A_i\mu_i$. Similarly, $G\mu$ (or the pair (G, μ)) is called a *type-abstracted negative clause*, and denotes the set of negative clauses obtained by replacing each X_i in G with a term in $\underline{p_i}$.

When G is of the form "$A_1, A_2, \ldots, A_n$", the type-abstracted atom $A_1\mu$ is called a *leftmost type-abstracted* atom of $G\mu$.

The purpose of type inference is to obtain type information on goals appearing in the top-down execution of a given goal. Let us formalize the top-down execution here. The top-down Prolog interpreter is modeled by OLD resolution. The OLD resolution is defined using only search trees, called OLD trees. (Because there is neither a solution table nor an association, we have no distinction of solution nodes and lookup nodes. All nodes are solution nodes.) The relation between a node and its child nodes in OLD trees is specified in the same way as the OLDT resolution in Section 2.1, except that we have no resolution using lookup nodes and solution tables, hence no manipulation of solution tables and associations.

An atom A appearing at the leftmost of the label of a node in some OLD tree of G is called *calling pattern of G*. Note that any calling pattern of G is an instance of some atom in the body of a clause in $P \cup \{G\}$. Each calling pattern corresponds to some key in the solution table of OLDT structure.

A solution $A\tau$ of a subrefutation in an OLD tree of G is called an *exiting pattern of G*. Note that any exiting pattern of G is also an instance of some atom in the body of a clause in $P \cup \{G\}$. Each exiting pattern corresponds to some solution in the solution lists of the OLDT structure.

Let $G\mu$ be a type-abstracted negative clause, $\mathcal{C}(G\mu)$ be the set of all calling patterns of negative clauses in $G\mu$ and $\mathcal{E}(G\mu)$ be the set of all exiting patterns of negative clauses in $G\mu$. The *type inference w.r.t. $G\mu$* is the problem to compute

(a) some list of type-abstracted atoms which is a superset of $\mathcal{C}(G\mu)$,

(b) some list of type-abstracted atoms which is a superset of $\mathcal{E}(G\mu)$.

3.2 Abstract Hybrid Interpretation for Polymorphic Type Inference
3.2.1 OLDT Structure for Type Inference

A *search tree for type inference* is a tree with its nodes labeled with a pair of a (generalized) negative clause and a type substitution. (For brevity, we will sometimes omit the term "for type inference" hereafter in Section 3.) A *search tree of* (G, μ) is a search tree whose root node is labeled with (G, μ). The clause part of each pair is a sequence "$\alpha_1, \alpha_2, \ldots, \alpha_n$" consisting of either atoms in the body of $P \cup \{G\}$ or call-exit markers of the form $[A, \mu, \eta]$. A *refutation of* (G, μ) is a path in a search tree of (G, μ) from the root to a node labeled with $(\square, \nu)$. The *answer substitution of the refutation* is the type substitution ν, and the *solution of the refutation* is $G\nu$.

A *solution table for type inference* is a set of entries. Each entry consists of the *key* and the *solution list*. The key is a type-abstracted atom. The solution list is a list of type-abstracted atoms, called *solutions*, whose solutions are all greater than the key w.r.t. the instantiation ordering.

Let Tr be a search tree whose nodes labeled with non-null clauses are classified into either *solution nodes* or *lookup nodes*, and let Tb be a solution table. An *association for type inference* of Tr and Tb is a set of pointers pointing from each lookup node in Tr into some solution list in Tb such that the leftmost type-abstracted atom of the lookup node's label and the key of the solution list are variants of each other.

An *OLDT structure for type inference* is a three-part structure of a search tree, a solution table and an association. The relation between a node and its child nodes in a search tree is specified by *OLDT resolution for type inference* in Section 3.2.3

3.2.2 Overestimation of Data Types

Because the purpose of type inference is to compute supersets of the sets of calling patterns and exiting patterns using lists of type-abstracted atoms, we need to overestimate them somehow by manipulating type-abstracted atoms. We would like to do it by specifying the operations for type inference corresponding to those at step (A),(B) and (C) in Figure 2.2.1. In order to specify them, we need to consider the following situation: Let A be an atom, $X_1, X_2, \ldots, X_k$ all the variables in A, μ a type substitution of the form
$$< X_1 \Leftarrow \underline{p_1}, X_2 \Leftarrow \underline{p_2}, \ldots, X_k \Leftarrow \underline{p_k} >,$$
B an atom, $Y_1, Y_2, \ldots, Y_l$ all the variables in B, and ν a type substitution of the form
$$< Y_1 \Leftarrow \underline{q_1}, Y_2 \Leftarrow \underline{q_2}, \ldots, Y_l \Leftarrow \underline{q_l} >.$$
Then

   (a) How can we know whether $A\mu$ and $B\nu$ are unifiable, i.e., whether there is an atom in $A\mu \cap B\nu$?

   (b) If there is such an atom that $A\sigma = B\tau$, what terms are expected to be assigned to each Y_j by τ?

Example 3.2.1 The following two type-abstracted atoms
$$p(L_1, suc(N_1)) < L_1 \Leftarrow \underline{list\langle num \rangle}, N_1 \Leftarrow \underline{num} >,$$
$$p([X_2|L_2], N_2) < X_2 \Leftarrow \underline{any}, L_2 \Leftarrow \underline{any}, N_2 \Leftarrow \underline{any} >$$
are unifiable. Then, the common atom is of the form $p([X|L], suc(N))$, and terms in $\underline{num}$, $\underline{list\langle num \rangle}$ and $\underline{num}$ must be assigned to variables X, L and N.

(1) Overestimation of Unifiability

When two type-abstracted atoms $A\mu$ and $B\nu$ are unifiable, two atoms A and B must be unifiable in the usual sense. Let η be an m.g.u. of A and B of the form
$$< X_1 \Leftarrow t_1, X_2 \Leftarrow t_2, \ldots, X_k \Leftarrow t_k, Y_1 \Leftarrow s_1, Y_2 \Leftarrow s_2, \ldots, Y_l \Leftarrow s_l >.$$
If we can overestimate the type assigned to each occurrence of Z in t_i from the type substitution μ and that of Z in s_j from the type substitution ν, we can overestimate the type assigned to the

variable Z by taking the join $\vee$ w.r.t. the instantiation ordering for all occurrences of Z. If it is the emptyset $\emptyset$ for some variable, we can't expect that there exists an atom $A\sigma = B\tau$ in $A\mu \cap B\nu$.

When a term t containing an occurrence of variable Z is instantiated to a term in $\underline{p}$, we compute a type set containing all instances of the occurrence of Z as follows and denote it by $Z/ <t[Z] \Leftarrow \underline{p}>$.

$$
Z/ <t[Z] \Leftarrow \underline{p}> = \begin{cases} \underline{p}, & \text{when } t \text{ is } Z; \\ \underline{any}, & \text{when } \underline{p} \text{ is } any; \\ \overline{Z/ <t_i \Leftarrow \underline{p_i}>}, & \text{when } t \text{ is of the form } c(t_1,\ldots,t_n), \\ & Z \text{ is in } t_i, \\ & \underline{p} \text{ is a type } \underline{p}\langle u_1,\ldots,u_m\rangle, \\ & c \text{ is a constructor of } p\langle \alpha_1,\ldots,\alpha_m\rangle \text{ and} \\ & \underline{p_i} \text{ is a type assigned to } t_i; \\ \emptyset & \text{otherwise.} \end{cases}
$$

Example 3.2.2 Let num and $list$ be defined as before. Then,

$$A/ <[A|L] \Leftarrow \underline{list\langle num\rangle} > = \underline{num},$$
$$L/ <[A|L] \Leftarrow \underline{list\langle num\rangle} > = \underline{list\langle num\rangle}.$$

If we would like to check the unifiability of type-abstracted atoms $A\mu$ and $B\nu$ exactly, i.e., would like a procedure returning true *if and only if* they are unifiable, we can check it using the estimation $Z/ <t[Z] \Leftarrow \underline{p}>$. The exact unifiability check, however, takes more computational time because it can't be reduced to the unifiability of terms. But, if we would like just to overestimate the unifiability, i.e., would like a procedure returning true *if* they are unifiable, we may use the unifiability check of A and B instead of the more time-consuming one.

Example 3.2.3 We can check the unifiability of $p(X) <X \Leftarrow \underline{list} >$ and $p(suc(Y)) <Y \Leftarrow \underline{list} >$ by computing $Z/ < suc(Z) \Leftarrow \underline{list} >= \emptyset$ and $Z/ < Z \Leftarrow \underline{list} >= \underline{list}$, because an m.g.u. of $p(X)$ and $p(suc(Y))$ is $<X \Leftarrow suc(Z), Y \Leftarrow Z>$. If we use the unifiability check of $p(X)$ and $p(suc(Y))$ instead of the exact one, we would consider these type-abstracted atoms unifiable.

(2) One Way Propagation of Type Substitutions

Recall the situation we are considering. First, we will restrict our attentions to the case where $\nu =<>$. Suppose there is an atom $A\sigma = B\tau$ in $A\mu \cap B <>$. Then, what terms are expected to be assigned to variables in B by τ?

As we have just shown, we can overestimate the type assigned to the variable Z appearing in the m.g.u. η of A and B due to the type substitution μ. By collecting these type assignments for all variables, we can overestimate the type substitution λ for the variables in $t_1, t_2, \ldots, t_k$ substituted by the m.g.u. η. Then, if we can overestimate the type assigned to s_j, from the type substitution λ obtained above, we can obtain the type substitution ν'

$$<Y_1 \Leftarrow \underline{q_1'}, Y_2 \Leftarrow \underline{q_2'}, \ldots, Y_l \Leftarrow \underline{q_l'}>$$

by collecting the types for all variables $Y_1, Y_2, \ldots, Y_l$.

When each variable Z in term s is instantiated to a term in $\lambda(Z)$, we compute a type set containing all instances of s as follows and denote it by s/λ.

$$
s/\lambda = \begin{cases}
\emptyset, & \text{when } \lambda(Z) \text{ is } \emptyset \text{ for some } Z \text{ in } s; \\
\lambda(Z), & \text{when } s \text{ is a variable } Z; \\
\underline{q}\langle \emptyset, \ldots, \emptyset \rangle, & \text{when } s \text{ is a bottom element of} \\
& \quad q\langle \alpha_1, \alpha_2, \ldots, \alpha_m \rangle; \\
\underline{q}\langle \underline{u_1}, \ldots, \underline{u_m} \rangle & \text{when } s \text{ is of the form } c(s_1, \ldots, s_n), \\
& \quad c \text{ is a constructor of } q\langle \alpha_1, \ldots, \alpha_m \rangle \text{ and} \\
& \quad s_i/\lambda \subseteq \underline{q_i}, \text{ for any } s_i \ (1 \le i \le n), \\
& \quad \text{where } \underline{q_i} \text{ is the type condition of} \\
& \quad \text{the } i\text{-th argument of } c \text{ in } \underline{q}\langle \underline{any}, \ldots, \underline{any} \rangle, \\
& \quad u_j \text{ is a type obtained as below;} \\
\underline{any}, & \text{otherwise.}
\end{cases}
$$

Let q_i' $(1 \le i \le n)$ be the type condition of the i-th argument of c in $p\langle \alpha_1, \alpha_2, \ldots, \alpha_m \rangle$. Then, for all occurrences of a parameter α_j in all q_i''s, u_j $(1 \le j \le m)$ is a union w.r.t. the set inclusion ordering of the types. Each of these types is s_i/λ when an occurrence appears as a predicate of q_i', the corresponding type in a parameter part of s_i/λ when an occurrence appears in a parameter part of q_i'.

Example 3.2.4 Let num and $list$ be defined as before. Then,

$[\,]/\lambda = \underline{list}\langle \emptyset \rangle$, for any type substitution λ,

$[A|L]/ <A \Leftarrow \underline{num}, L \Leftarrow \underline{list}\langle \underline{num} \rangle > = \underline{list}\langle \underline{num} \rangle$,

$[A|L]/ <A \Leftarrow \underline{num}, L \Leftarrow \underline{list}\langle \underline{any} \rangle > = \underline{list}\langle \underline{any} \rangle$.

Let λ be a type substitution $\quad <A \Leftarrow \underline{num}, B \Leftarrow \underline{list}, L \Leftarrow \underline{list}\langle \emptyset \rangle >$.

Then, $[A|L]/\lambda$ is $\underline{list}\langle \underline{num} \rangle$ and $[B|L]/\lambda$ is $\underline{list}\langle \underline{list} \rangle$, but $[A, B|L]/\lambda$ and $[A|B]/\lambda$ are $\underline{list}\langle \underline{any} \rangle$.

Example 3.2.5 Let $\underline{tree}$ be defined as follows:

$\text{tree}\langle \alpha \rangle(\psi)$.

$\text{tree}\langle \alpha \rangle(\text{tr}(\text{L,N,R})) :- \text{tree}\langle \alpha \rangle(\text{L}), \alpha(\text{N}), \text{tree}\langle \alpha \rangle(\text{R}).$

and λ be a type substitution

$$<A \Leftarrow \underline{tree}\langle \underline{num} \rangle, B \Leftarrow \underline{list}, C \Leftarrow \underline{tree}\langle \underline{list} \rangle >.$$

And let $\alpha^{(1)}, \alpha^{(2)}$ and $\alpha^{(3)}$ be occurrences of the parameter α at $\text{tree}\langle \alpha \rangle(\text{L}), \alpha(\text{N})$ and $\text{tree}\langle \alpha \rangle(\text{R})$ respectively. Suppose that we compute $\text{tr}(\psi, B, C)/\lambda$. Then, the type obtained from $\alpha^{(1)}$ is $\emptyset$, because $\alpha^{(1)}$ appears in a parameter part of the type condition of the 1st argument, i.e., $\text{tree}\langle \alpha^{(1)} \rangle$, and ψ/λ is $\underline{tree}\langle \emptyset \rangle$. The type obtained from $\alpha^{(3)}$ is $\underline{list}$, because $\alpha^{(3)}$ appears in a parameter part of the type condition of the 3rd argument, i.e., $\text{tree}\langle \alpha_2 \rangle$, and C/λ is $\underline{tree}\langle \underline{list} \rangle$. The type obtained from $\alpha^{(2)}$ is B/λ, i.e., $\underline{list}$, because $\alpha^{(2)}$ appears as the predicate of the type condition of the 2nd argument. The union of these types is $\underline{list}$, therefore

$$\text{tr}(\psi, \text{B,C})/\lambda = \underline{tree}\langle \underline{list} \rangle.$$

Now suppose that we compute $\text{tr}(A, B, C)/\lambda$. The types obtained from $\alpha^{(1)}, \alpha^{(2)}, \alpha^{(3)}$ are $\underline{num}$, $\underline{list}$, $\underline{list}$ respectively because A/λ, B/λ, C/λ are $\underline{tree}\langle \underline{num} \rangle$, $\underline{list}$, $\underline{tree}\langle \underline{list} \rangle$ respectively. Then, because the union of these types is $\underline{any}$,

$$\text{tr}(A, B, C)/\lambda = \underline{tree}\langle \underline{any} \rangle.$$

Let A, B be atoms, μ a type substitution for the variables in A, and η an m.g.u. of A and B. The type substitution for the variables in B, that is obtained from μ and η using $Z/ <t[Z] \Leftarrow t>$ and s/λ above, is denoted by $propagate(\mu, \eta)$. (Note that $propagate(\mu, \eta)$ depends on μ and η.)

(3) Overestimation of Type Substitutions

As for the operation at step (A) for type inference, we can adopt the one-way propagation

$$propagate(\mu, \eta),$$

since the destination side type substitution is $<>$. As for the operations at step (B) and (C) for type inference where the destination side type substitution is not necessarily equal to $<>$, we can adopt the join w.r.t. the instantiation ordering

$$\mu \vee propagate(\nu, \eta)$$

i.e., elementwise join of the type assigned by the previous type substitution and the one by the one-way propagation.

3.2.3 OLDT Resolution for Type Inference

The relation between a node and its child nodes of a search tree is specified by *OLDT resolution for type inference* as follows.

A node of OLDT structure (Tr, Tb, As) labeled with $(\text{“}\alpha_1, \alpha_2, \ldots, \alpha_n\text{”}, \mu)$ is said to be *OLDT resolvable* $(n \geq 1)$ when it satisfies either of the following conditions.
(a) The node is a terminal solution node of Tr and there is some definite clause "B_0 :- $B_1, B_2, \ldots, B_m$" $(m \geq 0)$ in program P such that α_1 and B_0 are unifiable, say by an m.g.u. η.
(b) The node is a lookup node of Tr and there is some type-abstracted atom $B\nu$ in the associated solution list of the lookup node. Let η be the renaming of B to α_1.

The precise algorithm of OLDT resolution for type inference is shown in Figure 3.2.1. Note that the operations at steps (A), (B) and (C) in Figure 2.2.1 are modified.

OLDT-resolve(($\text{“}\alpha_1, \alpha_2, \ldots, \alpha_n\text{”}, \mu$) : label) :label ;
    $i := 0$;
    case
        when a solution node is OLDT resolved with "B_0 :- $B_1, B_2, \ldots, B_m$" in P
            let η be the m.g.u. of α_1 and B_0 ;
            let G_0 be a negative clause "$B_1, B_2, \ldots, B_m, [\![\alpha_1, \mu, \eta]\!], \alpha_2, \ldots, \alpha_n$";
            let ν_0 be $propagate(\mu, \eta)$ — (A)
        when a lookup node is OLDT resolved with "$B\nu$" in Tb
            let η be the renaming of B to α_1 ;
            let G_0 be a negative clause "$\alpha_2, , \ldots, \alpha_n$" ;
            let ν_0 be $\mu \vee propagate(\nu, \eta)$;   — (B)
    endcase
    while the leftmost of G_i is a call-exit marker $[\![A_{i+1}, \mu_{i+1}, \eta_{i+1}]\!]$ **do**
        let G_{i+1} be G_i other than the leftmost call-exit marker ;
        let ν_{i+1} be $\mu_{i+1} \vee propagate(\nu_i, \eta_{i+1})$;   — (C)
        add $A_{i+1}\nu_{i+1}$ to the last of $A_{i+1}\mu_{i+1}$'s solution list if it is not in it ;
        $i := i + 1$;
    endwhile
    $(G_{new}, \mu_{new}) := (G_i, \nu_i)$;
    return (G_{new}, μ_{new}).

Figure 3.2.1 OLDT Resolution for Type Inference

A node labeled with $(\text{“}\alpha_1, \alpha_2, \ldots, \alpha_n\text{”}, \mu)$ is a lookup node when a variant of $\alpha_1\mu$ is a key in the solution table, and a solution node otherwise $(n \geq 0)$.

The *initial OLDT structure*, *immediate extension of OLDT structure*, *extension of OLDT structure*, *answer substitution of OLDT refutation* and *solution of OLDT refutation* are defined similarly as in Section 2.2.

Remark. Our algorithm might generate an infinite number of solutions, but we can prevent it from infinite looping by always replacing types at nesting level d in type substitutions, i.e., types inside d-fold angle bracket "$\langle \cdots \langle \cdots \rangle \cdots \rangle$", with <u>any</u>.

3.3 An Example of Polymorphic Type Inference

We show a simple example of the polymorphic type inference. Recall the following definition of *map-plus* and *plus*.

map-plus([ ],M,[ ]).
map-plus([A|L],M,[C|N]) :- plus(A,M,C), map-plus(L,M,N).
plus(0,Y,Y).
plus(suc(X),Y,suc(Z)) :- plus(X,Y,Z).

Then the polymorphic type inference of *map-plus*(X_0, Y_0, Z_0) proceeds as follows, when it is executed with the second argument instantiated to a number.

First, the initial OLDT structure is generated. The root node is a solution node labeled with ("*map-plus*(L_0, M_0, N_0)", $< M \Leftarrow \underline{num} >$).

Secondly, the root node ("*map-plus*(L_0, M_0, N_0)", $< M \Leftarrow \underline{num} >$) is OLDT resolved using the program. The left child node gives a solution *map-plus*$(L_0, M_0, N_0) < M_0 \Leftarrow \underline{num}, L_0, N_0 \Leftarrow \underline{list}\langle \emptyset \rangle >$. The right child node is a solution node labeled with ("*plus*(A_2, M_2, C_2),*map-plus*(L_2, M_2, N_2)", $< M_2 \Leftarrow \underline{num} >$). (From now on, the quantities inside call-exit markers are omitted due to limited space so that they are depicted simply by $[ ]$.)

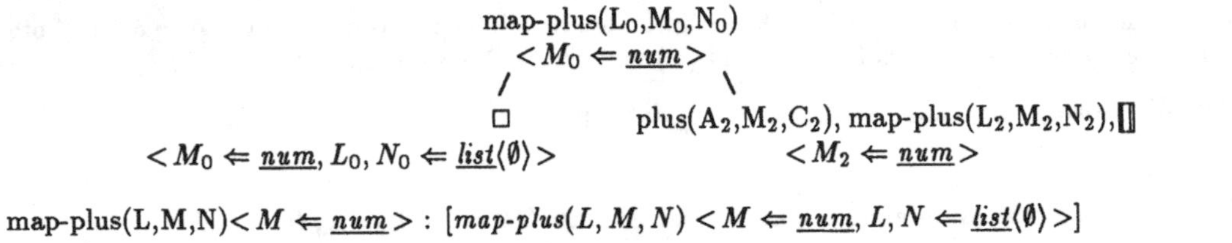

$$map\text{-}plus(L_0,M_0,N_0)$$
$$< M_0 \Leftarrow \underline{num} >$$

$$\square \qquad plus(A_2,M_2,C_2), map\text{-}plus(L_2,M_2,N_2), [ ]$$
$$< M_0 \Leftarrow \underline{num}, L_0, N_0 \Leftarrow \underline{list}\langle \emptyset \rangle > \qquad < M_2 \Leftarrow \underline{num} >$$

map-plus(L,M,N)$< M \Leftarrow \underline{num} >$: [$map\text{-}plus(L, M, N) < M \Leftarrow \underline{num}, L, N \Leftarrow \underline{list}\langle \emptyset \rangle >$]

Figure 3.3.1 Polymorphic Type Inference by Hybrid interpretation at Step 2

Thirdly, the solution node is OLDT resolved using the program. The left child node is a lookup node labeled with ("*map-plus*(L_2, M_2, N_2)", $< M_2 \Leftarrow \underline{num} >$), which gives a solution *plus*$(A_2, M_2, C_2) < A_2, M_2, C_2 \Leftarrow \underline{num} >$. The right child node is also a lookup node labeled with ("*plus*(A_3, M_3, C_3),*map-plus*(L_2, M_2, N_2)", $< M_3 \Leftarrow \underline{num} >$).

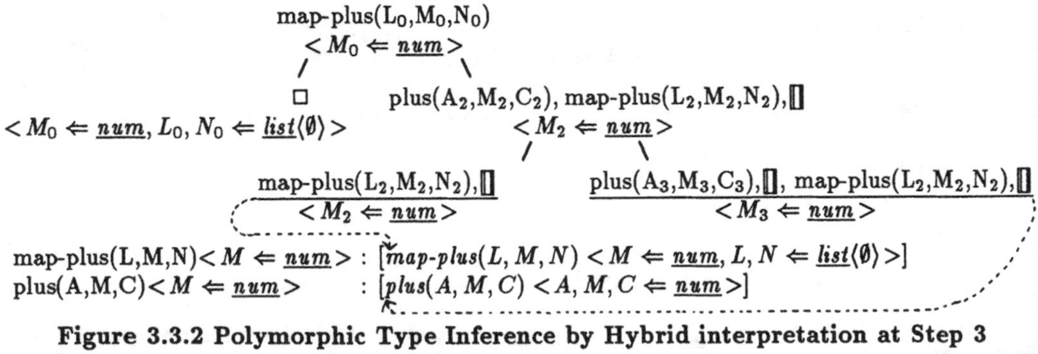

$$map\text{-}plus(L_0,M_0,N_0)$$
$$< M_0 \Leftarrow \underline{num} >$$

$$\square \qquad plus(A_2,M_2,C_2), map\text{-}plus(L_2,M_2,N_2), [ ]$$
$$< M_0 \Leftarrow \underline{num}, L_0, N_0 \Leftarrow \underline{list}\langle \emptyset \rangle > \qquad < M_2 \Leftarrow \underline{num} >$$

$$map\text{-}plus(L_2,M_2,N_2), [ ] \qquad plus(A_3,M_3,C_3), [ ], map\text{-}plus(L_2,M_2,N_2), [ ]$$
$$< M_2 \Leftarrow \underline{num} > \qquad < M_3 \Leftarrow \underline{num} >$$

map-plus(L,M,N)$< M \Leftarrow \underline{num} >$: [$map\text{-}plus(L, M, N) < M \Leftarrow \underline{num}, L, N \Leftarrow \underline{list}\langle \emptyset \rangle >$]
plus(A,M,C)$< M \Leftarrow \underline{num} >$: [$plus(A, M, C) < A, M, C \Leftarrow \underline{num} >$]

Figure 3.3.2 Polymorphic Type Inference by Hybrid interpretation at Step 3

Fourthly, The left lookup node is OLDT resolved further using the solution table. The child node gives a new solution *map-plus*$(L_0, M_0, N_0) < M_0 \Leftarrow \underline{num}, L_0, N_0 \Leftarrow \underline{list}\langle num \rangle >$.

Fifthly, the right lookup node is OLDT resolved using the solution table. The child is a lookup node labeled with ("*map-plus*(L_2, M_2, N_2)", $< M_2 \Leftarrow \underline{num} >$), which gives a solution *plus*$(A_3, M_3, C_3) < A_3, M_3, C_3 \Leftarrow \underline{num} >$.

Lastly, the lookup node is OLDT resolved using the solution table. Because the generated child node gives no new solution, the execution process stops.

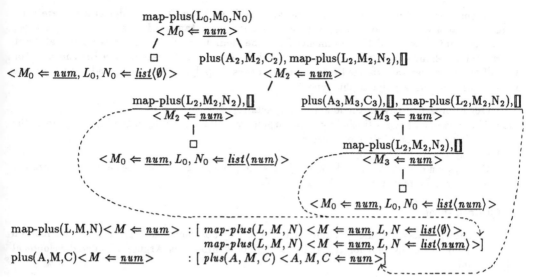

Figure 3.3.3 Polymorphic Type Inference by Hybrid interpretation at Step 6

4. Discussion

Type inference for functional programs has been studied by several researchers, while a few attempts to introduce types into Prolog have been done [1],[9],[10].

Bruynooghe [1] discussed the addition of type and mode information to Prolog in order to increase the reliability and readability of the programs. They made a method which checks the consistency using data flow analysis. Mycroft et al. [10] showed a type system for Prolog based on Milner's type polymorphism [8]. In their system, type declarations are considered as the syntactical restrictions on arguments of predicates, and the consistency between type declarations and programs is checked. Both of their systems are type checking systems, not type inference systems. Their slogan is "Well-typed programs do not go wrong." Note that their notion of "wrong" is independent of success, failure or looping. For example [10], $plus(suc(0), suc(suc(0)), suc(0))$ is well-typed but fails, while $eqnum(foo, foo)$ is ill-typed but succeeds, where $plus$ and $eqnum$ are defined with type declarations by

      type-declaration plus($\underline{num},\underline{num},\underline{num}$).
         plus(0,Y,Y).
         plus(suc(X),Y,suc(Z)) :- plus(X,Y,Z).
      type-declaration eqnum($\underline{num},\underline{num}$).
         eqnum(X,X).

In contrast, Mishra [9] considered types as sets of terms which were described by some regular expressions, and gave an algorithm for inferring types from Prolog programs. He didn't require either type declarations or any other type annotations. He claimed that no atom can succeed when its arguments are not the terms described by the types of its predicate. That is, his slogan is "Ill-typed program can't succeed." But his approach is monomorphic and it is not clear whether his idea can be easily extended to polymorphic cases. Zobel [13] showed the polymorphic approach on the same lines. He described types as rewriting rules, and gave an algorithm which derived the type for each variable in a Prolog clause. He also proved that a goal couldn't succeed if his algorithm couldn't derive a type for some variable in the goal.

In our approach, types are considered as the set of all terms satisfying the definition of type predicates. Although we need to define type predicates, we don't require type declarations. That is, our type definitions are used only to classify a set of all terms (the Herbrand universe) into various sets of terms (types), while Bruynooghe's or Mycroft's type declarations are used to assert that a goal should succeed with each argument instantiated to a term in some type. Our system infers types of the arguments from the definition of the predicates using abstract interpretation. Hence, our approach is closer to Mishra's or Zobel's rather than Bruynooghe's or Mycroft's. Moreover we extended monomorphic types to polymorphic ones, and gave a precise algorithm for inferring polymorphic types.

Our approach is new in the following respects :
(1) The meaning of types (including polymorphic types) is clear due to the introduction of the explicit definition of type predicates.
(2) Our system can infer polymorphic types.
(3) Our system can work on goals of any forms, i.e., the goals whose types are inferred are not necessarily in general form $p(X_1, X_2, \ldots, X_n)$.

5. Conclusions

We have shown a polymorphic type inference method by abstracted interpretation. This method is an element of our system for the analysis of Prolog programs Argus/A under development [3],[4],[5],[6].

Acknowledgments

Our analysis system Argus/A under development is a subproject of the Fifth Generation Computer System(FGCS) "Intelligent Programming System." The authors would like to thank Dr. K. Fuchi (Director of ICOT) for the opportunity of doing this research and Dr. K. Furukawa (Vice Director of ICOT), Dr. T. Yokoi (Former Vice Director of ICOT) and Dr. H. Ito (Chief of ICOT 3rd Laboratory) for their advice and encouragement.

References

[1] Bruynooghe, M., "Adding Redundancy to Obtain More Reliable and More Readable Prolog Programs," Proc. of 1st International Logic Programming Conference, pp. 129-133, 1982.

[2] Cousot, P. and R. Cousot, "Abstract Interpretation : A Unified Lattice Model for Static Analysis of Programs by Construction or Approximation of Fixpoints," Conference Record of the 4th ACM Symposium on Principles of Programming Languages, Los Angeles, pp. 238-252, 1977.

[3] Kanamori, T. and T. Kawamura, "Analyzing Success Patterns of Logic Programs by Abstract Interpretation," ICOT Technical Report TR-279, 1987.

[4] Kanamori, T. and K. Horiuchi, "Detecting Functionality of Logic Programs Based on Abstract Interpretation," ICOT Technical Report, 1987.

[5] Kanamori, T., K. Horiuchi and T. Kawamura, "Detecting Termination of Logic Programs Based on Abstract Interpretation," ICOT Technical Report, 1987.

[6] Maeji, M. and T. Kanamori, "Top-down Zooming Diagnosis of Logic Programs," ICOT Technical Report TR-290, 1987.

[7] Mellish, C. S., "Abstract Interpretation of Prolog Programs," Proc. of 3rd International Conference on Logic Programming, 1986.

[8] Milner, R. "A Theory of Type Polymorphism in Programming," J. Computer and Systems Science, 17, pp. 348-375, 1978.

[9] Mishra, P., "Towards a Theory of Types in Prolog," Proc. of 1984 International Symposium on Logic Programming, pp. 289-298, 1984.

[10] Mycroft, A. and R. A. O'Keefe, "A Polymorphic Type System for Prolog," Artificial Intelligence, 23, pp. 295-307, 1984.

[11] Pereira, L. M., F. C. N. Pereira and D. H. D. Warren, "User's Guide to DECsystem-10 Prolog," Occasional Paper 15, Dept. of Artificial Intelligence, Edinburgh, 1979.

[12] Tamaki, H. and T. Sato, "OLD Resolution with Tabulation," Proc. of 3rd International Conference on Logic Programming, pp. 84-98, London, 1986.

[13] Zobel, J, "Derivation of Polymorphic Types for Prolog," Logic Programming : Proc. of 4th International Conference, pp. 817-838, The MIT Press, 1987.

Proving Partial Correctness of
Guarded Horn Clauses Programs

Masaki Murakami

Institute for New Generation Computer Technology,
Mita Kokusai Building, 21F.
4-28, Mita, 1-Chome, Minato-Ku, Tokyo, 108, Japan

ABSTRACT: Guarded Horn Clauses (GHC) [Ueda 85] is a
parallel programming language based on Horn logic. A
verification method of partial correctness for GHC
programs is discussed here. The author investigated a
Hoare-like axiomatic system for proving partial correctness
of GHC programs. This paper presents fragments of the
axiomatic system. Programs which generate processes
dynamically during the execution or which contain
control of nondeterminism by the guard mechanism are
verified by these systems.

1. Introduction

During the last few years, several parallel programming languages based
on Horn logic, such as PARLOG [Clark 86],   Concurrent Prolog [Shapiro 86]
and Guarded Horn Clauses (GHC) [Ueda 85] have been investigated.   These
languages are designed to represent the notions of processes and to provide
mechanisms for communications and synchronization in the framework of logic
programming.   In these languages, Horn logic is extended in order to describe
these notions. For example, a GHC program consists of a finite set of Horn
clauses with 'guard' parts.   It is not enough in such languages to regard a
program as a set of Horn clauses to give semantics to the program.   For
example, [Takeuchi 86] introduced two GHC programs which are equivalent in the
declarative sense but the results of executions are not identical.
Results of the formal semantics of such languages have been reported in
several sources, particularly the semantics of their synchronization
mechanisms [Ueda 86, Takeuchi 86, Levi 85, 87, Saraswat 85, 87]. However,
most of them are based on the operational or an extension of the
declarative approach.   It is too difficult to apply these semantics to

prove the properties of given programs. On the other hand, several verification methods have been reported for pure Horn logic programming languages, for example, the method which is based on extended execution [Kanamori 86]. However, in most of them, programs which can be proved are 'pure' programs which do not contain any extra logical feature such as the cut '!' operator. In GHC, the synchronization of processes is achieved by the guard part. Nondeterminism of a program is controlled by guard mechanism. Since the result of the execution of programs is affected by guard mechanism control, it does not seem a good way to extend the verification methods for pure Prolog programs to GHC programs.

This paper adopts the axiomatic approach to give a logical framework as a verification method of GHC programs. A Hoare-like axiomatic system for proving the partial correctness of programs is modified and extended for GHC programs. Several verification systems have been reported for traditional parallel programming languages such as communicating sequential processes (CSP) [Saundararajan 84, Murakami 86], but not have been reported for parallel programming languages based on Horn logic. Verification systems for languages such as GHC need to have different features from the verification systems of traditional parallel programming languages. In the systems for traditional programming languages already reported, the number of processes is bounded irrespective to input value before a program is executed and processes cannot be generated dynamically during its execution. It is difficult to formalize in an axiomatic way the programming languages which contain dynamic generation of processes. In GHC, processes are presented as goals, so they are generated dynamically. An example is the program to find the maximum element from a given list in the tournament manner (see Section. 3). A verification system for GHC programs should be powerful enough to prove such program.

The author investigated an axiomatic system for proving partial correctness of GHC programs. This paper presents fragments of the axiomatic system. Section 2 of this paper contains a brief introduction of GHC and a definition of partial correctness. Section 3 introduces a fragment of the axiomatic system with a simple example of proof. It is an elementary part of the system. The section shows how the partial correctness of programs which contain dynamic generation of processes are proved using a kind of induction method. Section 4 presents a refinement of the proof system by which programs with control of nondeterminism by guard mechanisms can be verified.

2. Partial correctness of GHC

2.1 Guarded Horn Clauses

Guarded Horn Clauses (GHC) [Ueda 85] is a parallel logic programming language. For a set of predicate symbols PRED, function symbols FUN and variable symbols VAR, a program of GHC consists of a finite set of guarded clauses. A guarded clause has the form:

$$H :- B1, \cdots, Bn \mid A1, \cdots, Am.$$

where H is called the head of the clause. H, B1, $\cdots$, Bn is the guard part, and A1,$\cdots$,Am is the body part. Note that a clause head is included in a guard. Each Bi (1 $\leq$ i $\leq$ n) has the form 'true', T - S, T $\neq$ S or T< (>) S, where T and S are in the set of terms TERM constructed from FUN and VAR. Each Aj (1 $\leq$ j $\leq$ m) has a form of p(T1,$\cdots$,Tk) or T - S, where p $\in$ PRED and Ti (1$\leq$i$\leq$k) $\in$ TERM. H has the form p(T1,$\cdots$, Tk) and all variables appear in T1, $\cdots$, Tk are distinct. The operator 'l' is called a commitment operator. Note that nested guards are not allowed. A goal clause has the form of a body part and is denoted as:

$$G1, \cdots, Gh$$

where each Gi (1$\leq$i$\leq$h) is called a goal. The computation rule of GHC program is as follows. To execute a program is to refute a given goal by means of input resolution using the clauses forming the program. This can be done in a fully parallel manner i.e. each Gi (1 $\leq$ i $\leq$ h) is solved in parallel and each clause is tested in parallel for each Gi under the following rules.

(a) Solving the guard part: For a goal G and a clause C : H:- B1, $\cdots$, Bn l A1, $\cdots$, Am if G and H can unify without instantiating any variable term in G and B1, $\cdots$, Bn is solved without instantiating any variable in G then the guard part of C succeeds.

(b) Suspend: For a goal G and a clause C if B1, $\cdots$, Bn or unification between G and H cannot succeed without instantiating variable terms in G, then G suspends with C until the variable terms in G are instantiated by some other goal.

(c) Commitment: For a goal G and a clause C, when the guard part of C succeeds, it is first confirmed that no other clause has been

committed for G. If confirmed, C is selected exclusively for the
exeqution. Unification invoked in the active part of clause C cannot
instantiate the goal G until C is committed to G.

A goal which has the form 'true', T - S or T > (<) S is solved as a
built-in predicate.

Example:

The following is an example of a GHC program that takes lists in first
and second arguments as inputs, merges them and returns the result to the
third argument. Lists are denoted using the syntax as DEC-10 Prolog.

```
merge([A!Ix], Iy, O) :- true ! O - [A!Out], merge(Ix, Iy, Out).
merge(Ix, [A!Iy], O) :- true ! O - [A!Out], merge(Ix, Iy, Out).
merge(Ix, [], O) :- true ! Ix - O.
merge([], Iy, O) :- true ! Iy - O.
```

If the goal has the form of:

$$\text{merge}([1,2], V, Z)$$

where V and Z are variable terms, then only the first clause can commit
with this goal and the second and the third clause suspend. The fourth
clause does not match the goal. Thus, non-determinism of the program
is controlled by the guard mechanism. After the first clause is committed, the
subsequent goal has following form:

$$Z - [1!Out], \text{merge}([2], V, Out).$$

□

2.2 Partial Correctness

In GHC, the direction for execution of a program is indicated implicitly by
the guard part. For the example of 'merge(X, Y, Z)' in the previous
section, X and Y are for inputs and Z is for output. In the case of
defining partial correctness, the explicit description of the execution
direction of programs is useful. The description of execution direction of
programs is expressed by annotating each argument in the head parts
with + (input argument) or - (output argument). For a program with annotated

head parts, an invocation of a clause C by a goal G is consistent with the annotation if C is invoked by G with variable terms in all arguments annotated with -. For example, when the 'append' program is annotated as:

```
append(X+, Y+, Z-) :- X = [] | Y = Z.
append(X+, Y+, Z-) :- X = [A|X1] | append(X1, Y, Z1), Z = [A|Z1].
```

then 'append([1, 2], [3, 4], X)' and 'append([a], U, V)' are consistent with the above annotation, and append([1, 2, 3], W, [1, 2, 3, 4, 5])' is not.

In the axiomatic approach to give semantics for conventional programming languages, the partial correctness of a program is represented in a formula like the following.

input condition {program} output condition

The partial correctness of GHC programs is represented in a similar way. Input conditions and output conditions are predicates over the domain on which the program is defined. In this paper, the Herbrand universe constructed from a set of function symbols FUN is taken for the domain. The semantics of these predicates are relations over the Herbrand universe.   An expression representing a set of goal clauses appears in the 'program' part.

Def. 1 : goal form

Let D be a set of guarded clauses. The expression g defined below is said to be a <u>goal form</u>.

$$g = p(t1, \cdots, tn)$$

where p is a n-ary predicate name in PRED which is defined in D, $t1, \cdots,$ tn are terms which are defined from FUN and VAR, and Var. 'Var' is a set of meta variables over TERMS. In this paper, 'variable' means abstract variables appearing in goal forms, which are denoted by lower case letters u, v, $z1$, $z2$, $\cdots$ which are not in VAR. Variable terms appearing during the execution of a program which are in VAR (and in TERM) are denoted by upper case letters U, V, $\cdots$. Elements of VAR appearing in clauses in D are considered as variables for convenience. In this paper, 'term' means an element of TERM. A term containing an element of Var is called a 'term form'. The set of term forms constructed from Var, VAR and FUN is denoted as Term'.

For a goal form g, an individual goal G is derived by applying a substitution Σ : Var $\rightarrow$ TERM. The following is an example of a goal form.

$$merge(x, y, z)$$

From this goal form, the following goals are derived by applying substitution Σ:

$$\Sigma merge(x, y, z) = merge([1,2,3], Y, Z)$$

where:

$$\Sigma = \{[1,2,3] / x, Y/y, Z/z\}.$$

A goal form g can be considered to represent a set of goals |g| as follows.

$$|g| = \{G | \exists \Sigma : Var \rightarrow TERM, G = \Sigma g\}$$

A sequence of goal forms is called a <u>goal clause form</u>. A goal clause form represents a set of goal clauses.

Example: For g: merge(x, [y, y], z) the set of goals is defined as follows.

$$|g| = \{merge(X, [Y,Y], Z), merge(1, [0,0], W),$$
$$merge(X, [0,0], [0,1,0]), merge([1], [0,0],[]), \cdots\}$$

Note that an unsuccessful goal is included.

[Def. 2] normal success
  Let D be a set of guarded clauses:

$$H1:- B11,\cdots, B1n1 \mid A11, \cdots, A1m1.$$
$$H2:- B12,\cdots, B1n2 \mid A12, \cdots, A1m2.$$
$$\vdots$$
$$\vdots$$
$$Hs:- B1s,\cdots, B1ns \mid A1s, \cdots, A1ms.$$

Each argument of H1, $\cdots$,Hs is annotated by + or -.

Let G1, ⋯, Gk be a goal clause. A computation of G1, ⋯, Gk is
<u>normally successful</u> when it is successful computation and all invocation
of subgoals which appears in the computation are consistent with the annotation
in H1, ⋯, Hs.

In the above definition, the notions of 'computation' and 'success' are
used.   Strictly speaking, these notions should be defined based on
operational semantics of GHC [Takeuchi 86]. For a successful computation, the
result of computation is defined as a substitution σ : VAR → TERM.

[Def. 3] partial correctness

Let D be a set of guarded clauses as Def. 2 and Φ and Ψ be input and
output condition respectively. g1, ⋯, gk is partially correct wrt Φ and
Ψ iff for any substitution Σ : Var → TERM, and for any computation of Σ
g1, ⋯, Σ gk which is normally successful, if $\Sigma\Phi$ is true then $\sigma\Sigma\Psi$ is
true where σ is the result of the computation.

The above situation is denoted as :

$$\Phi \ \{ g1, \ \cdots, \ gk \}_D \ \Psi.$$

D after } is ommited if there is no confusion.

[Example]
For following GHC program:

```
reverse(X+, Y-) :- true ı rev1(X, [], Y).
rev1(E+, Y+, Z-) :- E = [] ı Y = Z.
rev1(C+, Y+, Z-) :- C = [AıY] ı rev1(X, [AıY], Z).
```

'reverse(u, v), reverse(v, w)' is partially correct wrt input condition
'true' and output condition 'u = w'. In other words:

$$\text{true } \{ \text{reverse(u, v), reverse(v, w)} \} \ u = w.$$

□

2.3 Inference Rules

This section shows an elementary fragment of the set of inference rules.

<Substitution>

$$\frac{\Phi \ \{g1, \ \cdots, \ gn\} \ \Psi}{\sigma \Phi \ \{\sigma g1, \cdots, \ \sigma gn\} \ \sigma \Psi}$$

where σ is a substitution.

<Consequence 1>

$$\frac{\Phi \ \{g1, \ \cdots, \ gn\} \ \Psi \qquad \Psi \Rightarrow \Psi'}{\Phi \ \{g1, \ \cdots, \ gn\} \ \Psi'}$$

<Consequence 2>

$$\frac{\Phi' \Rightarrow \Phi \qquad \Phi \ \{g1, \ \cdots, \ gn\} \ \Psi}{\Phi' \ \{g1, \ \cdots, \ gn\} \ \Psi}$$

<Derivation 1>

$$\frac{\Phi \ \wedge \ T=S \ \Rightarrow \ \Psi}{\Phi \ \{T=S\} \ \Psi}$$

<Derivation 2>

$$\frac{P1, \ \cdots, \ Ps}{\Phi \ \{g\} \ \Psi}$$

where $P1, \ \cdots, \ Ps$ is the sequence of all formulas defined as following. There is a guarded clause:

$$Hj :- Bj1, \ \cdots, \ Bj \ h_j \ | \ Aj1, \ \cdots, \ Aj \ m_j. \quad (1 \leqq j \leqq s)$$

in D such that Hj is unifiable with g ($\sigma_j \ g = \sigma_j \ Hj$) .
σ_j does not substitute any variable appearing in Φ for variables in arguments of Hj annotated with -. Then Pj has the following form:

$$Pj \equiv \bigwedge_{k=1, \ h_j} \sigma_j \ Bjk \ \wedge \ \sigma_j \Phi \ \{\sigma_j \ Aj1, \ \cdots, \ \sigma_j \ Aj \ m_j\} \ \sigma_j \ \Psi$$

where any variable appearing in the term form which is unified with a term form appearing in an argument annotated '-' does not appear at the left of ' {'.

<Parallel>

$$\frac{\Phi 1 \ \{g1\} \ \Psi 1, \ \cdots, \ \Phi n \ \{gn\} \ \Psi n}{\bigwedge_{i=1,n} \Phi i \ \{g1, \ \cdots, \ gn\} \ \bigwedge_{i=1,n} \Psi i}$$

where Φi and Φj (Ψi and Ψj) do not share any variable for all i, j ($1 \leq i, j \leq n$, $i \neq j$).

In this system, all formulas which are true in the domain of the program are regarded as an axiom like usual Hoare like system.

2.4   Proof Schema

In most Hoare like proof systems, a proof schema is defined as a tree in which each of the leaves corresponds to an axiom and the root corresponds to the formula which expresses partial correctness. In this system, in addition to axioms, 'the hypothesis of induction' can appear as a leaf. Such definition of proof schema is found in [Murakami 86].

[Def. 2]
A proof schema of formula Φ { g1, $\cdots$, gn } Ψ is a tree such that:

1) The root of the tree corresponds to Φ { g1, $\cdots$, gn } Ψ .

2) For every node n , one of a) or b) following is true.

   a) For some inference rule (shown in 2.3), n is an instance of a conclusion and each child of n corresponds to a premise.

   b) n is a leaf and one of following is true,

      (i) n is an axiom. In other words, n is a theorem without {, } -part.
      (ii) n is identical to one of its ancestors n' and Derivation 2) rule is used at least once on the path from n' to n .

2.5 Example of Proof

This is a program to find the maximum element from a binary tree. For example, the result of 'max([[[1],[4]],[3]], X)' is X = 4.

```
max([x, y]+, z-) :- y ≠ [] ∣ max(x, z1), max(y, z2), max2(z1, z2, z).
max([x]+, z-) :- x ≠ [], x ≠ [_∣_] ∣ z = x.
```

Now the proof of following formula is described:

$$\text{binary}(u) \; \{ \; \max(u, v) \; \} \; v \; \in \; |u| \; \wedge \; (\forall x \in |u| \Rightarrow v \geq x)$$

------------ (0)

where 'binary(u)' is true if u is the form of [a] for some atom a or u is the form of [x, y] and both of binary(x) and binary(y) are true. 'max2(z1, z2, z)' takes z1 and z2 as input and returns the greater element of them as z. The definition and correctness proof of this predicate are omitted. |u| means the set of elements of list 'u'.

It is easy to show that:

$$\text{binary}([y1]) \; \wedge \; y1 \neq [] \; \wedge \; y1 \neq [\_\mid\_] \Rightarrow (\forall \; x \in |[y1]| \Rightarrow y1 \geq x).$$

--------- (1)

From (1) :

$$\text{binary}([y1]) \; \wedge \; y1 \neq [] \; \wedge \; y1 \neq [\_\mid\_]$$
$$\Rightarrow (m = y1 \Rightarrow (\forall \; x \in |[y1]| \Rightarrow m \geq x)).$$

----------- (2)

Applying the rule <Derivation 1> :

$$\text{binary}([y1]) \; \wedge \; y1 \neq [] \; \wedge \; y1 \neq [\_\mid\_]$$
$$\{ \; m = y1 \; \} \; (\forall \; x \in |[y1]| \Rightarrow m \geq x). \;\text{----- (3)}$$

For 'max2', it is easy to show:

$$\text{true} \; \{ \; \max2(z1', z2', z3') \; \} \; ((z1' = z3' \; \wedge \; z1' \geq z2') \; \vee$$
$$(z2' = z3' \; \wedge \; z2' \geq z1')).$$

----- (4)

On the other hand, applying substitutions $\sigma1 = \{ \; u1/u, v1/v \; \}$ and $\sigma2 = \{ \; u2/u, v2/v \; \}$ to (0):

binary(u1) { max(u1, v1) } v1 ∈ ∣u1∣ ∧ (∀x ∈ ∣u1∣ ⇒ v1 ≧ x)

--------- (5)

binary(u2) { max(u2, v2) } v2 ∈ ∣u2∣ ∧ (∀x ∈ ∣u2∣ ⇒ v2 ≧ x).

--------- (6)

From (4), (5), (6) and the rule <Parallel> :

true ∧ binary(u1) ∧ binary(u2)
            { max(u1, v1), max(u2, v2), max2(z1', z2', z3') }
                        v1 ∈ ∣u1∣ ∧ (∀x ∈ ∣u1∣ ⇒ v1 ≧ x) ∧
                        v2 ∈ ∣u2∣ ∧ (∀x ∈ ∣u2∣ ⇒ v2 ≧ x) ∧
                        ((z1' = z3' ∧ z1' ≧ z2') ∨
                        (z2' = z3' ∧ z2' ≧ z1')). -- (7)

Applying <Substitution> to (7) with σ3 = { v1/z1', v2/z2', m/z3' } :

true ∧ binary(u1) ∧ binary(u2)
            { max(u1, v1), max(u2, v2), max2(v1, v2, m) }
                        v1 ∈ ∣u1∣ ∧ (∀x ∈ ∣u1∣ ⇒ v1 ≧ x) ∧
                        v2 ∈ ∣u2∣ ∧ (∀x ∈ ∣u2∣ ⇒ v2 ≧ x) ∧
                        ((v1 = m ∧ v1 ≧ v2) ∨ (v2 = m ∧ v2 ≧ v1)).

--------- (8)

(9) and (10) can easily be shown from the properties of binary trees.

v1 ∈ ∣u1∣ ∧ (∀x ∈ ∣u1∣ ⇒ v1 ≧ x) ∧
v2 ∈ ∣u2∣ ∧ (∀x ∈ ∣u2∣ ⇒ v2 ≧ x) ∧
((v1 = m ∧ v1 ≧ v2) ∨ (v2 = m ∧ v2 ≧ v1))
            ⇒ m ∈ ∣[u1, u2]∣ ∧ (∀x ∈ ∣[u1, u2]∣ ⇒ m ≧ x)

----------- (9)

binary([u1, u2]) ⇒ binary(u1) ∧ binary(u2)   --- (10)

Applying <Consequence 1> and <Consequence 2> to (8), (9), (10) :

binary([u1, u2])
            { max(u1, v1), max(u2, v2), max2(v1, v2, m) }
                        m ∈ ∣[u1, u2]∣ ∧ (∀x ∈ ∣[u1, u2]∣ ⇒ m ≧ x).

------------------ (11)

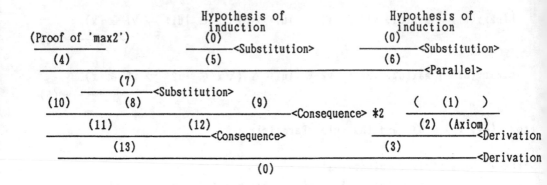

Fig. 1

(12) is trivial.

$$binary([u1, u2]) \land u2 \neq [] \Rightarrow binary([u1, u2])$$

------ (12)

From (11) and (12), applying <Consequence 2> :

$$binary([u1, u2]) \land u2 \neq []$$
$$\{ max(u1, v1), max(u2, v2), max2(v1, v2, m) \}$$
$$m \in |[u1, u2]| \land (\forall x \in |[u1, u2]| \Rightarrow m \geq x)$$

----------- (13)

From (3) and (13), applying <Derivation 2> :

$$binary(u) \{ max(u, v) \} v \in |u| \land (\forall x \in |u| \Rightarrow v \geq x)$$

This formula is identical to (0). Thus the proof schema is constructed. Fig. 1 shows the whole proof schema. □

3. Control of nondeterminism with suspend

3.1 ↑ annotation

This section shows how to prove partial correctness of programs which contain control of nondeterminism with the guard mechanism.   The following program is a example which contains a process controlled by the guard mechanism.

```
top(In+, Out-) :- true | merge(In, Y, O1), head2(O1, Out).

head2([U, V|X]+, W-) :- true | W = [U, V].

merge([U|X]+, Y+, W-) :- true | W = [U|V], merge(X, Y, V).
merge(X+, [U|Y]+, W-) :- true | W = [U|V], merge(X, Y, V).
merge(X+, []+, W-) :- true | X = W.
merge([]+, Y+, W-) :- true | Y = W.
```

When 'top' is invoked, 'merge' is invoked with a variable term in its
a second argument and executed with 'head2' in parallel subsequently. So when
'merge' is invoked, the first clause commits first in any case.
   As in this example, it often happens that only the invocation in which
some arguments are variable terms should be considered. In particular,
it is essential when discussing the effect of synchronization. Such
situation is represented using 'var' predicate as the input condition. For
example:

$$\text{list}(x) \wedge \text{var}(y) \ \{\text{merge}(x, y, z)\} \ \Psi$$

However, all input and output conditions are restricted to ordinary first
order predicates, i. e. their semantics should be defined as relations on the
Harbrand universe. So the 'meta' predicates such that 'var(y)' are not allowed.
   In this section, the situation that some variables are variable terms is
described by annotating the variables with ↑. For example, the invocation
of 'merge' with the variable term in the second argument is described as:

$$\text{merge}(u, v\uparrow, w).$$

The notion of partial correctness is redefined as follows for goals
containing a variable annotated with ↑.

[Def. 4]   partial correctness with ↑:
   Let D be a set of guarded clauses as [Def. 3] , and Φ and Ψ be the
input and output conditions.   For a goal clause form $g1, \cdots, gk$ which
contains variables $x1, \cdots, xs$ which are annotated with ↑:

$$\Phi \ \{g1, \cdots, gk\}_D \ \Psi$$

is true if and only if for any substitution Σ : Var $\to$ TERM which does not instantiate $x1, \cdots, xs$, for any normally successful computation of $\Sigma g1, \cdots, \Sigma gk$, if $\Sigma \Phi$ is true then $\sigma \Sigma \Psi$ is true where σ is the result of the computation.

New inference rules for the formula containing variables annotated with $\uparrow$ are introduced in the following section. When variable x is annotated at some occurrence in $g1, \cdots, gk$, x is annotated at all occurrence in $g1, \cdots, gk$. The result of unification of x and $y \uparrow$ is $y \uparrow$ when y occurs in $g1, \cdots, gk$.

3.2 Inference Rules for Formulas with $\uparrow$ Annotation

The following rules are introduced instead of <Substitution> and <Derivation 2> in Section 2.3.

<Substitution'>

$$\frac{\Phi \{g1, \cdots, gn\} \ \Psi}{\sigma \Phi \{\sigma g1, \cdots, \ \sigma gn\} \ \sigma \Psi}$$

where σ does not instantiate the variable annotated with $\uparrow$.

<Derivation 2'>

$$\frac{P1, \cdots, Ps}{\Phi \{g\} \ \Psi}$$

where $P1, \cdots, Ps$ is the sequence of all Pj $(1 \leq j \leq s)$ defined as follows:

There is a guarded clause:

$Hj :- Bj1, \cdots, Bjh_j \mid Aj1, \cdots, Ajm_j$. $(j = 1, s)$

in D such that Hj is unifiable with g $(\sigma_j \ g = \sigma_j Hj)$.
σ_j does not substitute any variable appearing in Φ for variables in arguments of Hj annotated with $-$, and σ_j does not instantiate the variable annotated with $\uparrow$ in the unification of a term appearing in g, and does not substitute a term form appears in Hj as an argument annotated with $+$. Then Pj has the following form:

$$P_j \equiv \bigwedge_{k=1, \; h_j} \sigma_j \, B_{jk} \wedge \; \sigma_j \, \Phi \; \{ \sigma_j \, A_{j1}, \; \cdots \; , \sigma_j \, A_{jm} \} \; \sigma_j \, \Psi$$

where any variable appearing in the term form which unified with an argument annotated – does not appear at the left of {, and for each B_{jk} (k=1, h_j), there is a substitution λ_{jk} such that $\lambda_{jk} B_{jk}$ is true and does not instantiate any variable in B_{jk} annotated with ↑.

A formula containing variables annotated with ↑ can be inferred by following rules:

1) If x is annotated in the premises then x is also annotated in the conclusion.

2) A variable x appearing in g of Φ {g} Ψ can be annotated with ↑ if Φ {g} Ψ is a conclusion of <Derivation 2'> and for any j ($1 \leqq j \leqq$ s) σ_j does not substitute a non-variable term form for x.

3) A variable x appearing in S = T of Φ {S = T} Ψ can be annotated if Φ {S = T} Ψ is a conclusion of <Derivation 1>.

4) A variable x appearing in g of Φ {g} Ψ can be annotated if Φ {g} Ψ appears in a proof schema as a hypothesis of induction.

All other inference rules and the definition of proof schema is similar to previous section.

3.3 Example of proof 2

In this section, the proof of following formula for GHC program in section 3.1 is given.

[a, b] = u {merge(u, v↑, w), head2(w, out)} out = [a, b]

From:

$$\text{true} \wedge v = v1 \Rightarrow v = v1 \qquad \text{------------------- (1)}$$

applying <Derivation 1> and rule for introducing '↑', 3):

$$\text{true} \quad \{v\uparrow - v1\} \quad v - v1 \ . \qquad \text{---------------- (2)}$$

On the other hand, from:

$$\text{true} \ \wedge \ o1 - [b1!o2] \Rightarrow o1 - [b1!o2] \qquad \text{------(3)}$$

applying <Derivation 1>:

$$\text{true} \ \{o1 - [b1!o2]\} \ o1 - [b1!o2]. \qquad \text{-------- (4)}$$

From (2), applying <Derivation 2'>:

$$\text{true} \quad \{ \ \text{merge}([], \ v\uparrow, \ v1) \ \} \ v - v1. \qquad \text{----- (5)}$$

From (4) and (5), applying <Parallel>:

$$\text{true} \ \{o1 - [b1!o2], \ \text{merge}([], \ v\uparrow, \ v1) \ \} \ v - v1 \ \wedge \ o1 - [b1!o2].$$
$$\text{---------------- (6)}$$

Applying <Substitution'> with $\sigma \ = \ \{o2 \ / \ v1\}$

$$\text{true} \ \{o1 - [b1!o2], \ \text{merge}([], \ v\uparrow, \ o2) \ \} \quad v - o2 \ \wedge \ o1 - [b1!o2].$$
$$\text{--------------------(7)}$$

From:
$$[b1] - [b1] \Rightarrow \text{true},$$
$$v - o2 \ \wedge \ o1 - [b1!o2] \Rightarrow o1 - [b1!v]$$
$$\text{----------------------(8)}$$

applying <Consequence 1> and <Consequence 2>:

$$[b1] - [b1] \ \{o1 - [b1!o2], \ \text{merge}([], \ v\uparrow, \ o2) \ \} \ o1 - [b1!v].$$
$$\text{------------- (9)}$$

On the other hand, from:

$$[b1] - [] \ \wedge \ v - o1 \Rightarrow o1 - [b1!v] \qquad \text{-------(10)}$$

applying <Derivation 1>:

$$[b1] - [] \ \{v\uparrow - o1 \ \} \ o1 - [b1!v]. \qquad \text{-------- (11)}$$

From (9) and (11), applying <Derivation 2'>:

$$[b1] - i1 \ \{merge(i1, v\uparrow, o1)\} \ o1 - [b1!v] \qquad\qquad --- (12)$$

Furthermore from:

$$true \ \wedge \ w - [a1!o11] \ \Rightarrow \ (o11 - [b11!v1] \Rightarrow w - [a1, b11!v1])$$
$$--------------------(13)$$

applying <Derivation 1>:

$$true \ \{ w - [a1!o11] \} \ (o11 - [b11!v1] \Rightarrow w - [a1, b11!v1]).$$
$$---------------- (14)$$

From (12) and (14), applying <Parallel>:

$$[b1] - i1 \ \{w - [a1!o11], merge(i1, v\uparrow, o1)\}$$
$$o1 - [b1!v] \ \wedge \ (o11 - [b11!v1] \Rightarrow w - [a1, b11!v1])$$
$$-----------------------(15)$$

Applying <Substitution> with $\sigma' = \{o1/o11, b1/b11, v/v1\}$:

$$[b1] - i1 \ \{w - [a1!o1], merge(i1, v\uparrow, o1)\}$$
$$o1 - [b1!v] \ \wedge \ (o1 - [b1!v] \Rightarrow w - [a1, b1!v]).$$
$$-----------------------(16)$$

From:

$$o1 - [b1!v] \ \wedge \ (o1 - [b1!v] \Rightarrow w - [a1, b1!v]) \ \Rightarrow \ w - [a1, b1!v]$$

$$[a1, b1] - [a1!i1] \ \Rightarrow \ [b1] - i1$$
$$---------------------------(17)$$

applying <Consequence 1> and <Consequence 2>:

$$[a1, b1] - [a1!i1] \ \{w - [a1!o1], merge(i1, v\uparrow, o1)\} \ w - [a1, b1!v].$$
$$------------ (18)$$

On the other hand from:

$$[a1, b1] - [] \ \wedge \ v - w \ \Rightarrow \ w - [a1, b1!v]$$
$$---------------------------(19)$$

applying <Derivation 1> and $\uparrow$ introduction rule:

$$[a1, b1] - [] \ \{v\uparrow - w \} \ w - [a1, b1!v]. \qquad ----- (20)$$

From (18) and (20), applying <Derivation 2'>:

$$[a1, b1] - i2 \{merge(i2, v\uparrow, w)\} \quad w - [a1, b1!v].\qquad\text{---------- (21)}$$

On the other hand, the proof of the correctness of 'head2' is as following. At first, it is easy to show:

$$true \wedge out1 - [a4, b4] \Rightarrow ([a4, b4!\_] - [a3, b3!v2] \Rightarrow out1 - [a3, b3]).$$
$$\text{-----------------------(22)}$$

Applying <Derivation 1>:

$$true \{out1 - [a4, b4]\} ([a4, b4!\_] - [a3, b3!v2] \Rightarrow out1 - [a3, b3]).$$
$$\text{--------------------(23)}$$

Applying <Derivation 2>:

$$true \{head2(w1, out1)\} w1 - [a3, b3!v2] \Rightarrow out1 - [a3, b3].$$
$$\text{---------------- (24)}$$

From (21) and (24), applying <Parallel>:

$$[a1, b1] - i2 \{merge(i2, v\uparrow, w), head2(w1, out1)\}$$
$$w - [a1, b1!v] \wedge (w1 - [a3, b3!v2] \Rightarrow out1 - [a3, b3]$$
$$\text{---------------- (25)}$$

Applying <Substitution>

$$[a1, b1] - i2 \{merge(i2, v\uparrow, w), head2(w, out)\}$$
$$w - [a1, b1!v] \wedge (w - [a1, b1!v] \Rightarrow out - [a1, b1]).$$
$$\text{---------------- (26)}$$

From:

$$w - [a1, b1!v] \wedge (w - [a1, b1!v] \Rightarrow out - [a1, b1]) \Rightarrow out - [a1, b1]$$
$$\text{----------------(27)}$$

applying <Consequence 1>:

$$[a1, b1] - i2 \{merge(i2, v\uparrow, w), head2(w, out)\} \quad out - [a1, b1]$$
$$\text{------------------(28)}$$

The result is derived applying <Substitution> with

$$\sigma'' = \{a/a1, b/b1, u/i2\} \ .$$

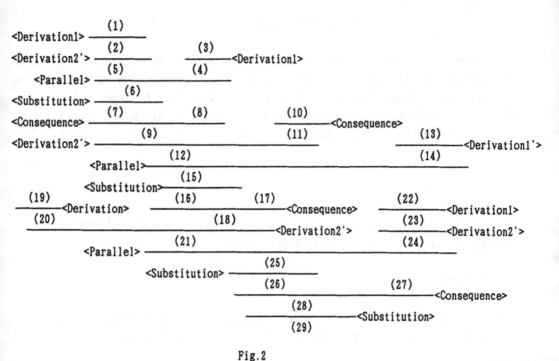

Fig.2

$$[a, b] = u \; \{merge(u, v\uparrow, w), head2(w, out)\} \; out = [a, b]$$
$$-----------------(29)$$

Fig. 2 shows the whole proof schema.   □

4. Conclusion

This paper introduced fragments of an axiomatic system for proving partial correctness. These are the most elementary parts. It is not enough to prove partial correctness for stronger output condition. For example, in Brock-Ackermann's anomaly, the following can be proved in the fragment system introduced here:

$$n = [a] \; \{t2(n, o)\} \; o = [a, a] \lor o = [a, s(a)].$$

However, the following cannot be proved in this system although this formula is true:

$$n = [a] \quad \{t2(n, o)\} \quad o = [a, a].$$

To prove a correctness property like this, a method to formalize effects of synchronization is needed. This is done by introducing a new notation representing communications between processes explicitly and refinement of the inference rule <Parallel>. This refinement of axiomatic system and examples of the proof appear in [Murakami 87].

Acknowledgments

I would like to thank Dr. K. Furukawa and all other members of First Laboratory. of ICOT for many useful discussions.

[References]

[Clark 86] K. L. Clark and S. Gregory, PARLOG: Parallel programming in logic, ACM Trans. on Programming Language and Systems 86, 1986

[Kameyama 87] Y. Kameyama, Axiomatic System for Concurrent Logic Programming Languages, Master's Thesis of the University of Tokyo 1987

[Kanamori 86] T. Kanamori and H. Seki, Verification of Prolog Programs Using an Extension of Execution, Lecture Notes in Comp. Sci., No. 225, 1986

[Levi 85] G. Levi and C. Palamidessi, The Declarative Semantics of Logical Read-only Variables, Prc. of Symp. on Logic Programming 85 1985

[Levi 87] G. Levi and C. Palamidessi, An Approach to The Declarative Semantics of Synchronization in Logic Language, to appear in Proc. of International Conf. on Logic Programming 87, 1987

[Murakami 86] M.Murakami and Y. Inagaki, Verification System for Partial Correctness of Communicating Sequential Processes, Systems and Computers in Japan, 1986

[Murakami 87] M. Murakami, Toward Axiomatic Semantics of Guarded Horn Clauses, 2nd France-Japan Artificial Intelligence and Computer Science Symposium, 1987

[Saraswat 85] V. A. Saraswat, Partial Correctness Semantics for CP [↓ , ! , &], Lecture Notes in Comp. Sci., no. 206, 1985

[Saraswat 87] V. A. Saraswat, GHC: Operational Semantics, Problems, and Relationships with CP (↓ , |) , Prc. of Symp. on Logic Programming 87 1987

[Saundararajan 84] N. Saundararajan, Axiomatic Semantics of Communicating Sequential Processes, ACM Trans. on Programming Languages and Systems, Vol. 6, No. 4, 1984

[Shapiro 86] E. Y. Shapiro, Concurrent Prolog: A progress report, Lecture Notes in Comp. Sci. No. 232, 1986

[Takeuchi 86] A. Takeuchi, Towards a Semantic Model of GHC, Tec. Rep. of IECE, COMP86-59, 1986

[Ueda 85] K. Ueda, Guarded Horn Clauses, Tec. Rep. of ICOT, TR-103, 1985

[Ueda 86] K. Ueda, On Operational Semantics of Guarded Horn Clauses, Tec. Memo of ICOT, TM-0160, 1986

KNOWLEDGE REPRESENTATION AND INFERENCE
BASED ON FIRST-ORDER MODAL LOGIC

Koji Iwanuma and Masateru Harao

Department of Information Engineering
Yamagta University, Yonezawa-shi, 992, Japan

Abstract: In this paper, we present a knowledge representation system based on a first-order modal logic and discuss the deductive inference mechanism of this system. A possible-world model, which is used in discussing the semantics of a modal logic, can be regarded as structured knowledge, and modal operators can be used to describe various kinds of properties on a possible-world model. In this paper, we introduce a new concept, "viewpoints of modalities", in order to describe the knowledge structure effectively and compactly. We also show that schema formulas available in this framework are useful for the description of metaknowledge such as property inheritance. Therefore, a modal logic is suitable for representing both structured knowledge and metaknowledge. We construct a knowledge representation system based on a subset of a first-order modal logic, and give a complete deductive inference rule which is as effective as SLD resolution.

1. Introduction

One of the most important problems in artificial intelligence is to design a knowledge representation language which can describe effectively knowledge structures and metaknowledge. Until now, lots of knowledge representation systems have been proposed. Roughly speaking, we can divide them into three classes: production systems; frame systems; and first-order logical systems. A production system is a language which treats only the "if-then-else" type of procedural knowledge, and we can realize efficient inference systems using it. But the knowledge representation ability of a production system is limited to some extent, since the "if-then-else" type of expression is not enough, by itself, to deal explicitly with complex structured knowledge and metaknowledge.

A frame system has very flexible and general expressive power for knowledge representation. In a frame system, the knowledge structures are described with a graph. Also various kinds of knowledge, such as property inheritance, daemons, or metaknowledge, can be described by assignment to each node of this graph. And the inference on a frame system can be regarded as a search over its graph; therefore, it is relatively fast. But we should note that a frame system, as proposed by Minsky, is fundamentally a programming paradigm. Though lots of efforts have been devoted to realize it in a concrete form, unfortunately, it has an insufficient theoretical basis. Therefore, the semantics of knowledge and the concept of inference in a frame system are not so clear; and we also tend to use tricky methods in using a frame system. Generally speaking, it is very hard to discuss theoretical properties of a frame system.

A system based on first-order logic, such as Prolog[11], has a fundamental mathematical theory and clear semantics. In these days, a lot of systems have been developed based on first-order logic. But, historically, first-order logic has been developed in order to describe mathematics, so it is suitable for representing properties which never change over time and space. There is no mechanism for representing the structure and hierarchy of knowledge. This causes inconvenience for practical knowledge representation. And it causes the hypothesis space of first-order logic to be uniform, which, in turn, causes inference on first-order logic to be ineffective. In order to design a knowledge representation language based on first-order logic, it is necessary to introduce the mechanism of treating both structured knowledge and metaknowledge.

The structure of knowledge can be regarded as a kind of space. We have proposed a first-order modal logic[12] which can treat both temporal and spatial modalities, and investigated some of its fundamental properties. In this paper, we will extend a knowledge representation system based on first-order logic by using a first-order spatial modal logic, which is a subsystem of our logic. Our modal logic has some useful mechanisms which first-order logic alone does not possess. At first, we show that a possible-world model used in our spatial modal logic can be regarded as structured knowledge and that modal operators are very useful in describing knowledge structures. We introduce a new concept, "viewpoints of modalities"[12], which makes it easier to describe knowledge structure. Also, we show the usefulness of schema formulas for representing such metaknowledge as property inheritance. Next, in accord with the above considerations, we construct a knowledge representation system which is based on a subset of our spatial modal logic, and give a complete deductive inference rule which is as effective as SLD resolution.

This paper is organized as follows: In Chapter 2, we show the usefulness of: a possible-word model; viewpoints of modalities; and schema formulas. In Chapter 3, we construct a knowledge representation system based on a first-order modal logic. At first, we contemplate some properties of a first-order modal logic in order to give an effective inference rule to our system. Next, we give the formal definition of our system, in accord with the above considerations. In Chapter 4, we give a deductive inference rule for our system, and show its completeness and soundness. In Chapter 5, we compare our system with other knowledge representation systems. Chapter 6 is the conclusion.

238

2. Possible-World Models and Schema Formulas

2.1 Possible-World Models and Structured Knowledge

A modal logic is a logic for treating two kinds of modalities: "necessity" and "possibility". In this paper, we introduce a new concept, "viewpoints of modalities"[12], and investigate its applicability to knowledge representation. The modalities of necessity and possibility under the viewpoint 'a' are expressed by the modal operators [a] and <a> respectively as follows:

[a]p   <==>   p is true in all situations related under the viewpoint 'a'.

<a>p   <==>   p is true in some situation related under the viewpoint 'a'.

Modal formulas are interpreted in a model, called a possible-world model, which takes the form of a directed graph. One example of possible-world models is shown in Fig.1, where each node is called a possible world and represents a situation. A possible world is an assignment of truth values to modal formulas. In Fig.1, P is true in the world W_1 and both P and Q are true in the world W_2. Directed arcs represent a relation, called an accessibility relation. The labels of these arcs are the names of the accessibilities, that is, they represent the viewpoints of modalities. We say the world w is accessible from the world y under the viewpoint 'a' if w is connected to y by a directed arc labeled with 'a'. In Fig.1, the worlds W_1 and W_2 are accessible from the world W_0 under the viewpoint 'A', and the worlds W_2 and W_3 are accessible from W_0 under the viewpoint 'B'.

The truth values of modal formulas are defined in the possible worlds. We write w |= p if the formula p is true in the world w. The truth values of the formulas [a]p and <a>p are defined respectively as follows:

w |= [a]p   <==> p is true in all worlds which are accessible from w under the viewpoint a.

w |= <a>p   <==> there is a world y such that y is accessible form w under the viewpoint a and p is true in y.

In Fig.1, the formulas [A]P, [B]Q, <A>P and <B>P are true in the world W_0. On the other hand, [A]Q and [B]P are false in W_0.

A possible-world model with the

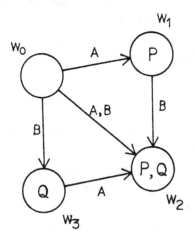

Fig.1: A Possible-World Model

viewpoints of modalities resembles a frame system. A possible world can be regarded as the module of knowledge which corresponds to the concept of a frame. The accessibility relations and the viewpoints of modalities correspond to the connections between frames and the names of these connections, respectively. Therefore, by these correspondences, a possible-world model can be regarded as a frame system, where slot values are represented by logical formulas. In addition, the inference rules of a modal logic can be regarded as those of a frame system. The computation of the truth value of a formula including modal operators involves a search over the skeleton graph of a possible-world model, and the viewpoints represent the names of the search paths.

We show that a kind of mechanical theorem proving for a modal logic can be considered as a question-answering computation for a frame system. We give an example of this kind of theorem proving in the possible-world model in Fig.2. Because all of the formulas holding in this model take the forms of definite clauses, inference like SLD resolution is possible. At first, we ask "How many legs does taro have ?" to the possible world (that is, the frame) "animal" by using the following question clause:

?- animal where <u>number legs(taro,y)</u>.

The underlined body of this clause can be unified with the head of the following clauses in "animal":

number_legs(x,y) <-- <ako⁻>num_legs(x,y).

After the unification, the body of the above clause changes to "<ako⁻>num_legs(taro,y)", which should be tested at the next step. This unified body is

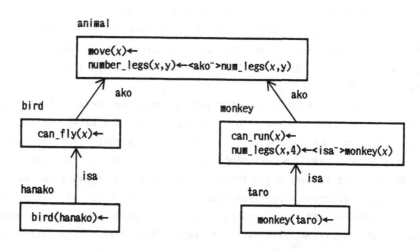

Fig.2: A Possible-World Model

the procedure which examines whether "num_legs(taro,y)" holds in some frame which is accessible from "animal" under the viewpoint "ako". The clause

num_legs(x,4) <-- <isa‾>monkey(x)

holds in the possible world "monkey" which is accessible from "animal" under "ako", and the head of this clause be unified with "num_legs(taro,y)". The next step is to determine the truth value of "<isa‾>monkey(taro)". It is enough to examine whether "monkey(taro)" holds in some frame which is accessible from "monkey" under the viewpoint "isa". In the model, the unit clause

monkey(taro) <--

holds in the world "taro", which is accessible from "monkey" under "isa". Because this clause has no body, the further inference is not necessary. Thus, the computation halts at this point. Note that it is possible to give the answer "y = 4" to the first question, by memorizing all unifiers used in this computation.

In general, it is very difficult and (has not yet been achieved) to furnish an effective inference system for the full first-order modal logic; but, we think, it is possible for that subsystem all of whose modal formulas take the forms of definite clauses.

2.2 Schema formulas and Meta Knowledge

Metaknowledge is knowledge which deals with knowledge. Therefore, if knowledge is expressed by a logical formula at a certain level of fomalization, then its metaknowledge should be expressed by a higher-level logical formula. In the higher-order logic, we can treat the different level formulas uniformly, so it is a very natural framework for dealing with meta knowledge. But, unfortunately, it is very difficult to construct symbolic computation rules for the higher-order logic.   For example, it is impossible to construct any complete axiom systems for higher-order logic, in the usual sense[8]; also, the unification problem for second-order formulas is not decidable[5].

In this paper, we use schema formulas to describe metaknowledge instead of higher-order formulas. Schema axioms are regarded as the knowledge for formulas, that is, metaknowledge.   Therefore, a knowledge representation system based on first-order logic can be extended to a system which can deal with some metaknowledge,   by introducing a framework for treating schema formulas.   In this paper, in order to treat schema formulas, we use three kinds of special variables: function, predicate and atom variables. These variables express the symbols which are names of functions, predicates or atoms. Note they don't directly express functions or predicates themselves. They are used only for syntactical matching between the sequences of alphabets.

We give an example to show the usefulness of the schema formulas. Consider the following axiom schema in Fig.2.

$$AP \leftarrow \langle (\text{isa} \cup \text{ako})^* \rangle AP$$

This formula implies that the property AP must hold on the frame w_0 if AP holds in a frame which is accessible from w_0 under the viewpoints "isa" or "ako". Therefore, this axiom schema expresses the property of inheritance in a frame system. For example, the formula "move(x)" isn't true in the frame "bird", but it is true in the frame "animal", which is the super concept of the frame "bird". If the above schema formula is assumed to be an axiom, then the frame "bird" inherits "move(x)" from "animal"; that is, "move(x)" holds in the frame "bird".

Mechanical theorem proving with schema formulas can also be easily established. The following inference is possible for the question "how many legs does taro have ?" to the frame "taro", by using the above axiom schema. At first, the question clause

?- taro where <u>num legs(taro,y)</u>

is sent to the frame "taro". Its body, which is underlined, can be unified with the head of the above axiom schema. After the unification, the body of the axiom schema changes into

$$\langle (\text{isa} \cup \text{ako})^* \rangle \text{num\_legs(taro,y)}.$$

The next step is to examine this body, which is true if "num_legs(taro,y)" holds in a frame which is accessible from "taro" under "isa" or "ako". In the frame "monkey", there is the clause

$$\text{num\_legs}(x,4) \leftarrow \langle \text{isa}^- \rangle \text{monkey}(x),$$

whose head can be unified with the above body. The unfinished tasks of this inference are the same as those of Section 2.1. As a result, this inference will succeed, and the unifiers through this inference will give the answer y=4 to the first question.

3. A Knowledge Representation System Based on a Modal Logic

3.1 System Architecture of a Knowledge Representation Language

A knowledge representation system based on first-order logic acquires the ability for treating both structured knowledge and metaknowledge, by introducing into it the frameworks of: possible-worlds; viewpoints of modalities; and schema formulas. In this chapter, we construct a knowledge representation system based on a first-order modal logic. But there are some problems to be anticipated in using first-order modal logic.

1) There is no canonical form of modal formulas.

2) It is very difficult to determine the truth values of modal formulas.

For example, in principle, it is impossible to construct a complete deductive system for first-order temporal logic with $\bigcirc$ (next) and $\diamondsuit$ (eventual) operators[12].   Also, many researchers have investigated the applicability of the resolution principle to various kinds of first-order modal logics[1,2,9]; but until now, no fruitful result has been achieved. Considering these difficulties, some restrictions on our logical system are necessary in order to establish effective inference rules. For example, we should contemplate the ability of modal operators used in our system, or the conditions on the skeleton structures of possible-world models treated in our system, etc.

According to these considerations, we construct a knowledge representation language and give to it an inference system as follows: At first, the formulas used in our system are restricted to definite (modal) clauses; that is, our language is a subset of a usual modal logic. This restriction makes it possible to construct an effective inference rule for our system. Secondly, because one purpose of our system is to have the ability for the natural description of structured knowledge, we require the following assumption on our system: knowledge expressions and the skeleton graph of a possible-world model, on which knowledge expressions should be interpreted, are both given to our system. A skeleton graph of a possible-world model is defined by a set of possible worlds and an accessibility relation among these possible worlds (it corresponds to the space structure of our temporal and spatial modal logic). Improvement on speed of inference can be expected as a consequence, because the system knows the skeleton of the model in advance.

Also, in our system, the domain for variables is assumed to be common over all possible worlds, and the interpretations of function constant symbols and variables are independent of possible worlds. These restrictions have been assumed in the examples of inferences shown in the previous chapter; therefore, we consider these assumptions to be not too severe for practical knowledge descriptions. The unary operator "(v_i)", which denotes the world v_i where its argument formula must hold, is introduced into our system, besides the operators used in the previous chapter. Regular expressions of links are used to express the viewpoints of modalities so that various search paths can be expressed in our system.

3.2 Syntax

Atomic symbols consist of: frame names v_1, v_2, $\cdots$, including the special frame name "any"; link names A_1, A_2, $\cdots$; individual variables x, y, $\cdots$; function constants f^n, g^n, $\cdots$; predicate constants p^n, q^n, $\cdots$; function variables F^n, G^n, $\cdots$; predicate variables P^n, Q^n, $\cdots$; and atom variables AP, AQ, $\cdots$. Also, we use {, }, <, >, [,], (,), ;, *, $\cup$, -, where and Frame_structure as subsidiary symbols.

Def.1 (Links and frame structures) Links and frame structures are inductively defined as follows:

1) If v_i and v_j are frame names and A_k is a link name, then $A_k(v_i,v_j)$ is a link.

2) If $L_1,\cdots,L_n$ are links, then Frame_structure($L_1,\cdots,L_n$) is a frame structure. []

Def.2 (Viewpoints of modalities) A viewpoint over the set of link names is a regular expression over the set of link names with the operators ";", "*", " $\cup$ ", and the unary operator "-". []

Def.3 (Knowledges) A knowledge is inductively defined as follows:

1) A term is an expression defined as usual from individual variables, function constants and function variables.

2) An atom is an atom variable, or an expression defined as usual from terms, predicate constants and predicate variables.

3) If A is an atom, v_i is a frame name and 'a' is a viewpoint, then

$$A, \quad [a]A, \quad \langle a \rangle A, \quad (v_i)A, \quad (v_i)[a]A, \quad (v_i)\langle a \rangle A$$

are modal atoms.

4) If A is an atom and $MA_1,\cdots,MA_n$ are modal atoms, then an expression

$$A \longleftarrow MA_1,\cdots,MA_n$$

is a definite clause.

5) If v_i is a frame name and $C_1,\cdots,C_n$ are definite clauses, then an expression

$$v_i \text{ where } \{ C_1,\cdots,C_n \}$$

is a knowledge of v_i, and is denoted by K_{vi}.

6) If $K_{v1},\cdots,K_{vn}$ are knowledges of the frames $v_1,\cdots,v_n$ appearing in a frame structure F, respectively, and K_{any} is a knowledge of the frame "any", where all links appearing in $K_{v1},\cdots,K_{vn}$ and K_{any} are also appearing in F, then an expression

$$\{ K_{v1},\cdots, K_{vn}, K_{any} \}$$

is a knowledge of F, and is denoted by K_F.

7) If v_i is a frame name and $MA_1,\cdots,MA_n$ are modal atoms, then an expression

$$?- v_i \text{ where } MA_1,\cdots,MA_n$$

is a goal clause for v_i, and is denoted by G_{vi}. []

We use the word "expression" as the generic name for terms, atoms, modal atoms, clauses and knowledges. An expression including some of function variables, predicate variables or atom variables is called a schema expression. An expression not including them is called a concrete expression. A concrete expression which doesn't include any individual variables is called a ground expression.

We give an example of a knowledge representation corresponding to the possible-world model of Fig.2.

```
Frame_structure {
         ako(bird,animal), ako(monkey,animal),
         isa(taro,monkey), isa(hanako,bird)
         }
animal where {
         move(x),
         number_legs(x,y) <-- <ako⁻>num_legs(x,y)
         }
bird where {    can_fly(x)      }
monkey where {
         can_run(x),
         num_legs(x,4) <-- <isa⁻>monkey(x)
         }
hanako where {    bird(hanako)    }
taro where {    monkey(taro)    }
any where {    AP <-- <(isa∪ako)*>AP    }
```

We have constructed a simple inference system in Prolog with the deductive inference rules stated in Chapter 4. Here, we show some examples of simple question-answering computations in our system.

```
?- animal where number_legs(taro,y).      ----- 1
y = 4;
no
?- taro where number_legs(taro,y).        ----- 2
y = 4;
no
?- bird where AP.                          ----- 3
AP = can_fly(x)
AP = move(x);
AP = number_legs(taro,4);
no
?- taro where [(isa∪ako)*]AP.             ----- 4
AP = move(x);
AP = number_legs(taro,4);
no
?- X where can_fly(hanako).                ----- 5
X = bird;
X = hanako;
no
```

The first two questions were explained in the previous chapter. In the third

question, we ask what holds in the frame "bird". The answers are the atoms
"can_fly(x)", "move(x)" and "number_legs(taro,4)". The last two answers are
inherited from the frame "animal", because the schema formula "AP <-- <(isa ∪
ako)*>AP" is assumed to be an axiom. The fourth question is what holds in all
frames which are super-concept frames of "taro". In the fifth question, we ask
where the atom "can_fly(hanako)" holds, by using a frame name variable X, which is
not treated in this paper in order to simplify our discussion. The answers are the
two frames "bird" and "hanako", because the frame "hanako" inherits
"can_fly(hanako)" form the frame "bird".

3.3   Semantics

Def.4 (Interpretations of frame structures) A model of a frame structure F is a
directed connected graph $G_F = \langle V_F, L_F, E_F \rangle$ with labeled arcs, where V_F is the set
of the frame names appearing in F, L_F is the set of the link names appearing in F,
and $E_F: \sum_F \rightarrow 2^{VF \times VF}$ is a function satisfying the following conditions:
1) $\sum_F$ is the set of the viewpoints over L_F,
2) $E_F(A_k) = \{ \langle v_i, v_j \rangle \mid A_k(v_i, v_j) \in F \}$
3) $E_F(a;b) = E_F(a) \circ E_F(b)$ (composition of relations)
4) $E_F(a \cup b) = E_F(a) \cup E_F(b)$ (union of relations)
5) $E_F(a^*) = E_F(a)^*$ (reflex and transitive closure of a relation)
6) $E_F(a^-) = \{ \langle v_i, v_j \rangle \mid \langle v_j, v_i \rangle \in E_F(a) \}$ []

The frame structure F defines the skeleton of a possible-world model. G_F is
abbreviated as F if no confusion arises.

We will give a kind of Herbrand interpretation to the knowledge K_F. It is
possible to prove the equivalence between the two definitions of this interpretation
and the usually used interpretation[2,7], but we omit the proof here. At first, as
stated in Section 3.1, the interpretation of the function constants is assumed to be
independent of the possible worlds, and so is the interpretation of variables.
Function constants are interpreted as the constructors over the Herbrand universe,
and variables are interpreted with substitutions as usual. The interpretation of
predicate constants must be dependent on the possible worlds, so we define the
Herbrand base for K_F as follows.

Def.5 (Herbrand universes and bases) Let K_F be a knowledge of a frame structure F.
The Herbrand universe H_{KF} for K_F is the set of all ground terms which can be
constructed with the function constants appearing in K_F. Also, the Herbrand base
B_{KF} for K_F is the following set:
$$B_{KF} = \{ (v_i)p^n(t_1, \cdots, t_n) \mid t_1, \cdots, t_n \in H_{KF}, \text{ the frame name } v_i \text{ and}$$
$$\text{the predicate constant } p^n \text{ appears in } F \text{ or } K_F \}   []$$

Def.6 (Interpretations of knowledges) Let K_F be a knowledge of a frame structure F. An interpretation I for K_F is a subset of the Herbrand base B_{KF} for K_F. []

$(v_i)p^n(t_1, \cdots, t_n) \in I$ means that $p^n(t_1, \cdots, t_n)$ is true in the frame v_i under the interpretation I. We will extend the usual definition of substitutions in order to deal with function, predicate and atom variables.

Def.7 (Substitutions) A substitution θ is a finite set of the form $\{ \alpha_1/\beta_1, \cdots, \alpha_n/\beta_n \}$, where each pair of α_i/β_i satisfies the following conditions:
1) α_i is an individual variable and β_i is a term distinct from α_i, or
2) α_i is a n-ary function variable and β_i is an n-ary function constant or an n-ary function variable distinct from α_i, or
3) α_i is an n-ary predicate variable and β_i is an n-ary predicate constant or an n-ary predicate variable distinct from α_i, or
4) α_i is an atom variable and β_i is an atom distinct from α_i. []

A substitution θ is called a substitution over a knowledge K_F if all constant symbols appearing in θ also appear in K_F. If $E\theta$ is a ground term, then θ is called a ground substitution.

All substitutions used in this paper are assumed to be substitutions over a knowledge K_F. The composition of substitutions and the most general unifier (mgu), etc. are defined in the same way as in first-order logic.

Def.8 (Truth values of knowledges) We write $I,v_i \models_F E$ if the expression E is true in the frame v_i under the interpretation I for the knowledge K_F. The truth values of ground modal atoms are inductively defined as follows:
1) $I,v_i \models_F p^n(t_1, \cdots, t_n)$ iff $(v_i)p^n(t_1, \cdots, t_n) \in I$
2) $I,v_i \models_F [a]A$ iff $I,v_k \models_F A$ for all v_k such that $\langle v_i,v_k \rangle \in E_F(a)$
3) $I,v_i \models_F \langle a \rangle A$ iff there is a v_k such that $\langle v_i,v_k \rangle \in E_F(a)$ and $I,v_k \models_F A$
4) $I,v_i \models_F (v_j)A$ iff $I,v_j \models_F A$
5) $I,v_i \models_F (v_j)[a]A$ iff $I,v_k \models_F A$ for all v_k such that $\langle v_j,v_k \rangle \in E_F(a)$
6) $I,v_i \models_F (v_j)\langle a \rangle A$ iff there is a v_k such that $\langle v_j,v_k \rangle \in E_F(a)$ and $I,v_k \models_F A$
   The truth values of definite clauses are defined as follows:
7) $I,v_i \models_F A \leftarrow MA_1, \cdots, MA_n$ iff for all ground substitutions θ,
$$\text{if } I,v_i \models_F MA_1\theta, \cdots, I,v_i \models_F MA_n\theta, \text{ then } I,v_i \models_F A\theta$$
   We write $I \models_F K_{vi}$ if the knowledge $K_{vi} = v_i$ where $\{C_1, \cdots, C_n\}$ is true under the interpretation I.
8) $I \models_F K_{vi}$ iff $I,v_i \models_F C_i$ for all $C_i \in K_{vi}$
   In particular, we define the truth values of the knowledge K_{any} as follows:
9) $I \models_F K_{any}$ iff $I,v_i \models_F C_i$ for all $v_i \in V_F$ and $C_i \in K_{any}$,
   We write $I \models_F K_F$ if the knowledge $K_F = \{ K_{v1}, \cdots, K_{vn}, K_{any} \}$ of the frame

structure F is true under the interpretation I.

10) $I \models_F K_F$ iff $I \models_F K_{vi}$ for all $K_{vi} \in K_F$, and $I \models_F K_{any}$ []

Function, predicate and atom variables are treated in Definition 8-7), where the values of these variables are restricted to the constant symbols appearing in K_F, because all substitutions used in this paper are assumed to be substitutions over K_F.

Def.9 (Models) A model I on F for K_F is an interpretation I such that $I \models_F K_F$. []

A minimal model can be defined, because the model intersection property holds.

Def.10 (Minimal models) The minimal model M_{KF} on F for K_F is the intersection $\bigcap_j I_j$ of all models I_j on F for K_F. []

Def.11 (Validities of goal clauses) Let K_F be a knowledge of F and $G_{vi} = ?- vi$ where $MA_1, \cdots, MA_n$ be a goal clause for v_i. G_{vi} is said to be true under the model I on F for K_F if G_{vi} satisfies the following condition:

For every ground substitution θ, $I, v_i \models_F MA_1\theta, \cdots, I, v_i \models_F MA_n\theta$

G_{vi} is said to be valid on K_F if G_{vi} is true under all models on F for K_F. []

Lemma 1 (Correctness of minimal models) Let M_{KF} be the minimal model on F for K_F and G_{vi} be a goal clause. Then the following holds:

       G_{vi} is valid on K_F iff G_{vi} is true under M_{KF} []

Def.12 (Correct answer substitutions) Let K_F be a knowledge and G_{vi} be a goal clause. A correct answer substitution θ for G_{vi} on K_F is a substitution satisfying the following condition:

     θ is a substitution for variables of G_{vi} and $G_{vi}\theta$ is valid on K_F. []

Def.13 (A function T_{KF}) Let K_F be a knowledge of F. A function $T_{KF} : 2^{B_{KF}} \rightarrow 2^{B_{KF}}$ for K_F is defined as follows:

    $T_{KF}(I) = \{ (v_i)A \quad B_{KF} \mid A \leftarrow MA_1, \cdots, MA_n$ is a ground instance of a clause

                    of K_{vi} or K_{any} and $I, v_i \models_F MA_1, \cdots, I, v_i \models_F MA_n\}$ []

The function T_{KF} is continuous on the complete lattice B_{KF}. The following theorem holds when $T_{KF} \uparrow n$ is defined as the ordinal powers of T_{KF} as usual[7].

Theorem 1 (The minimal model for K_F and the least fixpoint of T_{KF})
Let K_F be a knowledge on F. Then the following holds:

$$M_{KF} = lfp(T_{KF}) = T_{KF} \uparrow \omega \quad []$$

4. An Inference System and Its Soundness and Completeness

In this chapter, we give a deductive inference system for our language and show its soundness and completeness. Though it is possible to translate our knowledge representations to an equivalent many-sorted Prolog program, we will investigate a variant of SLD resolution here, because it is directly applicable to our language.

Def.14 Let v_i be a frame name and MA be a modal atom. Then we define the modal atom $\overline{(v_i)MA}$ as follows:

$$\overline{(v_i)MA} = \begin{cases} (v_j)MB & \text{if MA has the form } (v_j)MB \\ (v_i)MA & \text{otherwise.} \quad [] \end{cases}$$

Clearly, the following lemma holds.

Lemma 2 Let K_F be a knowledge, v_i and v_k be the frame names appearing in F and MA be a modal atom. Then the following statements are equivalent:
1) A goal ?- v_k where $\overline{(v_i)MA}$ is valid on K_F,
2) A goal ?- v_i where MA is valid on K_F. []

Def.15 (Resolvents) Let K_F be a knowledge, G_{vi}^{i} = ?- v_i where $MA_1, \cdots, MA_m, \cdots, MA_k$ be a goal and CS_{i+1} be a set of definite clauses. Then the goal G_{vi}^{i+1} satisfying the following conditions is said to be the resolvent obtained from G_{vi}^{i} and CS_{i+1} using the mgu θ_{i+1} on the selected atom MA_m:
1) if MA_m is an atom B, then
   a) CS_{i+1} is a set consisting of exactly one clause $A \leftarrow MB_1, \cdots, MB_n$ of K_{vi} or K_{any},
   b) θ_{i+1} is a mgu such that $B\theta_{i+1} = A\theta_{i+1}$.
   c) G_{vi}^{i+1} = ?- v_i where $(MA_1, \cdots, MA_{m-1}, MB_1, \cdots, MB_n, MA_{m+1}, \cdots, MA_k)\theta_{i+1}$.
2) if MA_m is a modal atom $(v_j)B$, then
   a) CS_{i+1} is a set consisting of exactly one clause $A \leftarrow MB_1, \cdots, MB_n$ of K_{vj} or K_{any},
   b) θ_{i+1} is a mgu such that $B\theta_{i+1} = A\theta_{i+1}$.
   c) G_{vi}^{i+1} = ?- v_i where $(MA_1, \cdots, MA_{m-1}, \overline{(v_j)MB_1}, \cdots, \overline{(v_j)MB_n}, MA_{m+1}, \cdots, MA_k)\theta_{i+1}$.
3) if MA_m is a modal atom $\langle a \rangle B$ (or $(v_j)\langle a \rangle B$) and v_r is a frame such that $\langle v_i, v_r \rangle \in E_F(a)$ (respectively, $\langle v_j, v_r \rangle \in E_F(a)$), then
   a) CS_{i+1} is a set consisting of exactly one clause $A \leftarrow MB_1, \cdots, MB_n$ of K_{vr} or K_{any},
   b) θ_{i+1} is a mgu such that $B\theta_{i+1} = A\theta_{i+1}$.
   c) G_{vi}^{i+1} = ?- v_i where $(MA_1, \cdots, MA_{m-1}, \overline{(v_r)MB_1}, \cdots, \overline{(v_r)MB_n}, MA_{m+1}, \cdots, MA_k)\theta_{i+1}$
4) if MA_m is a modal atom $[a]B$ (or $(v_j)[a]B$) and $v_r = v_1, \cdots, v_h$ are all frames satisfying the condition $\langle v_i, v_r \rangle \in E_F(a)$ (respectively, $\langle v_j, v_r \rangle \in E_F(a)$), then

a) CS_{i+1} is a set $\{C_{v1}, \cdots, C_{vh}\}$ such that each C_{vr} belongs to K_{vr} or K_{any}.

Suppose that each C_{vr} has the form $A_{vr} \langle -MB_{1_{vr}}, \cdots, MB_{n_{vr}}$. Then

b) θ_{i+1} is a mgu such that $B\theta_{i+1} = A_{v1}\theta_{i+1} = \cdots = A_{vh}\theta_{i+1}$

c) $G_{vi}^{i+1} = ?- v_i$ where $(MA_1, \cdots, MA_{m-1}, \overline{[(v_1)MB_1}]_{v_1}, \cdots, \overline{(v_1)MB_{n}}]_{v_1}], \cdots,$
$\overline{[(v_h)MB_1}]_{v_h}, \cdots, \overline{(v_h)MB_{n}}]_{v_h}], MA_{m+1}, \cdots, MA_k) \theta_{i+1}.$ []

Def.16 (Derivations and Refutations) Let K_F be a knowledge and G_{vi} be a goal. A derivation of G_{vi} on K_F consists of a sequence $G_{vi}^0 = G_{vi}$, G_{vi}^1, G_{vi}^2, $\cdots$ of goals, a sequence CS_1, CS_2, $\cdots$ of sets of clauses and a sequence θ_1, θ_2, $\cdots$ of mgu's such that G_{vi}^{i+1} is a resolvent obtained from G_{vi}^i and CS_{i+1} using θ_{i+1} on a selected atom in G_{vi}^i. A refutation of G_{vi} on K_F is a finite derivation of G_{vi} on K_F which has the empty clause as the last goal in the derivation. []

Def.17 (Computed answer substitutions) Let K_F be a knowledge and G_{vi} be a goal. A computed answer substitution θ for G_{vi} on K_F is the substitution obtained by restricting the composition $\theta_1 \cdots \theta_n$ to the variables of G_{vi}, where $\theta_1, \cdots, \theta_n$ is the sequence of mgu's in a refutation for G_{vi} on K_F. []

We can prove the following two theorems by using Theorem 1, Lemma 1 and 2, though their proofs are omitted here. We refer the reader to [7,13] for detailed proofs.

Theorem 2 (Soundness of computed answer substitutions) Let K_F be a knowledge and G_{vi} be a goal. Then every computed substitution for G_{vi} on K_F is a correct answer substitution. []

Theorem 3 (Completeness of computed answer substitution) Let K_F be a knowledge and G_{vi} be a goal. For every correct answer substitution θ for G_{vi} on K_F, there is a computed answer substitution σ for G_{vi} on K_F and a substitution γ such that $\theta = \sigma\gamma$. []

5. Modal Logic and Knowledge Representation

There are two kinds of research into the application of modal logics to knowledge representation. One of them is represented by the logics of belief or knowledge[3,6], where metaknowledges such as "believe" or "know" are represented by modal operators. In this case, the concept of possible worlds is hidden from the representation of such knowledge. The other is research[4,10,11] introducing into logics the framework for expressing the concept of possible worlds explicitly in order to describe the structure of knowledge. Modal operators are used for describing properties over the structure. Our research belongs to the latter category.

In other systems, the concept corresponding to our "viewpoint" is not investigated. Consequently, our system furnishes a stronger capability for describing knowledge structures than do others. Also, there are few researches concerning: the metaknowledge over knowledge structure; formal inference rules; and their soundness, completeness and effectiveness.

Sakakibara[10] conducted research into the programming based on a first-order modal logic. His philosophy is the same as ours. But he proposed only an outline of his language and its programming style. He neither discussed the formal semantics of his language nor gave any formal inference system. In his language, names of the relations over the set of possible worlds are assumed to be unique, so the viewpoints of modalities in this paper can be regarded as its extension. Also, the modal operators $\Box$ (necessity) and $\Diamond$ (possibility) are allowed to be at the heads of definite clauses in his language. It is used to express property inheritance over possible worlds. But the operator $\Diamond$ at the head doesn't guarantee the uniqueness of the models of knowledge expressions; that is, it has the effect that some knowledge expressions may have some least models instead of exactly one minimal model. Perhaps we can construct a linear resolution method that refutes a goal iff there is a least model making the goal valid; but we conjecture that its computation will become very complex, so that this approach is not practical. In this paper, we don't allow the operator <> at the head of a definite clause in order to achieve the effectiveness of inference.

6. Conclusion

In this paper, we have shown that structured knowledge and metaknowledge can be naturally described in our knowledge representation system, which is based on a first-order modal logic and has both the concept of viewpoints of modalities and the framework of possible-world models and schema formulas. Also, we have given a complete deductive system which is as effective as SLD resolution. Its simple inference system has been constructed in Prolog.

If the description of a property which isn't discussed in this paper, (for example, the innermost inheritance of properties) is necessary, then it is enough to introduce a new operator corresponding to that property (such as an innermost search operator). Such an extension is very easy. Also, in a sense, our research can offer a theoretical fomalization of frame systems which are intuitively defined by Minsky. For example, by using the concept of minimal models, the equivalence between two knowledge expressions in the form of a frame system can be discussed clearly and formally. Adopting a first-order modal logic as the base logic, we can formalize frame systems in a very natural way.

In the future, we will discuss the applicability of higher-order types to various kinds of metaknowledge representations. Additionally, we will investigate the problem of inductive inference for structured knowledge which is represented in our logical system. Also we have the plan to investigate the possibility of parallel processing in a processor network like a cellular machine, in which each processor corresponds to one possible world.

Acknowledgment: We would like to thank Mitunori Fukuju for helping us to write this paper, and we would like also to thank Kazuhisa Takeda for constructing the first-version of our inference system in Prolog.

References

[1] M.Abadi and Z.Manna; "A Timely Resolution", Proc. of the Symp. on Logic in Computer Science, Cambridge, MA, June (1986)
[2] M.Abadi and Z.Manna; "Modal Theorem Proving", 8th Int. Conf. on Automated Deduction, LNCS.230, pp.172-189, (1986)
[3] R.Fagin, J.Y.Halpern and M.Y.Yardi; "A Model Theoretical Analysis of Knowledge", 25th FOCS, pp.268-278, (1984)
[4] F.del Cerro.L; "MOLOG: A System That Extends PROLOG with Modal Logic", New Generation Computing, Vol.3, pp.359-383, (1985)
[5] W.D.Goldfarb; "The Undecidability of the Second-Order Unification Problem", TCS, Vol.13, pp.225-230, (1981)
[6] H.J.Levesque; "A Logic of Implicit and Explicit Belief", AAAI-84, pp.198-202, (1984)
[7] J.W.Lloyd; Foundations of Logic Programming, Springer-Verlag, (1984)
[8] D.A.Miller; "Proofs in Higher-Order Logic", Ph.D.Thesis, Carnegie-mellon Univ. (1983)
[9] G.Ventatesh; "A Decision Method for Temporal Logic Based on Resolution", Found. of Soft. Tech. & Theore. Comput. Sci., LNCS.206, pp.273-288, (1985)
[10] H.Sakakibara; "Programming in Modal Logic", Proc. of the Logic Programming '86, pp.119-126, Tokyo, (1986)
[11] H.Nakazima; Knowledge Representation and Prolog/KR, Sangyou-Tosyo, (1985)
[12] K.Iwanuma and M.Harao; "First-Order Modal Logic for Time and Space and Its Incompleteness and Relative Completeness", IEICE.(D), Vol.J70-D, No.5, pp.859-869, (1987)
[13] K.Iwanuma and M.Harao; "Knowledge Representation Based on First-Order Modal Logic", Technical Reports of IEICE, COMP86-74, (1987)

Manipulation of Embedded Context Using the Multiple World Mechanism

Akiko Kurata
University of Tsukuba
and
Hideyuki Nakashima
Electrotechnical Laboratory

Abstract

We describe a way of handling reasoning with embedded context which is created by attitude verbs such as "think" and "believe".

The meaning of the embedded sentence differs when it is extracted to the outside of the context of the attitude verb. Furthermore, some verbs enable certain kind of reasoning available within the context.

We use the multiple world mechanism of Uranus to implement the reasoning in embedded context.

1 Introduction

We describe a way of handling reasoning with embedded context which is created by attitude verbs such as "think" and "believe". We use the multiple world mechanism of Uranus to implement the reasoning mechanism.

The meaning, and thus the truth value, of a sentence embedded by attitude verb differs from the original one. For example, even when the following sentence (1) is true, we cannot say that (2) is also true. On the other hand, we can infer (4) from (1) and (3), provided that Mary has an arbitrary reasoning ability.

Mary **thinks** John is a philosopher.	(1)
John is a philosopher.	(2)
Mary **thinks** a philosopher is mortal.	(3)
Mary **thinks** John is mortal.	(4)

When the verb is "hear" instead of "think", however, we cannot infer (7) from (5) and (6). The axiom which we used to conclude (4) from (1) and (2) does not apply to (5) and (6). This means that we have to change axioms for reasoning according to the main verb of the sentence.

Louis **hears** Clark is a superman.   (5)
Louis **hears** a superman is immortal.   (6)
Louis **hears** Clark is immortal.   (7)

In this paper, we describe our attempt to use the multiple world mechanism to implement the above mechanism when given a set of attitude verbs and axioms corresponding to those verbs. The following axioms are proposed [Tee86][BP83]:

Axiom 1: $p(x,Q) \rightarrow Q$
   example: I see that a superman flies.
   $\Longrightarrow$ A superman flies.

Axiom 2: $p(x,Q \wedge R) \leftrightarrow p(x,Q) \wedge p(x,R)$
   example: I think that Clark is a male and Louis is a female.
   $\Longleftrightarrow$ I think that Clark is a male and I think that Louis is a female.

Axiom 3: $p(x,Q \vee R) \leftrightarrow p(x,Q) \vee p(x,R)$
   example: I think that Clark can fly or Jimmy can walk.
   $\Longleftrightarrow$ I think that Clark can fly or I think that Jimmy can walk.

Axiom 4: $p(x,Q \vee R) \leftarrow p(x,Q) \wedge p(x,R)$
   example: I doubt that Clark is a superman and I doubt that Jimmy is a superman.
   $\Longrightarrow$ I doubt that Clark is a superman or Jimmy is a superman.

Axiom 5: $p(x,Q(t/y)) \leftarrow p(x,Q(t/z)) \wedge p(x,y=z)$
   example: I think that he is Adam and I think that Adam ate his apple.
   $\Longrightarrow$ I think that Adam ate his apple.

Axiom 6: $p(x,Q(t/y)) \leftarrow p(x,Q(t/z)) \wedge y=z$
   example: This was an apple and you saw that he ate this.
   $\Longrightarrow$ You saw that he ate an apple.

Axiom 7: $p(x,Q) \leftarrow p(x,Q \leftarrow R) \wedge p(x,R)$
   example: I think that a lady is kind and I think taht Louis is a lady.
   $\Longrightarrow$ I think that Louis is kind.

Axiom 8: $p(x,p(x,Q)) \leftarrow p(x,Q)$
   example: I believe that Adam is a male.
   $\Longrightarrow$ I believe that I believe that Adam is a male.

Axiom 9: $p(x,\neg p(x,Q)) \leftarrow \neg p(x,Q)$
   example: I don't believe that a superman is a male.
   $\Longrightarrow$ I believe that I don't believe that a superman is a male.

Axiom 10: $\neg p(x,Q) \leftarrow p(x,\neg Q)$
   example: I think that Adam is not a human.
   $\Longrightarrow$ I don't think that Adam is a human.

In the above example, x, y and z represent the names of agents; p represents a⸀ attitude verb; Q and R represent arbitrary statements; ← and → represent logica⸀ consequences; ↔ represents logical equivalence.

We decided to use only axioms 1, 2, 4, 7, 8, 9 and 10. We did not use axiom 3, because we did not fully agreed on that. However, there should be no technic⸀ difficulty to introduce that. It is coded just like axioms 2 and 4. Axioms 5 an⸀ 6 addresses the problem of anaphora. Introducing them not only complicates th⸀ system but also is outside the scope of this paper.

We chose the following attitude verbs:

think	axiom set = {2, 7, 8, 9, 10}
believe	axiom set = {2, 7, 8, 9, 10}
know	axiom set = {1, 2, 7, 8, 9, 10}
see	axiom set = {1, 2}
doubt	axiom set = {4}

The system we describe here is implemented on Uranus [Nak86] and attacks th⸀ problem of reasoning in embedded contexts. This system accepts users input i⸀ English. If the input is a declarative sentence, it changes its database according t⸀ the information. If the input is a query, it answers according to its database.

The system consists of two parts: syntactic analysis and semantic analysis. Fo⸀ the syntax analysis, we use DCG (Definite Clause Grammars). Only the semantica⸀ treatment is described in this paper.

2 Structure of Database

The database consists of sub-databases which corresponds to different models ⸀ speakers. The multiple world mechanism of Uranus is used to implement those hier⸀ archical database. In other words, the database, into which information from inpu⸀ sentences are stored, consists of Uranus worlds. A *world* can be thought of as "con⸀ text" or "segment of database" here. Each world contains a set of Uranus clause⸀
1

2.1 Models Created by Embedded Sentences

When a person is given information on how the other is thinking about yet anothe⸀ people like:

Clark thought that Louis was angry.
Clark thought that Louis saw that Clark flew.
Clark thought that Louis thought that Clark loves her.
Louis is Clark's friend.

one may create a model according to the information as shown in figure 1.

---

[1] A Uranus clause corresponds to a Prolog clause, which is a Horn clause.

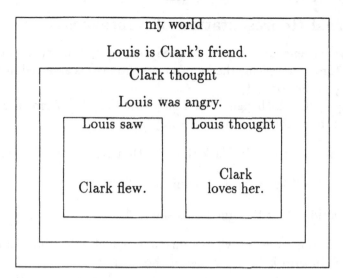

Figure 1: Nested Model of Embedded Contexts

In the figure, all the information contained in the model can be visible from outside with proper main sentence added. For example, "Louis was angry" in the model of "Clark thought" is referred to from "system's world" as "Clark thought Louis was angry".

2.2 The Multiple World Mechanism of Uranus

Uranus supports the multiple world mechanism which looks like figure 1. In Uranus terminology, those models are called "worlds". A world is referred to as:

> (with *world-name* ...)

For example, information in the world **Louis-thought** may be referred to as:

> (with Louis-thought (true (loves Clark Louis)))

The nesting of worlds in Uranus is controlled by a program and determined at the run-time of the program. On the other hand, the model people creates has a static structure of relation among worlds. The crucial difference here is that a world A is unique in Uranus while a model of A differs in human mind according to the model which contains A as its sub-model. For example, models for "Clark knows" in "Jimmy thinks" and that in "Louis thinks" may contain different information.

We provided a predicate **try** to access a unique world for each context. **try** takes a list of worlds, representing the nesting of models, and accesses its contents. By

> (try (Jimmy-think Clark-think) ...)

and

> (try (Louis-think Clark-think) ...)

we access two completely different worlds.

2.3　Internal Representation of Sentences

When the system encounters a embedded sentence, the inner-most sentence (th
internal structure representing the innermost sentence) is asserted in the proper worl
corresponding to the context.

For example, "Clark thought that Louis saw that Φ." forms a doubly embedde
context. It can be decomposed in three ways:

1. In the outermost world: Clark thought that Louis saw that Φ.

2. In the world (Clark-thought): Louis saw that Φ.

3. In the world (Clark-thought Louis-saw): Φ.

The fact Φ is in the model of what Louis saw, which is in the model of what Clar
thought, which in turn is in the model of the hearer.

We represent the above sentence by placing Φ in the world: Louis-saw, whic
exists in the world: Clark-thought, which is at the toplevel, because we assume tha
the whole model is the model of the hearer or the system. There is no "real world
in our system.

When we retrieve information, we strip the embedding sentence and goes into th
world designated by the very sentence. At the same time, we will also use the axiom
designated by the verb of the embedding sentence. In our system, the axiom set t
be used in reasoning is also stored in separate worlds.

3　Inference Mechanism

An embedded context deserves special treatment on inference used to retrieve info.
mation. In a flat sentence, we only use inference rules of the first order logic. [2] In a
embedded context, on the other hand, we use additional axioms determined by th
verb of the embedding sentence. This applies recursively to the level of embedding

3.1　Representation of Axiom Sets

During the inference, we should be able to switch axiom sets according to the verb
the embedding sentence. We regard the switching of axioms as a shift of context. A
inference of Uranus is carried out in the context of world nesting, we simply switc
the outer world and keep the program for inference (inference engine) the same. I
other words, when we encounter a new sentence, we just switch into the world whic
contains axioms for the verb, and keep going.

Let's take "think" as an example. In the context of "think", we can use axiom
2, 7, 8, 9 and 10. We define a world thinkgroup and put the corresponding inferen
rules [3] in it.

---

[2]To be precise, we use inference mechanism of Uranus, which is the same as SLD-resolution us
in Prolog.

[3]See the next section for how we represent those axioms.

When the system encounters a sentence: "Does Louis think that Clark is a human?", it sets a goal:

```
(try () (true (think Louis (human Clark))))
```

(try *context goal*) tries to solve *goal*, or to prove *goal* true in logical terms, in the context of *context*. If *context* is (), then it is tried at the top-level.

Since no direct information is available about think at the outermost world (top-level), the system goes into the world of Louis-think, and the next goal becomes:

```
(with thinkgroup (try (Louis-think) (true (human Clark))))
```

Now all the axioms on think is available to execute the goal:

```
(true (human Clark))
```

3.2 Implementation Examples of Axioms

As all the inference is achieved by the predicate try, axioms are defined in terms of try. That is, the behaviour of try differs if the axiom set is different.

We will explain implementations of several axioms in this section.

Axiom 1: $p(x,Q) \rightarrow Q$

This axiom needs special treatment, because it must be used outside the context.

This axiom does not apply to a sentence with particular verbs. On the contrary, it applies to all the sentences: When we want to know whether Q holds, we search for p(x, Q) where x ranges over verbs to which this axiom is applicable. The following program is used to realize Axiom 1:

```
0.    (assert
1.        (try *world (true* . *p))
2.        (group1 *group1)
3.        (member *act *group1)
4.        (world-name *w)
5.        (memberw (*agent (*act pt . *a) . *b) *w)
6.        (v-group2 *act *group2)
7.        (with *group2
8.               (try (*agent (*act pt . *a) . *world)
9.                    (true* . *p))))
```

The reason we use true* instead of true will be explained in the place for Axiom 7.

The essential part of this program is lines 0, 1, 7 – 9:

```
(assert
  (try *world (true* . *p))
  (with *group2
         (try (*agent (*act pt . *a) . *world)
              (true* . *p))))
```

which represents Axiom 1 directly. (*act pt . *a) is a list of a verb and it features. pt means that the verb is used in positive form.

All the other parts in the original program are computationally required details. Lines 2 and 3 searches for verbs to which this axiom applies. Lines 4 and 5 make it sure that the world to be searched by line 8 actually exists. world-name returns the names of all worlds (models) which exist.

Note that the axioms for the new verb is added by line 7. This enables all the axioms for the new verb be visible on the further inference activated by try.

Axiom 2: $p(x,Q \wedge R) \leftrightarrow p(x,Q) \wedge p(x,R)$

This axiom is divided into two rules:

$p(x,Q \wedge R) \leftarrow p(x,Q) \wedge p(x,R)$
$p(x,Q \wedge R) \rightarrow p(x,Q) \wedge p(x,R)$

If we provide both rules, the simple minded reasoning system of Uranus does not terminate by using those two rules back and forth. We treat the latter half at the time of assertion and use only the former part at the time of reasoning. In other words, when we have a sentence saying $Q \wedge R$, we assert two statements Q and R instead of $Q \wedge R$. This leaves us only the former part to program for the axiom:

```
(assert (try *world (true (and *p *q)))
        (try *world (true *p))
        (try *world (true *q)))
```

Axiom 7: $p(x,Q) \leftarrow p(x,Q \leftarrow R) \wedge p(x,R)$

This is the form of modus ponens and is the basic inference mechanism of Uranus. The internal representation of a sentence is expressed in terms of a predicate true. For example, sentences:

Jimmy is a man.	(8)
A man is mortal.	(9)

are of the form:

(true (man Jimmy))	(10)
(true (mortal *x) (man *x))	(11)

respectively.

We can use the inference mechanism of Uranus for (10) without any change provided that we have an assertion:

(assert (true (man Jimmy)))	(12)

On the other hand, (11) should be changed to

(assert (true (mortal *x)) (true (man *x)))	(13)

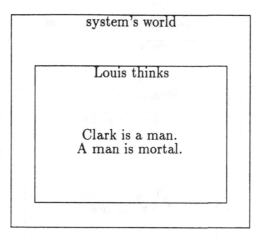

Figure 2: Initial Database

We will provide a mechanism to convert (11) into (13) where appropriate, that is, in the worlds whose corresponding verbs are those which Axiom 7 applies. By this, we can prevent the application of the inference mechanism to those verbs in which this axiom cannot be used, eg., "see".

The following definition of Axiom 7 does the job:

```
(assert (try *world (true* . *s))
        (try *world (true . *s)))
(assert (try *world (true* *s . *r))
        (try *world (true *s . *sr))
        (setdifference *sr *r *rest)
        (try *world (strans *rest)))
```

The first clause sees if the sentence is already in the database. If not, the second clause gets in action. It searches for the database with the same conclusion, and try to establish its antecedents. setdifference filters out those goals which are not satisfied by the database information. Those goals become new goals and are tried by try on the last line.

Axiom 8: $p(x,p(x,Q)) \leftarrow p(x,Q)$

This axiom applies when the same verb nests twice with same the actor. The following program is used to strip the outer world.

```
(assert (try (*agent (*act pt . *r) . *w)
        (true* ((*act pt . *r) *agent) . *sr)))
        (try *w
            (true* ((*act pt . *r) *agent) . *sr)))
```

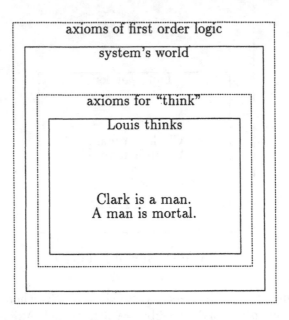

Figure 3: Setting of worlds for inference

3.3   An Example

We will explain the actual flow of reasoning with an example. Let us suppose the following input sentences:

Louis thinks that Clark is a man.	(14)
Louis thinks that a man is mortal.	(15)
Does Louis think that Clark is mortal?	(16)

Sentences (14) and (15) are declarative. They will simply be stored in the world of Louis's thought (fig 2).

On receiving the sentence (16), the system tries to infer the sentence from previous knowledge as shown in fig. 3. Axioms for the first order logic is added to the outer-most world, and axioms for the verb "think" is added to the world of "Louis thinks"(Fig. 3). Now, (17) can be derived from (14) and (15) using Axiom 7, which is included in the axiom set for "think".

Clark is mortal.   (17)

Furthermore, if we apply the conversion rule from world structure to sentence, it could be viewed like fig. 4. This is the end of the derivation of (16).

3.4   Amalgamation of Database and Inference

One of the advantages of this system is that you can plug-in various kind of axioms without changing other structure. If we regard the database with axioms as shown in fig. 4, we have no need to distinguish the derived knowledge from the knowledge

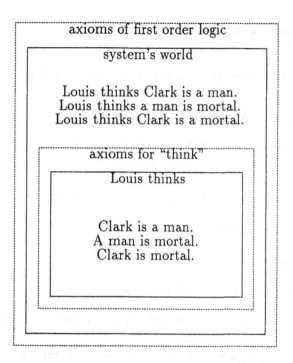

Figure 4: Final view of models

originally supplied. This fact of not distinguishing original information from derived one is also the case of human sentence recognition.

The major role of the inference mechanism provided here is to add proper axioms. All the rest should be done automatically performed by the inference mechanism of Uranus, although the system described here did not reach the point. Our final target is to get rid of the predicate **true**, so that we can use P instead of (**true** P).

4 Further Works

4.1 Reasoning between Different Worlds

In the current system, we focused on the reasoning within one linear nesting of worlds. Axiom 1 is the only exception. But it can hardly be said to use two different set of worlds, since it just exports the contents of a world.

What we left for future is reasoning employing more than one set of worlds at the same time. By this way we can handle reasoning among embedded contexts created with different verbs.

Examples follow:

I see that Clark is in Paris.   (18)

I think that Clark is in Paris.   (19)

I believe that I am a superman. (20)

I think that I am a superman. (21)

We should be able to infer (19) and (21) from (18) and (20) respectively.

4.2 Axioms for Multiply Embedded Context

At the moment, the system selects axioms according to the inner-most verb, even in the case of more than one nestings of embedded contexts. It is required to select the axioms by the set of those verbs.

For example, it is not certain that we can conclude

I think that Eve ate an apple. (22)

from

I think that Adam saw that Eve ate an apple. (23)

although the current system allows that. We may have to restrict the use of axioms inside the context of certain verbs.

We believe that the power of the multiple world mechanism should be used to attack this kind of problem. All we have done so far can be easily implemented within the scope of ordinary Prolog as shown in Teeple [Tee86]. In other words, axioms without considering its outer context are within the scope of Prolog. Our approach here is a more complex one in the hope of solving more complex problems such as shown here. Although we have not attacked them yet, we are confident of its success in the near future.

5 Conclusion

In this paper, we described an attempt to use the multiple world mechanism for the treatment of embedded context. The database of the system consists of multiple worlds which is similar to human's model that is constructed during conversation.

Axioms to be used in an embedded context is also grouped together using the multiple world mechanism. In this way, we can switch axioms easily. By the combination of the above two dimensions of separation of knowledge and axioms, we can handle reasoning in embedded contexts.

In the system, axioms and input data are represented as the same predicate. In this way, we don't have to distinguish input data and inferred sentence. This feature resembles human's not distinguishing derived semantic information from actual input sentence.

Although there are lots of future works left, we believe that this approach is useful in construction of conversational model. We also believe that this approach is extendable to handle reasoning regarding several layers of embedding at the same time.

References

[BP83] Jon Barwise and John Perry. *Situations and Attitudes*. MIT Press, 1983.

[Nak86] Hideyuki Nakashima. Uranus reference manual. *Bulletin of Electrotechnical Laboratory*, 50, 1986.

[Tee86] Douglus Teeple. *Reasoning in Embedded Contexts*. Technical Report, IBM, 1986.

Generating natural language responses appropriate to conversational situations
– In the case of Japanese –

Naohiko Noguchi   Masanori Takahashi   Hideki Yasukawa

Tokyo Research Laboratory
Matsushita Electric Industrial Co., Ltd.

17-15, Shinbashi 6-chome,
Minato-ku, Tokyo 105, Japan

Abstract

The goal of this work is to make human-machine interaction in natural language smooth and efficient. To realize this, the machine has to generate natural language sentences which are understood by users most easily. And it is important for this understandability that each sentence is appropriate to the conversational situation at the time of its utterance. In this paper, we will shed light on this appropriateness and consider how we can formalize the method to generate such appropriate sentences. First, we will define such appropriateness; second we will discuss some surface features of Japanese sentences and consider how people decide to add such features to their sentences depending on situational factors. Then we will show brief methods of deciding how to add suitable surface features to sentences in suitable situations. Finally, we will show an implementation of a conversational system which adopts these methods.

1   Introduction

In a conversational system which has some purposes and communicates with people(users) cooperatively in some natural language to achieve that purpose, it is important that the system makes the conversation with users as smooth as possible. And this enables the system to run effectively. To realize this aspect, such a system has to:

(1) Interpret user's input sentences correctly, and grasp his true intention;

In order that the system can deal with conversations similar to those which people make, the system has to grasp their true intention. Both the formalization and recognition of the speaker's intention are one of the major problems in the fields of linguistics and AI. The problem about formalizing the speaker's intention has been dealt with by the speech act theories [Searl 1969], and the problem about recognizing it has been dealt with by the plan-goal approaches [Allen 1983] based on the speech act theories.

(2) Decide the system's own response in accordance with its purposes and user's true intention;

After interpreting a user's input sentence, the system has to decide its own response. One of the criteria for deciding is to choose one response which will realize its purposes as fast as possible. And one of the necessary conditions for deciding is to have some accordance with the user's true intention which have been interpreted just before.

(3) Show the response in a natural language expression which users can understand most easily.

Finally, the system has to show its response in some natural language form. And it is a desirable aspect that users can easily understand the system's expression from the standpoint of continuation of the conversation. If this aspect is not realized, users may misunderstand the system's sentence. Then the system and the user must have further conversation in order to remove their misunderstanding, which decreases the efficiency of the whole conversation.

The system can do these three things only when it can refer to conversational situations at each point of the conversation. That is, to recognize a user's true intention from his sentence, it is necessary to take account of the things which have been understood from the previous conversation. And the system has to decide its own response based on the facts which had been recognized in the previous conversation. To show its response in a natural language expression users can easily understand, it is necessary to consider what had been communicated and what kind of expression had been used in the previous conversation.

In this paper, we will discuss (3) from above. In other words, we will consider, when the system has recognized the user's true intention correctly ((1) has been done) and has decided its response((2) has been done), how the system should express its response based on conversational situations at that time. To say more concretely, we are going to discuss

(a) what kind of factors in conversational situations should be parameterized for deciding the expression of its response and

(b) how are they used for deciding the expression.

Section 2 of this paper sheds light on the appropriateness of the expression which people generate in a conversation. The appropriateness is defined from the viewpoint of how easily people can understand that expression. In section 3, we consider some surface features of Japanese sentences and how can people decide to add these features to sentences appropriately. This appropriateness is evaluated in the meaning we define in section 2 and the methods are formalized in the form we stated above — some situational factors are used for deciding some surface features of Japanese sentences. Section 4 is related to implementation of these methods. Finally, section 5 summarizes this paper.

2 What is appropriateness?

What kinds of sentences are easily understood by people? Can we define concrete conditions for such sentences? Grice [Grice 1975] stated a principle and some maxims for cooperative conversations. They were described as rules which must be obeyed by all participants in a cooperative conversation. But they can be seen as the conditions for sentences in a conversation to be understood easily. In this paper, we define the conditions below, which are a slightly more concrete version of Grice's and which refer to levels of surface expressions.

The surface expressions of sentences in a conversation should :

(1) be consistent with what has been said before (corresponds to the Maxim of quality).

Do not use expressions which are inconsistent with the things which remarked and understood so far.

(2) offer as much information as needed to describe what the speaker really wants to say (corresponds to the Maxim of quantity).

Do not use expressions which offer more or less information than is required.

(3) have some relations to what has been said before (corresponds to the Maxim of relation).

Do use expressions which clearly show some relations to the conversation so far.

(4) be clear (corresponds to the Maxim of manner).

> Do not use ambiguous expressions and do use as clear expressions as possible.

We do not argue whether Grice's principle and maxims are valid or not. Throughout this paper, we assume that sentences which suit the conditions above are "appropriate" sentences in conversational situations.

3 Some linguistic phenomena in Japanese

In this section, we will describe some surface features of Japanese sentences and consider some relations between these features and conversational situations through the analysis of the related linguistic phenomena. In particular, we will consider the relation between the situation and the kind of surface features that sentences should have in order to satisfy the "appropriateness condition" stated in section 2. We deal with three categories of surface features of Japanese sentences here. They are

- style, topicalization and word-order variations,

- connectives,

- some referential expressions and ellipsis.

3.1 Style, topicalization and word-order variations

When we want to say something, there are many surface expressions which correctly describe what we want to say. For example, when we want to ask someone where he manufactures certain products, we can choose any sentence written below.

(1) **seihin-wo   doko-de   seizoushimasu-ka?**
products-ACC where-LOC manufacture-INT[1]
Where do you manufacture the products?

(2) **seihin-wo   seizousuru basho-wa doko-desu-ka?**
products-ACC manufacture place-TOP where-COP-INT
Where is it that you manufacture the products?

(3) **seihin-wa   doko-de   seizoushimasu-ka?**
products-TOP where-LOC manufacture-INT
As for the products, where do you manufacture these?

(4) **doko-de   seihin-wo   seizoushimasu-ka?**
where-LOC products-ACC manufacture-INT
Where do you manufacture the products?

---

[1]Through this paper, some abbreviations to express Japanese postpositions are used. They are
NOM: nominative,
ACC: accusative,
GEN: genitive,
PART: postposition which represents part-of relation,
LOC: locative,
TOP: postposition which marks topicalization,
INT: postposition which expresses an interrogative mood,
COP: copula,
CON: coordinating conjunction, and
COMP: complimentizer.

Sentences (1) and (2) differ in their style. For convenience, we call the style of sentence (1) "doushi-bun"(which corresponds to normal Japanese sentences in which the main verb is located at the end of the sentence), and the style of sentence (2), "meishi-bun" (which corresponds to the cleft sentences of English). In sentence (3), the accusative case "products" is topicalized and located at the beginning of the sentence; in sentence (1), it is also located at the beginning of the sentence but is not topicalized. Sentences (1) and (4) differ in their word-order. We will now discuss these differences and how these differences are related to the "appropriateness conditions" stated in section 2, illustrating the discussion with the following examples:

(5) **keisanki-no   memori-wo amerika-de   seizoushimasu.**
                           (wa)   **(de-wa)**
computer-PART memory-ACC America-LOC manufacture
                       (TOP)   (LOC-TOP)
I will manufacture the computer memory in America.

(6) **keisanki-no   memori-wo seizousuru basho-wa amerika-desu.**
computer-PART memory-ACC manufacture place-TOP America-COP
The place where I will manufacture the computer memory is America.
(It is America where I will manufacture the computer memory.)

(7) **keisanki-no   memori-wo amerika-de   seizoushimasu-ka?**
                           (wa)   **(de-wa)**
computer-PART memory-ACC America-LOC manufacture-INT
                       (TOP)   (LOC-TOP)
Will you manufacture the computer memory in America?

(8) **keisanki-no   memori-wo seizousuru basho-wa amerika-desuka?**
computer-PART memory-ACC manufacture place-TOP America-COP-INT
Is the place where you will manufacture the computer memory America?
(Is it America where you will manufacture the computer memory?)

(9) **keisanki-no   memori-wo doko-de   seizoushimasu-ka?**
                           (wa)
computer-PART memory-ACC where-LOC manufacture-INT
                       (TOP)
Where will you manufacture the computer memory?

(10) **keisanki-no   memori-wo seizousuru basho-wa doko-desu-ka?**
computer-PART memory-ACC manufacture place-TOP where-COP-INT
Where is the place in which you will manufacture the computer memory?
(Where is it in which you will manufacture the computer memory?)

Sentences (5),(7), and (9) are "doushi-bun" and sentences (6),(8), and (10) are "meishi-bun". First, we consider the difference between "doushi-bun" and "meishi-bun" in declarative sentences. (5) and (6) seem to mean exactly the same thing, but their true meaning is slightly different because of the difference of style. (5) states that the specific event in which the speaker manufactures the products is true, while (6) states that the place where the speaker manufactures the products and America are the same. That kind of difference is clarified if you imagine the situation in which one wants to manufacture the products in America and England. In such situation, it is possible to use such expressions as below.

keisanki-no   memori-wo amerika-de seizoushimasu.
computer-PART memory-ACC America-LOC manufacture
I will manufacture the computer memory in America.

keisanki-no   memori-wo amerika-to igirisu-de   seizoushimasu.
computer-PART memory-ACC America-CON England-LOC manufacture
I will manufacture the computer memory in America and England.

keisanki-no   memori-wo seizousuru basho-wa amerika-to   igirisu-desu.
computer-PART memory-ACC manufacture place-TOP America-CON England-COP
The places where I will manufacture the computer memory are America and England.

But (6) is not suitable for this situation. Because "The place where I will manufacture the computer memory" and "America" are not exactly the same. In (6), "keisanki-no memori-wo seizousuru basho (the place where I will manufacture the computer memory)" is topicalized, so we can recognize that the place is old information, i.e., someone has already referred to this place in the conversation. Only in the situation in which someone has already referred to the place where someone would manufacture the computer memory, can he use sentence (6) as an appropriate expression. On the other hand, (5) does not have such limitation.

Next, let's consider (7) and (8). In such yes/no-questions, there is an essential ambiguity — what does the speaker want to ask? For example, there are several possible interpretations of (7):

- Will you manufacture the computer memory or will you manufacture other things?

- Will you manufacture the computer memory in America or will you manufacture them in other places?

- Will you manufacture the computer memory in America or won't you manufacture them in America?

Ordinarily, one can change the order of postpositional phrases (PPs) or topicalize some PP to make the interpretation of the question clearer. Then, what is the relationship between this kind of ambiguities and these linguistic methods (topicalizations, word-order variations)? Since (7) has two PPs, we can make the sentences below from (7) by changing the order of PPs or topicalizing these PPs.

(11) **keisanki-no   memori-wa amerika-de seizoushimasu-ka?**
    computer-PART memory-TOP America-LOC manufacture-INT
    As for the computer memory, will you manufacture them in America?

This means that "will you manufacture the computer memory in America or will you manufacture them in another place?"

(12) **keisanki-no   memori-wo amerika-de-wa   seizoushimasu-ka?**
    computer-PART memory-ACC America-LOC-TOP manufacture-INT
    As for America, will you manufacture the computer memory there?

This sentence is appropriate only in the situation in which the speaker and the hearer know that the hearer will manufacture the computer memory in at least one country other than America, or that he won't manufacture them in at least one country other than America.(The latter is more ordinary.) It means "although you won't manufacture in that country, will you manufacture in America?"(this "wa" should be recognized as "contrastive-wa".)

(13) **amerika-de-wa   keisanki-no   memori-wo seizoushimasu-ka?**
    America-LOC-TOP computer-PART memory-ACC manufacture-INT
    As for America, will you manufacture the computer memory there?

This means "will you manufacture the computer memory in America or will you manufacture other products in America?"
It is presupposed that the hearer will manufacture something in America.

(14) **amerika-de keisanki-no memori-wa seizoushimasu-ka?**
America-LOC computer-PART memory-TOP manufacture-INT
As for the computer memory, will you manufacture them in America?

The meaning of this sentence is the same as (11).
This sentence is appropriate only in the situation in which the speaker and the hearer know that the hearer will manufacture at least one product other than the computer memory in America, or that he won't manufacture at least one product other than the computer memory in America. (The latter is more ordinary.) In this case, this sentence means "although you won't manufacture other products, will you manufacture the computer memory?"

(15) **keisanki-no memori-wa amerika-de-wa seizoushimasu-ka?**
computer-PART memory-TOP America-LOC-TOP manufacture-INT
As for the computer memory and as for America, will you manufacture them there?
As for the computer memory, will you manufacture them in America in contrast with any other country?

This sentence is appropriate only in the situation in which the speaker and the hearer know that the hearer will manufacture the computer memory in at least one country other than America, or that he won't manufacture them in at least one country other than America. (The former is more ordinary.)
It means "although you will manufacture in other countries, will you manufacture in America?"
It is presupposed that the hearer will manufacture the computer memory somewhere.

(16) **amerika-de-wa keisanki-no memori-wa seizoushimasu-ka?**
America-LOC-TOP computer-PART memory-TOP manufacture-INT
As for America and as for the computer memory, will you manufacture them there?
As for America, will you manufacture the computer memory in contrast with any other products there?

This sentence is appropriate only in the situation in which the speaker and the hearer know that the hearer will manufacture at least one product other than the computer memory in America, or that he won't manufacture at least one product other than the computer memory in America. (The former is more ordinary.) It means "although you will manufacture the other product, will you manufacture the computer memory?"
It is presupposed that the hearer will manufacture something in America.

According to above examples, we can understand that the PP which is topicalized and moved to the beginning of the sentence takes a role in the presupposed event. What the speaker wants to ask is clear in the sentence where some PP is topicalized, because its presupposed facts become more obvious. On the other hand, a PP located in front of the main verb is a sign of what the speaker wants to ask, but if the PP that is located in front of the main verb is topicalized, the situation may be changed. Although we can recognize it as such a sign by interpreting "wa" which marks that PP as the "contrastive-wa". (Especially in (12), we can only interpret it this way.) To sum up, when one utters a yes/no-question in "doushi-bun" style, one can make the sentence appropriate by topicalizing some PP or changing the order of PPs in relation to the presupposed facts at the time of the utterance. On the other hand, in (8), the speaker verifies the equality between "the place where you will manufacture the computer memory" and "America", so he presupposes that "there is a place where you will manufacture the computer memory" and also that "you will manufacture the computer memory". Therefore, we can't interpret this sentence as the speaker asking someone whether he will manufacture or not, and there is no ambiguity at all concerning what the speaker wants to ask. That is to say, in (7), the speaker verifies whether a specific event is true or not, or whether a specific role is valid to let a specific event be true, but in (8), he verifies the equality between two objects. We can understand this difference well by considering the situation in which the hearer will manufacture the computer memory in America and England. In such a situation, each pair of question-response described below is appropriate.

Q: **keisanki-no   memori-wo amerika-de seizoushimasu-ka?**
computer-PART memory-ACC America-LOC manufacture-INT
Will you manufacture the computer memory in America?

A: **hai, amerika-to igirisu-de   seizoushimasu.**
yes, America-CON England-LOC manufacture
Yes, I will manufacture them in America and England.

Q: **keisanki-no   memori-wo seizousuru-basho-wa amerika-desu-ka?**
computer-PART memory-ACC manufacture-place-TOP America-COP-INT
Is the place where you will manufacture the computer memory America?
(Is it America where you will manufacture the computer memory?)

A: **iie, amerika-to igirisu-desu.**
no, America-CON England-COP
No, it is America and England.

Finally, let's think about differences between (9) and (10), which are both wh-questions. There is also a difference between (9) and (10) which we have already considered in the case of yes/no-questions. That is to say, in (9), the speaker wants to ask about the location which makes the event that the hearer will manufacture the computer memory true, but in (10), he wants to ask whether the location is the same as the place where the hearer will manufacture the computer memory. This difference will be clearer with the examples below.

Q1: **keisanki-no   memori-wo doko-de   seizoushimasu-ka?**
computer-PART memory-ACC where-LOC manufacture-INT
Where will you manufacture the computer memory?

A1: **amerika-de seizoushimasu.**
America-LOC manufacture
I will manufacture in America.

Q2: **hoka-no basho-de-mo sore-wo   seizoushimasu-ka?**
other   place-LOC-also these-ACC manufacture-INT
Will you manufacture them in any other country?

A2: **hai, igirisu-de-mo   seizoushimasu.**
yes, England-LOC-also manufacture
Yes, I will manufacture in England, too.

Q: **keisanki-no   memori-wo seizousuru-basho-wa doko-desu-ka?**
computer-PART memory-ACC manufacture-place-TOP where-COP-INT
Where is the place in which you will manufacture the computer memory?

A: **amerika-to igirisu-desu.**
America-CON England-COP
America and England.

(17) **keisanki-no   memori-wo dokoka-de   seizoushimasu-ka?**
computer-PART memory-ACC somewhere-LOC manufacture-INT
Will you manufacture the computer memory somewhere and where is it?

We can interpret (17) as either a yes/no-question or a wh-question. If we interpret it as a yes/no-question, what the speaker wants to ask is whether the event in which one will manufacture the computer memory is true or not. And if we interpret it as a wh-question, its meaning is the same as that of (9). Because of this ambiguity, if the speaker uses a sentence like (17), he can ask whether the event described in the sentence becomes true or not, and if it's true, he can also ask where does it become true, when does it become true, what role is required for the event to become true, and so on. In (17), of course, it is not presupposed that the hearer will manufacture the computer memory.

So far, we have considered the differences between "doushi-bun" style sentences and "meishi-bun" style sentences. We have also considered the relationship between such differences and surface features of the sentences — word-order variations and topicalization. We conclude that when the speaker chooses an expression, his decision depends on the following situational factors:

1-a presupposed facts relating to the event which the speaker wants to describe, and

1-b the point about which the speaker wants to ask in the event which he wants to describe.

If one does not choose an expression depending on these factors correctly, one may create sentences which are inappropriate to the conversational situation. For example, he may say "keisanki-no memori-wo seizousuru basho-wa doko-desu-ka?" (Where is the place in which you will manufacture the computer memory?) in a situation where the hearer has no intention of manufacturing the computer memory.

3.2 Connectives

Connectives, which are located at the beginning of sentences, are used for expressing the relationship between previous utterances in the conversation and the present utterance. For example, connectives like "tokorode (by the way)" and "sate (well)" are used for changing a formerly discussed topic to a new one. Connectives like "soredewa (if so)", "sorede (then)" are used for maintaining formerly discussed topics or entering into details of these topics. For making the relationship between the previous conversation and the present utterance clear, it is necessary to use suitable connectives in the utterance in suitable situations. Then, what kind of situational information motivates the creation of "connective-added" sentences? There are two aspects of the relationship which the present utterance has in the conversation. They are:

A. relationship between the speaker's (one's own) last utterance and the present utterance and

B. relationship between the hearer's (the other's) last utterance and the present utterance.

The relationship which belongs to the category A comes to the surface when one participant (the speaker) has continued to lead the conversation. In ordinary question-answering conversation, the questioner has continued to lead and repeats the pair of "question-and-answer" utterances. In such a situation, the questioner chooses questions one by one from his prepared set of questions depending only upon his purpose. So the relationship between his last question and the present question is projected on the relationship between his last utterance and the present utterance. On the other hand, a category B relationship comes to the surface when the conversation goes in a direction which the speaker doesn't expect. When the other's answer is not sufficient, or when it is incorrect, or when the other says that he wants to take the lead in the conversation, the speaker should make some atypical conversation. In the first case, the speaker should say "please describe in detail." In the second case, he should say "you are wrong, because... and please answer it correctly." and In the last case, he should conform to the other's request. In such situations, the speaker should understand the other's true intention. The relationship between the previous utterances and the present utterance depends on how the speaker chooses his intention and the content of response according to the other's true intention. Here is an example:

Q1: **keisanki-no   memori-nikansuru tokkyo-wo tsukatteiru-no-desu-ka?**
computer-PART memory-concerning patent-ACC use-COP-INT
Have you used a patent for the computer memory?

A1: **hai.**
yes
Yes.

Q2: **sorede, sono-tokkyo-wa zenbude nanken-desu-ka?**
then   the-patent-TOP all   how many-COP-INT
Then, how many patents are there in all?

A2: **ikken-desu.**
one-COP
one.

Q3: **soredewa, sono-tokkyobangou-wa   irete-kudasai.**
then   the-number of the patent-TOP input-please
Then, please input the patent number.

A3: **nihontokkyo2312203.**
Japan patent 2312203
Japan patent 2312203.

Q4: **tokorode, keisanki-no   memori-wo seizoushiteiru-basho-wa doko-desu-ka?**
by the way computer-PART memory-ACC manufacture-place-TOP   where-COP-INT
By the way, where is it that you have manufactured the computer memory?

A4: **nihon-de seizoushi, nihon-to   amerika-de hanbaishiteiru.**
Japan-LOC manufacture Japan-CON America-LOC have sold
we have manufactured in Japan and sold in Japan and America.

Q5: **sousuruto, amerika-ni   yushutsushiteiru-no-desu-ne?**
so   America-LOC have exported-COMP-COP-INT
So, is it true that you have exported it into America?

A5: **hai.**
yes
Yes.

In the example, from Q1 to Q4, a category A relationship came to the surface of the conversation and connectives like "sorede", "soredewa" and "tokorode" appeared. That is, the questioner repeated questions in accordance with his purpose, and he maintained topics ("sorede"), or entered into details ("soredewa"), or changed topics ("tokorode"). But in Q5, because the answerer had said more than had been required, the questioner confirmed the result he inferred from the answerer's remarks (if one manufactures some products in Japan and sells them in Japan and America, it is probably true that he exports them from Japan to America). In such a situation, a category B relationship appeared and the connective "sousuruto" was added to the sentence.

To sum up, the speaker decides whether to add connectives to his utterance or not and what kind of connectives to add, depending on two situational factors:

2-a the structure of his prepared topics, and

2-b his choice of intention and content of his utterances in accordance with the other's previous true intention.

3.3 Some referential expressions and ellipsis

When people make conversation, they use many referential expressions, each of which is appropriate to the conversational situation at the time of their utterance. They also use ellipsis which is appropriate at that time. In this section, we will discuss how we assign referential expressions to some referents and how we choose to use ellipsis. We will also discuss what kind of situational factors are used for such decisions.

First, let's consider ellipsis.

In real conversations, participants hardly offer more information than is required. This is so when one is asked a question and one replies. For example, when you are asked,

"Where are you going to see the movie?"

it's more ordinary to reply

"Shibuya."

or

"Shinjuku."

than to reply

"I'm going to Shinjuku."

or

"I'm going to Shibuya to see a movie."

But if you know that the questioner doesn't know what movie you are going to see and you think that he wants to know the movie, you ordinary reply,

"I'm going to Shinjuku to see "Rocky-4""

which has more information than is asked. That is to say, when one replies to some question, it's ordinary to say only what he is asked. One offers more information only if the information has enough reason to be uttered in the situation at that time. This is so not only in this case (question-and-answer case) but in any other case. (It corresponds to Grice's "maxim of quantity".) Therefore, choosing to use ellipsis for some referent is reduced to examining whether there is enough reason for it to be uttered. And if there is no reason for it to be uttered, one can realize an appropriate utterance by using ellipsis for that referent. There are many reasons for some referents to be uttered, such as:

- referent which is a central topic in the conversation,

- referent which has never been uttered in the conversation before,

- referent which has a central role in the situation that corresponds to the speaker's utterance.

If a referent is not omitted from one's utterance, it can be referred to with several types of expressions. These types are:

(1) pronoun,

(2) specifier-added expression ("sono-tokkyo", "kono-hito", etc.),

(3) proper noun,

(4) common noun,

(5) expression with relative clause.

The speaker probably chooses one of these types of expressions for each referent, the one which is the most suitable to the situation at that time. Then, what is the relationship between that choice and conversational situations?

First, we will consider type (1) and (2) expressions. Generally, there are several ways to refer by noun phrases.

```
        ┌─────── specific reference ────────┬─────── unique reference
        │                                   │
        │                                   └─────── generic reference
        │
        └─────── non-specific reference
```

The sentences below are examples of these types of referring.

(18) **sono-tokkyo-wa boku-ga kakimashita.**
   the-patent-TOP   I-NOM   wrote
   The patent, I wrote.

(19) **tokkyo-wa aru-ittei-no kikan-wo   sugiru-to   mukou-ni-naru.**
   patent-TOP some-fixed   duration-ACC pass-COMP non effective-become
   Patents will be non-effective after some period.

(20) **wareware-wa ichinen-ni ikken tokkyo-wo kakanakereba-naranai.**
   we-TOP   one year-per one   patent-ACC write-must
   We must write one patent a year.

In (18), "sono-tokkyo (the patent)" refers to some specific patent which the speaker wrote. In (19), "tokkyo (patents)" refers to the generic class of patents. And in (20), "tokkyo (patent)" refers to one non-specific patent. That difference comes from the difference in the way the speaker grasps these referents. The specifier-added expression is only used for unique reference.

Moreover, all referents should be identified by the hearer. There are several types of context which the hearer can use for that identification process. They are:

```
        ┌─────── linguistic context
        │
        └─────── non-linguistic context ───────┬─────── direct
                                                │
                                                └─────── indirect (commonsense, mutual belief)
```

A referential expression which refers to a referent in the linguistic context is ordinarily called "anaphora". When it refers to a referent in the non-linguistic direct context, it is ordinarily called "deixis". A specifier-added expression can not be used for any referent in the non-linguistic indirect context. When the hearer identifies the referent and chooses a candidate from these contexts, he will choose one which has been introduced into the context most recently. Conversely, the speaker uses referential expressions considering the hearer's process of identification of the referent. Therefore, when the speaker uses a referential expression, he chooses the expression depending on how recently its referent has been introduced into the context.

Next, let's consider type (3),(4) and (5) expressions. The way to decide which type of these expressions the speaker uses mainly depends on how he grasps the referent and whether there is an indication act or not. It is generally accepted that all proper nouns indicate referents specifically which are in the non-linguistic indirect context. So when the speaker uses a proper noun to refer to the referent, there is an obvious indication act by him, and he grasps the referent as unique and specific object. On the other hand, when he uses a common noun to refer to the referent, it may not be so. It is not decidable from the referential expression how the speaker grasps the referent and whether there is an indication act or not. It depends on the conversational situation. Noun phrases with relative clauses guarantee that there is some identification act by the speaker, if the relative clauses are used restrictively. But it is not decidable from the referential expression only whether these are used restrictively or not. Some information contained in the conversational situations is needed. From the standpoint of the speaker, if he wants to indicate some object by a referential expression (i.e., if there is an indication act), he wants the hearer to identify the object correctly. Therefore, to communicate such an intention to the hearer and to let the hearer recognize that, the speaker should use referential expressions that express the existence of the indication act clearly. If it is realized, the speaker can make clearer sentences in the sense of Grice's maxim of manner. As a result, we have a general criterion, which defines the way to choose referential expressions, namely, when one wants to indicate some object, one should choose a referential expression that expresses the existence of the indication act more clearly.

We briefly summarize the points discussed here. In deciding which type of referential expression the speaker should use, he has to consider the situational factors described below:

3-a whether there is an indication act by the speaker or not,

3-b how does the speaker grasp the referent,

3-c what type of context is the referent in, and

3-d how recently has the referent been introduced into the context.

4 Implementation and some example

We are doing research on a conversational system named "ToR". It is a kind of computer-aided documentation system which helps people draw contracts. This system holds a conversation with the human user, extracts the user's intention and request, interprets them as contracting conditions and finally produces a form of the contract. We have developed a prototype of the system which is based on the discussion in this paper. Our conclusions are applied to the interface of ToR, which carries a conversation with the user in Japanese. More concretely, when ToR offers its response on the CRT-display to the user, ToR considers the conversational situation at that point of time to create sentences which the user can understand most easily. In this section, we will state how ToR creates sentences relating to what we have discussed in section 3. In 4.1 we will describe how to represent the information about conversational situations. In 4.2, we will describe the framework and the methods to decide on three surface features, which are discussed in section 3, based on that information. We will briefly review the implementation of ToR in 4.3. Finally, in 4.4, we will demonstrate an example and explain how ToR runs according to the example.

4.1 Representation of the information about conversational situations

In ToR, the content of the user's utterances, the concepts about contracts and the content of ToR's utterances are all represented in LAST (LAnguage based on Situations and Types), which is a kind of knowledge representation language based on Situation theory [Barwise 1987]. It has major functions required for a conversational system. [Yasukawa 1987] In ToR, the facts which are recognized through the conversation with the user are registered into the LAST database. For example, when the user says,

uchi-ga ICOT-no tokkyo-wo tsukatteiru.
we-NOM ICOT-GEN patent-ACC have used
we have used the ICOT's patents.

the instance of a situation type, where the user has used patents which are owned by ICOT in order to manufacture and sell something, is registered into the database as a fact. Figure 1 shows such an instance of a situation type.

X = use(agt:S1,obj:O,purpose:P),

Y = possess(agt:S2,obj:O),

S1 = USER,

S2 = ICOT,

O typeof patent,

P typeof product.

registered objects = [X,Y,S1,S2,O,P]

Figure 1: LAST expressions registered into the database

The content of ToR's response to the user is also represented in a set of intermediate expressions of LAST (i.e., expressions not registered in the database). For instance, the content of the utterance below

ICOT-no tokkyo-wo tsukatte, keisanki-no   memori-wo seizoushiteiru.
ICOT-GEN patent-ACC use   computer-PART memory-ACC have manufactured
we have manufactured the computer memory using ICOT's patents.

is represented in a set of intermediate LAST expressions described in Figure 2.

X = manufacture(agt:S1,obj:O1),

Y = use(agt:S1,obj:O2,purpose:O1),

Z = possess(agt:S2,obj:O2),

W = partof(obj1:O1,obj2:O3),

S1 = USER,

S2 = ICOT,

O1 typeof memory,

O2 typeof patent,

O3 typeof computer.

utterance content = [X,Y,Z,W,S1,S2,O1,O2,O3]

Figure 2: LAST expressions corresponding to the utterance content

The information about the conversational situation at the point of each utterance is basically contained in the LAST database. Referring to the conversational situation is reduced to observing the relationship between the intermediate LAST expressions which represent the utterance content and the LAST database. To observe such a relationship, LAST provides some built-in predicates such as:

hold(X):
examines whether the partially instantiated type X holds in the database or not.

hold_same_rel(Rel,Y):
  examines whether the specific relation Rel holds in the instantiated situation type Y in the database or not.

Using these predicates, we can examine the condition 1-a discussed in 3.1.

There are several sorts among the objects of LAST. They are:

- instance (unique object)

- generic (generic object)

- set

The sorts of LAST objects represent the different ways for ToR to grasp objects. Therefore this represents the information 3-b discussed in 3.3. We can get the sort of an object by the built-in predicate "sortof".

sortof(X,Sort):
  returns sort Sort of the object X.

But the LAST database contains only recognized facts flatly, so there is no distinction among the objects referred to in the real utterance and the ones deduced by inference. We don't know how recently each object has been introduced into the conversation. To represent these aspects, we construct some structured data such as:

(1) the list of LAST objects which are referred to in each utterance:

  it stores LAST objects which are referred to explicitly by either the user or ToR

(2) the list of LAST objects which are introduced into the conversation:

  it stores LAST objects which are introduced into the conversation relating to each utterance, and it also categorizes these objects according to the time they were introduced;
  1 objects which were introduced by the last user's utterance,
  2 objects which were introduced by ToR's last utterance, and
  3 objects which had been introduced in some previous utterances.

We can consider the objects in (1) as the objects in the linguistic context. We can consider the objects categorized in (2) as introduced into the attentional state of the participants by some utterances, so there also exist objects which have not been referred to explicitly. Categories 1,2, and 3 represent the time sequence of these objects. (This represents 3-c and 3-d discussed in 3.3)

We also construct some structured data relating to the continuity of the conversation such as:

(3) the retroactive records of topics which have been discussed in the conversation:

  ToR has a set of topics to ask, which are related to contracts. At the time of each utterance, ToR registers the central topic of the utterance.

(4) the retroactive records of intentions which each participant has at the time of each utterance:

  ToR registers intentions of the user and ToR at the time of each utterance. Categories of intentions are defined provisionally as described below. Categories of the user's intentions are:
  1 answering ToR's question,
  2 requesting some explanation,
  3 requesting to know some information about the contract which has been partially decided by the conversation so far, and
  4 requesting to know how the user answers ToR's question.
  Categories of ToR's intentions are:
  1 informing the user of some information,
  2 explaining,
  3 asking, and
  4 confirming.

These data represent 2-1 and 2-b discussed in 3.2.

4.2 How to choose surface features for ToR's responses

ToR generates Japanese sentences corresponding to the utterance content, which is represented in a set of LAST expressions, examining the relationship between the utterance content and the information about the conversational situations described in 4.1. Figure 3 is the framework of this process.

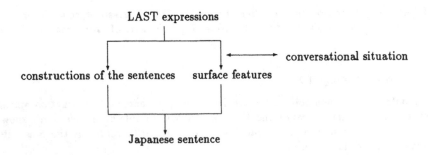

Figure 3: The framework of the process

Now, we will describe the methods which choose surface features for ToR's sentences from a set of LAST expressions.

4.2.1 Method to choose style, topicalized element and word-order

According to the discussion in 3.1, surface features such as style, topicalization and word-order are chosen based on conversational situations. The method to do this is described below:

1. In the case where there is some presupposed fact of the utterance content (this can be examined by the predicate "hold"),

   1-1. In the case where there is a point ToR wants to ask about especially,

      1-1-1. choose "meishi-bun" style and put the expression of the object, which corresponds to what ToR wants to ask about, at the end of the sentence,

      1-1-2. if we can't choose "meishi-bun" style because of some reason,
      - choose "doushi-bun" style,
      - topicalize the object which corresponds to the presupposed fact and
      - put the expression of the object, which corresponds to what ToR wants to ask about, just before the sentence predicate.

   1-2. In the case where there is no point ToR wants to ask about especially,
      - choose "doushi-bun" style and
      - topicalize the object which corresponds to the presupposed fact.

2. In the case where there is no presupposed fact of the utterance content,

   2-1. In the case where there is a point ToR wants to ask about especially,
      - choose "doushi-bun" style,

- put the expression of the object, which corresponds to what ToR wants to ask about, just before the sentence predicate and
- if the utterance content corresponds to the wh-question, choose an expression such as (17) — use "some-wh" in the sentence.

2-2. In the case where there is no point ToR wants to ask about especially, choose "doushi-bun" style.

4.2.2 Method to add suitable connectives

According to the discussion in 3.2, we can summarize how to decide whether to add suitable connectives to the sentences.

1. In the case where ToR has been leading the conversation, ToR should refer to the retroactive records of topics and should add an appropriate connective in accordance with the relationship of the current topic to the last topic. There are several kinds of relationships described below:

   - changing the topic,
   - maintaining the topic and
   - entering into the details of the last topic.

2. In the case where the user answers with something ToR didn't expect, ToR should refer to the retroactive records of utterance intentions and should add an appropriate connective in accordance with the relationship between the current ToR's intention and intentions so far.

4.2.3 Method to use ellipsis and to choose referential expressions

We describe how to use ellipsis and how to choose referential expressions as follows.

1. If there is some reason for an object not to be omitted from the sentence in the conversational situation at that time, choose a referential expression for it according to the method described in 2 (below). Otherwise, use ellipsis for the object. The following may be reasons for not omitting the object:

   - the object is what ToR wants to ask about.
   - the object is a kind of new information that has not been introduced in the conversation so far.
   - the object is what ToR wants to confirm.

2. For the objects which are not omitted,

   2-1. an object which is introduced by both ToR's last utterance and the user's last utterance and which is expressed explicitly in at least one of these utterances should be referred to by a pronoun.

   2-2. an object which has a proper name should be referred to by the proper name.

   2-3. an object which is introduced by either ToR's last utterance or the user's last utterance and which is expressed explicitly in at least one of these utterances should be referred to by a specifier-added expression.

   2-4. an object which was expressed explicitly in the former utterances should be referred to by the same expression.

   2-5. an object other than the ones described above should be referred to by a common noun which corresponds to the class of the object.

4.3 Implementation

ToR has been implemented in Quintus-PROLOG, which is running on Micro VAX 2. ToR can carry a simple conversation in Japanese with the user and then write out a draft of a contract in English. In this section, we will briefly explain the implementation, especially of the process which chooses surface features for ToR's responses. That process receives a set of LAST expressions which corresponds to ToR's sentence as an input and yields a rough construction of ToR's sentence and surface features which apply to the construction as an output. It consists of a group of production rules, a rule applier which selects suitable rules and applies these rules, and an information manager, which holds and manages information about the conversational situation. (It is depicted in Figure 4.)

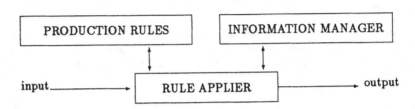

Figure 4: Process configuration

The format of the production rules is described below.

RULE_NAME::PRIORITY,
PATTERNS OF LAST EXPRESSION,
PATTERNS OF WORKING MEMORY,
CONDITIONS OF CONVERSATIONAL SITUATION
⟹ SURFACE FEATURES.

Figure 5 shows an example of that rule.

> style_concept_completion::15,
> [_,X,Sit],
> working([[utterance_type,[[question_type,concept_completion]]]]),
> discourse_condition([hold(Sit,Sit1)])
> ⟹ [additional_information,[[style,meishibun]]].

Figure 5: An example of the rule

The meaning of each item of the rule is:

(1) RULE_NAME: identifier of the rule,

(2) PRIORITY: priority of the rule,

(3) PATTERNS OF LAST EXPRESSION:
   patterns of a set of LAST expressions corresponding to ToR's utterance,

(4) PATTERNS OF WORKING MEMORY:
   patterns of a set of surface features which are chosen by the application of other rules,

(5) CONDITIONS OF CONVERSATIONAL SITUATION:
   conditions of the conversational situation at each point of time that enable the application of the rule,

(6) SURFACE FEATURES:

surface features of ToR's sentence which is concluded by the application of this rule.

For example, the meaning of the rule depicted in Figure 5 is,

> "If the set of LAST expressions which corresponds to ToR's utterance content represents that the utterance is a wh-question, and if the event which corresponds to ToR's utterance content is a presupposed fact, then choose "meishi-bun" style."

The rule applier selects the applicable rules and applies them one by one to choose surface features for ToR's sentence. If more than two rules are applicable at the same time, it choose one rule whose priority is the highest among these rules. When there is no applicable rule, surface features which have been chosen so far are the result.

4.4　How does ToR work?

Figure 6 shows an example of a conversation between ToR and the user. S*n*s are ToR's utterances, and U*n*s are the user's utterances.

S1: **konkai-wa donna goyou-desu-ka?**
　　What can I do for you?

U1: **ICOT-no　tokkyo-wo uchi-ga tsukatteiru.**
　　ICOT-GEN patent-ACC we-NOM have used
　　I have used ICOT's patents.

S2: **sono-tokkyo-wa nanken-desu-ka?**
　　that-patent-TOP how many-COP-INT
　　As for the patents, How many are there?

U2: **nihontokkyo2312203-to　　nihontokkyo2312201-no 2ken desu.**
　　Japanese patent 2312203-CON Japanese patent 2312201　two　COP
　　They are two, Japanese patent 2312203 and Japanese patent 2312201.

S3: **sore-wa　　donoyouna seihin-ni　　tsukatteimasu-ka?**
　　Them-TOP what kind　product-ACC have used-INT
　　What kind of products have you used them for ?

U3: **keisanki-no　　memori-desu.**
　　computer-PART memory-COP
　　The computer memory.

S4: **tokorode, sono-memori-wa dokoka-de　　seizoushiteimasu-ka?**
　　by the way the-memory-TOP　anywhere-LOC have manufactured-INT
　　By the way, as for the memory, have you manufactured them anywhere?

U4: **nihon-de　seizoushite, nihon-to　amerika-de　hanbaishiteiru.**
　　Japan-LOC manufacture Japan-CON America-LOC have sold
　　We have manufactured (them) in Japan and sold (them) in Japan and America.

S5: **amerika-ni　yushutsushiteimasu-ne?**
　　America-LOC have exported-INT
　　Is it true that you have exported (it) to America?

U5: **hai.**
　　yes
　　Yes.

Figure 6: An example of a conversation between ToR and USER

Now we will explain how ToR chooses surface features for its response in the above example.

In S2, ToR asked for the number of patents which the user had used. Because the patents which ToR referred to in S2 were the same as those which the user referred to in U1, ToR chose a specifier-added referential expression "sono-tokkyo (the patents)" in S2.

In S3, since the patents had been specified by the conversation before, ToR asked what products the user had manufactured using these patents. This time, ToR chose a pronoun to refer to ICOT's patents in place of a specifier-added expression. That is because the patents had been referred to in both S2 and U2. And at that point of the conversation, ToR had recognized that the user had used ICOT's patents based on the interpretation of U1, so it's appropriate to topicalize the patents in S3 ("sore-wa").

In S4, since both the patents and the products had been specified by the conversation so far, ToR changed topics and asked about manufacturing and selling the products. At that point, there had been a situation in which ToR had continued to lead the conversation and there was change of topics; therefore, ToR decided to add a connective "tokorode (by the way)" to S4. Also at that point, ToR had recognized that the user had used the patents in connection with the computer memory but it had not recognized that the user had manufactured and sold these products using these patents. Because of that situation, ToR chose the sentence S4. (The word "anywhere" was added at the end of the sentence.) That is to say, the meaning of S4 is, whether the user had manufactured or not, and if the user had manufactured, also where the user had manufactured. Moreover, the computer memory was topicalized ("sono-memori-wa") because of the fact that the computer memory were referred to in U3 by the expression "keisanki-no memori".

5 Summary and concluding remarks

We have analyzed the method which makes responses of the system more understandable to the user in order for the system to conduct efficient conversation with people. And we have considered these method from a standpoint of performance of language.

We have discussed the information in conversational situations needed for a decision on the choice of surface features of sentences. The correspondence between the conditions on appropriate sentence and surface features discussed in section 3 is described below:

(1) The correct choice of style, topicalized object and word-order makes the sentence consistent and clear.

(2) The insertion of appropriate connectives makes the relationship between the sentence and the previous utterances clear.

(3) The appropriate use of ellipsis appropriately makes the information conveyed by the sentence necessary and sufficient.

(4) The correct choice of referential expressions makes the sentence clear.

We have realized this method in the prototype of the contract making system(ToR) which we had already developed.

It seems that surface features of sentences are decided on according to many factors in conversational situations, so the method discussed in this paper is only one method and is restricted to only three surface features. But the framework in which surface features of sentences are decided on based on such situational factors is general. It can be applied to a future conversational system.

Acknowledgements

We would like to thank Masato Yamazaki and Katsuhiro Komorida for giving us a chance to do work and for their helpful comments and suggestions throughout this work. We would also like thank members of our laboratory for their interest in our discussions.

This work was done as one of the sub-projects of the Fifth Generation Computer System(FGCS) project.

References

[Allen 1983] J. Allen: *Recognizing intentions from natural language utterances*, in M. Brady and R.C. Berwick Eds., *Computational Models of Discourse*, MIT Press, 1983, pp.107-166.

[Barwise 1987] J. Barwise: *Notes on a model of a theory of situations, sets, types and propositions*, informal manuscript, 1987.

[Grice 1975] H. P. Grice: *Logic and Conversation*, in P. Cole and J.L. Morgan Eds., *Syntax and Semantics: Vol.3, Speech Acts*, Academic Press, 1975, pp.41-58.

[Kaplan 1983] J. Kaplan: *Cooperative responses from a portable natural language database query system*, in M. Brady and R.C. Berwick Eds., *Computational Models of Discourse*, MIT Press, 1983, pp.167-208.

[Searl 1969] J. R. Searl: *Speech Acts: an Essay in the Philosophy of Language*, Cambridge Univ. Press, 1969.

[Yasukawa 1987] H. Yasukawa and H. Suzuki: *Knowledge Representation Language based on Situation Theory*, France-Japan Artificial Intelligence and Computer Science Symposium '87(to be appeared).

An Approach to Speeding Up the Prolog-based Inference Engine KORE/IE

Toramatsu Shintani

International Institute for Advanced Study of Social Information Science (IIAS-SIS)
FUJITSU LIMITED, 140 Miyamoto, Numazu-shi, Shizuoka 410-03, Japan
e-mail: iia213@fujitsu.junet

ABSTRACT

In this paper, we propose an approach for speeding up the KORE/IE (Knowledge Oriented Reasoning Environment / Inference Engine) and discuss some features of the Prolog-based system. The main features provided by KORE/IE are (1)a mechanism of an inference engine on KORE, (2)cooperative problem solving among rule bases, and (3)a speedy inference mechanism. On Prolog, it is important to speed up inference engines without sacrificing flexible power for rule expressions. It is essential for constructing large scale application programs on the systems. In order to speed up the inference mechanism and realize the flexible rule expressions, we take advantage of a speedy refutation mechanism, partial evaluation techniques and fast searching for heads of clauses. At present, KORE/IE is implemented on C-Prolog and Quintus Prolog, and its efficiency of inferences is comparable with that of OPS5 on Franz Lisp.

1. Introduction

KORE/IE (Knowledge Oriented Reasoning Environment / Inference Engine) can function not only as the inference engine module of KORE(Shintani 1986), but also as an independent production system. The basic functions of KORE/IE are based on those of OPS5(Forgy 1981), and the system provides a rule-oriented programming environment (i.e. a tracer for rules, a stepper for inferences, and so on) in a similar manner as OPS5. Furthermore, its functions are extended by using the advantages of Prolog. As the system adopts a mechanism of a pure production system, the rules can be represented efficiently by considering the inference mechanism. Inference is attained by performing a sequence of operations called the recognize-act cycle:

    (1)Matching process: Determine a CS(conflict set) which includes rules
       whose LHSs (left-hand sides) have matched the current contents of working memory.
    (2)Conflict resolution process: Select one rule from CS; if CS is empty,
       halt the recognize-act cycle.
    (3)Act process: Perform the actions in the RHS (a right-hand side) of the
       selected rule.
    (4)Go to (1).

The components of a pure production system consist of WM(working memory), PM(production memory), and PSI(production system interpreter). In KORE/IE, PSI's functions are provided by Prolog system itself and the remaining components are realized by Prolog programs as shown in Fig.1. This architecture of the KORE/IE is the most important feature in speeding up the system because recognize-act cycles can be made faster by utilizing the fast refutation mechanism which is a basic computation mechanism for Prolog systems.

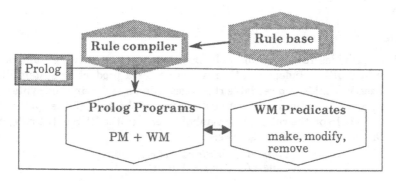

Fig.1. The architecture of the KORE/IE .

A Prolog system provides powerful pattern matching (that is, unification) and a flexible backtracking mechanism for constructing inference engines. Furthermore, the system itself can be utilized as a powerful inference engine based on a refutation mechanism(Kowalski 79).

Generally, in order to realize an inference system, we must construct an interpreter for executing inference rules. However, we can realize such a system simply by using a Prolog system as an inference engine in which the non-unit Prolog clauses are considered to be rules of the system and the rules are executed directly by the Prolog system. These clauses can be easily obtained by transforming the rules into the Prolog program. In logic programming, as a very straightforward method, this method is usually adopted to realize inference systems (e.g. BUP (Matsumoto 1983)).

There is an alternative method based on partial evaluation (Futamura 1983) of Prolog programs. In this method, an inference engine is partially evaluated with respect to inference rules and the result generates a specialized Prolog program for the rules. Then the inferences are realized by executing the program. This method is adopted in order to build an interpreter for the rules. This program can execute rules efficiently (Takeuchi 1985). The main advantage is easy maintenance of the rules. Its efficiency is due to the fast refutation mechanism of Prolog systems.

The above two methods for constructing inference systems do not actively exploit the internal mechanisms (e.g. recognize-act cycles, making and modifying WM, conflict resolution) of the system. We can further speed up the systems by making the internal mechanisms faster.

In this paper, we propose a new method for constructing a speedy inference system based on the techniques of the existing two methods mentioned above. In order to speed up the inference and realize the flexible rule expressions, we take advantage of features of Prolog systems, such as a speedy refutation mechanism, partial evaluation techniques and speedy searching for heads of clauses. The two existing methods directly transform rules into Prolog programs (that is, non-unit clauses), however the main feature of our approach corresponds to speeding up internal mechanism of the inference. At present, using the new method, KORE/IE is implemented on C-Prolog and Quintus Prolog, and its speed of the inference is comparable with that of OPS5 on Franz Lisp.

This paper consists of five sections. In Section 2 we sketch functions provided by KORE/IE. In Section 3, the main part of this paper, a new method for building an inference system is presented. In Section 4, experimental results of its performance are described. In Section 5, some concluding remarks are presented.

2. KORE/IE

2.1. The rule

KORE/IE provides functions for rule-oriented problem solving and knowledge representation in KORE. Independently it functions as a production system like OPS5. KORE/IE realizes a flexible and readable rule description by adopting the syntax of a term description in Prolog. A rule consists of (1)the name of the rule, (2)the symbol ":", (3)the symbol "if", (4)the LHS of the rule, (5)the symbol "then", (6)the RHS of the rule, and (7)the symbol ".". The rule is expressed as follows;

$$Rule\_name: \text{if } Conditions_1 \text{ \& } Conditions_2 \ldots$$
$$\text{then } Actions_1 \text{ \& } Actions_2 \ldots .$$

where the $Rule\_name$ is the name of the rule. $Condition_N$ is a condition element of the rule. It is called an LHS pattern. $Action_N$ is a rule action, which is used to change WM, to execute Prolog programs, and so on. It is called an RHS action. The symbol "&" is a delimiter. For example, a rule can be expressed as follows;

```
on_floor:
     if goal(status=active, type=(on;move), object_name=X) &
        monkey(on \= = floor)
     then
        modify(2, on=floor) &
        modify(1, status=satisfied).
```

As shown in the example, the LHS is composed of LHS patterns which correspond to compound terms of Prolog. The patterns are called declarative information in KORE. The patterns are described by a unified description for representing declarative information in KORE subsystems. For example, a WM is described by a set of declarative information, and it corresponds to a relational database which is managed by KORE/DB, a subsystem of KORE which provides functions for managing databases.

The LHS pattern consists of (1)a class name (which corresponds to a functor name of a term in Prolog) and (2)its arguments. The arguments are a sequence of one or more slot-value pairs. The pairs correspond to terms which have functors of arity 2 (e.g. =, = =, \= =, = <, > =). The arguments are called slot descriptions. The slot descriptions are used in the same manner as the basic predicates for comparison of terms in Prolog. For example, "on\= = floor" in the above example tests if the value of the slot "on" obtained from the current contents of WM and the value "floor" are not literally identical. In Prolog programs, the goals in the body of a clause are linked by the operator "," and the operator ";" which can be interpreted as conjunction ("and") and disjunction ("or") respectively. In the same manner as Prolog programs, we can also use a conjunctive and a disjunctive slot description in the slot description as follows:

Conjunctive slot description:
$$Slot = (Restriction_1, Restriction_2, \ldots, Restriction_N)$$

Disjunctive slot description:
$$Slot = (Value_1; Value_2; \ldots; Value_N)$$

The right side of a conjunctive slot description consists of some restrictions (or Prolog goals) which are used to indicate that the slot value in a WM element must satisfy the restrictions simultaneously. The right side of a disjunctive slot description consists of some values (or Prolog goals) which are used to specify that any of the contained values is acceptable as a match. Thus, "type=(on;move)" in the above example will match either "on" or "move".

In a rule, we can use a functional notation to enhance the readability of the rule. For example, the following predicate definition returns the result to the first argument "Result":

add_one(*Result, Number*) :- *Result* is *Number* + 1.

This definition can be used as a function in a slot description as follows;

slot = add_one(X).

The functional notation can be executed as a normal Prolog program since a rule containing functional notations is compiled into Prolog programs.

2.2. Mechanisms for cooperative problem solving

KORE consists of four subsystems including the KORE/IE, and provides an environment for cooperative problem solving by integrating the subsystems. They have a common internal representation in the form of relational tables on Prolog. A subsystem can support and use results of problem solving in the other subsystems by using the tables as a means of communication. The integration between the subsystems can be realized efficiently by using the tables and flags without constructing a meta-control mechanism. The flag is used for checking existence of subsystems. The relational table corresponds to a blackboard which is proposed in a "blackboard model(Lesser 1977)". It has the following two unique features: (1)it is used by subsystems, which have unique control strategies, as a means of communication, (2)it is a kind of a relational database managed by KORE/DB.

The cooperative problem solving can be applicable among rule bases in KORE/IE. It appears that the cooperation among KORE/IE rules corresponds to cooperative problem solving in the blackboard model. However, cooperative problem solving in KORE/IE can be realized efficiently without building a meta control mechanism, since a basic Prolog computation mechanism (that is, the refutation mechanism) can be used.

The internal mechanism for cooperative problem solving on rule bases in KORE/IE can be considered as generating optimum Prolog programs from rules in the rule bases and executing the programs in Prolog. In order to generate the programs, a rule compiler is applied. The rule compiler translates a rule into a uniform Prolog program. The program consists of an LHS program for the LHS and an RHS program for the RHS, and is realized as flat non-unit clauses of Prolog as shown in Fig.2.

A change in WM is transformed to a question for the LHS program. Then, applying the question by using the Prolog refutation mechanism corresponds to executing the matching process of the recognize-act cycle and generates instantiations as a result of the question (for further details, see Section 3). An instantiation is an object in a conflict set and an ordered pair of a rule name and a list of WM elements satisfying the rule's LHS. The instantiations are generated for every rule base and conflict sets are also generated for every rule base. A unique conflict resolution strategy for each rule base is applied to conflict sets for each rule base. After the conflict resolution, one instantiation for each rule base is selected for executing the RHS programs for each rule base. Execution of the RHS programs is achieved by applying questions for RHS for each rule base. The question is generated by transforming the selected instantiation. Applying the question in Prolog corresponds to performing an act process of the recognize-act cycle. An order for invoking rule bases is determined automatically according to the order of their compilation. Otherwise, the order can be determined explicitly by showing the order in the rule bases.

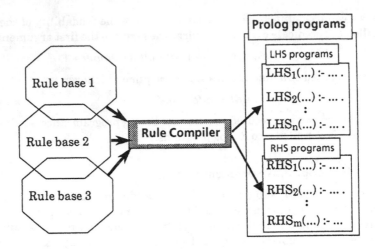

Fig.2. Rule compilation.

2.3. Definitions for conflict resolution strategies

KORE/IE provides functions for defining a conflict resolution strategy. The function is useful to realize flexible cooperative problem solving. The definition is specified by combining the following items; (1)the recency of the instantiations which is determined by using time tags of WM elements, (2)positions of time tags according to the instantiations, and (3)the number of undefined slots in LHS. For example, the MEA strategy provided in OPS5 can be defined as follows;

> define_strategy <u>mea</u> : =
>> select <u>latest</u> instantiation
>> by comparing <u>first</u> time tag.

where underscored words are specified by the user and the remaining ones are reserved for the system. The underscored "mea", "latest", and "first" represent the name of a strategy, indication of recency, and indication of position, respectively. The definition can be used by executing the following directive;

> ?- strategy(*Rule_base*,mea).

where the first and second arguments indicate a name of a rule base and a conflict resolution strategy respectively.

3. Speeding up inference engines

Inferences in KORE/IE are realized by performing recognize-act cycles. In order to speed up the inferences, we need to speed up a sequence of operations in the recognize-act cycle, which are matching, conflict resolution, and act processes. Generally, the matching process consumes more time than the other processes, and influences the efficiency of the inferences. In a straightforward pattern matcher all the WM elements are compared against all the LHS patterns for every rule on each cycle. In order to avoid iteration over the elements on each cycle and to realize an efficient matching process, the Rete Match algorithm (Forgy 1982) is used in OPS5. The algorithm was developed to eliminate extra work in the unoptimized pattern matcher. In the algorithm, LHS's are compiled into a tree structured sorting network by linking nodes together which test the slot values, and a matching process is realized by passing tokens into the network in which information of previous matching is stored. The token is a description of WM changes.

However, in logic programming, it is difficult to implement the kind of network structure efficiently. It requires appropriate data structures (e.g. pointers) to construct the network. Therefore, in order to speed up an inference engine, we make use of an efficient refutation mechanism in Prolog to match the techniques of the Rete Match algorithm which avoids iterating on matching processes.

3.1. The LHS program

An LHS program is a specialized program for matching process and is generated by transforming rules into Prolog programs which include information about variable bindings in the LHS. The programs are used for computing a conflict set. In the transformation, we use a technique for partial evaluation of Prolog programs. We call the transformation LHS compilation of rules. The technique is useful for generating the specialized program from rule descriptions and declarative data for defining skeletons of LHS patterns. The data can be asserted by using "literalize" command in KORE/IE. In the compilation, an LHS is transformed into Prolog programs by processing information about variable bindings. In a strict sense, it appears that the technique is not the partial evaluation (Futamura 1983), but it essentially utilizes the partial evaluation of Prolog programs which can evaluate parts of a program without some special evaluation scheme such as lazy evaluation. However, in a broad sense, it is a kind of partial evaluation since the LHS program is generated as a matching program from the data and the LHS pattern in which the unification mechanism of the Prolog system itself is considered a program required by the partial evaluation. In this approach the Prolog system corresponds to the PSI (production system interpreter). Thus, in order to realize fast inferences effectively, we need to utilize the advantages of Prolog systems and optimize the Prolog programs generated by the compilation. We utilize the following functions of Prolog systems: (1)fast head searching; clauses are hash-indexed according to functor name and its arity in the head of the clauses and (2)powerful backtracking for the search.

Function (2) can be used as a control mechanism for finding several instantiations at the time when the WM is changed. Using this function, the system can check all the LHS program according to changes of WM and then generate instantiations without building a particular control mechanism.

Function (1) is particularly important in speeding up inferences and can provide functions for realizing a root node of the network in the Rete Match algorithm. The root node is an entrance to the network and receives only the changes of WM and passes them to its successors. The node is used for utilizing only changes of WM in the matching process. In LHS programs, the functions of the root node can be realized easily by naming the functor name in the head of the clause according to the class name of the LHS pattern, because the clause is hash-indexed on the name. Each clause of the LHS program corresponds to a path from a root node to a terminal node (that is, production node) in the network because an LHS pattern is realized by using a Prolog clause. In the clause, functions of one-input nodes (which are used for comparing slot values) and two-input nodes (which are used for checking variable bindings) in the network are realized simply by using the refutation mechanism of the Prolog system as shown in Fig.3-1. Fig.3-2 is given to clarify the description in Fig.3-1. In the LHS program, for example, the skeleton of the LHS programs is generated by the LHS compilation. The functor "ie_lhs_class1" is named according to the class name "class1"

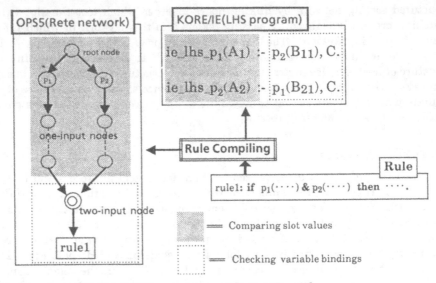

Fig.3-1. LHS program and Rete network.

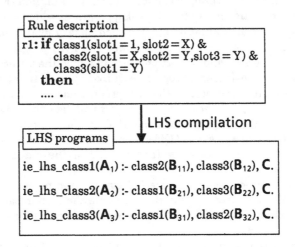

Fig.3-2. The LHS program.

of the LHS pattern. A_i represents a sequence of arguments in the head; A_i consists of a rule name, slot values, information of variable bindings , and so on. The bodies of the clauses in the LHS programs represent the other LHS patterns requested for satisfying the rule. The B_{ij} represents slot values of the other LHS patterns. The C represents constraints for variable bindings between A_i and B_{ij}. Details will be described in Section 3.2. By using the LHS program, We can perform a matching process according to changes of WM elements without iterations over the WM elements. A change of a WM element is transformed into a question for executing the LHS program as mentioned in Section 2.2. In Fig.3-2, for example, if a new WM element, whose class name is "class1", is built and added to WM, the first clause in the LHS programs is called and executed by performing the following question

$$?\text{- ie\_lhs\_class1}(A_1).$$

where A_1 can be determined by the new WM element.

A feature of the LHS program is that the matching process is run by the speedy refutation mechanism in Prolog systems, which is started by the question generated by the change of WM. The process in the Rete Match algorithm is performed by passing a token into the network. The token is an ordered pair of a tag (that is, + and - which indicate adding to WM and deleting from WM respectively) and a WM element. In the LHS programs, the matching process is realized without building a particular mechanism by directly using the refutation mechanism. The refutation mechanism is a basic computation mechanism in Prolog systems, hence we can utilize the efficiency of head searching in Prolog systems. In the Rete Match algorithm, when rules are compiled into the network, the order of nodes has direct effects upon efficiency of the matching process. The LHS program is not affected by the order since the efficiency of unification between terms is not quite affected by the order of the arguments. The network reduces memory use by using the structural similarity of rules. In the LHS program, memory use is not efficient since the clauses are generated for every LHS pattern. Improving the efficiency of memory use is a subject for a future study.

3.2. Rule compilation

In KORE/IE we speed up inferences by compiling (or transforming) the rules into Prolog programs. The compilation is realized by the rule compiler of KORE/IE. In the compilation, in order to speed up each step of a recognize-act cycle, the programs are generated according to LHS and RHS of rules as shown in Fig.4. We call the compilation for

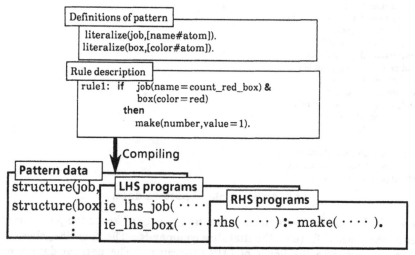

Fig.4. Generating Prolog programs by compiling a rule.

the LHS LHS compilation, and the compilation for the RHS RHS compilation. LHS compilation generates Prolog programs for speeding up the matching process as mentioned in Section 3.1. RHS compilation generates Prolog programs for speeding up the action process. In Fig.4 the patterns define class names, slot names and types of the slot values in the LHS patterns. This definition is realized by using the "literalize" command in KORE/IE and is used for standardizing LHS patterns by the compiler. By standardization of LHS patterns, positions of slots in LHS patterns are fixed, and this contributes to speeding up processing of LHS patterns. For example, the rule descriptions in Fig.5 is compiled into

(1)the pattern data in Fig.6 defined by the literalize commands, (2)the LHS programs in Fig.7 and (3)the RHS programs in Fig.8.

```
literalize(monkey, [at, on, holds]).
literalize(goal, [status, type, object_name, on, to]).
```

'At_Monkey': if
        goal + goal(status=active, type=at, object__name=nothing, to=*P1*) &
        monkey + monkey(on=floor, at \== *P1*, holds=nothing)
    then
        nl & write('Walk to ') & write(*P1*) & nl & nl &
        modify(monkey, at=*P1*) &
        modify(goal, status=satisfied).

Fig.5. An example of a rule description.

In Fig.6, the fact "structure" is used to keep information about standardized LHS patterns where the first and second arguments represent the class name and the database name respectively. The database name is used by KORE/DB. The third, fourth and fifth arguments represent the number of slots, the list of slot names ,and the list of types for slot values, respectively. The positions in the list which is the fourth argument correspond to the positions in the list which is the fifth argument. In KORE/IE, the class "start" is

```
structure(goal,goal,6,[time_tag,status,type,object_name,on,to],[number,non,non,non,non,non]).
structure(monkey,monkey,4,[time_tag,at,on,holds],[number,non,non,non]).
structure(start,start,2,[time_tag,order],[number,number]).

position(start,time_tag,number,1).
position(start,order,non,2).
position(monkey,time_tag,,number,1).
position(monkey,at,non,2).
position(monkey,on,non,3).
position(monkey,holds,non,4).
position(goal,time_tag,,number,1).
position(goal,status,non,2).
position(goal,type,non,3).
position(goal,object_name,non,4).
position(goal,on,non,5).
position(goal,to,non,6).

lhs__class(start,ie_lhs_start).
lhs__class(monkey,ie_lhs_monkey).
lhs__class(goal,ie_lhs_goal).
```

Fig.6. An example of pattern data.

defined by a default class for convenience. The fact "position" keeps the positions of slots of LHS patterns which are defined by the literalize commands. The fact "lhs_class" is used to keep the functor names in the heads of LHS programs. The pattern data are used to standardize patterns in KORE/IE and enable to speed up referring to slot values.

As shown in Fig.7, the compiler generates LHS programs. The number of the programs (or clauses) corresponds to the number of LHS patterns. Then, by using the programs, we can perform the matching process according to changes of WM as mentioned in Section 3.1. The programs can also check the variable bindings in the process. For example, let us see the LHS program, which is the first clause in Fig.7, according to the LHS pattern named "monkey", which is the second pattern in Fig.5. The LHS pattern can be named by using the operator " + ". The argument in the head of the clause can be shown as in Fig.7-1. Argument (3) in Fig.7-1 is used to represent a variable list which keeps all the variables occurred in the

```
ie_lhs_monkey('At_Monkey',r1,[A,B,B],[C,D],1,D,A,floor,nothing) :-
        goal(C,active,at,nothing,E,B),
        A \== B.

ie_lhs_goal('At_Monkey',r1,[A,B,B],[C,D],1,C,active,at,nothing,E,B) :-
        monkey(D,A,floor,nothing),
        A \== B.
```

Fig.7. An example of an LHS program.

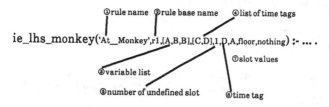

Fig.7-1. The head of the LHS program.

LHS patterns in the rule. In the example, the variable "B" corresponds to the variable "P1" in the LHS of the rule. The variable "A" is a dummy variable used in the slot description "at\== P1" of the second LHS pattern. The internal representation of the slot description is "at = $(X \== P1)$" where the dummy variable "X" corresponds to the variable "A". Argument (4) is a list of time tags which indicate satisfied WM elements in the matching process. Argument (5) is the number of undefined slots which are unused (or unfilled) slots in the LHS pattern in spite of definition in the literalize command. The number is used as information for conflict resolutions. Argument (6) is a time tag which indicates a WM element matched the LHS pattern. The rest of the arguments including Argument (7) is a sequence of slot values where the values are arranged in the order defined by the literalize command. In Fig. 7-1, as the slot "at" of the class "monkey" is undefined, a dummy variable "A" is placed at the position for the slot. Checking for variable bindings between LHS patterns is realized in the body of the program. In the example, it is the last goal "$A \== B$".

In Fig.8, the lists "[A,B,B]" and "[C,D]" in the head represent a list of variables occurred in the LHS program and a list of time tags respectively. The other variables "E","F","G" are used as flags for cooperative problem solving with the other KORE subsystems.

```
rhs('At_Monkey',r1,[A,B,B],[C,D],E,F,G) :-
        nl,
        write('Walk to '),
        write(B),
        nl,
        nl,
        modify(E,F,D,[at=B],G),
        modify(E,F,C,[status=satisfied],G),
        !.
```

Fig.8. An example of an RHS program.

The LHS programs are called by actions (that is, make, modify, and remove) which change WM. Let us take an example. The make command is defined as in Fig.9, which is used for building a new WM element and adding it to the WM. For example, the command is used as follows;

$$make(goal(status = active, type = at)).$$

As shown in Fig.9, in a process of the make command, to begin with, a time tag is given in part (1) and the input pattern is standardized in part (2). Then, in part (3) a new WM element is added to WM. In part (4), a question is generated by using the information from (1),(2), and (3). By executing the question instantiations can be composed in part (5).

```
make(Fact) :-
  (1)  Fact = .. [F|Atrs],
       Time_tag is cputime,
  (2)  structure(F,_,_,[_|ANL],[_|ATL]),
       reforming_make(F,Atrs,ANL,ATL,Reformed),
  (3)  FACT = .. [F,Time_Tag|Reformed],
       assert(FACT),
  (4)  lhs_class(F,FF),
       Call = .. [FF,Rule_Name,Rule_Base,VL,Instantiation,
                                    NUS,Time_Tag|Reformed],
  (5)  (call(CALL),
       strategy_rec(Rule_Base,_,Strategy),
       ass(Rule_Base,Rule_Name,Instantiation,NUS,Strategy,VL),
       fail ;
       true),
       !.
```

Fig.9. A Prolog definition of the make command.

The RHS program is also executed, by generating a question like the LHS program, as shown Fig.10. Fig.10 shows a definition of an inference stepper in KORE/IE. The RHS program is called in the definition. To begin with, in part (1) an instantiation is selected as a result of the conflict resolution. In part (2), a question is generated by using the information (1). By executing the question, the action process is realized.

```
running(N,off,Rule_base) :-
       now_running(Rule_Base,running),
       strategy_rec(Rule_Base,_,Strategy),
       retract(cs(Rule_Base,[[Rule_name1,Time_Tags1,STT1,NUS1,Var_List1]|CS])),
  (1)  conflict_resolution(Strategy,CS,
                      [Rule_Name1,Time_Tags1,STT1,NUS1,Var_List1],
                      [Rule_Name,Time_Tags,_,_,Var_List],New_CS),
       asserta(cs(Rule_Base,New_CS)),
       ie_to_eden(Rule_Name,Rule_Base,EDEN_Mode),
  (2)  rhs(Rule_Name,Rule_Base,Var_List,Time_Tags,off,EDEN_Mode,Time_Tags),
       NN is N - 1,
       !,
       running(NN,off,Rule_Base).
```

Fig.10. A Prolog definition of the inference stepper.

4. Experimental results

We conducted a few experiments to see how fast KORE/IE runs. It is generally considered that the speed for executing programs in Prolog systems is considerably slower than the speed in Lisp systems. To begin with, KORE/IE on C-prolog is compared with OPS5 on Franz Lisp. It is well known that OPS5 is the fastest system among production systems on interpretive languages. Likewise it is well known that C-prolog is one of the slowest

Prolog systems. Table 1 shows the comparison of the OPS5 on Franz Lisp (Opus 38.79) with KORE/IE on C-Prolog (version 1.4). For this test, we used a standard bench mark system which is also used in (Brekke 1986). The system is "Monkey and Bananas" which consists of 27 rules (Brownston 1985). In Table 1, the OPS5(compiled) is a compiled OPS5 system by using the Lisp compiler. The OPS5(interpreted) is a system which is loaded simply into Lisp system. The method of using OPS5(interpreted) corresponds to the method of KORE/IE on C-Prolog. As is evident in Table 1, KORE/IE is sufficiently faster than OPS5(interpreted) and the speed of KORE/IE is comparable with that of OPS5(compiled). It should be noted that the speed of KORE/IE is improved effectively if we use a more efficient Prolog system.

VAX11/780
OPS5 : Franz Lisp (Opus 38.79)
KORE/IE : C-prolog (version 1.4)

Table 1.	OPS5 (Compiled)	OPS5 (interpreted)	KORE/IE
Rule Execution time(Sec)	1.5	61.5	7.0

Table 2 shows the performances of KORE/IE on C-prolog and Quintus Prolog where we used the same example as for Table 1. The Table 2, the Quintus(compiled1) is where the KORE/IE system is compiled using a Prolog compiler. The Quintus(compiled2) is a system where LHS programs, RHS programs and pattern data generated by the compiler are also compiled using a Prolog compiler. What is evident from the table is that the performance of KORE/IE is improved effectively by using the Prolog compiler. However, since the mechanism for inputs and outputs in Prolog systems is inefficient, it seems that the improvement reaches a limit.

SUN3/52m
KORE/IE : C-prolog (version 1.4)
Quintus Prolog (Release 1.6)

Table 2.	Quintus (Compiled2)	Quintus (Compiled1)	C-Prolog
Rule Execution time(Sec)	2.0	2.5	4.1

Now, we test with an example without using inputs and outputs. As shown in Fig.11, the example is rules that modifies WM successively according to the number of rules. In the graph, the vertical axis indicates CPU time (seconds) required for each system, and the horizontal axis indicates the number of rules. The graph shows performances of Quintus(compiled2) and Quintus(compiled1) on SUN3/52m, and the performances of KORE/IE (the C-prolog version) and OPS5(compiled) on VAX11/780. As is evident from the graph, the Quintus(compiled2) realizes the efficiency of head searching in Prolog systems. The time required is linearly proportional to the number of rules. It seems that Quintus(compiled2) attains ideal performance in the Prolog system. The performance of the KORE/IE system on VAX11/780 is equal or superior to that of OPS5 on VAX11/780.

5. Conclusions

In this paper, we have proposed and discussed the following advantages of KORE/IE; (1) a mechanism for an inference engine for KORE, (2)cooperative problem solving among rule bases, (3)an efficient inference mechanism. By using (1) and (2), we have shown the flexible and powerful mechanisms of KORE/IE. The (3) is the most important subject in logic

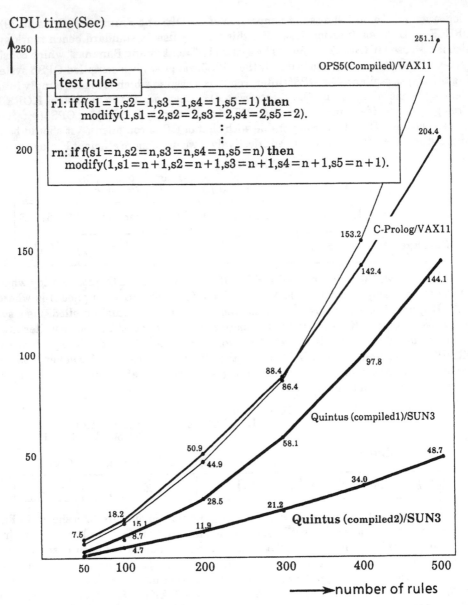

Fig.11. Evaluation of KORE/IE.

programming and also the main part of this paper. In KORE/IE, we have realized a speedy inference mechanism without restricting rule expressions by using advantages of Prolog systems. Specifically speaking, in order to realize the full speedy mechanism, we have utilized the features of the inference mechanism and the efficient refutation mechanism of Prolog systems. Namely, by compiling rules into optimized Prolog programs, recognize-act cycles are transformed into execution of the Prolog programs based on the speedy refutation mechanism. The programs consist of LHS programs and RHS programs. By using the LHS program we can realize an efficient matching process. It can be seen from the experimental results that the efficiency is superior to that of the Rete Match algorithm.

Acknowledgment

The author would like to acknowledge the continuing guidance and encouragements of Dr. Tosio Kitagawa, the president of IIAS-SIS, and Dr. Hajime Enomoto, the director of IIAS-SIS. The author is deeply grateful to Dr. Mitsuhiko Toda, IIAS-SIS, for reading the draft of this paper and giving him many valuable comments. Also many thanks to Mr. Yoshinori Katayama and Mr. Kunihiko Hiraishi, IIAS-SIS, for their useful comments. The author is also very grateful to Mr. Hiromichi Futagami for his computer programming with great competence and enthusiasm.

This research has been carried out as a part of Fifth Generation Computer Project.

References

Brownston L, Farrell E K, and Martin N(1985) Programming expert system in OPS5, Addison-Wesley

Brekke B(1986) Benchmarking Expert System Tool Performance, Ford Aerospace Tech Note

Forgy CL(1981) OPS5 User's Manual, CMU-CS-81-135,July

Forgy CL(1982) Rete: A Fast Algorithm for the Many Pattern/Many Object Pattern Match Problem, Artificial Intelligence 19: 17-37

Futamura Y (1983) Partial Computation of Programs, Lecture Notes in Computer Science 147, Springer-Verlag

Kowalski R (1977) Logic for Problem Solving, Elservier North Holland :49-74

Lesser VR and Erman LD (1977) A retrospective view of the HEARSAY-II architecture. Proc. IJCAI 5:790-800

Matsumoto Y, Tanaka H, and Kiyono M (1983) BUP: A Bottom-up Parser Embedded in Prolog, New Generation Computing 1,No.2 :

Shintani T, Katayama Y, Hiraishi K, and Toda M (1986) KORE: A Hybrid Knowledge Programming Environment for Decision Support based on a Logic Programming Language, Lecture Notes in Computer Science 264, Logic Programming '86 :22-33

Takeuchi A and Furukawa K (1985) Partial Evaluation of Prolog Programs and Its Application to Meta Programming, in Kuger, H.-J.(ed.): Information Processing 86, Dublin, Ireland 415-420., North-Holland

Test Generation for Large-Scale Combinational Circuits by using Prolog

Yoshihiro Tohma and Kenji Goto
Department of Computer Science
Tokyo Institute of Technology, Tokyo, Japan

Abstract

This paper presents a method to improve the execution of Prolog programs which generate tests of very large combinational circuits. Essentially, we restrict the area where the 4-valued unification will be performed and exploit the knowledge of tests for component modules of large circuits. Examples are given to demonstrate the improvement achieved by this method.

Index Terms - Prolog, Knowledge, Test, Module, Acceleration.

1. Introduction

The more significant the use of computer systems becomes, the more important is the reliability of computer systems. The test of computer systems is obviouly necessary for assuring the reliability of computer systems. Therefore, many efficient test generation algorithms like the D-algorithm have been well studied and practiced in real world. However, we are still facing difficulty in testing logic circuits, because the complexity of circuits to be tested is increasing more rapidly than the improvement of test generation algorithms.

Unification in Prolog has the property of bidirectional simulator [FUJ82],[KAN84] and therefore, Prolog is very convenient to write a program for the test generation of logic circuits [VAR87]. However, the performance of Prolog programs is not yet satisfactory.

This paper presents methods to improve the execution of Prolog programs for test generation, which is based on the D-algorithm in this paper. The key to the improvement is to reduce the number of possible backtrackings.

The D-algorithm uses four signal values, 0, 1, d and $\bar{d}$. However, the unification in test generation does not always need these four values. The four values are needed only for propagating $d/\bar{d}$ signal from a faulty line to primary output terminals. The consistency operation to determine values of primary input terminals uses only two signal values, 0 and 1. Therefore, a number of unnecessary backtrackings can be avoided by restricting area where the 4-valued unification will be carried out.

Further, since databases for test generation can be handled well by Prolog, we exploit the knowledge of component modules in the generation of the test of very large complicated circuits. This approach not only makes the test generation faster but also is comform with modular ways of designing very large circuits.

2. Definitions and Notations

Logic circuits to be tested may be sequential. However, a sequential circuit is usually decomposed into combinational one with, say, the scan-path mechanism [EIC77]. Thus, the test generation for sequential circuits can be rduced to the one for combinational circuits. In this paper, we assume that circuits are combinational ones made of AND, OR, NAND, NOR, and EXOR gates. Input terminals of a circuit directly controllable from the external are called *primary input* terminals. Output terminals of the circuit directly observable from the external are similarly called *primary output* terminals. A combination of signal values at input terminals is simply referred to as an *input*, while an output is a combination of signal values at output terminals. The relationship between primary inputs and primary outputs are defined by the input-output function.

All faults considered in this paper are of the *stuck-at-e* ($e = 0$ or 1) type, which may develop at an input or output line of a gate, or at a primary input or primary output line. We assume the occurrence of a single fault. The signal value at a faulty line may be correct or erroneous.

The faulty signal value of a line is denoted by d or $\bar{d}$. d means that the signal value of the line is 0 under the existence of the fault, but 1 without the development of the fault. In contrast, $\bar{d}$ is such a faulty signal value that it is 0 without the development of the fault, but 1 with the fault. When we confuse d with $\bar{d}$, the both are simply referred to as f.

A gate with its faulty output line is called a *detecting gate*. An input line of the detecting gate is referred to as a *detecting line*.

A (potential) *f-chaining path* is a signal path on which f may propagate from a faulty line to a primary output terminal. There may be many f-chaining paths even under the occurrence of a single fault. An input line of a gate on a f-chaining path is a *f-interface line*, if and only if it is not included in the f-chaining path itself.

A f-chaining path is said *sensitized*, when and only when f actually propagates through the path to its primary output terminal. This path is simply called *sensitized path*. An input line of a gate on a sensitized path is a *sensitizing line*, if and only if it is not included in the sensitized path itself. When all f-chaining paths are sensitized, every f-interface lines are sensitizing ones.

Examples of the above definitions are illustrated in Fig. 1.

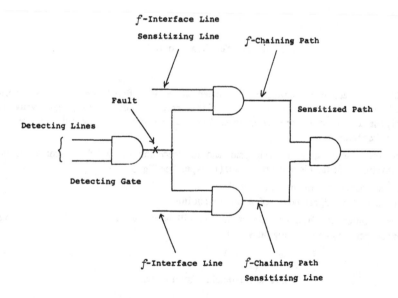

Fig. 1. Propagation of f.

We call a point where signal lines diverge a *fanout point*. *Bounded lines* are signal lines reachable from at least one fanout point. Further, a line which is not bounded but feeds directly bounded lines will be referred to as a *frontier line*. Note that a sub-circuit feeding a frontier line is tree-structured. These tree-structured segments will be called *front segments*, while the rest of the circuit is referred to as the *bounded segment*. See Fig. 2.

The test generation is just to choose sensitized path(s) with proper signal values of the sensitizing lines and the detecting lines. Then, signal values of primary input lines should be determined so as to realize the values of the above lines.

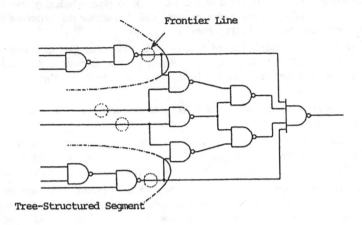

Fig. 2. Frontier Lines and Segments.

3. Primitive Test Generator (PT)

As described in Section 1, unification considered as a bidirectional simulator is quite effective for sensitizing a path(s) with proper signal values of sensitizing lines and for determining signal values of primary input lines consistent to those of the sensitizing lines. Thus, the procedure of the primitive test generation (PT) can be simply stated as follows:

(1) Cut the faulty line, assigning the succeeding side and the preceding side of the disconnected line d $(\bar{d})$ and $1(0)$, respectively, if the fault is of the stuck-at-0 (1) type. See Fig. 3.

(2) Assign d or $\bar{d}$ at least one of primary output terminals.

(3) Use unification to obtain signal values of primary input lines.

In this simple procedure, however, the unification will be carried out with four signal values and therefore, many unnecessary backtrackings may happen.

4. Acceleration of Prolog Programs

4.1 FIPM (Fault Information Propagating Method)

Unnecessary backtrackings can be avoided by performing the 4-valued unification on the set of all possible f-chaining paths only and the two-valued unification with 0 and 1 in the rest of the circuit, respectively, as shown in Fig. 4. However, this method is not enough, when many lines fanout from a gate near primary input line. In such a case, the set of f-chaining paths extends so that the 4-valued unification is required over most of the circuit area.

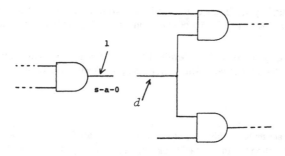

Fig. 3. Determination of $d / \bar{d}$.

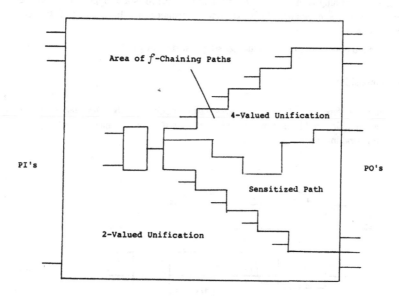

Fig. 4. Restriction of Area of 4-Valued Unification.

Therefore, we first choose the candidate of a sensitized path among possible f-chaining paths. Then, the 4-valued unification will be carried out on the chosen path, but the 2-valued unification in the rest of the circuit. Note that the choice of the sensitization here does not necessarily mean to take only one f-chaining path. We continue the choice of the sensitization until a test is found, taking simultaneous sensitization of multiple f-chaining paths into consideration. Of course, we first look at one possible path, and then simultaneous sensitization of two possible paths, three possible paths, and so on.

When the candidate sensitized paths fanout and reconverge at an EXOR gate, f-chaining path succeeding to this gate cannnot be sensitized. Similarly, if two chosen paths with f and $\bar{f}$ ($\bar{f}$ means the inverse of f) reconverge at an AND or OR gate, the succeeding f-chaining path never be sensitized. In these cases, the candidate sensitization will be discarded.

This situation could be found by the failure of the unification with respect to the reconverging gate. However, this way to detect such situations may need a lot of search on the database and therefore, we prepared clauses for the consistency check.

Further, contradictions may encounter in performing the forward/backward unification. In such a case, a backtracking occurs and the alternative sensitization of the path(s) will be chosen.

4.2 Segmentation

Since the front segments are mutually disjoint, primary inputs to all front segments can be determined simply by the (backward) unification with no backtracking, provided signal values at the frontier lines are given [FUJ85]. Therefore,

(1) when a fault develops at a bounded line, we first apply FIPM only to the bouded segment. After signal vaues at the frontier lines are obtained, primary inputs to all front segments will be determined by applying the two-valued unification to all front segments with the signal values of their frontier lines. On the other hand,

(2) When a fault develops at a primary input line, FIPM is applied to the front segment including the faulty primary input line, determining faulty value at the frontier line. FIPM is also applied to the succeeding bounded segment, assuming that the equivalent fault exists at the frontier line. In the rest of the circuit, the two-valued unification is used.

By this segmentation, we can avoid unnecessary backtrackings.

4.3 Modular Decomposition

The difficulty in generating the test for very large circuits may be alleviated by decomposing a complicated circuit into modules and by exploiting the knowledge of these modules [GEN82],[YOK86]. Prolog is again convenient for handling knowledges.

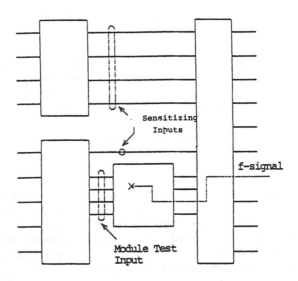

Fig. 5. Modular Decomposition.

As shown in Fig. 5, let us consider a circuit to consist of modules. Further, we assume that tests for component modules (we call it simply *module test*) and their input-output functions in terms of binary values of 0 and 1 (we call functions in terms of these values *2-valued functions*) are already known.

For a fault in a module, we know the test for this fault and at what output lines of the module $f / \bar{f}$'s appear. Note that even under the occurrence of a single fault, many $f / \bar{f}$'s may appear at multiple output lines of the module. Then, the sensitization of f-chaining path(s) in terms of modular strucuture is to determine signal values of input lines of the succeeding module, where $f / \bar{f}$'s do not appear, so as to propagate $f / \bar{f}$'s to some output lines of the succeeding module. These input lines of the succeeding module are the sensitizing lines.

Let s be input to input lines of a module, where $f / \bar{f}$'s appear, while a is the one to the the remaining input lines. Then, a is the sensitizing input, if and only if

$$F(a, s) \neq F(a, \bar{s})\qquad(1)$$

where $\bar{s}$ is the inverse of s and $F(a, s)$ is the 2-valued input-output function of a and s of the module. See Fig. 6.

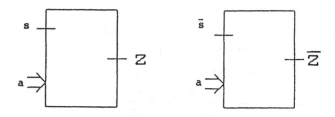

Fig. 6. Sensitizing Input.

As described earlier, $f / \bar{f}$ does not necessarily appear at only one input line of the succeeding module. Therefore, when we prepare sensitizing inputs for a given module in the database, we should consider all possible appearances of $f / \bar{f}$'s at its input lines. If the module has n input lines, the total number of such possible cases is

$$\sum_{k=1}^{n} {}_nC_k\, 2^{k-1}$$

where the distinction between f and $\bar{f}$ is ignoreded. Given an appearance of $f / \bar{f}$ at k input lines, we should check for all inputs at the remaining $n - k$ input lines whether they are the sensitizing input. Thus, the total number of cases to be checked is

$$\sum_{k=1}^{n} {}_nC_k\, 2^{k-1}\, 2^{n-k} = 2^{n-1}\,(2^n - 1)\qquad(2)$$

This is an enormous amount for large n.

There are two choices in dealing with this large n. The one is simply to prepare all possible sensitizing inputs, while the alternative is to compute them when required with the specific appearance of $f / \bar{f}$'s. In this paper, we take the former, providing the table of input-output function in terms of four values, 0, 1, d, $\bar{d}$ (we call functions in terms of these four values *4-valued functions*) for each module.

The appearance of $f / \bar{f}$'s at some input lines of a module is equivalent to the development of the faults at these lines. The propagation of $f / \bar{f}$'s to output lines of the module is just the module test for these faults. Thus, the sensitizing input(s) can be obtained by referring to the module test, if test inputs for multiple faults are provided.

Unfortunately, the module test is generally determined under the assumption of the occurrence of a single fault. When $f / \bar{f}$ appears at only one input line, the sensitizing input(s) can surely be found in the set of test inputs for the module.

Since all possible sensitizing inputs for each module are provided in the database, the inhibited reconvergence of sensitized paths that makes the succeeding sensitization impossible can be found by checking the 4-valued input-output function of the module where the sensitized paths reconverge.

As in the case of the gate-level unification, the forward as well as backward unification will be done by referring input-output functions of modules which are provided in the database.

5. Representation in Prolog

5.1 Gate

When only two values of 0 and 1 are considered, the predicate of a gate is as follows.

$$\text{element (GATETYPE, INPUTLIST, OUTPUTLIST).} \tag{3}$$

where

$$\text{GATETYPE ::= and I nand I or I nor I exor I inv I fanout}$$

$$\text{INPUTLIST ::= [INPUT \{, INPUT \}]}$$

$$\text{OUTPUTLIST ::= [OUTPUT \{, OUTPUT \}]}$$

$$\text{INPUT ::= LINE}$$

$$\text{OUTPUT ::= LINE}$$

$$\text{LINE ::= [LINENAME, LINEVALUE]}$$

$$\text{LINENAME ::= atom}$$

$$\text{LINEVLUE ::= 0 I 1 I variable} \tag{4}$$

GATETYPE represents type of the gate. INPUTLIST is the list of the input lines, OUTPUTLIST being that of the outputlines. Note that fanout points are considered here as gates. Signal lines are represented by combinations of LINENAME and LINEVALUE. LINENAME is an atom to identify the line, while LINEVALUE is a value of the line. It may be a constant or a variable. LINENAME is also used to define f-chaining paths. Examples of gate predicates are given below.

element (and, [[l1, L1], [l2, L2]], [[l3, L3]])

element (inv, [[l1, L1]], [[l2, L2]])

element (fanout, [[l1, L1]], [[l2, L2], [l3, L3]])

Their input-output functions are defined as facts or rules. The following are examples.

element (and, INPUTLIST, [[_, 0]]) : -

lgc (INPUTLIST), mbrl (0, INPUTLIST).

element (and, INPUTLIST, [[_, 1]]) : -

all (1, INPUTLIST).

element (inv, [[_, 0]], [[_, 1]]).

element (inv, [[_, 1]], [[_, 0]]).

element (fanout, [[_, 0]], OUTPUTLIST) : - all (0, OUTPUTLIST).

element (fanout, [[_, 1]], OUTPUTLIST) : - all (1, OUTPUTLIST).

In order to propagate f through gates, their 4-valued input-output functions must also be provided. In this case the predicate of a gate is named *delement*. For example,

$$delement (and, [[l1, L1], [l2, L2]], [[l3, L3]]). \tag{5}$$

Its 4-valued input-output function is defined as

delement (and, INPUTLIST, [[_, 0]]) : -

        alw (INPUTLIST),

        mbrl (0, INPUTLIST).

delement (and, INPUTLIST, [[_, 1]]) : -

        all (1, INPUTLIST).

delement (and, INPUTLIST, [[_, 0]]) : -

        alw (INPUTLIST),

        mbrl (d, INPUTLIST),

        mbrl ($\bar{d}$, INPUTLIST).

delement (and, INPUTLIST, [[_, d]]) : -

        lt1d (INPUTLIST),

        mbrl (d, INPUTLIST).

delement (and, INPUTLIST, [[_, $\bar{d}$]]) : -

        lt1$\bar{d}$ (INPUTLIST),

        mbrl ($\bar{d}$, INPULIST).

5.2 Module

Two predicates for a module are provided as for a gate.

element (MODULENAME, INPUTLIST, OUTPUTLIST).

delement (MODULENAME, INPUTLIST, OUTPUTLIST).   (6)

The knowledge of module tests is also provided. It is represented by predicates as

mdlts (MODULENAME, TESTLIST).   (7)

where

$$TESTLIST ::= [TEST \{ , TEST \}]$$
$$TEST ::= [IVAL \{ , IVAL \}, OVAL \{ , OVAL \}]$$
$$IVAL ::= 0 \mid 1 \mid d \mid \bar{d}$$
$$OVAL ::= 0 \mid 1 \mid d \mid \bar{d} \tag{8}$$

TESTLIST is a list of values. IVAL and OVAL take one of four values 0, 1, d, and $\bar{d}$. However, at least one d or $\bar{d}$ must exist in the list of OVAL's. The order of the placement of components of TEST is consistent with that in INPUTLIST and OUTPUTLIST of the module.

There may be many module tests for a fault. In principle, all of these possible modulle tests must be provided in the database. Due to the limitation to the amount of the database, however, only one module test for a fault is considered in the present implementation of our test generator. Therefore, there may be a case such that a module test may not be applied to the module and the fault should be detected by other module test which is currently not included in the database. Thus, the present implementation may not give us the test for a fault in a module, even though all faults are considered in each module test.

5.3 Circuit

A circuit is represented as follows

$$\text{cir (PILIST, MLLIST, POLIST, GATELIST)}. \tag{9}$$

where

PILIST ::= [LINENAME {, LINENAME }]

MLLIST ::= [LINENAME {, LINENAME }]

POLIST ::= [LINENAME {, LINENAME }]

GATELIST ::= [GATE {, GATE }]

$$\text{GATE ::= [GATETYPE, INPUTLIST, OUTPUTLIST]} \tag{10}$$

PILIST and POLIST are the lists of primary input lines and primary output lines of the circuit, while MLLIST is the list of the remaining lines. GATELIST is the list of component gates.

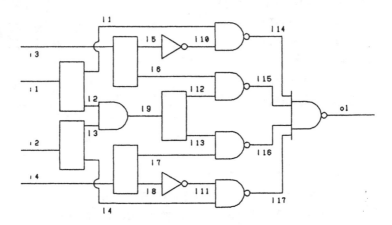

Fig. 7. Circuit.

For the circuit of Fig. 7

cir ([i1, i2, i3, i4], [l1, l2, l3, l4, l5, l6, l7, l8, l9, l10,
　　　l11, l12, l13, l14, l15, l16, l17], [o1],
　　　[[fanout, [[i1, l1]], [[l1, L1], [l2, L2]]],
　　　　[fanout, [[i2, l2]], [[l3, L3], [l4, L4]]],
　　　　[fanout, [[i3, l3]], [[l5, L5], [l6, L6]]],
　　　　[fanout, [[i4, l4]], [[l7, L7], [l8, L8]]],
　　　　[and, [[l2, L2], [l3, L3]], [[l9, L9]]],
　　　　[inv, [[l5, L5]], [[l10, L10]]],
　　　　[inv, [[l8, L8]], [[l11, L11]]],

[fanout, [[I9, L9]], [[I12, L12], [I13, L13]]],
[nand, [[I1, L1], [I10, L10]], [[I14, L14]]],
[nand, [[I16, L16], [I12, L12]], [[I15, L15]]],
[nand, [[I13, L13], [I7, L7]], [[I16, L16]]],
[nand, [[I11, L11], [I4, L4]], [[I17, L17]]],
[nand, [[I14, L14], [I15, L15], [I16, L16], [I17, L17]],
        [[o1, O1]]]]).

When a circuit consists of modules, GATELIST and GATE in the above representation should be replaced by MODULELIST and MODULE, respectively. MODULE here is a list of MODULENAME, INPUTLIST, and OUTPUTLIST. The circuit in Fig. 8 is represented as

cir ([i1, i2, i3, i4, i5], [l1, l2, l3, l4], [o1, o2],
    [[me, [[i1, X1], [i2, X2], [i3, X3]],
        [[l1, Y1], [l2, Y2]]],
      [mf, [[i4, X4], [i5, X5]],
        [[l3, Y3], [l4, Y4]]],
      [md, [[l1, Y1], [l2, Y2], [l3, Y3], [l4, Y4]],
        [[o1, Z1], [o2, Z2]]]]).

5.4 Description of FIPM

(1) In order to identify a detecting gate, predicate *fgate* such as

    fgate (FLN, [PILIST, MLLIST, POLIST, GATELIST], [GTN, IN, OUT]) : -
        ⊬ (mbr (FLN, PILIST)),
        mbr ([GTN, IN, OUT], GATELIST),
        mbr (FLN, OUT),
        !.
    fgate (FLN, [PILIST, MLLIST, POLIST, GATELIST], [ ]) : -
        mbr (FLN, PILIST),
        !.   (11)

is provided. FLN is the name of faulty line, while [GTN, IN, OUT] represents the detecting gate.

(2) Predicate *ipath* (FLN, CIR, IGAT, GI, PATH, [*d* | VALR]) is used to find a *f*-chaining path. IGAT is a list of GATETYPE's of gates on the *f*-chaining path, while GI is a list of their INPUTLIST's. The *f*-chaining path is represented by a list of LINENAME's in PATH and their *f* values in [*d* | VALUER]. A *f*-chaining path can be found by tracing gates from the faulty line to a primary output terminal. That is,

    ipath (FLN, CIR, IGAT, GI, PATH, [d | VALR]) : -
        ipathc (FLN, CIR, IGAT, GI, PATH, [d | VALR]).
    ipathc (FLN, [_, _, LNL3, GATEL], [[IGAN, IIN, IOUT] | ICIRR],
        GI, [FLN | PATHL], [VALF | [VALS | VALR]]) : -
        ⊬(mbr (FLN, LNL3)),

mbr ([IGAN, IIN, IOUT], GATEL),

mbr (FLN, IIN),

!,

dir (IGAN, VALF, VALS),

mbrf (NFLN, IOUT),

lfd (IIN, INL),

append (INL, GIR, GI),

delete ([IGAN, IIN, IOUT], GATEL, NGATEL),

ipathc (NFLN, [_, _, LNL3, NGATEL], ICIRR, GIR, PATHL,

[VALS I VALR]).

ipathc (FLN, [_, _, LNL3, GATEL], [ ], [ ], [FLN], [VALF]) : -

mbr (FLN, LNL3). $\qquad$ (12)

In the above

FLN: identifier of the faulty line,

CIR: circuit predicate,

IGAT: list of gates on the path,

GI: list of input lists of gates on the path,

PATH: list of line names on the path,

[d I VALR]: list of values of lines on the path.

Note that the above definition is recursive. For example, the definition says that if IGAT is a gate list of a path and the first element [IGAN, IIN, IOUT] of IGAT resides on the path, then the succeeding elements of the gate list must also be the elements of the path.

The set of f -chaining paths is obtained by taking *bagof.*

(3) Invalid reconvergence of the sensitized paths is detected by the consistency check or in the unification of signal values of a module where multiple sensitized paths reconverge. Further, when the unification at a signal line encouncters a conctradiction, a backtracking happens and the sensitized paths chosen will be discarded.

(4) Since it is unknown in the circuit description whether a gate is to be unified with 4 values or with 0 and 1, it is represented only by its gate type, list of input lines, and list of output lines. When a sensitized path is chosen, gates on this sensitized path will be unfied with the four values and the remaining gates with 0 and 1. Therefore, the representation of a gate should be changed to one of predicates of Eq.(3) and Eq.(5). For this purpose, predicates as

elmake ([ ], [ ]).

elmake ([NA I NB], [GATELA I GATELB] : -

GATELA = .. [element I NA],

elmake (NB, GATELB). $\qquad$ (13)

are provided. Similarly, we have predicate *delmake.*

(5) Predicate *lsttr* (CIR) such as

lsttr ([A I B]) : - A, lsttr (B).

lsttr ([ ]). $\qquad$ (14)

is used to check the completion of unification for all gates.

5.5 Test Generation Program

The test generation program represented by *tstgen* (TSTA) consists of predicates for finding test points and for generating the test of each test point. That is,

```
testgen ( TSTA ) : -
        find_tstp ( TSTP ),
        eachtstg ( TSTP, TST ),
        sort ( TST, TSTA ),
        :

        :
```
(15)

The main part of eachtstg is *onetstg*. It looks like

```
onetstg ( FLN, TSTL, SPATH ) :-
        cir ( IN, MD, OT, GA ),
        display ( FLN ), nl,
        fgate ( FLN, [ IN, MD, OT, GA ], FRE ),
        bagof ( [ GATEL, GI, PATH, PVAL ],
            ipath ( FLN, [ IN, MD, OT, GA ], GATEL, GI, PATH, PVAL ),
            BAGLIST),
        sort3e ( BAGLIST, [ GATEC, GIC, PATHC ] ),
        deletel ( PATHC, GIC, IPI ),
        asserta ( ga ( GA ) ),
        asserta ( bgl ( BAGLIST ) ),
        asserta ( fre ( FRE ) ),
        asserta ( gc ( GATEC ) ),
        :

        :

        areatst ( [ IN, OT ], IPI, FLN, SPATHL, TSTL ),
        retract ( ga ( GA ) ),
        retract ( bgl ( BAGLIST ) ),
        retract ( fre ( FRE ) ),
        retract ( gc ( GATEC ) ),
        :

        :

        !.
```
(16)

areatst classifies the test point, because the procedure of test generation is a little different from each other according to where the test point lies. In any case, areatst chooses a sensitized path from BAGLIST and generates predicates such as Eq.(5) by delmake for gates on the sensitized path, determining values of sensitizing lines of those gates. Finally, areatst generates predicates such as Eq.(3) by elmake for the remaining gates, determining signal values at primary input terminals by the unification with the values of the sensitizing lines.

6. Evaluation

Our test generators were run on SUN work station with C-Prolog. Table 1 shows examples of execution

Table 1. Experimental Result.

Circuit	#1	#2	#3	#4	#5	-
PT	735.7	11612.8	826.7	279.3	49.4	sec
FIPM	55.3	57.2	83.5	25.7	45.2	sec
PT/FIPM	13.3	203.0	9.9	10.9	1.1	-

times for several circuits. Entries in the row idendified by PT are times necessary for executing PT, while those in the row of FIPM are times spent by FIPM. The observed values themselves have little meaning, because they heavily depend on the operational speed of our SUN work station. (Its performance is around 1KLIPS.) The relative improvement by using FIPM is remarkable. We see FIPM is more than 50 times faster than PT in average.

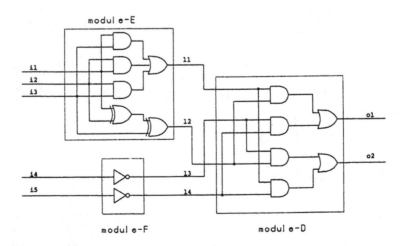

Fig. 8. Circuit.

The execution time for the circuit of Fig. 8 is 75.9 sec where all necessary knowledge of input-output functions, sensitizing inputs, and test inputs for each module was provided in advance. We compare this value to 416.7 sec, which is obtained for the same circuit by using FIPM. Thus, the improvement factor is about 5.5. When the test inputs and the sensitizing inputs were not provided for each module, we needed additional times 70.9 sec and 46.5 sec for the generation of the respective knowledges. If these times are added to 75.9 sec, the total time is 193.3 sec and still less than 416.7. The improvement factor even in this case is about 2.

Note that the modular approach can be applied recursively. A module can be decomposed in smaller sub-modules for obtaing its test inputs.

7. Concluding Remarks

We have proposed two methods, FIPM and the modular decomposition, to improve the execution of Prolog programs for generating tests of very large combinational circuits. We see from our experiment that our methods are promising. Since the machine limitation allowed us to make the experiment only for small circuits, the effectiveness of our methods should be proved by applying them to more complicated real examples.

Our modular approach could be improved by some way of obtaining sensitizing inputs of modules more efficiently. If we would need only to consider the single occurrence of f at an input line of each module in stead of the multiple occurrence of $f / \bar{f}$'s, the computation of sensitizing inputs of modules could be simplified greatly. This simplification would also contribute to make the database smaller and to get the test faster.

References

[FUJ82] M. Fujita, H. Tanaka, and T. Motooka: "Logic Design Verification by Using Temporal Logic and Prolog", Technical Report on Design Automation, IPS of Japan, 14-1, October 1982.

[KAN84] Juro Kaneda: "Bilateral Simulation for Logic Circuits Using Design Knowledge", Proc. Logic Programming Conference, June 1984.

[VAR87] P. Varma and Y. Tohma: "PROTEAN - A Knowledge-Based Test Generator", IEEE Custom Integrated Circuits Conference, May 1987.

[EIC77] E. B. Eichelberger and T. W. Williams: "A Logic Design Structure for LSI Testability", Proc. 14th Design Automation Conference, pp. 462 - 468, 1977.

[FUJ85] Hideo Fujiwara: "Logic Testing and Design for Testability", MIT Press, pp. 57-58, 1985.

[GEN82] Michael R. Genesereth: "Diagnosis Using Hierarchical Design Method", AAI-82, 1982.

[YOK86] H. Yokomizu and H. Mizoguchi: "Development of Diagnosing System for Logic Circuits Using Structural Information", Proc. Logic Programming Conference, 1986.

Acknowledgment

We appreciate Assoc. Prof. T. Nanya, Dr. T. Yoneda, Mr. A. Takahara, Mr. A. Kato, and other members of Computer Systems Lab at the Department of Computer Science, Tokyo Institute of Technology for their discussion and criticism in preparing this paper. We also thank Prof. H. Fujiwara of Meiji Univ. for his provision of circuit data. This work is partially supported by the Ministry of Education and Culture of Japan under the Grant of Scientific Research.

CONCURRENT EXECUTION OF PROLOG TRANSACTION

Makoto Takizawa and Katsumi Miyajima

Department of Information and Systems Engineering
Tokyo Denki University
Ishizaka, Hatoyama-cho, Saitama 350-03, Japan

ABSTRACT

Information systems are composed of multiple heterogeneous database systems and workstations interconnected by communication networks. Users want to manipulate data in multiple database systems in a common form. In our system, database systems are viewed to be fact base systems (FBSs), which provide sets of Prolog ground unit clauses, and retrieval and update operations on them. Transactions composed of multiple update operations on facts are written as Prolog rule clauses. In the Prolog system, atoms in a goal clause are selected from left to right. This means read/write operations on facts are sequentially executed. In this paper, we try to execute the transaction in parallel by multiple FBSs. In the sequence of atoms in the Prolog transaction, we define two types of meaningful sequences, i.e. conflict and flow ones. In this paper, we present how to decompose transactions into subtransactions, each of which is locally executed by one FBS, so as to preserve the meaningful sequences in the transaction. Also, we show that any parallel execution of the subtransactions is free of deadlock on send-receive relations.

1. INTRODUCTION

Information systems are composed of heterogeneous database systems and workstations interconnected by communication networks. Users want to manipulate these database systems independently of their heterogeneity and distribution. Logic languages like Prolog [15,17,21] have advantages to conventional database languages like SQL [9], i.e. data structures and procedures are defined recursively and uniformly. In our system [24-26], every database system is viewed to be a fact base system (FBS) which provides a set of ground unit clauses, and operations for manipulating them. That is, users can manipulate heterogeneous database systems in Prolog as if they were fact base systems. In our system, in stead of providing one integrated schema on multiple database systems [11,16,23], users define hierarchically and recursively their views on fact bases in Prolog. How to provide Prolog views on the relational database systems are discussed in [27 etc.]. Also, Prolog views on the network database systems are discussed in [24].

In addition to common interface on heterogeneous database systems, users want to manipulate multiple database systems. In our system, users write procedures which manipulate facts in multiple FBSs as Prolog rule clauses, called Prolog transactions. Transactions [12] are procedures composed of multiple update operations on facts, and are units of atomic executions. In the Prolog systems [15,17], atoms in a goal are selected from left to right. This means that the sequence of atoms in the goal denotes the execution sequence. In the atom sequence of Prolog transaction, we define two types of meaningful sequences, i.e. conflict and flow ones. In order to reduce the response time, it has to be concurrently executed by multiple FBSs. In this paper, we present how to decompose the transaction T into subtransactions, each of which references facts in one FBS, so as to preserve the meaningful sequences in T, and which are concurrently executed by the FBSs. Recently, Prolog programs have been tried to be executed in parallel [28,21,6 etc.]. In addition to input-output relation [21] among atoms, in our paper, read-write, write-read, write-write relations named conflict ones among atoms are introduced. Also, we show that our decomposition method never implies deadlock on send-receive synchronization. Update problems of a single database system through Prolog have been discussed by [19]. In our paper, update problems of multiple database systems are discussed.

In chapter 2, our system architecture is presented. In chapter 3, we present how to write transactions in Prolog. In chapter 4, we define what is a meaningful sequence of atoms in the transaction. In chapter 5, we discuss how to decompose Prolog transactions into subtransactions. In chapter 6, commitment controls for parallel executions of decomposed subtransactions are presented.

2. DISTRIBUTED FACT BASE SYSTEM

First, the overview of our system named DFBS (Distributed Fact Base System) is presented.

2.1 Logical Structure

Our system is composed of three hierarchical layers, i.e. local, local conceptual, and external layers, as shown in Fig.1. The lowest local layer provides the local conceptual layer with existing data models of database systems. This layer is viewed as a collection of database systems, each of which provides a data model, i.e. data structure, operations on the data structure, and integrity constraints. There are two stereo types of data models, relational [8] and network [5] models.

Next local conceptual layer provides the external layer with a fact base system (FBS) for each database system. An FBS is composed of a fact base (FB), that is a set of facts, and operations on the facts. In our system, every fact is a ground unit clause in Prolog. Facts are manipulated in a fact-at-a-time manner. This layer provides common

Prolog views of existing heterogeneous database systems. That is, users can see multiple heterogeneous database systems as if they were FBSs which provide sets of ground unit clauses and manipulation operations on them.

Users define their views on multiple FBSs in Prolog clauses. Also, views can be defined hierarchically and recursively on views. In this sense, our system is a federated system [14] rather than an integrated one [11,16,23]. The view defined by users is called an external fact base (EFB). Through this EFB, users can manipulate multiple heterogeneous database systems as if they were one FBS.

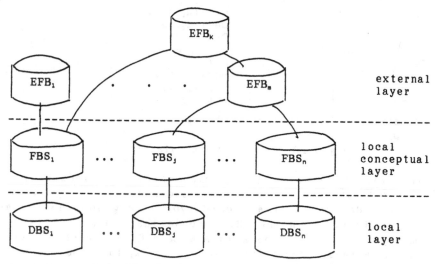

Fig.1   Hierarchical Structure.

Fact base systems (FBSs) can communicate with other FBSs by the communication network. Our communication network provides a reliable broadcast communication service [24,25] for the FBSs and workstations. That is, data units sent by one FBS are correctly received by every FBS in the same order.

2.2   Fact Base System

The FBS provides a fact base (FB) which is a set of facts. Each fact in the FB is a Prolog ground unit clause of a form $P(@p, v_1,\ldots,v_m)$, where P is an (m+1)-ary predicate symbol, @p and v_k (k=1,...,m) constant symbols, and @p denotes an identifier of the fact called a fact identifier (fid). We assume that each fact in our system is uniquely identified by its fid. When a fact is stored in the FB, its fid is given by the FBS.

A local conceptual view of the relational database [8] is a collection of ground unit clauses, each of which denotes a tuple. For each tuple $\langle v_1,\ldots,v_m \rangle$ in a relation R with tuple identifier (tid) k, a ground unit clause $R(k,v_1,\ldots,v_m)$ exists where R is an (m+1)-ary predicate symbol, $k,v_1,\ldots,v_m$ are constants. In Fig.2, an example of a relational database and its FB is shown. Here, each constant e_j denotes a tuple identifier.

```
+---+-----+------+----+          Emp(e₁, 1, a, 100).
|Emp| eno | ename| sal|
+---+-----+------+----+          Emp(e₂, 2, b, 210).
    |  1  |   a  | 100|
    |  2  |   b  | 210|          Emp(e₃, 3, c, 180).
    |  3  |   c  | 180|
    |  4  |   b  | 160|          Emp(e₄, 4, b, 160).
+----+------+------+----+
```

　a) relation   b) fact base (FB)

Fig.2 FB for a relational database

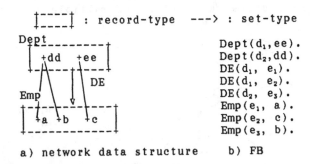

```
┆----┆ : record-type  ---> : set-type
```

```
Dept_____+              Dept(d₁,ee).
  ┆ +dd  +ee  ┆              Dept(d₂,dd).
  ├-----------┤              DE(d₁, e₁).
  ┆        DE ┆              DE(d₁, e₂).
Emp┆          ┆              DE(d₂, e₃).
  ┆-----------┆              Emp(e₁, a).
  ┆ +a +b +c  ┆              Emp(e₂, c).
  +-----------+              Emp(e₃, b).
```

　a) network data structure   b) FB

Fig.3 FB for a network database

An FB of the network database [5] is composed of two kinds of predi-
cates, record and set ones [24]. For each record occurrence $\langle v_1,\ldots, v_m\rangle$
with a database (db) key k in a record type R, a ground unit clause
$R(k,v_1,\ldots,v_m)$ is included in the FB. Suppose that there exists a set
type S from a parent record type A to a member B. For each set occurrence of S among a record occurrence with db key k_1 in A and one with k_2
in B, a ground unit clause $S(k_1,k_2)$ exists in the FB. Fig.3 shows an example of a network database and its FB. Here, d_j and e_k denote db keys.
A method for generating DML [20] procedures for goal clauses is
presented in [24]. In our method, meaningless backtrackings to find
refutations are prevented and redundant refutations to get all answer
substitutions are reduced.

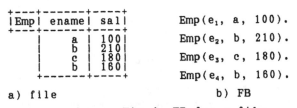

```
+---+------+----+          Emp(e₁, a, 100).
|Emp| ename| sal|
+---+------+----+          Emp(e₂, b, 210).
    |   a  | 100|
    |   b  | 210|          Emp(e₃, c, 180).
    |   c  | 180|
    |   b  | 160|          Emp(e₄, b, 160).
+------+----+
```

　a) file   b) FB

Fig.4 FB for a file.

A UNIX file [29] is a byte stream, which is structured as a sequence of
records. For each record $\langle v_1,\ldots,v_m\rangle$ in a file F with an offset k, a
ground unit clause $F(k,v_1,\ldots,v_m)$ is included in FB. Fig.4 shows the FB
for a conventional UNIX file. Here, e_j denotes an offset of a record
from the top of the file.

2.3   FBS Transaction

Facts in the FB are manipulated by fact-at-a-time operations, which correspond to conventional DMLs and tuple-at-a-time operations like cursors [9]. Let S_P be a set of facts of a predicate symbol P in the FB. S_P is totally ordered by some mechanism. The FBS provides the following fid-based sequential operations to read and write facts, and to communicate with other FBSs.

[FB Operations] Here, P is an (m+1)-ary predicate symbol, and K and X_j are terms.

(1) C_P = <u>open</u>(P). C_P is a variable which represents a cursor for P, i.e. C_P denotes a fact most recently accessed. Here, C_P points the top fact in S_P.

(2) $\langle K, X_1, \ldots, X_m \rangle$ = <u>read</u>(C_P). A fact $P(@p, v_1, \ldots, v_m)$ denoted by C_P is derived from the FB, and terms K and X_k are instantiated by @p and v_k (k=1,...,m), respectively. Then, C_P is changed to denote the fact next to P(@p,...) in S_P.

(3) <u>write</u>(P,K,X_1,...,X_m).

(3-1) If K is instantiated by a constant @p and X_k by a ground term a_k (k=1,...,m), a fact P(@p,...) is replaced with $P(@p, a_1, \ldots, a_m)$ in the FB.

(3-2) If K is not instantiated and every X_k is instantiated by a_k, a new fact $P(k, a_1, \ldots, a_m)$ is appended to the FB and K is instantiated by its fid @p.

(3-3) If K is instantiated by @p and X_k is not, P(@p,...) is deleted from the FB.□

An FBS communicates with other FBSs by sending and receiving messages at a service access pint (SAP) [30] provided by the communication network. A cluster is a set of SAPs where the same messages are received at every SAP in the same order [25,26]. Suppose that the SAP of C is identified by C in each FBS.

[Communication Operations](1) <u>send</u>(X, C) sends an X's value at C.
(2) X = <u>rec</u>(C) receives a message at C.□

Transactions [12] are sequences of read and write operations on a database, whose executions are atomic. An FBS transaction is a sequence of <u>read</u>, <u>write</u>, <u>send</u>, and <u>rec</u> operations encapsulated by <u>begin</u> and either <u>commit</u> or <u>abort</u>. We assume that every FBS provides some concurrency and reliability controls presented by [4].

[Transaction Operations](1) <u>begin</u> starts the transaction T.
(2) <u>commit</u> completes T, where the results updated by T are reflected to the FB permanently, i.e. they can be seen by the other transactions and are not be lost by failures the FBS suffers from.
(3) <u>abort</u> indicates an abnormal termination of T, whose intermediate results are never reflected to the FB.□

3.   PROLOG TRANSACTION

An external fact base (EFB) is a union of distributed fact bases. Users view multiple FBSs as one EFB without knowing where each fact is located. Here, we make the following assumptions.

[Assumptions](1) Every two FBs have no common predicate symbols.
(2) Let M_K be a model of the FB in the FBS_K. Every M_K has the same domain D. Also, M_K has the same constant mapping. That is, the same constant symbol in different FBs denotes the same individual in D.
(3) Every fact in the EFB has a unique identifier.□

In order to write transactions in Prolog, we introduce new predicate symbols, Begin, Commit, Abort, and Write. Their procedural meanings are as follows.

[Procedural meanings](1) When Begin is selected, the resolution always succeeds. This means the transaction starts.
(2) When Commit is selected, the resolution always succeeds and the transaction completes. After that, we cannot backtrack to resolutions from the selection of Begin to this Commit. Facts written by the transaction are made permanent, i.e. updated facts can be seen by other transactions and survive various failures of the FBS.
(3) When Abort is selected, the resolution fails, and we backtrack to the last resolution where Begin is selected. This means that update effects by the transaction are erased from the FB.
(4) When Write([P,K,X_1,...,X_m]) where P is a predicate symbol in the FB and K and X_k are terms (k=1,...,m) is selected,
(4-1) if K and X_k are instantiated by @p and a_k (k=1,...,m), respectively, the fact P(@p,...) is replaced with P(@p,a_1,...,a_m),
(4-2) if K is not instantiated and X_k is instantiated by a_k (k=1,...,m), P(@p,a_1,...,a_m) with new fid @p is appended to the FB and K is instantiated by @p,
(4-3) if K is instantiated by @p and every X_k is not (k=1,...,m), P(@p,...) is deleted from the FB.
Variables like K which take fids as values are said to be primary.
(5) When a fact atom P(E_1,...,E_m) is selected, a fact unifiable with it is read from the FB, and uninstantiated variables in it are instantiated by the unification. □

Write is different from retract and assert of Prolog [7] in a point that effects of Write are removed from the fact base (FB) by backtracking. Let us consider an example of funds transfer. Let A, B, and C be three persons. Suppose that FBS_1 and FBS_2 have facts Acct1 including A's account CA and B's CB, and Acct2 including C's account CC, respectively.
(1) shows a Prolog transaction which transfers (CA-CB)/3 from C to B if CA < CB. Selection of the atom Acct1 (K1,A,CA) in the resolution means that a fact about A is derived from FBS_1. The selection of Write([Acct1,K3,C,CC-(CA-CB)/3]) means that C's account in Acct1 is decremented by (CA-CB)/3.

```
trans(A, B) :- Begin, Acct1(K1,A,CA), Acct2(K2,B,CB), Acct1(K3,C,CC),
    acheck(CA,CB), Write([Acct1,K3,C,CC-
    (CA-CB)/3]), Write([Acct2,K2,B,CB+(CA-CB)/3]), Commit.
acheck(X,Y) :- X < Y, Abort.
acheck(X,Y) :-.                                          ... (1)
```

The transaction includes nondeterminacy in the selection of input clauses as shown in (1). Transactions composed of subtransactions are said to be nested [18]. Since it is difficult to implement nondeterminacy and nested transactions, we consider one class of transactions which neither include nondeterminacy nor are nested.

[Definition] A simple transaction is an ordered goal clause in a form ?- Begin, $A_1,...,A_m$, Commit, where each A_k is either a fact atom, write atom, or evaluable atom (for k=1,...,m).□
The procedural meaning of the simple transaction is a sequential execution of write operations denoted by Write atoms and read ones by fact atoms. (2) shows a simple transaction where acheck is removed from (1).

```
?- Begin, Acct1(K1,A,CA), Acct2(K2,B,CB), Acct1(K3,C,CC),
   Write([Acct1,K3,C,CC-(CA-CB)/3]),
   Write([Acct2,K2,B,CB+(CA-CB)/3]), Commit.          ...(2)
```

4. MEANINGFUL ORDERING

For a simple transaction T, we try to find a meaningful partial ordering of atoms from the atom sequence in T in order to decompose T. A simple transaction T = ?- Begin, $A_1,...,A_m$, Commit is considered to be a totally ordered set $(AA,<)$, where AA is a set $\{A_1,...,A_m\}$ of atoms and for every A_k and A_j in AA, $A_k < A_j$ iff (if and only if) k < j. For example, Acct1(K1,A,CA) < Write([Acct2, K2,B,CB-(CA-CB)/3]) in (2). Let us define what is a meaningful ordering on atoms in T. Here, two atoms A and B in T are said to share a variable X iff they include X in common.

[Definition] Let A and B be two atoms in a simple transaction. A and B are said to conflict iff at least one of them is a Write atom and they share some primary variable on fid.□
[Definition] For a simple transaction T = $(AA,<)$, a conflict relation → $\underline{C}$ < is one such that, for every A and B in AA, A → B iff 1) A < B and 2) A and B conflicts.□
For example, Acct1(K3,C,CC) and Write([Acct1,K3,...]) in (2) conflict because they have the same primary variable K3. Also, Acct1 (K3,C,CC) → Write([Acct1,K3,C,CC-(CA-CB)/3]) holds in (2). This means that a fact denoted by the atom Acct1 is updated by the atom Write. When A → B holds in T, selection sequence of A and B cannot be exchanged. If exchanged, the results are different from T. The conflict relation represents read-write, write-read, and write-write relation [12].

Next, we define a flow relation which represents an input-output relation among the atoms in the transaction.
[Definition] For a simple transaction T = $(AA,<)$, an atom A in AA is said to be a first atom of a variable X iff A includes X and there is no atom B such that B includes X and B < A. □
[Definition] For T = $(AA,<)$, a flow relation ⇒ $\underline{C}$ < is one such that, for every A and B in AA, A ⇒ B iff 1) A < B, 2) A and B share a variable X, 3) A is a non-Write atom, and 4) A is the f-atom of X. □

A ⇒ B denotes an information flow from an A's fact into a B's fact. For example, since Acct1(K1,A,CA) is a first atom of CA, Acct1(K1,A,CA) ⇒ Write([Acct1,K3,C,CC-(CA-CB)/3]) on CA holds in (2). This means that a value CA read from Acct1 is written to the fact denoted by K3. Like the conflict relation, if A ⇒ B in T, the selection sequence of A and B cannot be exchanged.

[**Definition**] For a simple transaction T = (**AA**,<), intrasite flow relation ⇒ C < and intersite flow relation ⇒> C < are ones such that for every A ⇒ B in T,
  (1) A ⇒> B iff A and B are in different FBSs, and
  (2) A ⇒ B iff A and B are in the same FBS. □
For example, an intrasite flow Acct1(K1,A,CA) ⇒ Write([Acct1,K3, C,CC-(CA-CB)/3]) on CA and an intersite flow Acct1(K1,A,CA) ⇒> Write([Acct2,K2,B,CB+(CA-CB)/3]) on CA hold in (2).

In the Prolog system, as [21] stated, every variable is instantiated only once. This means that a single assignment property [1] holds in the resolution. Hence, it is easy to find the meaningful sequences in the simple transaction.

5. DECOMPOSITION OF PROLOG TRANSACTION

Next problem is how to resolve Prolog transactions which reference facts in multiple fact base systems (FBSs).

5.1 Approaches

There are two approaches to resolving the transactions. In the first one, the workstation executes the SLD resolution. When facts are required as input clauses, the facts are derived from the FBSs and returned to it. Facts are obtained by handshaking of the workstation to the FBSs. In this approach, resolutions are sequentially executed in the workstations like conventional Prolog systems. This approach is called a server one.

In the second parallel approach, the resolutions of the transactions are concurrently executed by multiple FBSs. In this approach, first, transactions are decomposed into subtransactions, each of which references facts in one FBS. Then, these subtransactions are concurrently executed by FBSs by communicating with each other.

Although the first approach is simple, transactions are not efficiently executed, since the workstation blocks during the handshaking and due to the overhead of fact-at-a-time communications. Hence, we take the parallel approach, i.e. parallel execution of subtransactions.

5.2 Transaction Graph

To decompose a transaction T into subtransactions, atoms in T are partially ordered so as to preserve the T's meaningful ordering. Here, a subtransaction is a transaction which includes atoms from one FBS. First, we define a transaction (T) graph.

[Definition] For a simple transaction T = (AA,<), a transaction (T) graph TG is a directed graph obtained by the following procedure:
(1) generate a node A for every atom A in AA, and
(2) if A -> B in T, generate a conflict edge —> from the node A to B, if A==>B, generate an intrasite flow edge ++> from A to B, and if A=>>B, generate an intersite flow edge **> from A to B. □
For example, a T graph for (2) is shown in Fig.5, where labels on edges show shared variables. The T graph shows the meaningful ordering of atoms in the transaction.

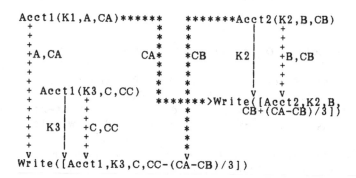

```
Acct1(K1,A,CA)******        *******Acct2(K2,B,CB)
+                    *    *         |    +
+                    *    *         |    +
+                    *    *         |    +
+A,CA           CA*  *CB       K2|  +B,CB
+                    *    *         |    +
+                    *    *         |    +
+ Acct1(K3,C,CC)     *    *         v    v
+        |      +    *******>Write([Acct2,K2,B,
+        |      +         *         CB+(CA-CB)/3])
+    K3|   +C,CC          *
+        |      +         *
+        |      +         *
v        v      v         v
Write([Acct1,K3,C,CC-(CA-CB)/3])
```

—>: conflict edge

+++>: intrasite flow edge   ***>: intersite flow edge

Fig.5 Transaction graph

Here, new predicate symbols Send and Rec are introduced for communication. They have the following procedural meanings.

[Communication Predicates](1) When Send(X,M) is selected, the resolution always succeeds and a variable M is instantiated by X.
(2) When Rec(M,X) is selected, the resolution blocks until a term M is instantiated. When instantiated, the resolution succeeds and X is instantiated by M.□
Here, M is a communication variable. Even if multiple Rec predicates include the same communication variable M, they can be resolved when one Send atom including M is resolved. By using the Send and Rec atoms, intersite flow edges are replaced.

[Definition] For a T graph TG of a simple transaction T = (AA,<), a modified transaction G is a graph obtained by the following procedures:
For every A **> B on a variable X in TG,
    (1) select unused variable V called a communication variable,
    (2) add two nodes denoting atoms Send(X, V) and Rec(V, X),
    (3) add an intrasite flow edge A ++> Send(X,V) and Rec(V,X) ++> B,
    (4) delete the edge A **> B on X from TG. □
For example, Fig.6 shows a modified transaction of Fig.5.

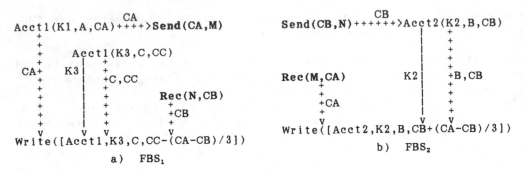

Fig.6 Transaction graph

5.3 Deadlock-Free Decomposition of Transactions

From a modified transaction **G**, subtransactions are generated by the
following procedure.
[Decomposition] For a modified transaction **G** of T = (**AA**,⟨),
(1) decompose **G** into connected subgraphs $G_1, \ldots, G_n$,
(2) for each G_k, construct a sequence of nodes, which represents a sub-
    transaction T_k, so as to preserve the conflict and flow relations in
    T, and
(3) for each G_k, rename variables in G_k except for communication vari-
    ables so as to be different from other subtransactions.□

It is clear that each decomposed subtransaction includes atoms in an
FBS, since it includes no intersite flow relations. For example, from
a) and b) in Fig.6, subtransactions T_1 and T_2 are constructed as (3) and
(4), respectively.

T_1 ?- Begin, Acct1(K1,A,AA), **Rec(N,BB)**, Acct1(K3,C,CC),
       Send(AA,M), Write([Acct1,K3,C,CC-(AA-BB)/3]), Commit. ... (3)
T_2 ?- Begin, Acct2(K2,B,CB), **Rec(M,AA)**, **Send(CB,N)**,
       Write([Acct2,K2,B,CB+(AA-CB)/3]), Commit.   ... (4)

It is clear that conflict and flow relations in (2) are preserved in
(3) and (4). The resolution of (3) is executed at the FBS$_1$ and (4) at
the FBS$_2$. Here, we have a deadlock problem caused by intersite communication, i.e. (3) waits for instantiation of N by the resolution of
Rec(N,BB) and (4) for M by Rec(M,AA).

[Subtransaction construction] Let $G_1, \ldots, G_n$ be decomposed subgraphs for
T = (**AA**,⟨). For every G_k, a subtransaction T_k is a partially ordered set
(**BB**$_k$,⟨$_k$) which is constructed as follows:
(1) for every node A in G_k, an atom A is included in BB$_k$,
(2) if A ⟶ B or A ⁑⟩ B in G_k, A ⟨$_k$ B in T_k, and
(3) if A ↦⟩Send(X,M) and Rec(N,Y)↦⟩B in G_k, and A ⟨ B in T, then Send
    (X,M) ⟨$_k$ Rec(N,Y) in T_k. □
For example, Fig.7 shows a T graph for Fig.6, which includes precedence
edges ↛⟩ among Send and Rec nodes iff Send ⟨$_k$ Rec. A subtransaction T_k =
(**BB**$_k$,⟨$_k$) can be executed concurrently by a parallel machine FBS$_k$ if ⟨$_k$ is

preserved. Subtransactions (5) and (6) are constructed from Fig.7 by the above procedure. Since Acct1(K1,...) < Write(K2,...) in (2), Send(CA,M) <₁ Rec(N,BB) in (5). Also, Send(CB,N) <₂ Rec(M,AA) in (6).

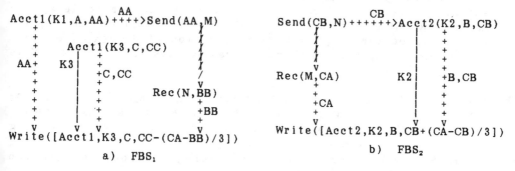

```
            AA                                   CB
Acct1(K1,A,AA)++++>Send(AA,M)        Send(CB,N)++++++>Acct2(K2,B,CB)
   +                  /                     /              +
   +      Acct1(K3,C,CC)                   /               +
   +         +        /                   /                +
 AA+    K3|  +       /              Rec(M,CA)      K2|    +B,CB
   +      |  +C,CC  /                   +          |       +
   +      |  +     /                    +CA        |       +
   +      |  +  Rec(N,BB)               +          |       +
   +      |  +     +                    +          |       +
   v      v  v     +BB                  v          v    v  v
Write([Acct1,K3,C,CC-(CA-BB)/3])   Write([Acct2,K2,B,CB+(CA-CB)/3])

        a)  FBS₁                              b)  FBS₂
```

Fig.7 Transaction graph

T_1 ?- Begin, Acct1(K1,A,AA), **Send(AA,M)**, **Rec(N,BB)**, Acct1(K3,C,CC),
   Write([Acct1,K3,C,CC-(AA-BB)/3]), Commit.   ... (5)
T_2 ?- Begin, Acct2(K2,B,CB), **Send(CB,N)**, **Rec(M,CA)**,
   Write([Acct2,K2,B,CB+(CA-CB)/3]), Commit.   ... (6)

[Proposition] Any executions of subtransactions decomposed by our procedure are deadlock-free.
[Proof] Let T be a simple transaction, and $T_1,...,T_n$ be subtransactions decomposed from T. We construct a following graph P, called a precedence graph, from $T_1,...,T_n$.
(1) For every atom A in T_k, construct a node A.
(2) For every atoms A and B in T_k, construct a directed edge A —> B among the nodes A and B, iff A $<_k$ B in T_k.
(3) For every Send(X,M) in T_k and Rec(M,Y) in T_j, construct a directed edge Send(X,M) —> Rec(M,Y).
If deadlock occurs, P includes a directed cycle. Hence, it is sufficient to show that a precedence graph of our decomposed subtransactions includes no directed cycle. Suppose that some directed cycle for two subtransactions T_k and T_j is included as shown in Fig.8. According to the definition of our procedure, B < Send(Y,N) < Rec(N,Z) < D and E< Send(W,M) < Rec(M,X)< A have to hold in T. Sine A < B in T_k, E < A < B < D. However, D < E in T_j. This is a contradiction. Hence, since no directed cycle is included, our procedure never results deadlock. The case of more than two subtransactions are proved in the same manner.∎

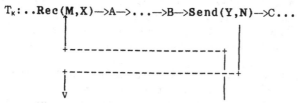

```
Tₖ:..Rec(M,X)—>A—>...—>B—>Send(Y,N)—>C...
       |                         |
       +-------------------+     |
                           |     |
       +-------------------|-----+
       |                   |
       v                   |
Tⱼ:..Rec(N,Z)—>D—>...—>E—>Send(W,M)—>F...
```

Fig.8 Precedence graph P

5.4 Exchange Rule

Let us consider subtransactions for sequential machine FBS. The selection of Rec(M,X) blocks the resolution of the transaction until M is instantiated, i.e. M is received. Hence, it is better to delay the selection of Rec(M,X) and instead select an atom A such that Rec(M,X) < A. Also, it is better to promote the selection of Send(X,M) as possible, because it may cause blocked subtransactions which wait for M to execute.

[Exchange rule] Let T_k be a subtransaction $A_1 <_k ... <_k A_p$. For j = 1,...,p-1, if one of the following conditions holds, A_j and A_{j+1} are exchanged:
(1) A_j is Rec(M,X), there exists no meaningful ordering relation among them, and A_{j+1} is not a Send atom.
(2) A_{j+1} is Send(X,M), there exists no meaningful ordering relation among them, and A_j is not a Rec atom.
If they are exchanged, j=j-1, else j=j+1. While j<p, 1) and 2) are repeated. □
For example, atoms Rec and Acct1 in (5) are exchanged as shown in (7). By this procedure, since Send is selected as earlier as possible and rec as later as possible, the duration of waiting for the instantiation of rec can be reduced.

T_1 ?- Begin, Acct1(K1,A,CA), **Send(CA,M)**, Acct1(K3,C,CC),
       Rec(N,BB), Write([Acct1,K3,C,CC-(CA-BB)/3]), Commit. ... (7)

Lastly, for each subtransaction T_k, a local FBS transaction is constructed. Atoms Begin, Commit, Send(...), Rec(...), Write(...) are translated to the FBS operations <u>begin</u>, <u>commit</u>, <u>send</u>, <u>rec</u>, <u>write</u>, respectively. Also, a fact atom P(...) is translated to a read operation. Backtracking in the refutation procedure is represented by while-loop. For example, (7) is translated into an FBS transaction (8).

```
T₁: begin; k1 = open(Acct1);
    while ( (<K1,A,CA> = read(k1)) is not end )
    { send(CA,M); k2 = open(Acct1);
      while ( (<K1,C,CC> = read(k2)) is not end )
      { BB = rec(N); write(Acct1,K3,C,CC-(CA-BB)/3);
        commit; } }                                    ... (8)
```

5.5 Correctness of Decomposition

Now, we show the correctness of our decomposition of the transaction.
[Definition] Let T_k be a subtransaction $(BB_k, <_k)$ of T = $(AA, <)$ (for k=1,...,n). A global log L of $T_1,...,T_n$ is a partially ordered set $(BB, <<)$ such that 1) $BB = BB_1 \cup ... \cup BB_n$, and 2) for every A and B in T_k, if A $<_k$ B, then A << B in L, and for Send(X,M) in T_k and Rec(M,Y) in T_j, Send(X,M) << Rec(M,Y). □
[Definition] A global log L of $T_1,...,T_n$ is said to be serializable to T iff all meaningful ordering relations in T are held in L. □
The serializability gives the criteria of correctness of parallel executions of subtransactions, since T is assumed to be correct.

[Proposition] Any global log of decomposed subtransactions are serializable.

[Proof] Let T be a simple transaction, $T_1,...,T_n$ be decomposed subtransactions of T, and L a global log (BB, $\ll$) of T. According to the decomposition procedure, the conflict and intrasite flow relations in T are held in subtransactions. For an intersite flow relation A $\Longrightarrow$ B, subtransaction T_k has A $\Longrightarrow$ Send(X,M) and T_j has Rec(M,X) $\Longrightarrow$ B. Since Send(X,M) $\ll$ Rec(M,X) in L, A $\Longrightarrow$ Send(X,M) $\ll$ Rec(M,Y) $\Longrightarrow$ B. Hence, A $\ll$ B in L.∎

Hence, our decomposition is correct. That is, the result of L is the same as the serial execution of T.

6. COMMITMENT CONTROL

Commitment control is one for guaranteeing that all updates on facts by the transaction are either completely done or none of them. In the distributed systems, two-phase commitment (2PC) protocol [13] is widely used. One problem in the 2PC is how to reduce the communication overhead.

Here, suppose that the network provides reliable broadcast communication [25,26]. By using the reliable broadcast network, the 2PC protocol can be easily implemented [23,25,26]. For every subtransaction T_k, Commit is replaced by a sequence of atoms: Send(prc, PC_k), Rec([$PC_1,...,PC_n$],_), Commit. This means that T_k first broadcasts a "precommitted(prc)" message and waits for all prc's from T_j (j=1,...,n). Then, on receipt of prc from all subtransactions, i.e., all communication variables $PC_1,...,PC_n$ are instantiated, T_k commits. For example, (9) and (10) shows the subtransactions of (2) with 2PC protocol.

T_1 ?- Begin, Acct1(K1,A,AA), Send(AA,M), Acct1(K3,C,CC), Rec(N,BB),
Write([Acct1,K3,C,CC-(AA-BB)/3]), Send(prc,PC), Rec(PC,_),
Commit.   ... (9)

T_2 ?- Begin, Acct2(K2,B,CB), Send(CB,N), Rec(M,CA), Write([Acct2,
K2,B,CB+(CA-CB)/3]), Send(prc,PC), Rec(PC,_), Commit.   ...(10)

Finally, the following two FBS transactions are obtained.

```
T₁: begin; k1 = open(Acct1);
    while ( (<K1,A,AA> = read(k1)) is not end )
    { send(AA,M);  k2 = open(Acct1);
        while ( (<K3,C,CC> = read(k2)) is not end)
        { BB = rec(N); write(Acct1,K3,C,CC-(AA-BB)/3);
            send(prc,PC); X1 = rec(PC); commit; } }          ...(11)
T₂: begin;  k1 = open(Acct2);
    while ( <K2,B,CB> = read(Acct2,K2,B,CB) is not end )
    { send(CB,N); CA = rec(M);
        write(Acct2,K2,B,CB+(CA-CB)/3); send(prc,PC);
        X2 = rec(PC); commit;  }                              ...(12)
```

7. CONCLUDING REMARKS

In this paper, we discussed how to decompose Prolog transactions to subtransactions in order to concurrently execute the subtransactions. First, we defined two types of meaningful sequences, conflict and flow ones. The conflict relations represent read-write, write-read, and write-write conflict relations in the conventional concurrency control [2,3,4,12]. The flow relations represent the input-output relations among the atoms. In the resolution in Prolog, a variable is instantiated only one time. This means a single assignment property of data flow languages [1]. By this property, it is easy to find the input-output relation. Also, we showed the method to decompose the transactions into deadlock-free subtransactions on send-receive relation. At present, we try to extend our method to nondeterminacy.

ACKNOWLEDGMENT

We would like to thank Mr. A. Ishihara, graduate student of Tokyo Denki University, for his helpful cooperation of implementation of our system.

REFERENCES

[1] Ackerman, W.B. and Dennis, J.B., "VAL - Value-Oriented Algorithmic Language," LCS/TR-218, MIT, 1979.

[2] Bernstein, P.A. and Goodman, N., "Concurrency Control in Distributed Database Systems," ACM Computing Surveys, Vol.13, No.2, 1981.

[3] Bernstein, P.A. and Goodman, N., "Multiversion Concurrency Control - Theory and Algorithms," ACM TODS, Vol.8, No.4, 1983.

[4] Bernstein, P.A. et al., "Concurrency Control and Recovery in Database Systems," Addison-Wesley, 1986.

[5] Codasyl, "Report of the CODASYL Data Definition Language Committee," Journal of Development, 1973.

[6] Clark, K.L. and Gregory, S., "PARLOG: Parallel Programming in Logic," Research Report DOC 84/4, Imperial College of Science and Technology, London, 1984.

[7] Clocksin, W.F. and Mellish, C.S., "Programming in Prolog," Springer-Verlag, 1984.

[8] Codd, E.F., "A Relational Model of Data for Large Shared Data Banks, " CACM, Vol.13, No.6, 1970.

[9] Date, C.J., " Introduction to Database Systems," Addison-Wesley, 1983.

[10] CODASYL DBTG Committee, "CODASYL Data Description Language," Journal of Development, 1973.

[11] Ferrier, A. and Stangret, C., "Heterogeneity in the Distributed Database Management System Sirius-Delta," Proc. VLDB 82, 1982.

[12] Gray, J., "The Notions of Consistency and Predicate Locks in a Database System," CACM, Vol.19, No.11, 1976.

[13] Gray, J., "Notes on Data Base Operating Systems," Operating Systems: An advanced Course (Bayer,R. ed.), Springer-Verlag, 1979.

[14] Heimbigner, D. and McLeod, D. "A Federated Architecture for Information Management," ACM TOIS, Vol.3, No.3, 1985, pp.253-278.

[15] Kowalski, R.A., "Logic for Problem Solving," Elsevier North Holland, 1979.

[16] Landers, T. and Rosenberg, R.L., "An Overview of Multibase," North-Holland, 1982.

[17] Lloyd, J.W., "Foundation of Logic Programming," Springer-Verlag, 1984.

[18] Moss, J.E.B., "Nested Transactions," MIT Press, 1985.

[19] Naish, L., Thom, J.A., and Ramamohanarao, "Concurrent Database Updates in Prolog," Proc. of the Fourth International Conf. on Logic Programming, 1987, pp.178-195.

[20] Olle, T., "The CODASYL Approach to Data Base Management," John Wiley and Sons, 1978.

[21] Shapiro, E., "Concurrent Prolog: A progress Report," Foundation of Artificial Intelligence, Springer-Verlag, 1986.

[22] Shapiro, E., "The Art of Prolog," MIT Press, 1986.

[23] Takizawa, M., "Distributed Database System - JDDBS," JARECT, Vol.7, Ohmsha and North-Holland, 1983.

[24] Takizawa, M., Ito, H., and Moriya, K., "Logic Interface System on the Navigational Database System," Lecture Notes in Computer Science, No.264, 1987, pp.70-80.

[25] Takizawa, M., "Highly Reliable Broadcast Communication Protocol," Proc. of IEEE COMPSAC, Tokyo, 1987, pp.731-740.

[26] Takizawa, M., "Cluster Control Protocol for Highly Reliable Broadcast Communication," Proc. of the IFIP Conf. on Distributed Processing, Amsterdam, 1987.

[27] Ueda, K., "Guarded Horn Clauses," Lecture Notes in Computer Science, 221, Springer-Verlag, 1986.

[28] Ullman, D., "Implementation of Logical Query Language for Databases," ACM TODS, Vol.10, No.3, 1985, pp.289-321.

[29] Quarterman, J.S., Silberschatz, A., and van Renesse, R., "4.2BSD and 4.3BSD as Examples of the UNIX System," ACM Computing Surveys, Vol.17, No.4, 1985, pp.379-418.

[30] "Data Processing - Open Systems Interconnection - Basic Reference Model," DP7498, 1980.